Free Video  **Free Video**

Essential Test Tips Video from Trivium Test Prep

Dear Customer,

Thank you for purchasing from Trivium Test Prep! We're honored to help you prepare for your PSAT exam.

To show our appreciation, we're offering a **FREE *PSAT Essential Test Tips* Video by Trivium Test Prep.*** Our video includes 35 test preparation strategies that will make you successful on the SAT. All we ask is that you email us your feedback and describe your experience with our product. Amazing, awful, or just so-so: we want to hear what you have to say!

To receive your **FREE *PSAT Essential Test Tips* Video**, please email us at 5star@ triviumtestprep.com. Include "Free 5 Star" in the subject line and the following information in your email:

1. The title of the product you purchased.
2. Your rating from 1 – 5 (with 5 being the best).
3. Your feedback about the product, including how our materials helped you meet your goals and ways in which we can improve our products.
4. Your full name and shipping address so we can send your **FREE *PSAT Essential Test Tips* Video**.

If you have any questions or concerns please feel free to contact us directly at 5star@ triviumtestprep.com.

Thank you!

– Trivium Test Prep Team

*To get access to the free video please email us at 5star@triviumtestprep.com, and please follow the instructions above.

PSAT 10 Prep 2021-2022 with Practice Tests

Study Guide with Practice Questions for the PSAT/NMSQT College Board Exam

Table of Contents

Online Resources

To help you fully prepare for your PSAT, Accepted, Inc. includes online resources with the purchase of this study guide.

PRACTICE TESTS

In addition to the practice test included in this book, we also offer an online exam. Since many exams today are computer based, getting to practice your test-taking skills on the computer is a great way to prepare.

FLASH CARDS

A convenient supplement to this study guide, Accepted Inc.'s flash cards enable you to review important terms easily on your computer or smartphone.

CHEAT SHEETS

Review the core skills you need to master the exam with easy-to-read Cheat Sheets.

FROM STRESS to SUCCESS

Watch "From Stress to Success," a brief but insightful YouTube video that offers the tips, tricks, and secrets experts use to score higher on the exam.

REVIEWS

Leave a review, send us helpful feedback, or sign up for Accepted, Inc. promotions—including free books!

Access these materials at: **https://www.acceptedinc.com/psat-online-resources**

Introduction

Congratulations on choosing to take the PSAT/NMSQT or PSAT 10! By purchasing this book, you've taken the first step toward SAT preparation and your college career. This guide will provide you with a detailed overview of the PSAT/NMSQT and PSAT 10 so you know exactly what to expect on test day. We'll take you through all the concepts covered on the test and give you the opportunity to test your knowledge with practice questions. Even if it's been a while since you took a major test, don't worry; we'll make sure you're more than ready!

What is the PSAT?

The PSAT (Preliminary Scholastic Aptitude Test) is an achievement test designed to assess what you've learned in school. Colleges won't be able to see your score, but taking the PSAT does offer advantages.

There are two versions of the PSAT: the PSAT/NMSQT and the PSAT 10.

Students who take the **PSAT/NMSQT** may qualify for a **National Merit Scholarship**. That's why you'll sometimes see this test referred to as the NMSQT—the National Merit Scholarship Qualifying Test. The PSAT/NMSQT is offered in the fall.

The **PSAT 10** is offered to sophomore students during the spring semester. PSAT 10 scores will not qualify examinees for the National Merit Scholarship, but taking the test is a good way to become familiar with the format of the SAT, so that you can do your best.

Both the PSAT/NMSQT and the PSAT 10 help you prepare for the SAT. The material covered on all the tests is virtually identical, so taking the PSAT will allow you to see how you'll do on the SAT. On the PSAT, you'll see the same types of questions as those that appear on the SAT. You'll also get to experience the same testing conditions.

What's on the PSAT?

The PSAT consists of three sections: Reading, Writing and Language, and Mathematics.

The Mathematics section is further broken down into two parts: one that's taken with a calculator and one taken without. You will have a reference sheet with common formulas for each math test.

The Reading and Writing sections include only multiple-choice questions, while the Mathematics section includes multiple-choice and grid-ins (shown below). Each test section has a time limit (as specified in the following table), for a total of 139 questions and two hours and forty-five minutes of testing.

What's on the PSAT?			
Section	**Concepts**	**Number of Questions**	**Time**
Reading	understanding and analyzing nonfiction and fiction passages; interpreting graphs and charts; vocabulary in context	47 questions	60 minutes
Writing and Language	identifying errors in basic grammar, punctuation, usage, and style; rhetorical skills	44 questions	35 minutes
Mathematics	mathematical reasoning and performing calculations using algebra, geometry, and basic statistics	17 questions (without calculator)	25 minutes
		31 questions (with calculator)	45 minutes
Total		**139 questions**	**2 hours and 45 minutes**

How is the PSAT Scored?

Every question on the PSAT is worth one point. There is no guess penalty, meaning there is no penalty for choosing an incorrect answer. So be sure to guess if you do not know the answer to a question; you might get it right!

You scores for the Reading Test and the Writing and Language Test will be combined to one quantity called "Evidence-Based Reading and Writing."

The total number of questions you answer correctly is your raw score. This score will then be scaled from 120 – 720. You'll receive a single score between 120 and 720 for

Evidence-Based Reading and Writing, and another score for the Mathematics section. So, the combined score for all three sections will range from 240 – 1440.

Your score report will also reflect other metrics to show how well you performed on specific types of questions like scientific analysis, historical analysis, algebra, conventions of Standard English, and more. Use your score report to learn your strengths and weaknesses.

For the PSAT/NMSQT, all scores are automatically sent to the National Merit Scholarship Corporation unless students opt out.

How is the PSAT Administered?

Both the PSAT/NMSQT and the PSAT 10 are administered by schools. Students take the exams at school. Students can only register to take the test through the school administering it—you cannot register online. The exams are pencil-and-paper tests.

▶ The PSAT/NMSQT is administered by schools in the fall. It is offered to sophomores and juniors.

▶ The PSAT 10 is administered by schools in the spring. It is offered to sophomores only.

On the day of your test, arrive early and be sure to bring proper identification and your admission ticket (which is emailed to you after you register). You are required to put away all personal belongings before the test begins. Cell phones and other electronic, photographic, recording, or listening devices are not permitted in the testing center at all.

You are allowed pencils, erasers, and a four-function or scientific calculator on your desk during the test. Calculators may only be used during the designated mathematics section. A watch that will not sound during the test is also allowed. For more details on what to expect on testing day, refer to the College Board website.

About This Guide

This guide will help you to master the most important test topics and also develop critical test-taking skills. We have built features into our books to prepare you for your tests and increase your score. Along with a detailed summary of the format, content, and scoring of the PSAT, we offer an in-depth overview of the content knowledge required to pass the exam. In the review you'll find sidebars that provide interesting information, highlight key concepts, and review content so that you can solidify your understanding of the exam's concepts. You can also test your knowledge with sample questions throughout the text and practice questions that reflect the content and format of the exams. We're pleased you've chosen Accepted, Inc. to be a part of your journey!

PART I
Evidence-Based Reading and Writing

Reading: 47 questions ¦ 60 minutes

Writing: 44 questions ¦ 35 minutes

The Evidence-Based Reading and Writing part of the PSAT includes two tests: 1) the Reading Test and 2) the Writing and Language Test. The Reading Test will include four single passages and one set of paired passages that cover a range of topics. You'll likely see at least one fictional passage and also excerpts from works on science, history, and social studies. Some of these passages will be accompanied by tables or graphs. Each passage or set of passages will be followed by ten or eleven questions that cover the following topics:

▶ the main idea of a passage

▶ the role of supporting details in a passage

▶ adding supporting details to a passage

▶ the structure of a passage

▶ the author's purpose

▶ logical inferences that can be drawn from a passage

▶ comparing passages

▶ vocabulary and figurative language

The Writing and Language Test asseses your knowledge of basic grammar, punctuation, and rhetoric. The test will include four passages with various words, phrases, and sentences underlined. The corresponding questions will ask you to revise the underlined text; you can choose to leave the text as-is or replace it with another option. Topics you'll see on the test include:

▶ matching pronouns with their antecedents

▶ matching verbs with their subjects

▶ ensuring that verbs are in the correct tense

▶ correcting sentence structure

▶ placing sentences logically within the passage

▶ determining if sentences belong within a passage

CHAPTER ONE
Reading

The Main Idea

The main idea of a text is the author's purpose in writing a book, article, story, etc. Being able to identify and understand the main idea is a critical skill necessary to comprehend and appreciate what you're reading.

Consider a political election. A candidate is running for office and plans to deliver a speech asserting her position on tax reform. The topic of the speech—tax reform—is clear to voters, and probably of interest to many. However, imagine that the candidate believes that taxes should be lowered. She is likely to assert this argument in her speech, supporting it with examples proving why lowering taxes would benefit the public and how it could be accomplished. While the topic of the speech would be tax reform, the benefit of lowering taxes would be the main idea. Other candidates may have different perspectives on the topic; they may believe that higher taxes are necessary, or that current taxes are adequate. It is likely that their speeches, while on the same topic of tax reform, would have different main ideas: different arguments likewise supported by different examples. Determining what a speaker, writer, or text is asserting about a specific issue will reveal the MAIN IDEA.

One more quick note: the exam may also ask about a passage's THEME, which is similar to but distinct from its topic. While a TOPIC is usually a specific *person*, *place*, *thing*, or *issue*, the theme is an *idea* or *concept* that the author refers back to frequently. Examples of common themes include ideas like the importance of family, the dangers of technology, and the beauty of nature.

There will be many questions on the exam that require you to differentiate between the topic, theme, and main idea of a passage. Let's look at an example:

QUICK REVIEW

Topic: The subject of the passage.

Theme: An idea or concept the author refers to repeatedly.

Main idea: The argument the writer is making about the topic.

Babe Didrikson Zaharias, one of the most decorated female athletes of the twentieth century, is an inspiration for everyone. Born in 1911 in Beaumont, Texas, Zaharias lived in a time when women were considered second-class to men, but she never let that stop her from becoming a champion. Babe was one of seven children in a poor immigrant family, and was competitive from an early age. As a child she excelled at most things she tried, especially sports, which continued into high school and beyond. After high school, Babe played amateur basketball for two years, and soon after began training in track and field. Despite the fact that women were only allowed to enter in three events, Babe represented the United States in the 1932 Los Angeles Olympics, and won two gold medals and one silver for track and field events.

In the early 1930s, Babe began playing golf which earned her a legacy. The first tournament she entered was a men's only tournament; however she did not make the cut to play. Playing golf as an amateur was the only option for a woman at this time, since there was no professional women's league. Babe played as an amateur for a little over a decade, until she turned pro in 1947 for the Ladies Professional Golf Association (LPGA) of which she was a founding member. During her career as a golfer, Babe won eighty-two tournaments, amateur and professional, including the U.S. Women's Open, All-American Open, and British Women's Open Golf Tournament. In 1953, Babe was diagnosed with cancer, but fourteen weeks later, she played in a tournament. That year she won her third U.S. Women's Open. However by 1955, she didn't have the physicality to compete anymore, and she died of the disease in 1956.

The topic of this passage is obviously Babe Zaharias—the whole passage describes events from her life. Determining the main idea, however, requires a little more analysis. The passage describes Babe Zaharias' life, but the main idea of the paragraph is what it says about her life. To figure out the main idea, consider what the writer is saying about Babe Zaharias. The writer is saying that she's someone to admire—that's the main idea and what unites all the information in the paragraph. Lastly, what might the theme of the passage be? The writer refers to several broad concepts, including never giving up and overcoming the odds, both of which could be themes of the passage.

Two major indicators of the main idea of a paragraph or passage follow below:

▶   It is a general idea; it applies to all the more specific ideas in the passage. Every other sentence in a paragraph should be able to relate in some way to the main idea.

▶   It asserts a specific viewpoint that the author supports with facts, opinions, or other details. In other words, the main idea takes a stand.

EXAMPLE

It's easy to puzzle over the landscapes of our solar system's distant planets—how could we ever know what those far-flung places really look like? However, scientists utilize a number of tools to visualize the surfaces of many planets. The topography of Venus, for example, has been explored by several space probes, including the Russian Venera landers and NASA's Magellan orbiter. These craft used imaging and radar to map the surface of the planet, identifying a whole host of features including volcanoes, craters, and a complex system of channels. Mars has likewise been mapped by space probes, including the famous Mars Rovers, which are automated vehicles that actually landed on the planet's surface. These rovers have been used by NASA and other space agencies to study the geology, climate, and possible biology of the planet.

In addition to these long-range probes, NASA has also used its series of orbiting telescopes to study distant planets. These four massively powerful telescopes include the famous Hubble Space Telescope as well as the Compton Gamma Ray Observatory, Chandra X-Ray Observatory, and the Spitzer Space Telescope. These allow scientists to examine planets using not only visible light but also infrared and near-infrared light, ultraviolet light, x-rays and gamma rays.

Powerful telescopes aren't just found in space: NASA makes use of Earth-bound telescopes as well. Scientists at the National Radio Astronomy Observatory in Charlottesville, VA, have spent decades using radio imaging to build an incredibly detailed portrait of Venus' surface. In fact, Earth-bound telescopes offer a distinct advantage over orbiting telescopes because they allow scientists to capture data from a fixed point, which in turn allows them to effectively compare data collected over a long period of time.

1. Which of the following sentences best describes the main idea of the passage?
   A) It's impossible to know what the surfaces of other planets are really like.
   B) Telescopes are an important tool for scientists studying planets in our solar system.
   C) Venus' surface has many of the same features as the Earth's, including volcanoes, craters, and channels.
   D) Scientists use a variety of advanced technologies to study the surface of the planets in our solar system.

TOPIC and SUMMARY SENTENCES

The main idea of a paragraph usually appears within the topic sentence. The TOPIC SENTENCE introduces the main idea to readers; it indicates not only the topic of a passage, but also the writer's perspective on the topic.

Notice, for example, how the first sentence in the text about Babe Zaharias states the main idea: *Babe Didrikson Zaharias, one of the most decorated female athletes of the twentieth century, is an inspiration for everyone.*

Even though paragraphs generally begin with topic sentences due to their introductory nature, on occasion writers build up to the topic sentence by using supporting details in order to generate interest or build an argument. Be alert for paragraphs when writers do not include a clear topic sentence at all; even without a clear topic sentence, a paragraph will still have a main idea. You may also see a **SUMMARY SENTENCE** at the end of a passage. As its name suggests, this sentence sums up the passage, often by restating the main idea and the author's key evidence supporting it.

EXAMPLE

The Constitution of the United States establishes a series of limits to rein in centralized power. Separation of powers distributes federal authority among three competing branches: the executive, the legislative, and the judicial. Checks and balances allow the branches to check the usurpation of power by any one branch. States' rights are protected under the Constitution from too much encroachment by the federal government. Enumeration of powers names the specific and few powers the federal government has. These four restrictions have helped sustain the American republic for over two centuries.

2. In the above paragraph, what are the topic and summary sentences?

IMPLIED MAIN IDEA

A paragraph without a clear topic sentence still has a main idea; rather than clearly stated, it is implied. Determining the implied main idea requires some detective work: you will need to look at the author's word choice and tone in addition to the content of the passage to find his or her main idea. Let's look at an example paragraph.

EXAMPLES

One of my summer reading books was *Mockingjay*. Though it's several hundred pages long, I read it in just a few days. I was captivated by the adventures of the main character and the complicated plot of the book. However, I felt like the ending didn't reflect the excitement of the story. Given what a powerful personality the main character has, I felt like the ending didn't do her justice.

3. Even without a clear topic sentence, this paragraph has a main idea. What is the writer's perspective on the book—what is the writer saying about it?
    A) *Mockingjay* is a terrific novel.
    B) *Mockingjay* is disappointing.
    C) *Mockingjay* is full of suspense.
    D) *Mockingjay* is a lousy novel.

Read the following paragraph:

Fortunately, none of Alyssa's coworkers have ever seen inside the large filing drawer in her desk. Disguised by the meticulous neatness of the rest of her workspace, the drawer betrayed no sign of the chaos within. To even open it, she had to struggle for several minutes with the enormous pile of junk jamming the drawer, until it would suddenly give way, and papers, folders, and candy wrappers spilled out onto the floor. It was an organizational nightmare, with torn notes and spreadsheets haphazardly thrown on top of each other and melted candy smeared across pages. She was worried the odor would soon waft to her coworkers' desks, revealing her secret.

4. Which sentence best describes the main idea of the paragraph above?

   A) Alyssa wishes she could move to a new desk.

   B) Alyssa wishes she had her own office.

   C) Alyssa is glad none of her coworkers know about her messy drawer.

   D) Alyssa is sad because she doesn't have any coworkers.

Supporting Details

SUPPORTING DETAILS provide more support for the author's main idea. For instance, in the Babe Zaharias example, the writer makes the general assertion that *Babe Didrikson Zaharias, one of the most decorated female athletes of the twentieth century, is an inspiration for everyone.* The rest of the paragraph provides supporting details with facts showing why she is an inspiration: the names of the challenges she overcame, and the specific years she competed in the Olympics.

Be alert for SIGNAL WORDS, which indicate supporting details and so can be helpful in identifying supporting details. Signal words can also help you rule out sentences that are not the main idea or topic sentence: if a sentence begins with one of these phrases, it will likely be too specific to be a main idea.

Questions on the SAT will ask you to find details that support a particular idea and also to explain why a particular detail was included in the passage. In order to answer these questions, you must have a solid understanding of the passage's main idea. With this knowledge, you can determine how a supporting detail fits in with the larger structure of the passage.

DID YOU KNOW?
The SAT questions almost always refer to specific lines in the text, so you don't need to read the entire passage before you start answering the questions.

EXAMPLES

It's easy to puzzle over the landscapes of our solar system's distant planets—how could we ever know what those far-flung places really look like? However, scientists utilize a number of tools to visualize the surfaces of many planets. The topography of Venus, for example, has been explored by several space probes, including the Russian Venera landers and NASA's Magellan orbiter. These craft used imaging and radar to map the surface of the planet, identifying a whole host of features including volcanoes, craters, and a complex system of channels. Mars has likewise been mapped by space probes, including the famous Mars Rovers, which are automated vehicles that actually landed on the planet's surface. These rovers have been used by NASA and other space agencies to study the geology, climate, and possible biology of the planet.

In addition to these long-range probes, NASA has also used its series of orbiting telescopes to study distant planets. These four massively powerful telescopes include the famous Hubble Space Telescope as well as the Compton Gamma Ray Observatory, Chandra X-Ray Observatory, and the Spitzer Space Telescope. These allow scientists to examine planets using not only visible light but also infrared and near-infrared light, ultraviolet light, x-rays and gamma rays.

Powerful telescopes aren't just found in space: NASA makes use of Earth-bound telescopes as well. Scientists at the National Radio Astronomy Observatory in Charlottesville, VA, have spent decades using radio imaging to build an incredibly detailed portrait of Venus' surface. In fact, Earth-bound telescopes offer a distinct advantage over orbiting telescopes because they allow scientists to capture data from a fixed point, which in turn allows them to effectively compare data collected over a long period of time.

5. Which sentence from the text best develops the idea that scientists make use of many different technologies to study the surfaces of other planets?

    A) These rovers have been used by NASA and other space agencies to study the geology, climate, and possible biology of the planet.

    B) It's easy to puzzle over the landscapes of our solar system's distant planets—how could we ever know what those far-flung places really look like?

    C) In addition to these long-range probes, NASA has also used its series of orbiting telescopes to study distant planets.

    D) These craft used imaging and radar to map the surface of the planet, identifying a whole host of features including volcanoes, craters, and a complex system of channels.

6. If true, which sentence could be added to the passage above to support the author's argument that scientists use many different technologies to study the surface of planets?

    A) Because the Earth's atmosphere blocks x-rays, gamma rays, and infrared radiation, NASA needed to put telescopes in orbit above the atmosphere.

    B) In 2015, NASA released a map of Venus which was created by compiling images from orbiting telescopes and long-range space probes.

    C) NASA is currently using the Curiosity and Opportunity rovers to look for signs of ancient life on Mars.

    D) NASA has spent over $2.5 billion to build, launch, and repair the Hubble Space Telescope.

7. The author likely included the detail that Earth-bound telescopes offer a distinct advantage over orbiting telescopes because they allow scientists to capture data from a fixed point in order to

   A) explain why it has taken scientists so long to map the surface of Venus

   B) suggest that Earth-bound telescopes are the most important equipment used by NASA scientists

   C) prove that orbiting telescopes will soon be replaced by Earth-bound telescopes

   D) demonstrate why NASA scientists rely on many different types of scientific equipment

Text Structure

Authors can structure passages in a number of different ways. These distinct organizational patterns, referred to as **TEXT STRUCTURE**, use the logical relationships between ideas to improve the readability and coherence of a text. The most common ways passages are organized include:

- ▶ **PROBLEM-SOLUTION:** The author presents a problem and then discusses a solution.

- ▶ **COMPARE-CONTRAST:** The author presents two situations and then discusses their similarities and differences.

- ▶ **CAUSE-EFFECT:** The author presents an action and then discusses the resulting effects.

- ▶ **DESCRIPTIVE:** The author describes an idea, object, person, or other item in detail.

EXAMPLE

The issue of public transportation has begun to haunt the fast-growing cities of the southern United States. Unlike their northern counterparts, cities like Atlanta, Dallas, and Houston have long promoted growth out and not up—these are cities full of sprawling suburbs and single-family homes, not densely concentrated skyscrapers and apartments. What to do then, when all those suburbanites need to get into the central business districts for work? For a long time it seemed highways were the twenty-lane wide expanses of concrete that would allow commuters to move from home to work and back again. But these modern miracles have become time-sucking, pollution-spewing nightmares. They may not like it, but it's time for these cities to turn toward public transport like trains and buses if they are to remain livable.

8. The organization of this passage can best be described as:

   A) a comparison of two similar ideas

   B) a description of a place

   C) a discussion of several effects all related to the same cause

   D) a discussion of a problem followed by the suggestion of a solution

The Author's Purpose

Whenever an author writes a text, she always has a purpose, whether that's to entertain, inform, explain, or persuade. A short story, for example, is meant to entertain, while an online news article would be designed to inform the public about a current event. Each of these different types of writing has a specific name:

► **NARRATIVE WRITING** tells a story. (novel, short story, play)

► **EXPOSITORY WRITING** informs people. (newspaper and magazine articles)

► **TECHNICAL WRITING** explains something. (product manual, directions)

► **PERSUASIVE WRITING** tries to convince the reader of something. (opinion column on a blog)

On the exam, you may be asked to categorize a passage as one of these types, either by specifically naming it as such or by identifying its general purpose.

You may also be asked about primary and secondary sources. These terms describe not the writing itself but the author's relationship to what's being written about. A **PRIMARY SOURCE** is an unaltered piece of writing that was composed during the time when the events being described took place; these texts are often written by the people directly involved. A **SECONDARY SOURCE** might address the same topic but provide extra commentary or analysis. These texts are written by outside observers and may even be composed after the event. For example, a book written by a political candidate to inform people about his or her stand on an issue is a primary source. An online article written by a journalist analyzing how that position will affect the election is a secondary source; a book by a historian about that election would be a secondary source, too.

EXAMPLE

Elizabeth closed her eyes and braced herself on the armrests that divided her from her fellow passengers. Take-off was always the worst part for her. The revving of the engines, the way her stomach dropped as the plane lurched upward; it made her feel sick. Then, she had to watch the world fade away beneath her, getting smaller and smaller until it was just her and the clouds hurtling through the sky. Sometimes (but only sometimes) it just had to be endured, though. She focused on the thought of her sister's smiling face and her new baby nephew as the plane slowly pulled onto the runway.

9. This passage is reflective of which type of writing?
   A) narrative
   B) expository
   C) technical
   D) persuasive

Facts vs. Opinions

On the SAT you might be asked to identify a statement in a passage as either a fact or an opinion, so you'll need to know the difference between the two. A FACT is a statement or thought that can be proven to be true. The statement *Wednesday comes after Tuesday* is a fact—you can point to a calendar to prove it. In contrast, an OPINION is an assumption that is not based in fact and cannot be proven to be true. The assertion that television is more entertaining than feature films is an opinion—people will disagree on this, and there's no reference you can use to prove or disprove it.

DID YOU KNOW?
Keep an eye out for answer choices that may be facts, but which are not stated or discussed in the passage.

EXAMPLE

Exercise is critical for healthy development in children. Today, there is an epidemic of unhealthy children in the United States who will face health problems in adulthood due to poor diet and lack of exercise in childhood. This is a problem for all Americans, especially with the rising cost of health care.

It is vital that school systems and parents encourage their children to engage in a minimum of thirty minutes of cardiovascular exercise each day, mildly increasing their heart rate for a sustained period. This is proven to decrease the likelihood of developmental diabetes, obesity, and a multitude of other health problems. Also, children need a proper diet rich in fruits and vegetables so that they can grow and develop physically, as well as learn healthy eating habits early on.

10. Which of the following is a fact in the passage, not an opinion?
    A) Fruits and vegetables are the best way to help children be healthy.
    B) Children today are lazier than they were in previous generations.
    C) The risk of diabetes in children is reduced by physical activity.
    D) Children should engage in thirty minutes of exercise a day.

Drawing Conclusions

In addition to understanding the main idea and factual content of a passage, you'll also be asked to take your analysis one step further and anticipate what other information could logically be added to the passage. In a non-fiction passage, for example, you might be asked which statement the author of the passage would agree with. In an excerpt from a fictional work, you might be asked to anticipate what a character would do next.

To answer these questions, you must have a solid understanding of the topic, theme, and main idea of the passage; armed with this information, you can figure out which of the answer choices best fits within those criteria (or alternatively, which ones do not). For example, if the author of the passage is advocating for safer working conditions in textile factories, any supporting details that would be added to the passage should support that idea. You might add sentences that contain information about the number of accidents that occur in textile factories or that outline a new plan for fire safety.

EXAMPLES

Today, there is an epidemic of unhealthy children in the United States who will face health problems in adulthood due to poor diet and lack of exercise during their childhoods. This is a problem for all Americans, as adults with chronic health issues are adding to the rising cost of healthcare. A child who grows up living an unhealthy lifestyle is likely to become an adult who does the same.

Because exercise is critical for healthy development in children, it is vital that school systems and parents encourage their children to engage in a minimum of thirty minutes of cardiovascular exercise each day. Even this small amount of exercise has been proven to decrease the likelihood that young people will develop diabetes, obesity, and other health issues as adults. In addition to exercise, children need a proper diet rich in fruits and vegetables so that they can grow and develop physically. Starting a good diet early also teaches children healthy eating habits they will carry into adulthood.

11. The author of this passage would most likely agree with which statement?
- **A)** Parents are solely responsible for the health of their children.
- **B)** Children who do not want to exercise should not be made to.
- **C)** Improved childhood nutrition will help lower the amount Americans spend on healthcare.
- **D)** It's not important to teach children healthy eating habits because they will learn them as adults.

Elizabeth closed her eyes and braced herself on the armrests that divided her from her fellow passengers. Take-off was always the worst part for her. The revving of the engines, the way her stomach dropped as the plane lurched upward; it made her feel sick. Then, she had to watch the world fade away beneath her, getting smaller and smaller until it was just her and the clouds hurtling through the sky. Sometimes (but only sometimes) it just had to be endured, though. She focused on the thought of her sister's smiling face and her new baby nephew as the plane slowly pulled onto the runway.

12. Which of the following is Elizabeth least likely to do in the future?

    A)   Take a flight to her brother's wedding.

    B)   Apply for a job as a flight attendant.

    C)   Never board an airplane again.

    D)   Get sick on an airplane.

Meaning of Words and Phrases

On the Reading section you may be asked to provide definitions or intended meanings for words within passages. You may have never encountered some of these words before the test, but there are tricks you can use to figure out what they mean.

CONTEXT CLUES

A fundamental vocabulary skill is using context to determine the meaning of a word. There are two types of context that can help you understand unfamiliar words: situational context and sentence context. Regardless of which context you encounter, these types of questions are not really testing your knowledge of vocabulary; rather, they test your ability to comprehend the meaning of a word through its usage.

SITUATIONAL CONTEXT helps you determine the meaning of a word through the setting or circumstances in which that word or phrase occurs. Using **SENTENCE CONTEXT** requires analyzing only the sentence in which the new word appears to understand it. To figure out words using sentence context clues, you should first identify the most important words in the sentence.

There are four types of clues that can help you understand the context, and therefore the meaning of a word:

▶ **RESTATEMENT CLUES** occur when the definition of the word is clearly stated in the sentence.

▶ **POSITIVE/NEGATIVE CLUES** can tell you whether a word has a positive or negative meaning.

▶ **CONTRAST CLUES** include the opposite meaning of a word. Words like *but, on the other hand*, and *however* are tip-offs that a sentence contains a contrast clue.

▶ **SPECIFIC DETAIL CLUES** provide a precise detail that can help you understand the meaning of the word.

It is important to remember that more than one of these clues can be present in the same sentence. The more there are, the easier it will be to determine the meaning of the word. For example, the following sentence uses both restatement and positive/negative clues: *Janet suddenly found herself destitute, so poor she could barely afford to eat.* The second part of the sentence clearly indicates that destitute is a negative word. It also restates the meaning: very poor.

EXAMPLES

13. I had a hard time reading her <u>illegible</u> handwriting.
    A) neat
    B) unsafe
    C) sloppy
    D) educated

14 The dog was <u>dauntless</u> in the face of danger, braving the fire to save the girl trapped inside the building.
    A) difficult
    B) fearless
    C) imaginative
    D) startled

15. Beth did not spend any time preparing for the test, but Tyrone kept a <u>rigorous</u> study schedule.
    A) strict
    B) loose
    C) boring
    D) strange

ANALYZING WORDS

As you no doubt know, determining the meaning of a word can be more complicated than just looking in a dictionary. A word might have more than one DENOTATION, or definition; which one the author intends can only be judged by examining the surrounding text. For example, the word *quack* can refer to the sound a duck makes, or to a person who publicly pretends to have a qualification which he or she does not actually possess.

A word may also have different CONNOTATIONS, which are the implied meanings and emotions a word evokes in the reader. For example, a cubicle is simply a walled desk in an office, but for many the word implies a constrictive, uninspiring workplace. Connotations can vary greatly between cultures and even between individuals.

Lastly, authors might make use of FIGURATIVE LANGUAGE, which is the use of a word to imply something other than the word's literal definition. This is often done by comparing two things. If you say *I felt like a butterfly when I got a new haircut*, the listener knows you don't resemble an insect but instead felt beautiful and transformed.

WORD STRUCTURE

Although you are not expected to know every word in the English language for the PSAT, you can use deductive reasoning to determine the answer choice that is the best match for the word in question by breaking down unfamiliar vocabulary. Many complex words can be broken down into three main parts:

> **PREFIX — ROOT — SUFFIX**

ROOTS are the building blocks of all words. Every word is either a root itself or has a root. Just as a plant cannot grow without roots, neither can vocabulary, because a word must have a root to give it meaning. The root is what is left when you strip away all the prefixes and suffixes from a word. For example, in the word *unclear*, if you take away the prefix *un–*, you have the root *clear*.

Roots are not always recognizable words; they generally come from Latin or Greek words like *nat*, a Latin root meaning *born*. The word *native*, which describes a person born in a referenced place, comes from this root, as does the word *prenatal*, meaning before birth. It's important to keep in mind, however, that roots do not always match the exact definitions of words, and they can have several different spellings.

Prefixes are syllables added to the beginning of a word, and suffixes are syllables added to the end of the word. Both carry assigned meanings and can be attached to a word to completely change the word's meaning or to enhance the word's original meaning.

Take the word *prefix* itself as an example: *fix* means to place something securely, and *pre–* means before. Therefore, *prefix* means to place something before or in front of. Now let's look at a suffix: in the word *portable*, *port* is a root which means to move or carry. The suffix *–able* means that something is possible. Thus, *portable* describes something that can be moved or carried.

Although you cannot determine the meaning of a word by a prefix or suffix alone, you can use this knowledge to eliminate answer choices; understanding whether the word is positive or negative can give you the partial meaning of the word.

Comparing Passages

In addition to analyzing single passages, the PSAT will also require you to compare two passages. Usually these passages will discuss the same topic, and it will be your task to identify the similarities and differences between the authors' main ideas, supporting details, and tones.

EXAMPLES

Read Passages One and Two, and then answer questions 16 and 17.

Passage One

Today, there is an epidemic of unhealthy children in the United States who will face health problems in adulthood due to poor diet and lack of exercise during their childhoods: in 2012, the Centers for Disease Control found that 18 percent of students aged 6-11 were obese. This is a problem for all Americans, as adults with chronic health issues are adding to the rising cost of healthcare. A child who grows up living an unhealthy lifestyle is likely to become an adult who does the same.

Because exercise is critical for healthy development in children, it is vital that school systems and parents encourage their children to engage in a minimum of thirty minutes of cardiovascular exercise each day. Even this small amount of exercise has been proven to decrease the likelihood that young people will develop diabetes, obesity, and other health issues as adults. In addition to exercise, children need a proper diet rich in fruits and vegetables so that they can grow and develop physically. Starting a good diet early also teaches children healthy eating habits they will carry into adulthood.

Passage Two

When was the last time you took a good, hard look at a school lunch? For many adults, it's probably been years—decades even—since they last thought about students' midday meals. If they did stop to ponder, they might picture something reasonably wholesome if not very exciting: a peanut butter and jelly sandwich paired with an apple, or a traditional plate of meat, potatoes, and veggies. At worst, they may think, kids are making due with some pizza and a carton of milk.

The truth, though, is that many students aren't even getting the meager nutrients offered up by a simple slice of pizza. Instead, schools are serving up heaping helpings of previously frozen, recently fried delicacies like french fries and chicken nuggets. These high-carb, low-protein options are usually paired with a limp, flavorless, straight-from-the-freezer vegetable that quickly gets tossed in the trash. And that carton of milk? It's probably a sugar-filled chocolate sludge, or it's been replaced with a student's favorite high-calorie soda.

So what, you might ask. Kids like to eat junk food—it's a habit they'll grow out of soon enough. Besides, parents can always pack lunches for students looking for something better. But is that really the lesson we want to be teaching our kids? Many of those children aren't going to grow out of bad habits; they're going to reach adulthood thinking that ketchup is a vegetable. And students in low-income families are particularly impacted by the sad state of school food. These parents rely on schools to provide a warm, nutritious meal because they don't have the time or money to prepare food at home. Do we really want to be punishing these children with soggy meat patties and salt-soaked potato chips?

16. Both authors are arguing for the importance of improving childhood nutrition. How do the authors' strategies differ?

    A) Passage 1 presents several competing viewpoints while Passage 2 offers a single argument.

    B) Passage 1 uses scientific data while Passage 2 uses figurative language.

    C) Passage 1 is descriptive while Passage 2 uses a cause-effect structure.

    D) Passage 1 has a friendly tone while the tone of Passage 2 is angry.

17. Both authors argue that

    A) children should learn healthy eating habits at a young age.

    B) low-income students are disproportionately affected by the low-quality food offered in schools.

    C) teaching children about good nutrition will lower their chances of developing diabetes as adults.

    D) schools should provide children an opportunity to exercise every day.

Answer Key

1. A) can be eliminated because it directly contradicts the rest of the passage, which goes into detail about how scientists have learned about the surfaces of other planets. Answers B) and C) can also be eliminated because they offer only specific details from the passage; while both choices contain details from the passage, neither is general enough to encompass the passage as a whole. **Only answer D) provides an assertion that is both supported by the passage's content and general enough to cover the entire passage.**

2. **The topic sentence is the first sentence in the paragraph.** It introduces the topic of discussion, in this case the constitutional limits on centralized power. The summary sentence is the last sentence in the paragraph. It sums up the information that was just presented: here, that constitutional limits have helped sustain the United States of America for over two hundred years.

3. **B) is correct**: the novel is disappointing. The process of elimination will reveal the correct answer if that is not immediately clear. While the paragraph begins with positive commentary on the book—*I was captivated by the adventures of the main character and the complicated plot of the book*—this positive idea is followed by the contradictory transition word *however*. A) cannot be the correct answer because the author concludes that the novel was poor. Likewise, D) cannot be correct because it does not encompass all the ideas in the paragraph; despite the negative conclusion, the author enjoyed most of the book. The main idea should be able to encompass all of the thoughts in a paragraph; choice D) does not apply to the beginning of this paragraph. Finally, choice C) is too specific; it could only apply to the brief description of the plot and adventures of the main character. That leaves choice B) as the best option. The author initially enjoyed the book, but was disappointed by the ending, which seemed unworthy of the exciting plot and character.

4. Clearly, Alyssa has a messy drawer, and **C) is the right answer**. The paragraph begins by indicating her gratitude that her coworkers do not know about her drawer (*Fortunately, none of Alyssa's coworkers have ever seen inside the large filing drawer in her desk*). Plus, notice how the drawer is described: *it was an organizational nightmare*, and it apparently doesn't even function properly: *to even open the drawer, she had to struggle for several minutes...* The writer reveals that it even has an odor, with old candy inside.

    Alyssa is clearly ashamed of her drawer and fearful of being judged by her coworkers about it.

5. You're looking for details from the passage that supports the main idea—scientists make use of many different technologies to study the surfaces of other planets. Answer A) includes a specific detail about rovers, but does not offer any details that support the idea of multiple technologies being used. Similarly, answer D) provides another specific detail about space probes. Answer B) doesn't provide any supporting details; it simply introduces the topic of the passage. **Only answer C) provides a detail that directly supports**

the author's assertion that scientists use multiple technologies to study the planets.

6. You can eliminate answers C) and D) because they don't address the topic of studying the surface of planets. Answer A) can also be eliminated because it only addresses a single technology. **Only choice B) would add support to the author's claim about the importance of using multiple technologies.**

7. **Only answer D) relates directly to the author's main argument.** The author doesn't mention how long it has taken to map the surface of Venus (answer A), nor does he say that one technology is more important than the others (answer B). And while this detail does highlight the advantages of using Earth-bound telescopes, the author's argument is that many technologies are being used at the same time, so there's no reason to think that orbiting telescopes will be replaced (answer C).

8. You can exclude answer choice C) because the author provides no root cause or a list of effects. From there this question gets tricky, because the passage contains structures similar to those described above. For example, it compares two things (cities in the North and South) and describes a place (a sprawling city). However, if you look at the overall organization of the passage, you can see that it starts by presenting a problem (transportation) and then presents a solution (trains and buses), making **answer D) the only choice that encompasses the entire passage**.

9. The passage is telling a story—we meet Elizabeth and learn about her fear of flying—so **it's a narrative text, answer choice A)**. There is no factual information presented or explained, nor is the author trying to persuade the reader of anything.

10. Choice B) can be discarded immediately because it is negative (recall that particularly negative answer statements are generally wrong) and is not discussed anywhere in the passage. Answers A) and D) are both opinions—the author is promoting exercise, fruits, and vegetables as a way to make children healthy. (Notice that these incorrect answers contain words that hint at being an opinion such as best, should, or other comparisons.) **Answer C), on the other hand, is a simple fact stated by the author**; it appears in the passage with the word *proven*, indicating that you don't just need to take the author's word for it.

11. **The author would most likely support answer C)**: he mentions in the first paragraph that poor diets are adding to the rising cost of healthcare. The main idea of the passage is that nutrition and exercise are important for children, so answer B) doesn't make sense—the author would likely support measures to encourage children to exercise. Answers A) and D) can also be eliminated because they are directly contradicted in the text. The author specifically mentions the role of school systems, so he doesn't believe parents are solely responsible for their children's health. He also specifically states that children

who grow up with unhealthy eating habits will become adults with unhealthy eating habits, which contradicts D).

12. It's clear from the passage that Elizabeth hates flying, but is willing to endure it for the sake of visiting her family. Thus, it seems likely that she would be willing to get on a plane for her brother's wedding, making A) and C) incorrect answers. The passage also explicitly tells us that she feels sick on planes, so D) is likely to happen. We can infer, though, that she would not enjoy being on an airplane for work, so she's very unlikely to apply for a job as a flight attendant, which is **choice B)**.

13. Already, you know that this sentence is discussing something that is hard to read. Look at the word that illegible is describing: handwriting. Based on context clues, you can tell that illegible means that her handwriting is hard to read.

    Next, look at the answer choices. Choice A), *neat*, is obviously a wrong answer because neat handwriting would not be difficult to read. Choices B) and D), *unsafe* and *educated*, don't make sense. Therefore, **choice C), *sloppy*, is the best answer**.

14. **Demonstrating bravery in the face of danger would be B), fearless.** In this case, the restatement clue (*braving the fire*) tells you exactly what the word means.

15. In this case, the contrast word *but* tells us that Tyrone studied in a different way than Beth, which means it's a contrast clue. If Beth did not study hard, then Tyrone did. **The best answer, therefore, is choice A).**

16. The first author uses scientific facts (*the Centers for Disease Control found...* and *Even this small amount of exercise has been proven...*) to back up his argument, while the second uses figurative language (the *ironic delicacies* and the metaphor *sugar-filled chocolate sludge*), so **the correct answer is B)**. Answer A) is incorrect because the first author does not present any opposing viewpoints. Answer C) is incorrect because Passage 2 does not have a cause-effect structure. And while the author of the second passage could be described as angry, the first author is not particularly friendly, so you can eliminate answer D) as well.

17. **Both authors argue children should learn healthy eating habits at a young age (answer A).** The author of Passage 1 states that a child who grows up living an unhealthy lifestyle is likely to become an adult who does the same, and the author of Passage 2 states that many of those children aren't going to grow out of bad habits—both of these sentences argue that it's necessary to teach children about nutrition early in life. Answers C) and D) are mentioned only by the author of Passage 1, and answer B) is only discussed in Passage 2.

CHAPTER TWO
Writing and Language

Parts of Speech

The first step in getting ready for the Writing and Language Test is to review parts of speech and the rules that accompany them. The good news is that you have been using these rules since you first began to speak; even if you don't know a lot of the technical terms, many of these rules may be familiar to you.

DID YOU KNOW?
Remember that you can write on the test booklet—cross out wrong answer choices and other parts of the text you may find confusing.

NOUNS and PRONOUNS

NOUNS are people, places, or things. For example, in the sentence *The hospital was very clean*, the noun is *hospital*; it is a place. Pronouns replace nouns and make sentences sound less repetitive. Take the sentence *Sam stayed home from school because Sam was not feeling well*. The word *Sam* appears twice in the same sentence. To avoid repetition and improve the sentence, use a pronoun instead: *Sam stayed at home because he did not feel well*.

Because pronouns take the place of nouns, they need to agree both in number and gender with the noun they replace. So, a plural noun needs a plural pronoun, and a feminine noun needs a feminine pronoun. In the first sentence of this paragraph, for example, the plural pronoun *they* replaced the plural noun *pronouns*. There will usually be several questions on the PSAT Writing and Language Test that cover pronoun agreement, so it's good to get comfortable spotting pronouns.

QUICK REVIEW
Singular pronouns:
▶ I, me, mine, my
▶ you, your, yours
▶ he, him, his
▶ she, her, hers
▶ it, its

Plural pronouns:
▶ we, us, our, ours
▶ they, them, their, theirs

EXAMPLES

1. Which sentence below is correct?
   A) If a student forgets their homework, it is considered incomplete.
   B) If a student forgets his or her homework, it is considered incomplete.

2. Which sentence below is correct?
   A) Everybody will receive their paychecks promptly.
   B) Everybody will receive his or her paycheck promptly.

3. Which sentence below is correct?
   A) When a nurse begins work at a hospital, you should wash your hands.
   B) When a nurse begins work at a hospital, he or she should wash his or her hands.

4. Which sentence below is correct?
   A) After the teacher spoke to the student, she realized her mistake.
   B) After Mr. White spoke to his student, she realized her mistake. (she and her referring to student)
   C) After speaking to the student, the teacher realized her own mistake. (her referring to teacher)

VERBS

A **VERB** is the action of a sentence: verbs *do* things. A verb must be conjugated to match the context of the sentence; this can sometimes be tricky because English has many irregular verbs. For example, *run* is an action verb in the present tense that becomes *ran* in the past tense; the linking verb *is* (which describes a state of being) becomes *was* in the past tense.

Table 2.1. Conjugation of the Verb *To Be*

	PAST	PRESENT	FUTURE
singular	was	is	will be
plural	were	are	will be

QUICK REVIEW
Think of the subject and the verb as sharing a single *s*. If the noun ends with an *s*, the verb shouldn't and vice versa.

Verb tense must make sense in the context of the sentence. For example, the sentence *I was baking cookies and eat some dough* probably sounds strange. That's because the two verbs *was baking* and *eat* are in different tenses. *Was baking* occurred in the past; *eat*, on the other hand, occurs in the present. To correct this error, conjugate *eat* in the past tense: *I was baking cookies and ate some dough.*

Like pronouns, verbs must agree in number with the noun they refer back to. In the example above, the verb *was* refers back to the singular *I*. If the subject of the sentence was plural, it would need to be modified to read *They were baking cookies and ate some dough*. Note that the verb *ate* does not change form; this is common for verbs in the past tense.

QUICK REVIEW
If the subject is separated from the verb, cross out the phrases between them to make conjugation easier.

EXAMPLES

5. Which sentence below is correct?

   A) The cat chase the ball while the dogs runs in the yard.

   B) The cat chases the ball while the dogs run in the yard.

6. Which sentence below is correct?

   A) The cars that had been recalled by the manufacturer was returned within a few months.

   B) The cars that had been recalled by the manufacturer were returned within a few months.

7. Which sentence below is correct?

   A) The deer hid in the trees.

   B) The deer are not all the same size.

8. Which sentence below is correct?

   A) The doctor and nurse work in the hospital.

   B) Neither the nurse nor her boss was scheduled to take a vacation.

   C) Either the patient or her parents complete her discharge paperwork.

9. Which sentence below is correct?

   A) Because it will rain during the party last night, we had to move the tables inside.

   B) Because it rained during the party last night, we had to move the tables inside.

ADJECTIVES and ADVERBS

ADJECTIVES are words that describe a noun. Take the sentence *The boy hit the ball*. If you want to know more about the noun *ball*, then you could use an adjective to describe him: *The boy hit the red ball*. An adjective simply provides more information about a noun in a sentence.

Like adjectives, **ADVERBS** provide more information about a part of a sentence. Adverbs can describe verbs, adjectives, and even other adverbs. For example, in the sentence

The doctor had recently hired a new employee, the adverb *recently* tells us more about how the action *hired* took place. Often, but not always, adverbs end in *–ly*. Remember that adverbs can never describe nouns—only adjectives can.

Adjectives, adverbs, and *modifying phrases* (groups of words that together modify another word) should always be placed as close as possible to the word they modify. Separating words from their modifiers can result in incorrect or confusing sentences.

EXAMPLES

10. Which sentence below is correct?
    A) Running through the hall, the bell rang and the student knew she was late.
    B) Running through the hall, the student heard the bell ring and knew she was late.

11. Which sentence below is correct?
    A) The terrifyingly lion's loud roar scared the zoo's visitors.
    B) The lion's terrifyingly loud roar scared the zoo's visitors.

OTHER PARTS of SPEECH

PREPOSITIONS generally help describe relationships in space and time; they may express the location of a noun or pronoun in relation to other words and phrases in a sentence. For example, in the sentence *The nurse parked her car in a parking garage*, the preposition *in* describes the position of the car in relation to the garage. The noun that follows the preposition is called its *object*. In the example above, the object of the preposition *in* is the noun *parking garage*.

CONJUNCTIONS connect words, phrases, and clauses. The conjunctions summarized in the acronym FANBOYS—for, and, nor, but, or, yet, so—are called **COORDINATING CONJUNCTIONS** and are used to join independent clauses. For example, in the sentence *The nurse prepared the patient for surgery, and the doctor performed the surgery*, the conjunction *and* joins the two independent clauses together. **SUBORDINATING CONJUNCTIONS**, like *although, because,* and *if,* join together an independent and dependent clause. In the sentence *She had to ride the subway because her car was broken*, the conjunction *because* joins together the two clauses. (Independent and dependent clauses are covered in more detail below.)

INTERJECTIONS, like *wow* and *hey*, express emotion and are most commonly used in conversation and casual writing. They are often followed by *exclamation points*.

Constructing Sentences
PHRASES and CLAUSES

A PHRASE is a group of words acting together that contain either a subject or verb, but not both. Phrases can be constructed from several different parts of speech. For example, a prepositional phrase includes a preposition and the object of that preposition (e.g., *under the table*), and a verb phrase includes the main verb and any helping verbs (e.g., *had been running*). Phrases cannot stand alone as sentences.

A CLAUSE is a group of words that contains both a subject and a verb. There are two types of clauses: INDEPENDENT CLAUSES can stand alone as sentences, and DEPENDENT CLAUSES cannot stand alone. Again, dependent clauses are recognizable as they begin with subordinating conjunctions.

EXAMPLE

12. Classify each of the following as a phrase, independent clause, or dependent clause:
   1) I have always wanted to drive a bright red sports car
   2) under the bright sky filled with stars
   3) because my sister is running late

TYPES of SENTENCES

A sentence can be classified as simple, compound, complex, or compound-complex based on the type and number of clauses it has.

SENTENCE TYPE	NUMBER OF INDEPENDENT CLAUSES	NUMBER OF DEPENDENT CLAUSES
	Table 2.2. Sentence Classification	
simple	1	0
compound	2+	0
complex	1	1+
compound-complex	2+	1+

A SIMPLE SENTENCE consists of only one independent clause. Because there are no dependent clauses in a simple sentence, it can be as short as two words, a subject and a verb (e.g., *I ran.*). However, a simple sentence may also contain prepositions, adjectives, and adverbs. Even though these additions can extend the length of a simple sentence, it is still considered a simple sentence as long as it doesn't contain any dependent clauses.

COMPOUND SENTENCES have two or more independent clauses and no dependent clauses. Usually a comma and a coordinating conjunction (*for, and, nor, but, or, yet,* and *so*) join the independent clauses, though semicolons can be used as well. For example, the sentence *My computer broke, so I took it to be repaired* is compound.

COMPLEX SENTENCES have one independent clause and at least one dependent clause. In the complex sentence *If you lie down with dogs, you'll wake up with fleas*, the first clause is dependent (because of the subordinating conjunction *if*), and the second is independent.

COMPOUND-COMPLEX SENTENCES have two or more independent clauses and at least one dependent clause. For example, the sentence *City traffic frustrates David because the streets are congested, so he is seeking an alternate route home*, is compound-complex. *City traffic frustrates David* is an independent clause, as is *he is seeking an alternate route home*; however the subordinating conjunction *because* indicates that *because the streets are so congested* is a dependent clause.

EXAMPLES

13. Classify the following sentence: *San Francisco is one of my favorite places in the United States.*
    A) A simple sentence
    B) A compound sentence
    C) A complex sentence
    D) A compound-complex sentence

14. Classify the following sentence: *I love listening to the radio in the car because I enjoy loud music on the open road.*
    A) A simple sentence
    B) A compound sentence
    C) A complex sentence
    D) A compound-complex sentence

15. Classify the following sentence: *I wanted to get a dog, but I got a fish because my roommate is allergic to pet dander.*
    A) A simple sentence
    B) A compound sentence
    C) A complex sentence
    D) A compound-complex sentence

16. Classify the following sentence: *The game was canceled, but we will still practice on Saturday.*

  A) A simple sentence

  B) A compound sentence

  C) A complex sentence

  D) A compound-complex sentence

CLAUSE PLACEMENT

In addition to the classifications above, sentences can also be defined by the location of the main clause. In a periodic sentence, the main idea of the sentence is held until the end. In a cumulative sentence, the independent clause comes first, and any modifying words or clauses follow it. (Note that this type of classification—periodic or cumulative—is not used in place of the simple, compound, complex, or compound-complex classifications. A sentence can be both cumulative and complex, for example.)

EXAMPLES

17. Classify the following sentence: *The GED, the TASC, the SAT, the ACT—this dizzying array of exams proved no match for the determined students.*

  A) A cumulative sentence

  B) A periodic sentence

18. Classify the following sentence: *Jessica was well prepared for the test, for she had studied for weeks, taken practice exams, and reviewed the material with other students.*

  A) A cumulative sentence

  B) A periodic sentence

Punctuation

The basic rules for using the major punctuation marks are given in Table 2.3.

Table 2.3. Basic Punctuation Rules		
PUNCTUATION	PURPOSE	EXAMPLE
period	ending sentences	Periods go at the end of complete sentences.
question mark	ending questions	What's the best way to end a sentence?

Table 2.3. Basic Punctuation Rules (continued)

Punctuation	Purpose	Example
exclamation point	indicating interjections or commands; ending sentences that show extreme emotion	Help! I'll never understand how to use punctuation!
comma	joining two independent clauses (always with a coordinating conjunction)	Commas can be used to join independent clauses, but they must always be followed by a coordinating conjunction in order to avoid a comma splice.
	setting apart introductory and nonessential words and phrases	Commas, when used properly, set apart extra information in a sentence.
	separating three or more items in a list	My favorite punctuation marks include the colon, semicolon, and period.
semicolon	joining together two independent clauses (never with a conjunction)	I love semicolons; they make sentences so concise!
colon	introducing a list, explanation, or definition	When I see a colon I know what to expect: more information.
apostrophe	form contractions	It's amazing how many people can't use apostrophes correctly.
	show possession	The students' grammar books are out of date, but the school's principal cannot order new ones yet.
quotation marks	indicate a direct quote	I said to her, "Tell me more about parentheses."

EXAMPLES

19. Which sentence below is correct?

A) Her roommate asked her to pick up milk, and a watermelon from the grocery store.

B) Her roommate asked her to pick up milk and a watermelon from the grocery store.

20. Which sentence below is correct?

A) The softball coach—who had been in the job for only a year, quit unexpectedly on Friday.

B) The softball coach—who had been in the job for only a year—quit unexpectedly on Friday.

C) The softball coach, who had been in the job for only a year, quit unexpectedly on Friday

21. Which sentence below is correct?

A) I'd like to order a hamburger, with extra cheese, but my friend says I should get a fruit salad instead.

B) I'd like to order a hamburger with extra cheese, but my friend says I should get a fruit salad instead.

Point of View

A sentence's **POINT OF VIEW** is the perspective from which it is written. Point of view is described as either first, second, or third person.

Table 2.4. Point of View			
PERSON	**PRONOUNS**	**WHO'S ACTING?**	**EXAMPLE**
first	I, we	the writer	I take my time when shopping for shoes.
second	you	the reader	You prefer to shop online.
third	he, she, it, they	the subject	She buys shoes from her cousin's store.

First person perspective appears when the writer's personal experiences, feelings, and opinions are an important element of the text. Second person perspective is used when the author directly addresses the reader. Third person perspective is most common in formal and academic writing; it creates distance between the writer and the reader. A sentence's point of view must remain consistent.

EXAMPLE

22. Which sentence below is correct?

A) If someone wants to be a professional athlete, you have to practice often.

B) If you want to be a professional athlete, you have to practice often.

C) If someone wants to be a professional athlete, he or she has to practice often.

Active and Passive Voice

Sentences can be written in active voice or passive voice. **ACTIVE VOICE** means that the subjects of the sentences are performing the action of the sentence. In a sentence written in **PASSIVE VOICE**, the subjects are being acted on. The sentence *Justin wrecked my car* is in the active voice because the subject (*Justin*) is doing the action (*wrecked*). The sentence can be rewritten in passive voice by using a to be verb: *My car was wrecked by Justin.* Now the subject of the sentence (*car*) is being acted on. It's also possible to write the sentence so that the person performing the action is not identified: *My car was wrecked.*

Generally, good writing will avoid using passive voice. However, when it is unclear who or what performed the action of the sentence, passive voice may be the only option.

EXAMPLES

23. Rewrite the following sentence in active voice: *I was hit with a stick by my brother.*

24. Rewrite the following sentence in passive voice: *My roommate made coffee this morning.*

Transitions

TRANSITIONS connect two ideas and also explain the logical relationship between them. For example, the transition *because* tells you that two things have a cause and effect relationship, while the transitional phrase *on the other hand* introduces a contradictory idea. On the PSAT Writing and Language Test you may be asked to identify the best transition for a particular sentence, and you will definitely need to make good use of transitions in your essay.

DID YOU KNOW?
Don't be afraid to choose "No Change"—it will be the correct choice around a quarter of the time!

Table 2.5. Common Transitions	
CAUSE AND EFFECT	AS A RESULT, BECAUSE, CONSEQUENTLY, DUE TO, IF/THEN, SO, THEREFORE, THUS
Similarity	also, likewise, similar, between
Contrast	but, however, in contrast, on the other hand, nevertheless, on the contrary, yet
Concluding	briefly, finally, in conclusion, in summary, to conclude
Addition	additionally, also, as well, further, furthermore, in addition, moreover
Examples	in other words, for example, for instance, to illustrate
Time	after, before, currently, later, recently, since, subsequently, then, while

EXAMPLES

Choose the transition word or words that would best fit in the blank.

25. Clara's car breaks down frequently. _____, she decided to buy a new one.

   A) However

   B) For example

   C) While

   D) Therefore

26. Chad scored more points than any other player on his team. _____, he is often late to practice, so his coach won't let him play in the game Saturday.

   A) However

   B) For example

   C) While

   D) Therefore

27. Miguel will often eat his lunch outside. _____, on Wednesday he took his sandwich to the park across from his office.

   A) However

   B) For example

   C) While

   D) Therefore

28. Alex set the table _____ the lasagna finished baking in the oven.

   A) however

   B) for example

   C) while

   D) therefore

Wordiness and Redundancy

Sometimes sentences can be grammatically correct but still be confusing or poorly written. Often this problem arises when sentences are wordy or contain redundant phrasing (i.e., when several words with similar meanings are used). Often such phrases are used to make the writing seem more serious or academic when actually they can confuse the reader. On the test, you might be asked to clarify or even remove such phrases.

Some examples of excessive wordiness and redundancy include:

► I'll meet you in the *place where I parked my car.* → I'll meet you in the *parking lot.*

► *The point I am trying to make is that* the study was flawed. → The study was flawed.

► A memo was sent out *concerning the matter of* dishes left in the sink. → A memo was sent out *about* dishes left in the sink.

► The email was *brief and to the point.* → The email was *terse.*

► I don't think I'll ever *understand or comprehend* Italian operas. → I don't think I'll ever *understand* Italian operas.

EXAMPLES

Rewrite each of the following sentences to eliminate wordiness and redundancy.

29. The game was canceled due to the fact that a bad storm was predicted.

30. The possibility exists that we will have a party for my mother's birthday.

31. With the exception of our new puppy, all of our dogs have received their vaccinations.

32. We threw away the broken microwave that didn't work.

33. It was an unexpected surprise when we won the raffle.

Answer Key

1. **B)** *Student* is a singular noun, but *their* is a plural pronoun, making the first sentence grammatically incorrect. To correct it, replace *their* with the singular pronoun *his* or *her*.

2. **B)** *Everybody* is a singular noun, but *their* is a plural pronoun; the first sentence is grammatically incorrect. To correct it, replace *their* with the singular pronoun *his* or *her*.

3. **B)** This sentence begins in third-person perspective and finishes in second-person perspective. To correct it, ensure the sentence finishes with third-person perspective.

4. **B) and C)** This sentence refers to a teacher and a student. But to whom does *she* refer, the teacher or the student? To improve clarity, use specific names or state more clearly who spotted the mistake.

5. **B)** *Cat* is singular, so it takes a singular verb (which confusingly ends with an s); *dogs* is plural, so it needs a plural verb.

6. **B)** Sometimes the subject and verb are separated by clauses or phrases. Here, the subject *cars* is separated from the verb phrase *were returned*, making it more difficult to conjugate the verb correctly; this results in a number error.

7. **A) and B)** The subject of these sentences is a collective noun, which describes a group of people or things. This noun can

be singular if it is referring to the group as a whole or plural if it refers to each item in the group as a separate entity.

8. **A), B), and C)** When the subject contains two or more nouns connected by *and*, that subject is plural and requires a plural verb. Singular subjects joined by *or, either/or, neither/nor,* or *not only/but also* remain singular; when these words join plural and singular subjects, the verb should match the closest subject.

9. **B)** All the verb tenses in a sentence need to agree both with each other and with the other information in the sentence. In the first sentence, the tense doesn't match the other information in the sentence: *last night* indicates the past (rained) not the future (will rain).

10. **B)** The phrase *running through the hall* should be placed next to *student*, the noun it modifies.

11. **B)** While the lion may indeed be terrifying, the word *terrifyingly* is an adverb and so can only modify a verb, an adjective or another adverb, not the noun *lion*. In the second sentence, *terrifyingly* is modifying the adjective *loud*, telling us more about the loudness of the lion's roar—so loud, it was terrifying.

12. **1 is an independent clause—it** has a subject (*I*) and a verb (*have wanted*) and has no subordinating conjunction. **2 is a phrase** made up of a preposition (*under*), its

object (*sky*), and words that modify sky (*bright, filled with stars*), but lacks a conjugated verb. **3 is a dependent clause**—it has a subject (*sister*), a verb (*is running*), and a subordinating conjunction (*because*).

13. **A)** Although the sentence is lengthy, it is simple because it contains only one subject and verb (*San Francisco... is*) modified by additional phrases.

14. **C)** The sentence has one independent clause (*I love... car*) and one dependent (*because I... road*), so it is complex.

15. **D)** This sentence has three clauses: two independent (*I wanted... dog* and *I got a fish*) and one dependent (*because my... dander*), so it is compound-complex.

16. **B)** This sentence is made up of two independent clauses joined by a conjunction (*but*), so it is compound.

17. **B)** In this sentence the main independent clause—*this... students*—is held until the very end, so it's periodic. Furthermore, despite its length the sentence is simple because it has only one subject (*dizzying array*) and verb (*proved*).

18. **A)** Here, the main clause *Jessica... test* begins the sentence; the other clauses modify the main clause, providing more information about the main idea and resulting in a cumulative sentence. In addition, the sentence is compound as it links two independent clauses together with a comma and the coordinating conjunction *for*.

19. **B)** Commas are only needed when joining three items in a series; this sentence only has two (milk and watermelon).

20. **B) and C)** When setting apart nonessential words and phrases, you can use either dashes or commas, but not both.

21. **B)** Prepositional phrases are usually essential to the meaning of the sentence, so they don't need to be set apart with commas. Here, the prepositional phrase *with extra cheese* helps the reader understand that the speaker wants a particularly unhealthy meal; however, the friend is encouraging a healthier option. Removing the prepositional phrase would limit the contrast between the burger and the salad. Note that the second comma remains because it is separating two independent clauses.

22. **B) and C)** In the first sentence, the person shifts from third (*someone*) to second (*you*). It needs to be rewritten to be consistent.

23. First, identify the person or object performing the action (usually given in a prepositional phrase— here, *by my brother*) and make it the subject; the subject of the original sentence (*I*) becomes the object. Remove the *to be* verb: *My brother hit me with a stick.*

24. Here, the object (*coffee*) becomes the subject; move the original subject (*my roommate*) to a prepositional phrase at the end of the sentence. Add the *to be* verb: *The coffee was made this morning by my roommate.*

25. **D)** The sentence is describing a cause (*her car breaks down*) and an effect (*she'll buy a new one*), so the correct transition is *therefore*.

26. **A)** The sentence includes a contrast: it would make sense for Chad to play in the game, but he isn't, so the best transition is *however*.

27. **B)** In the sentence, the clause after the transition is an example, so the best transition is *for example*.

28. **C)** In the sentence, two things are occurring at the same time, so the best transition is *while*.

29. The game was canceled because a bad storm was predicted.

    Replace the long phrase *due to the fact that* with the much shorter *because*.

30. We might have a party for my mother's birthday.

    By rearranging the sentence, we can replace the phrase *the possibility exists that* with the word *might*.

31. All of our dogs have been vaccinated except our new puppy.

    The sentence can be rearranged to replace *with the exception of* with *except*. The phrase *receive their vaccinations* has also been shortened to *been vaccinated*.

32. We threw away the broken microwave.

    If something is broken that means it doesn't work, so the phrase *that didn't work* can be removed.

33. It was a surprise when we won the raffle.

    By definition, a surprise is always unexpected, so the word *unexpected* can be removed.

PART II
Mathematics
13 questions ¦ 20 minutes (without calculator)

25 questions ¦ 40 minutes (with calculator)

The Mathematics section of the PSAT tests your knowledge of math concepts taught through the tenth grade, including geometry, algebra, statistics, probability, and trigonometry. The majority of the questions will require you to use complex reasoning to work through multiple steps—you won't simply be performing calculations. Instead, you can expect to perform tasks like building equations from word problems, comparing expressions, and interpreting figures.

The first thirteen questions of the Mathematics section have to be done without a calculator; you may use a calculator on the final twenty-five questions. You can use any calculator that can't access the internet, including graphing calculators. Note that you cannot use the calculator on your tablet or phone.

There are two types of questions on the Mathematics section: multiple-choice and grid-in. For the grid-in questions, you will be required to provide an answer—no answer choices will be provided for you. A couple of notes about grid-in answers:

- ▶ Answers cannot be given as mixed numbers—you must convert the answer to a decimal or improper fraction.

- ▶ Decimal numbers must be rounded to fit in the grid. Do not include the zero before the decimal point; instead you can place the decimal point in the left-most column.

- ▶ There are no negative answers on the grid-in questions.

- ▶ You will only receive credit for answers that are bubbled in; you will NOT get credit if you only write the answer in the box at the top of the grid.

CHAPTER THREE
Numbers and Operations

In order to do any type of math—whether it's basic geometry or advanced calculus—you need to have a solid understanding of numbers and operations. The specific operations the PSAT will test you on are covered in this chapter. However, we won't be covering basic arithmetic operations like adding fractions or long division, since you'll be able to perform these on your calculator during the test.

Types of Numbers

INTEGERS are whole numbers, including the counting numbers, the negative counting numbers and zero. 3, 2, 1, 0, –1, –2, –3 are examples of integers. **RATIONAL NUMBERS** are made by dividing one integer by another integer. They can be expressed as fractions or as decimals. Three divided by 4 makes the rational number $\frac{3}{4}$ or 0.75. **IRRATIONAL NUMBERS** are numbers that cannot be written as fractions; they are decimals that go on forever without repeating. The number π (3.14159…) is an example of an irrational number.

Imaginary numbers are numbers that, when squared, give a negative result. Imaginary numbers use the symbol i to represent $\sqrt{-1}$, so $3i = 3\sqrt{-1}$ and $(3i)^2 = -9$. **COMPLEX NUMBERS** are combinations of real and imaginary numbers, written in the form $a + bi$, where a is the real number and bi is the imaginary number. An example of a complex number is $4 + 2i$. When adding complex numbers, add the real and imaginary numbers separately: $(4 + 2i) + (3 + i) = 7 + 3i$.

EXAMPLES

1. Is $\sqrt{5}$ a rational or irrational number?

2. What kind of number is $-\sqrt{64}$?

3. Solve: $(3 + 5i) - (1 - 2i)$

Working with Positive and Negative Numbers

Adding, multiplying, and dividing numbers can yield positive or negative values depending on the signs of the original numbers. Knowing these rules can help determine if your answer is correct.

(+) + (–) = the sign of the larger number

(–) + (–) = negative number

(–) × (–) = positive number

(–) × (+) = negative number

(–) ÷ (–) = positive number

(–) ÷ (+) = negative number

EXAMPLES

4. Find the product of –10 and 47.

5. What is the sum of –65 and –32?

6. Is the product of –7 and 4 less than –7, between –7 and 4, or greater than 4?

7. What is the value of –16 divided by 2.5?

Order of Operations

Operations in a mathematical expression are always performed in a specific order, which is described by the acronym PEMDAS:

1. Parentheses
2. Exponents
3. Multiplication
4. Division

5. Addition

6. Subtraction

Perform the operations within parentheses first, and then address any exponents. After those steps, perform all multiplication and division. These are carried out from left to right as they appear in the problem. Finally, do all required addition and subtraction, also from left to right as each operation appears in the problem.

EXAMPLES

8. Solve: $[-(2)^2 - (4 + 7)]$

9. Solve: $(5)^2 \div 5 + 4 \times 2$

10. Solve the expression: $15 \times (4 + 8) - 3^3$

11. Solve the expression: $\left(\frac{5}{2} \times 4\right) + 23 - 4^2$

Units of Measurement

You are expected to memorize some units of measurement. These are given below. When doing unit conversion problems (i.e., when converting one unit to another), find the conversion factor, then apply that factor to the given measurement to find the new units.

Table 3.1. Unit Prefixes		
PREFIX	SYMBOL	MULTIPLICATION FACTOR
tera	T	1,000,000,000,000
giga	G	1,000,000,000
mega	M	1,000,000
kilo	k	1,000
hecto	h	100
deca	da	10
base unit	--	--
deci	d	0.1
centi	c	0.01
milli	m	0.001
micro	μ	0.0000001
nano	n	0.0000000001
pico	p	0.0000000000001

Table 3.2. Units and Conversion Factors

Dimension	American	SI
length	inch/foot/yard/mile	meter
mass	ounce/pound/ton	gram
volume	cup/pint/quart/gallon	liter
force	pound-force	newton
pressure	pound-force per square inch	pascal
work and energy	cal/British thermal unit	joule
temperature	Fahrenheit	kelvin
charge	faraday	coulomb

Conversion Factors

1 in = 2.54 cm	1 lb = 0.454 kg
1 yd = 0.914 m	1 cal = 4.19 J
1 mile = 1.61 km	$1\ °F = \frac{5}{9}\ (°F - 32)$
1 gallon = 3.785 L	$1\ cm^3 = 1\ mL$
1 oz = 28.35 g	1 hour = 3600 s

EXAMPLES

12. A fence measures 15 ft. long. How many yards long is the fence?

13. A pitcher can hold 24 cups. How many gallons can it hold?

14. A spool of wire holds 144 in. of wire. If Mario has 3 spools, how many feet of wire does he have?

15. A ball rolling across a table travels 6 inches per second. How many feet will it travel in 1 minute?

16. How many millimeters are in 0.5 meters?

17. A lead ball weighs 38 g. How many kilograms does it weigh?

18 How many cubic centimeters are in 10 L?

19. Jennifer's pencil was initially 10 centimeters long. After she sharpened it, it was 9.6 centimeters long. How many millimeters did she lose from her pencil by sharpening it?

Decimals and Fractions
ADDING and SUBTRACTING DECIMALS

When adding and subtracting decimals, line up the numbers so that the decimals are aligned. You want to subtract the ones place from the ones place, the tenths place from the tenths place, and so on.

EXAMPLES

20. Find the sum of 17.07 and 2.52.

21. Jeannette has 7.4 gallons of gas in her tank. After driving, she has 6.8 gallons. How many gallons of gas did she use?

MULTIPLYING and DIVIDING DECIMALS

When multiplying decimals, start by multiplying the numbers normally. You can then determine the placement of the decimal point in the result by adding the number of digits after the decimal in each of the numbers you multiplied together.

When dividing decimals, you should move the decimal point in the divisor (the number you're dividing by) until it is a whole number. You can then move the decimal in the dividend (the number you're dividing into) the same number of places in the same direction. Finally, divide the new numbers normally to get the correct answer.

EXAMPLES

22. What is the product of 0.25 and 1.4?

23. Find 0.8 ÷ 0.2.

24. Find the quotient when 40 is divided by 0.25.

WORKING with FRACTIONS

FRACTIONS are made up of two parts: the NUMERATOR, which appears above the bar, and the DENOMINATOR, which is below it. If a fraction is in its SIMPLEST FORM, the numerator and the denominator share no common factors. A fraction with a numerator larger than its denominator is an IMPROPER FRACTION; when the denominator is larger, it's a PROPER FRACTION.

Improper fractions can be converted into proper fractions by dividing the numerator by the denominator. The resulting whole number is placed to the left of the fraction, and the remainder becomes the new numerator; the denominator does not change. The new number is called a **MIXED NUMBER** because it contains a whole number and a fraction. Mixed numbers can be turned into improper fractions through the reverse process: multiply the whole number by the denominator and add the numerator to get the new numerator.

EXAMPLES

25. Simplify the fraction $\frac{121}{77}$.

26. Convert $\frac{37}{5}$ into a proper fraction.

MULTIPLYING and DIVIDING FRACTIONS

To multiply fractions, convert any mixed numbers into improper fractions and multiply the numerators together and the denominators together. Reduce to lowest terms if needed.

DID YOU KNOW?
Inverting a fraction changes multiplication to division:
$$\frac{a}{b} \div \frac{c}{d} = \frac{a}{b} \times \frac{d}{c} = \frac{d}{bc}$$

To divide fractions, first convert any mixed fractions into single fractions. Then, invert the second fraction so that the denominator and numerator are switched. Finally, multiply the numerators together and the denominators together.

EXAMPLES

27. Find $\frac{7}{8} \div \frac{1}{4}$.

28. What is the product of $\frac{1}{12}$ and $\frac{6}{8}$?

29. Find the quotient: $\frac{2}{5} \div 1\frac{1}{5}$.

30. A recipe calls for $\frac{1}{4}$ cup of sugar. If 8.5 batches of the recipe are needed, how many cups of sugar will be used?

ADDING and SUBTRACTING FRACTIONS

Adding and subtracting fractions requires a **COMMON DENOMINATOR**. To find the common denominator, you can multiply each fraction by the number 1. With fractions, any number over itself (e.g., $\frac{5}{5}$, $\frac{12}{12}$) is equivalent to 1, so multiplying by such a fraction can change the denominator without changing the value of the fraction. Once the denominators are the same, the numerators can be added or subtracted.

DID YOU KNOW?
The phrase *simplify the expression* just means you need to perform all the operations in the expression.

To add mixed numbers, first add the whole numbers and then the fractions. To subtract mixed numbers, convert each number to an improper fraction, then subtract the numerators.

EXAMPLES

31. Simplify the expression: $\frac{2}{3} - \frac{1}{5}$.

32. Find $2\frac{1}{3} - \frac{3}{2}$.

33. Find the sum of $\frac{9}{16}$, $\frac{1}{2}$, and $\frac{7}{4}$.

34. Sabrina has $\frac{2}{3}$ of a can of red paint. Her friend Amos has $\frac{1}{6}$ of a can. How much red paint do they have combined?

CONVERTING FRACTIONS to DECIMALS

Calculators are not allowed on a portion of the PSAT, which can make handling fractions and decimals intimidating for many test takers. However, there are several helpful techniques you can use to navigate between the two forms.

The first thing to do is simply memorize common decimals and their fractional equivalents; a list of these is given below. With these values, it's possible to convert more complicated fractions as well. For example, $\frac{2}{5}$ is just $\frac{1}{5}$ multiplied by 2, so $\frac{2}{5} = 0.2 \times 2 = 0.4$.

Table 3.3. Fractions to Decimals	
FRACTION	**DECIMAL**
$\frac{1}{2}$	0.5
$\frac{1}{3}$	$0.\overline{33}$
$\frac{1}{4}$	0.25
$\frac{1}{5}$	0.2
$\frac{1}{6}$	$0.1\overline{66}$
$\frac{1}{7}$	$0.\overline{142857}$
$\frac{1}{8}$	0.125
$\frac{1}{9}$	$0.\overline{11}$
$\frac{1}{10}$	0.1

Knowledge of common decimal equivalents to fractions can also help you estimate. This skill can be particularly helpful on multiple-choice tests like the PSAT, where excluding incorrect answers is just as helpful as knowing how to find the right one. For example, to find $\frac{5}{8}$ in decimal form for an answer, you can eliminate any answers less than 0.5 because $\frac{4}{8}$ = 0.5. You may also know that $\frac{6}{8}$ is the same as $\frac{3}{4}$ or 0.75, so anything above 0.75 can be eliminated as well.

Another helpful trick is to check if the denominator is easily divisible by 100; for example in the fraction $\frac{9}{20}$, you know 20 goes into 100 five times, so you can multiply the top and bottom by 5 to get $\frac{45}{100}$ or 0.45.

If none of these techniques work, you'll need to find the decimal by dividing the denominator by the numerator using long division.

EXAMPLES

35. Write $\frac{8}{18}$ as a decimal.

36. Write the fraction $\frac{3}{16}$ as a decimal.

CONVERTING DECIMALS to FRACTIONS

Converting a decimal into a fraction is more straightforward than the reverse process is. To convert a decimal, simply use the numbers that come after the decimal as the numerator in the fraction. The denominator will be a power of 10 that matches the place value for the original decimal. For example, the denominator for 0.46 would be 100 because the last number is in the hundredths place; likewise, the denominator for 0.657 would be 1000 because the last number is in the thousandths place. Once this fraction has been set up, all that's left is to simplify it.

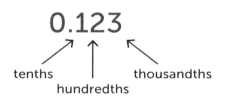

Figure 3.1. Decimal Places

EXAMPLE

37. Convert 0.45 into a fraction.

Ratios

A ratio describes the quantity of one thing in relation to the quantity of another. Unlike fractions, ratios do not give a part relative to a whole; instead, they compare two values. For example, if you have 3 apples and 4 oranges, the ratio of apples to oranges is 3 to 4. Ratios can be written using words (3 to 4), fractions $\left(\frac{3}{4}\right)$, or colons (3:4).

It's helpful to rewrite a ratio as a fraction expressing a part to a whole. For instance, in the example above you have 7 total pieces of fruit, so the fraction of your fruit that is apples is $\frac{3}{7}$, while oranges make up $\frac{4}{7}$ of your fruit collection.

When working with ratios, always consider the units of the values being compared. On the PSAT, you may be asked to rewrite a ratio using the same units on both sides. For example, you might have to rewrite the ratio 3 minutes to 7 seconds as 180 seconds to 7 seconds.

EXAMPLES

38. There are 90 voters in a room, and each is either a Democrat or a Republican. The ratio of Democrats to Republicans is 5:4. How many Republicans are there?

39. The ratio of students to teachers in a school is 15:1. If there are 38 teachers, how many students attend the school?

Proportions

A proportion is an equation that equates two ratios. Proportions are usually written as two fractions joined by an equal sign $\left(\frac{a}{b} = \frac{c}{d}\right)$, but they can also be written using colons (a:b::c:d). Note that in a proportion, the units must be the same in both numerators and in both denominators.

Often you will be given three of the values in a proportion and asked to find the fourth. In these types of problems, you can solve for the missing variable by cross-multiplying—multiply the numerator of each fraction by the denominator of the other to get an equation with no fractions as shown below. You can then solve the equation using basic algebra. (For more on solving basic equations, see *Algebraic Expressions*.)

$$\frac{a}{b} = \frac{c}{d} \rightarrow ad = bc$$

EXAMPLES

40. A train traveling 120 miles takes 3 hours to get to its destination. How long will it take for the train to travel 180 miles?

41. One acre of wheat requires 500 gallons of water. How many acres can be watered with 2600 gallons?

42. If 35:5::49:x, find x.

Percentages

A percent is the ratio of a part to the whole. Questions may give the part and the whole and ask for the percent, or give the percent and the whole and ask for the part, or give the part and the percent and ask for the value of the whole. The equation for percentages can be rearranged to solve for any of these:

$$\text{percent} = \frac{\text{part}}{\text{whole}}$$

$$\text{part} = \text{whole} \times \text{percent}$$

$$\text{whole} = \frac{\text{part}}{\text{percent}}$$

In the equations above, the percent should always be expressed as a decimal. In order to convert a decimal into a percentage value, simply multiply it by 100. So, if you've read 5 pages (the part) of a 10-page article (the whole), you've read $\frac{5}{10}$ = .50 or 50%. (The percent sign (%) is used once the decimal has been multiplied by 100.)

Note that when solving these problems, the units for the part and the whole should be the same. If you're reading a book, saying you've read 5 pages out of 15 chapters doesn't make any sense.

EXAMPLES

43. 45 is 15% of what number?

44. Jim spent 30% of his paycheck at the fair. He spent $15 for a hat, $30 for a shirt, and $20 playing games. How much was his check? (Round to the nearest dollar.)

45. What percent of 65 is 39?

46. Greta and Max sell cable subscriptions. In a given month, Greta sells 45 subscriptions and Max sells 51. If 240 total subscriptions were sold in that month, what percent were not sold by Greta or Max?

47. Grant needs to score 75% on an exam. If the exam has 45 questions, at least how many does he need to answer correctly to get this score?

PERCENT CHANGE

Percent change problems ask you to calculate how much a given quantity has changed. The problems are solved in a similar way to regular percent problems, except that instead of using the *part* you'll use the *amount of change*. Note that the sign of the *amount of change* is important: if the original amount has increased the change will be positive; if it has decreased the change will be negative. Again, in the equations below the percent is a decimal value; you need to multiply by 100 to get the actual percentage.

$$\text{percent change} = \frac{\text{amount of change}}{\text{original amount}}$$

$$\text{amount of change} = \text{original amount} \times \text{percent change}$$

$$\text{original amount} = \frac{\text{amount of change}}{\text{percent change}}$$

EXAMPLES

48. A computer software retailer marks up its games by 40% above the wholesale price when it sells them to customers. Find the price of a game for a customer if the game costs the retailer $25.

49. A golf shop pays its wholesaler $40 for a certain club, and then sells it to a golfer for $75. What is the markup rate?

50. A shoe store charges a 40% markup on the shoes it sells. How much did the store pay for a pair of shoes purchased by a customer for $63?

51. An item originally priced at $55 is marked 25% off. What is the sale price?

52. James wants to put an 18 foot by 51 foot garden in his backyard. If he does, it will reduce the size of his yard by 24%. What will be the area of the remaining yard space?

Comparison of Rational Numbers

Number comparison problems present numbers in different formats and ask which is larger or smaller, or whether the numbers are equivalent. The important step in solving these problems is to convert the numbers to the same format so that it is easier to compare them. If numbers are given in the same format, or after converting them, determine which number is smaller or if the numbers are equal. Remember that for negative numbers, higher numbers are actually smaller.

EXAMPLES

53. Is $4\frac{3}{4}$ greater than, equal to, or less than $\frac{18}{4}$?

54. Which of the following numbers has the greatest value: 104.56, 104.5, or 104.6?

55. Is 65% greater than, less than, or equal to $\frac{13}{20}$?

Exponents and Radicals

Exponents tell us how many times to multiply a base number by itself. In the example 2^4, 2 is the base number and 4 is the exponent. $2^4 = 2 \times 2 \times 2 \times 2 = 16$. Exponents are also called powers: 5 to the third power $= 5^3 = 5 \times 5 \times 5 = 125$. Some exponents have special names: x to the second power is also called "x squared" and x to the third power is also called "x cubed." The number 3 squared $= 3^2 = 3 \times 3 = 9$.

Radicals are expressions that use roots. Radicals are written in the form $\sqrt[a]{x}$ where a = the **RADICAL POWER** and x = **THE RADICAND**. The solution to the radical $\sqrt[3]{8}$ is the number that, when multiplied by itself 3 times, equals 8. $\sqrt[3]{8} = 2$ because $2 \times 2 \times 2 = 8$. When the radical power is not written we assume it is 2, so $\sqrt{9} = 3$ because $3 \times 3 = 9$. Radicals can also be written as exponents, where the power is a fraction. For example, $x^{\frac{1}{3}} = \sqrt[3]{x}$.

Review more of the rules for working with exponents and radicals in the table below.

Table 3.4. Exponents and Radicals Rules

RULE	EXAMPLE
$x^0 = 1$	$5^0 = 1$
$x^1 = x$	$5^1 = 5$
$x^a \times x^b = x^{a+b}$	$5^2 \times 5^3 = 5^5 = 3125$
$(xy)^a = x^a y^a$	$(5 \times 6)^2 = 5^2 \times 6^2 = 900$
$(x^a)^b = x^{ab}$	$(5^2)^3 = 5^6 = 15{,}625$
$\left(\dfrac{x}{y}\right)^a = \dfrac{x^a}{y^a}$	$\left(\dfrac{5}{6}\right)^2 = \dfrac{5^2}{6^2} = \dfrac{25}{36}$
$\dfrac{x^a}{x^b} = x^{a-b} \ (x \neq 0)$	$\dfrac{5^4}{5^3} = 5^1 = 5$
$x^{-a} = \dfrac{1}{x^a} \ (x \neq 0)$	$5^{-2} = \dfrac{1}{5^2} = \dfrac{1}{25}$
$x^{\frac{1}{a}} = \sqrt[a]{x}$	$25^{\frac{1}{2}} = \sqrt[2]{25} = 5$
$\sqrt[a]{x \times y} = \sqrt[a]{x} \times \sqrt[a]{y}$	$\sqrt[3]{8 \times 27} = \sqrt[3]{8} \times \sqrt[3]{27} = 2 \times 3 = 6$
$\sqrt[a]{\dfrac{x}{y}} = \dfrac{\sqrt[a]{x}}{\sqrt[a]{y}}$	$\sqrt[3]{\dfrac{27}{8}} = \dfrac{\sqrt[3]{27}}{\sqrt[3]{8}} = \dfrac{3}{2}$
$\sqrt[a]{x^b} = x^{\frac{b}{a}}$	$\sqrt[2]{5^4} = 5^{\frac{4}{2}} = 5^2 = 25$

56. Simplify the expression $2^4 \times 2^2$

57. Simplify the expression $(3^4)^{-1}$

58. Simplify the expression $\left(\frac{9}{4}\right)^{\frac{1}{2}}$

Matrices

A **MATRIX** is an array of numbers aligned into horizontal rows and vertical columns. A matrix is described by the number of rows (m) and columns (n) it contains. For example, a matrix with 3 rows and 4 columns is a 3×4 matrix, as shown below.

$$\begin{bmatrix} 2 & -3 & 5 & 0 \\ 4 & -6 & 2 & 11 \\ 3.5 & 7 & 2.78 & -1.2 \end{bmatrix}$$

To add or subtract 2 matrices, simply add or subtract the corresponding numbers in each matrix. Only matrices with the same dimensions can be added or subtracted, and the resulting matrix will also have the same dimensions.

In order to multiply 2 matrices, the number of columns in the first must equal the number of rows in the second. To multiply the matrices, multiply the numbers in each row of the first by the numbers in the column of the second and add. The resulting matrix will have the same number of rows as the first matrix and same number of columns as the second. Note that the order of the matrices is important when they're being multiplied: **AB** is not the same as **BA**.

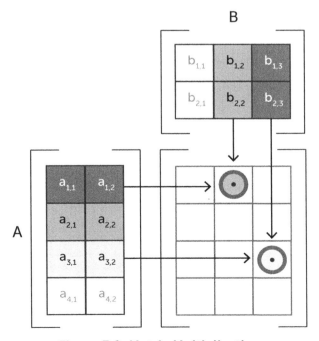

Figure 3.2. Matrix Multiplication

To multiply a matrix by a single number or variable, simply multiply each value within the matrix by that number or variable.

EXAMPLES

59. Simplify: $\begin{bmatrix} 6 & 4 & -8 \\ -3 & 1 & 0 \end{bmatrix} + \begin{bmatrix} 5 & -3 & -2 \\ -3 & 4 & 9 \end{bmatrix}$

60. Solve for x and y: $\begin{bmatrix} x & 6 \\ 4 & y \end{bmatrix} + \begin{bmatrix} 3 & 2 \\ 8 & -1 \end{bmatrix} = \begin{bmatrix} 11 & 8 \\ 12 & 4 \end{bmatrix}$

61. If $\mathbf{A} = \begin{bmatrix} 1 & 3 & 0 \\ 6 & 2 & 4 \end{bmatrix}$ and $\mathbf{B} = \begin{bmatrix} 5 & 3 \\ 2 & 1 \\ 4 & 7 \end{bmatrix}$, what is $\mathbf{AB}$?

62. Simplify: $6x \begin{bmatrix} 2 & -3 \\ 6 & 4 \end{bmatrix}$

Answer Key

1. $\sqrt{5}$ is an irrational number because it cannot be written as a fraction of two integers. It is a decimal that goes on forever without repeating.

2. $-\sqrt{64}$ can be rewritten as the negative whole number −8, so it is an **integer**.

3. Subtract the real and imaginary numbers separately.

   $3 - 1 = 2$

   $5i - (-2i) = 5i + 2i = 7i$

   Solve $(3 + 5i) - (1 - 2i) = 2 + 7i$

4. $(-) \times (+) = (-)$

   $-10 \times 47 = \mathbf{-470}$

5. $(-) + (-) = (-)$

   $-65 + -32 = \mathbf{-97}$

6. $(-) \times (+) = (-)$

   $-7 \times 4 = -28$, which is **less than −7**

7. $(-) \div (+) = (-)$

   $-16 \div 2.5 = \mathbf{-6.4}$

8. First, complete operations within parentheses:

   $-(2)^2 - (11)$

   Second, calculate the value of exponential numbers:

   $-(4) - (11)$

   Finally, do addition and subtraction:

   $-4 - 11 = \mathbf{-15}$

9. First, calculate the value of exponential numbers:

   $(25) \div 5 + 4 \times 2$

   Second, calculate division and multiplication from left to right:

   $5 + 8$

   Finally, do addition and subtraction:

   $5 + 8 = \mathbf{13}$

10. First, complete operations within parentheses:

    $15 \times (12) - 3^3$

    Second, calculate the value of exponential numbers:

    $15 \times (12) - 27$

    Third, calculate division and multiplication from left to right:

    $180 - 27$

    Finally, do addition and subtraction from left to right:

    $180 - 27 = \mathbf{153}$

11. First, complete operations within parentheses:

    $(10) + 23 - 4^2$

    Second, calculate the value of exponential numbers:

    $(10) + 23 - 16$

    Finally, do addition and subtraction from left to right:

    $(10) + 23 - 16$

    $33 - 16 = \mathbf{17}$

12. 1 yd. = 3 ft.

    $\frac{15}{3} = \mathbf{5\ yd.}$

13. 1 gal. = 16 cups

    $\frac{24}{16} = \mathbf{1.5\ gal.}$

14. 12 in. = 1 ft.

    $\frac{144}{12} = 12\ ft.$

    12 ft. × 3 spools = **36 ft. of wire**

15. This problem can be worked in two steps: finding how many inches are covered in 1 minute, and then converting that value to feet. It can also be worked the opposite way, by finding how many feet it travels in 1 second and then converting that to feet traveled per minute. The first method is shown below.

   1 min. = 60 sec.

   $\frac{6 \text{ in.}}{\text{sec.}} \times 60 \text{ s} = 360 \text{ in.}$

   1 ft. = 12 in.

   $\frac{360 \text{ in.}}{12 \text{ in.}} = \textbf{30 ft.}$

16. 1 meter = 1000 mm

   0.5 meters = **500 mm**

17. 1 kg = 1000 g

   $\frac{38 \text{ g}}{1000 \text{ g}} = \textbf{0.038 kg}$

18. $1 \text{ L} = 1000 \text{ cm}^3$

   $10 \text{ L} = 1000 \text{ cm}^3 \times 10$

   $10 \text{ L} = \textbf{10,000 cm}^3$

19. 1 cm = 10 mm

   10 cm − 9.6 cm = 0.4 cm lost

   0.4 cm = 10 mm × 0.4 = **4 mm were lost**

20.   17.07
     + 2.52
   = **19.59**

21.   7.4
     − 6.8
   = **0.6 gal.**

22. 25 × 14 = 350

   There are 2 digits after the decimal in 0.25 and one digit after the decimal in 1.4. Therefore the product should have 3 digits after the decimal: **0.350 is the correct answer.**

23. Change 0.2 to 2 by moving the decimal one space to the right.

   Next, move the decimal one space to the right on the dividend. 0.8 becomes 8.

   Now, divide 8 by 2. 8 ÷ 2 = **4**

24. First, change the divisor to a whole number: 0.25 becomes 25.

   Next, change the dividend to match the divisor by moving the decimal two spaces to the right, so 40 becomes 4000.

   Now divide: 4000 ÷ 25 = **160**

25. 121 and 77 share a common factor of 11. So, if we divide each by 11 we can simplify the fraction:
   $\frac{121}{77} = \frac{11}{11} \times \frac{11}{7} = \mathbf{\frac{11}{7}}$

26. Start by dividing the numerator by the denominator:

   37 ÷ 5 = 7 with a remainder of 2.

   Now build a mixed number with the whole number and the new numerator:
   $\frac{37}{5} = \mathbf{7\frac{2}{5}}$

27. For a fraction division problem, invert the second fraction and then multiply and reduce:
   $\frac{7}{8} \div \frac{1}{4} = \frac{7}{8} \times \frac{4}{1} = \frac{28}{8} = \mathbf{\frac{7}{2}}$

28. This is a fraction multiplication problem, so simply multiply the numerators together and the denominators together and then reduce:
   $\frac{1}{12} \times \frac{6}{8} = \frac{6}{96} = \mathbf{\frac{1}{16}}$
   Sometimes it's easier to reduce fractions before multiplying if you can:
   $\frac{1}{12} \times \frac{6}{8} = \frac{1}{12} \times \frac{3}{4} = \frac{3}{48} = \mathbf{\frac{1}{16}}$

29. This is a fraction division problem, so the first step is to convert the

mixed number to an improper fraction:

$$1\tfrac{1}{5} = \tfrac{5 \times 1}{5} + \tfrac{1}{5} = \tfrac{6}{5}$$

Now, divide the fractions. Remember to invert the second fraction, and then multiply normally:

$$\tfrac{2}{5} \div \tfrac{6}{5} = \tfrac{2}{5} \times \tfrac{5}{6} = \tfrac{10}{30} = \mathbf{\tfrac{1}{3}}$$

30. This is a fraction multiplication problem: $\tfrac{1}{4} \times 8\tfrac{1}{2}$.

    First, we need to convert the mixed number into an improper fraction:

    $$8\tfrac{1}{2} = \tfrac{8 \times 2}{2} + \tfrac{1}{2} = \tfrac{17}{2}$$

    Now, multiply the fractions across the numerators and denominators, and then reduce:

    $$\tfrac{1}{4} \times 8\tfrac{1}{2} = \tfrac{1}{4} \times \tfrac{17}{2} = \mathbf{\tfrac{17}{8}} \textbf{ cups of sugar}$$

31. First, multiply each fraction by a factor of 1 to get a common denominator.

    How do you know which factor of 1 to use? Look at the other fraction and use the number found in that denominator:

    $$\tfrac{2}{3} - \tfrac{1}{5} = \tfrac{2}{3}\left(\tfrac{5}{5}\right) - \tfrac{1}{5}\left(\tfrac{3}{3}\right) = \tfrac{10}{15} - \tfrac{3}{15}$$

    Once the fractions have a common denominator, simply subtract the numerators:

    $$\tfrac{10}{15} - \tfrac{3}{15} = \mathbf{\tfrac{7}{15}}$$

32. This is a fraction subtraction problem with a mixed number, so the first step is to convert the mixed number to an improper fraction:

    $$2\tfrac{1}{3} = \tfrac{2 \times 3}{3} + \tfrac{1}{3} = \tfrac{7}{3}$$

    Next, convert each fraction so they share a common denominator:

    $$\tfrac{7}{3} \times \tfrac{2}{2} = \tfrac{14}{6}$$

    $$\tfrac{3}{2} \times \tfrac{3}{3} = \tfrac{9}{6}$$

Now, subtract the fractions by subtracting the numerators:

$$\tfrac{14}{6} - \tfrac{9}{6} = \mathbf{\tfrac{5}{6}}$$

33. For this fraction addition problem, we need to find a common denominator. Notice that 2 and 4 are both factors of 16, so 16 can be the common denominator:

    $$\tfrac{1}{2} \times \tfrac{8}{8} = \tfrac{8}{16}$$

    $$\tfrac{7}{4} \times \tfrac{4}{4} = \tfrac{28}{16}$$

    $$\tfrac{9}{16} + \tfrac{8}{16} + \tfrac{28}{16} = \mathbf{\tfrac{45}{16}}$$

34. To add fractions, make sure that they have a common denominator. Since 3 is a factor of 6, 6 can be the common denominator:

    $$\tfrac{2}{3} \times \tfrac{2}{2} = \tfrac{4}{6}$$

    Now, add the numerators:

    $$\tfrac{4}{6} + \tfrac{1}{6} = \mathbf{\tfrac{5}{6}} \textbf{ of a can}$$

35. The first step here is to simplify the fraction:

    $$\tfrac{8}{18} = \tfrac{4}{9}$$

    Now it's clear that the fraction is a multiple of $\tfrac{1}{9}$, so you can easily find the decimal using a value you already know:

    $$\tfrac{4}{9} = \tfrac{1}{9} \times 4 = 0.\overline{11} \times 4 = \mathbf{0.\overline{44}}$$

36. None of the tricks above will work for this fraction, so you need to do long division:

```
         0.1875
   16 ) 3.0000
      − 1.6000
        1.40
      − 1.28
        0.120
      − 0.112
        0.0080
      − 0.0080
        0.0000
```

The decimal will go in front of the answer, so now you know that $\tfrac{3}{16}$ = **0.1875.**

37. The last number in the decimal is in the hundredths place, so we can easily set up a fraction:

$0.45 = \frac{45}{100}$

The next step is simply to reduce the fraction down to the lowest common denominator. Here, both 45 and 100 are divisible by 5. 45 divided by 5 is 9, and 100 divided by 5 is 20. Therefore, you're left with:

$\frac{45}{100} = \mathbf{\frac{9}{20}}$

38. We know that there are 5 Democrats for every 4 Republicans in the room, which means for every 9 people, 4 are Republicans.

$5 + 4 = 9$

Fraction of Democrats: $\frac{5}{9}$
Fraction of Republicans: $\frac{4}{9}$
If $\frac{4}{9}$ of the 90 voters are Republicans, then:
$\frac{4}{9} \times 90 =$ **40 voters are Republicans**

39. To solve this ratio problem, we can simply multiply both sides of the ratio by the desired value to find the number of students that correspond to having 38 teachers:

$\frac{15 \text{ students}}{1 \text{ teacher}} \times 38 \text{ teachers} = 570$ students

The school has **570 students.**

40. Start by setting up the proportion:
$\frac{120 \text{ mi}}{3 \text{ hrs}} = \frac{180 \text{mi}}{x \text{ hr}}$
Note that it doesn't matter which value is placed in the numerator or denominator, as long as it is the same on both sides. Now, solve for the missing quantity through cross-multiplication:

$120 \text{ mi} \times x \text{ hr} = 3 \text{ hrs} \times 180 \text{ mi}$

Now solve the equation:

$x \text{ hours} = \frac{3 \text{ hrs} \times 180 \text{ mi}}{120 \text{ mi}}$

$x = \mathbf{4.5 \text{ hrs}}$

41. Set up the equation:

$\frac{1 \text{ acre}}{500 \text{ gal}} = \frac{x \text{ acres}}{2600 \text{ gal}}$

Then solve for x:

$x \text{ acres} = \frac{1 \text{ acre} \times 2600 \text{ gal}}{500 \text{ gal}}$

$x = \frac{26}{5}$ acres or **5.2 acres**

42. This problem presents two equivalent ratios that can be set up in a fraction equation:

$\frac{35}{5} = \frac{49}{x}$

You can then cross-multiply to solve for x:

$35x = 49 \times 5$

$\mathbf{x = 7}$

43. Set up the appropriate equation and solve. Don't forget to change 15% to a decimal value:

$\text{whole} = \frac{\text{part}}{\text{percent}} = \frac{45}{0.15} = \mathbf{300}$

44. Set up the appropriate equation and solve:

$\text{whole} = \frac{\text{part}}{\text{percent}} = \frac{15 + 30 + 20}{.30} = $ **\$217.00**

45. Set up the equation and solve:

$\text{percent} = \frac{\text{part}}{\text{whole}} = \frac{39}{65} = $ **0.6 or 60%**

46. You can use the information in the question to figure out what percentage of subscriptions were sold by Max and Greta:

$percent = \frac{part}{whole} = \frac{51 + 45}{240} = \frac{96}{240} = $ 0.4 or 40%

However, the question asks how many subscriptions weren't sold by Max or Greta. If they sold 40%, then the other salespeople sold $100\% - 40\% = 60\%$.

47. Set up the equation and solve. Remember to convert 75% to a decimal value:

part = whole × percent = 45 × 0.75 = 33.75, so **he needs to answer at least 34 questions correctly.**

48. Set up the appropriate equation and solve:

amount of change = original amount × percent change →

25 × 0.4 = 10

If the amount of change is 10, that means the store adds a markup of $10, so the game costs:

$25 + $10 = **$35**

49. First, calculate the amount of change:

75 − 40 = 35

Now you can set up the equation and solve. (Note that markup rate is another way of saying percent change):

percent change = $\frac{\text{amount of change}}{\text{original amount}}$

→ $\frac{35}{40}$ = 0.875 = **87.5%**

50. You're solving for the original price, but it's going to be tricky because you don't know the amount of change; you only know the new price. To solve, you need to create an expression for the amount of change:

If original amount = x

Then amount of change = 63 − x

Now you can plug these values into your equation:

original amount = $\frac{\text{amount of change}}{\text{percent change}}$

$x = \frac{63 - x}{0.4}$

The last step is to solve for x:

0.4x = 63 − x

1.4x = 63

x = 45 → **The store paid $45 for the shoes.**

51. You've been asked to find the sale price, which means you need to solve for the amount of change first:

amount of change = original amount × percent change =

55 × 0.25 = 13.75

Using this amount, you can find the new price. Because it's on sale, we know the item will cost less than the original price:

55 − 13.75 = 41.25

The sale price is **$41.25**.

52. This problem is tricky because you need to figure out what each number in the problem stands for. 24% is obviously the percent change, but what about the measurements in feet? If you multiply these values you get the area of the garden (for more on area see *Area and Perimeter*):

18 ft. × 51 ft. = 918 ft.²

This 918 ft.² is the amount of change—it's how much area the yard lost to create the garden. Now you can set up an equation:

original amount = $\frac{\text{amount of change}}{\text{percent change}}$

= $\frac{918}{.24}$ = 3825

If the original lawn was 3825 ft.² and the garden is 918 ft.², then the remaining area is:

3825 − 918 = 2907

The remaining lawn covers 2907 ft.²

53. These numbers are in different formats—one is a mixed fraction and the other is just a fraction. So, the first step is to convert the mixed fraction to a fraction:

$$4\frac{3}{4} = \frac{4 \times 4}{4} + \frac{3}{4} = \frac{19}{4}$$

Once the mixed number is converted, it is easier to see that

$\frac{19}{4}$ **is greater than** $\frac{18}{4}$.

54. These numbers are already in the same format, so the decimal values just need to be compared. Remember that zeros can be added after the decimal without changing the value, so the three numbers can be rewritten as:

104.56

104.50

104.60

From this list, it is clear that **104.60 is the greatest** because 0.60 is larger than 0.50 and 0.56.

55. The first step is to convert the numbers into the same format—65% is the same as $\frac{65}{100}$.

Next, the fractions need to be converted to have the same denominator because it is difficult to compare fractions with different denominators. Using a factor of $\frac{5}{5}$ on the second fraction will give common denominators:

$\frac{13}{20} \times \frac{5}{5} = \frac{65}{100}$. Now it is easy to see that **the numbers are equivalent.**

56. When multiplying exponents in which the base number is the same, simply add the powers:

$$2^4 \times 2^2 = 2^{(4+2)} = 2^6$$

$$2^6 = 2 \times 2 \times 2 \times 2 \times 2 \times 2 = \mathbf{64}$$

57. When an exponent is raised to a power, multiply the powers:

$$(3^4)^{-1} = 3^{-4}$$

When the exponent is a negative number, rewrite as the reciprocal of the positive exponent:

$$3^{-4} = \frac{1}{3^4}$$

$$\frac{1}{3^4} = \frac{1}{3 \times 3 \times 3 \times 3} = \mathbf{\frac{1}{81}}$$

58. When the power is a fraction, rewrite as a radical:

$$\left(\frac{9}{4}\right)^{\frac{1}{2}} = \sqrt{\frac{9}{4}}$$

Next, distribute the radical to the numerator and denominator:

$$\sqrt{\frac{9}{4}} = \frac{\sqrt{9}}{\sqrt{4}} = \mathbf{\frac{3}{2}}$$

59. Add each corresponding number:

$$\begin{bmatrix} 6+5 & 4+(-3) & (-8)+(-2) \\ (-3)+(-3) & 1+4 & 0+9 \end{bmatrix} = \begin{bmatrix} \mathbf{11} & \mathbf{1} & \mathbf{-10} \\ \mathbf{-6} & \mathbf{5} & \mathbf{9} \end{bmatrix}$$

60. Add each corresponding number to create 2 equations:

$$\begin{bmatrix} x+3 & 6+2 \\ 4+8 & y+(-1) \end{bmatrix} = \begin{bmatrix} 11 & 8 \\ 12 & 4 \end{bmatrix}$$

$x + 3 = 11$

$y - 1 = 4$

Now, solve each equation:

$x = 8, y = 5$

61. First, check to see that they can be multiplied: **A** has 3 columns and **B** has 3 rows, so they can. The resulting matrix will be 2 × 2. Now multiply the numbers in the first row of **A** by the numbers in the first column of **B** and add the results:

$$\begin{bmatrix} 1 & 3 & 0 \\ 6 & 2 & 4 \end{bmatrix} \times \begin{bmatrix} 5 & 3 \\ 2 & 1 \\ 4 & 7 \end{bmatrix} = \begin{bmatrix} (1 \times 5)+(3 \times 2)+(0 \times 4) & \square \\ \square & \square \end{bmatrix} = \begin{bmatrix} 11 & \square \\ \square & \square \end{bmatrix}$$

Now, multiply and add to find the 3 missing values:

$$\begin{bmatrix} 1 & 3 & 0 \\ 6 & 2 & 4 \end{bmatrix} \times \begin{bmatrix} 5 & 3 \\ 2 & 1 \\ 4 & 7 \end{bmatrix} =$$

$$\begin{bmatrix} (1 \times 5)+(3 \times 2)+(0 \times 4) & (1 \times 3)+(3 \times 1)+(0 \times 7) \\ (6 \times 5)+(2 \times 2)+(4 \times 4) & (6 \times 3)+(2 \times 1)+(4 \times 7) \end{bmatrix} = \begin{bmatrix} \mathbf{11} & \mathbf{6} \\ \mathbf{50} & \mathbf{48} \end{bmatrix}$$

62. Multiply each value inside the matrix by 6x.

$$6x \begin{bmatrix} 2 & -3 \\ 6 & 4 \end{bmatrix} = \begin{bmatrix} 6x \times 2 & 6x \times (-3) \\ 6x \times 6 & 6x \times 4 \end{bmatrix} = \begin{bmatrix} \mathbf{12x} & \mathbf{-18x} \\ \mathbf{36x} & \mathbf{24x} \end{bmatrix}$$

CHAPTER FOUR
Algebra

Algebraic Expressions

Algebraic expressions and equations include **VARIABLES**, or letters standing in for numbers. These expressions and equations are made up of **TERMS**, which are groups of numbers and variables (e.g., $2xy$). An **EXPRESSION** is simply a set of terms (e.g., $\frac{2x}{3yz} + 2$). When those terms are joined only by addition or subtraction, the expression is called a polynomial (e.g., $2x + 3yz$). When working with expressions, you'll need to use many different mathematical properties and operations, including addition/subtraction, multiplication/division, exponents, roots, distribution, and the order of operations.

EVALUATING ALGEBRAIC EXPRESSIONS

To evaluate an algebraic expression, simply plug the given value(s) in for the appropriate variable(s) in the expression.

EXAMPLE

1. Evaluate $2x + 6y - 3z$ if $x = 2$, $y = 4$, and $z = -3$.

ADDING and SUBTRACTING EXPRESSIONS

Only **LIKE TERMS**, which have the exact same variable(s), can be added or subtracted. **CONSTANTS** are numbers without variables attached, and those can be added and subtracted together as well. When simplifying an expression, like terms should be added or subtracted so that no individual group of variables occurs in more than one term. For example, the expression $5x + 6xy$ is in its simplest form, while $5x + 6xy - 11xy$ is not because the term xy appears more than once.

EXAMPLE

2. Simplify the expression: $5xy + 7y + 2yz + 11xy - 5yz$

MULTIPLYING and DIVIDING EXPRESSIONS

To multiply a single term by another, simply multiply the coefficients and then multiply the variables. Remember that when multiplying variables with exponents, those exponents are added together. For example: $(x^5y)(x^3y^4) = x^8y^5$.

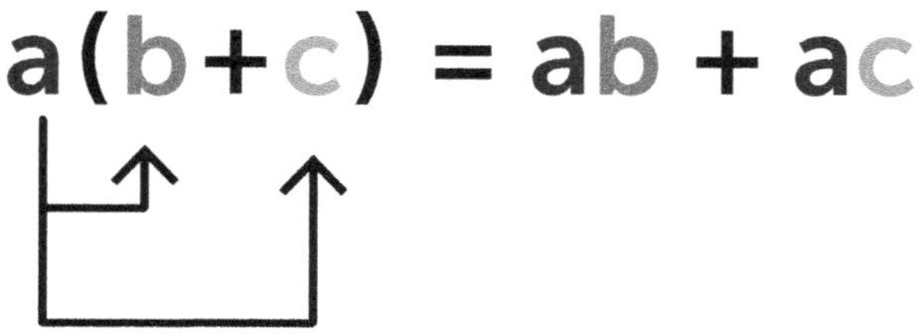

$$a(b+c) = ab + ac$$

Figure 4.1. Distribution

When multiplying a term by a set of terms inside parentheses, you need to distribute to each term inside the parentheses as shown in Figure 4.1.

When variables occur in both the numerator and denominator of a fraction, they cancel each other out. So, a fraction with variables in its simplest form will not have the same variable on the top and bottom.

EXAMPLES

3. Simplify the expression: $(3x^4\,y^2z)(2y^4z^5)$

4. Simplify the expression: $(2y^2)(y^3 + 2xy^2z + 4z)$

5. Simplify the expression: $(5x + 2)(3x + 3)$

6. Simplify the expression: $\frac{2x^4y^3z}{8x^2z^2}$

FACTORING EXPRESSIONS

Factoring is splitting one expression into the multiplication of two expressions. It requires finding the highest common factor and dividing terms by that number. For example, in the expression $15x + 10$, the highest common factor is 5 because both terms are divisible by 5: $\frac{15x}{5} = 3x$ and $\frac{10}{5} = 2$. When you factor the expression you get $5(3x + 2)$.

Sometimes it is difficult to find the highest common factor. In these cases, consider whether the expression fits a polynomial identity. A polynomial is an expression with more than one term. If you can recognize the common polynomials listed below, you can easily factor the expression.

- ▶ $a^2 - b^2 = (a + b)(a - b)$
- ▶ $a^2 + 2ab + b^2 = (a + b)\,(a + b) = (a + b)^2$
- ▶ $a^2 - 2ab + b^2 = (a - b)(a - b) = (a - b)^2$
- ▶ $a^3 + b^3 = (a + b)(a^2 - ab + b^2)$
- ▶ $a^3 - b^3 = (a - b)(a^2 + ab + b^2)$

EXAMPLES

7. Factor the expression: $27x^2 - 9x$

8. Factor the expression: $25x^2 - 16$

9. Factor the expression: $100x^2 + 60x + 9$

Linear Equations

An **EQUATION** is a statement saying that two expressions are equal to each other. They always include an equal sign (e.g., $3x + 2xy = 17$). A **LINEAR EQUATION** has only two variables; on a graph, linear equations form a straight line.

SOLVING LINEAR EQUATIONS

To solve an equation, you need to manipulate the terms on each side to isolate the variable, meaning if you want to find x, you have to get the x alone on one side of the equal sign. To do this, you'll need to use many of the tools discussed above: you might need to distribute, divide, add, or subtract like terms, or find common denominators.

Think of each side of the equation as the two sides of a see-saw. As long as the two people on each end weigh the same amount (no matter what it is) the see-saw will be balanced: if you have a 120 pound person on each end, the see-saw is balanced. Giving each of them a 10 pound rock to hold changes the weight on each end, but the see-saw itself stays balanced. Equations work the same way: you can add, subtract, multiply, or divide whatever you want as long as you do the same thing to both sides.

DID YOU KNOW?
If you're stumped, try plugging the answer choices back into the original problem to see which one works.

Most equations you'll see on the PSAT can be solved using the same basic steps:

1. distribute to get rid of parentheses
2. use LCD to get rid of fractions
3. add/subtract like terms on either side
4. add/subtract so that constants appear on only one side of the equation
5. multiply/divide to isolate the variable

EXAMPLES

10. Solve for x: $25x + 12 = 62$

11. Solve the following equation for x: $2x - 4(2x + 3) = 24$

12. Solve the following equation for x: $\frac{x}{3} + \frac{1}{2} = \frac{x}{6} - \frac{5}{12}$

13. Find the value of x: $2(x + y) - 7x = 14x + 3$

GRAPHING LINEAR EQUATIONS

Linear equations can be plotted as straight lines on a coordinate plane. The **x-AXIS** is always the horizontal axis and the **y-AXIS** is always the vertical axis. The x-axis is positive to the right of the y-axis and negative to the left. The y-axis is positive above the x-axis and negative below. To describe the location of any point on the graph, write the coordinates in the form (x, y). The origin, the point where the x- and y-axes cross, is $(0, 0)$.

The **y-INTERCEPT** is the y coordinate where the line crosses the y-axis. The **SLOPE** is a measure of how steep the line is. Slope is calculated by dividing the change along the y-axis by the change along the x-axis between any two points on the line.

Linear equations are easiest to graph when they are written in **POINT-SLOPE FORM**: $y = mx + b$. The constant m represents slope and the constant b represents the y-intercept. If you know two points along the line (x_1, y_1) and (x_2, y_2), you can calculate slope using the following equation: $m = \frac{y_2 - y_1}{x_2 - x_1}$. If you know the slope and one other point along the line, you can calculate the y-intercept by plugging the number 0 in for x_2 and solving for y_2.

When graphing a linear equation, first plot the y-intercept. Next, plug in values for x to solve for y and plot additional points. Connect the points with a straight line.

EXAMPLES

14. Find the slope of the line: $\frac{3y}{2} + 3 = x$

15. Plot the linear equation: $2y - 4x = 6$

SYSTEMS of EQUATIONS

A system of equations is a group of related questions sharing the same variable. The problems you see on the PSAT will most likely involve two equations that each have two variables, although you may also solve sets of equations with any number of variables as long as there are a corresponding number of equations (e.g., to solve a system with four variables, you need four equations).

DID YOU KNOW?
The math section will always include a set of questions that require you to understand and manipulate a real-life equation (usually related to physics).

There are two main methods used to solve systems of equations. In **SUBSTITUTION**, solve one equation for a single variable, then substitute the solution for that variable into the second equation to solve for the other variable. Or, you can use **ELIMINATION** by adding equations together to cancel variables and solve for one of them.

16. Solve the following system of equations: $3y - 4 + x = 0$ and $5x + 6y = 11$

17. Solve the system: $2x + 4y = 8$ and $4x + 2y = 10$

BUILDING EQUATIONS

Word problems describe a situation or a problem without explicitly providing an equation to solve. It is up to you to build an algebraic equation to solve the problem. You must translate the words into mathematical operations. Represent the quantity you do not know with a variable. If there is more than one unknown, you will likely have to write more than one equation, then solve the system of equations by substituting expressions. Make sure you keep your variables straight!

EXAMPLES

18. David, Jesse, and Mark shoveled snow during their snow day and made a total of $100. They agreed to split it based on how much each person worked. David will take $10 more than Jesse, who will take $15 more than Mark. How much money will David get?

19. The sum of three consecutive numbers is 54. What is the middle number?

20. There are 42 people on the varsity football team. This is 8 more than half the number of people on the swim team. There are 6 fewer boys on the swim team than girls. How many girls are on the swim team?

Linear Inequalities

INEQUALITIES look like equations, except that instead of having an equal sign, they have one of the following symbols:

>   greater than: the expression left of the symbol is larger than the expression on the right

<   less than: the expression left of the symbol is smaller than the expression on the right

≥   greater than or equal to: the expression left of the symbol is larger than or equal to the expression on the right

≤   less than or equal to: the expression left of the symbol is less than or equal to the expression on the right

SOLVING LINEAR INEQUALITIES

Inequalities are solved like linear and algebraic equations. The only difference is that the symbol must be reversed when both sides of the equation are multiplied by a negative number.

EXAMPLE

21. Solve for x: $-7x + 2 < 6 - 5x$

GRAPHING LINEAR INEQUALITIES

Graphing a linear inequality is just like graphing a linear equation, except that you shade the area on one side of the line. To graph a linear inequality, first rearrange the inequality expression into $y = mx + b$ form. Then treat the inequality symbol like an equal sign and plot the line. If the inequality symbol is < or >, make a broken line; for ≤ or ≥, make a solid line. Finally, shade the correct side of the graph:

> For $y < mx + b$ or $y \leq mx + b$, shade **below** the line.
>
> For $y > mx + b$ or $y \geq mx + b$, shade **above** the line.

EXAMPLE

22. Plot the inequality: $-3 \geq 4 - y$

Quadratic Equations

A quadratic equation is any equation in the form $ax^2 + bx + c = 0$. In quadratic equations, x is the variable and a, b, and c are all known numbers. a cannot be 0.

SOLVING QUADRATIC EQUATIONS

There is more than one way to solve a quadratic equation. One way is by **FACTORING**. By rearranging the expression $ax^2 + bx + c$ into one factor multiplied by another factor, you can easily solve for the **ROOTS**, the values of x for which the quadratic expression equals 0. Another way to solve a quadratic equation is by using the **QUADRATIC FORMULA**:

$$x = \frac{-b \pm \sqrt{b^2 - 4ac}}{2a}$$

The expression $b^2 - 4ac$ is called the **DISCRIMINANT**; when it is positive you will get two real numbers for x, when it is negative you will get one real number and one imaginary number for x, and when it is zero you will get one real number for x.

EXAMPLES

23. Factor the quadratic equation $-2x^2 = 14x$ and find the roots.

24. Use the quadratic formula to solve for x: $3x^2 = 7x - 2$.

GRAPHING QUADRATIC EQUATIONS

Graphing a quadratic equation forms a **PARABOLA**. A parabola is a symmetrical, horseshoe-shaped curve; a vertical axis passes through its vertex. Each term in the equation $ax^2 + bx + c = 0$ affects the shape of the parabola. A bigger value for a makes the curve narrower, while a smaller value makes the curve wider. A negative value for a flips the parabola upside down. The **AXIS OF SYMMETRY** is the vertical line $x = \frac{-b}{2a}$. To find the y-coordinate for the **VERTEX** (the highest or lowest point on the parabola), plug this value for x into the expression $ax^2 + bx + c$. The easiest way to graph a quadratic equation is to find the axis of symmetry, solve for the vertex, and then create a table of points by plugging in other numbers for x and solving for y. Plot these points and trace the parabola.

EXAMPLE

25. Graph the equation: $x^2 + 4x + 1 = 0$

Functions

FUNCTIONS describe how an input relates to an output. Linear equations, sine, and cosine are examples of functions. In a function, there must be one and only one output for each input. $\sqrt{x}$ is not a function because there are two outputs for any one input: $\sqrt{4} = 2, -2$.

DESCRIBING FUNCTIONS

Functions are often written in $f(x)$ form: $f(x) = x^2$ means that for input x the output is x^2. In relating functions to linear equations, you can think of $f(x)$ as equivalent to y. The **DOMAIN** of a function is all the possible inputs of that function. The **RANGE** of a function includes the outputs of the inputs. For example, for the function $f(x) = x^2$, if the domain includes all positive and negative integers the range will include 0 and only positive integers. When you graph a function, the domain is plotted on the x-axis and the range is plotted on the y-axis.

EXAMPLES

26. Given $f(x) = 2x - 10$, find $f(9)$.

27. Given $f(x) = \frac{4}{x}$ with a domain of all positive integers except zero, and $g(x) = \frac{4}{x}$ with a domain of all positive and negative integers except zero, which function has a range that includes the number -2?

EXPONENTIAL FUNCTIONS

An **EXPONENTIAL FUNCTION** is in the form $f(x) = a^x$, where $a > 0$. When $a > 1$, $f(x)$ approaches infinity as x increases and zero as x decreases. When $0 < a < 1$, $f(x)$ approaches zero as x increases and infinity as x increases. When $a = 1$, $f(x) = 1$. The graph of an exponential function where $a \neq 1$ will have a horizontal asymptote along the x-axis; the graph will never cross below the x-axis. The graph of an exponential function where $a = 1$ will be a horizontal line at $y = 1$. All graphs of exponential functions include the points $(0, 1)$ and $(1, a)$.

EXAMPLES

28. Graph the function: $f(x) = 3^x$.

29. Given $f(x) = 2^x$, solve for x when $f(x) = 64$.

LOGARITHMIC FUNCTIONS

A **LOGARITHMIC FUNCTION** is the inverse of an exponential function. Remember the definition of a log: if $\log_a x = b$, then $a^b = x$. Logarithmic functions are written in the form $f(x) = \log_a x$, where a is any number greater than 0, except for 1. If a is not shown, it is assumed that $a = 10$. The function $\ln x$ is called a **NATURAL LOG**, equal to $\log_e x$. When $0 < a < 1$, $f(x)$ approaches infinity as x approaches zero and negative infinity as x increases. When $a > 1$, $f(x)$ approaches negative infinity as x approaches zero and infinity as x increases. In either case, the graph of a logarithmic function has a vertical asymptote along the y-axis; the graph will never cross to the left of the y-axis. All graphs of logarithmic functions include the points $(1, 0)$ and $(a, 1)$.

EXAMPLES

30. Graph the function $f(x) = \log_4 x$.

31. Given $f(x) = \log_{\frac{1}{3}} x$, solve for $f(81)$.

ARITHMETIC and GEOMETRIC SEQUENCES

SEQUENCES are patterns of numbers. In most questions about sequences you must determine the pattern. In an **ARITHMETIC SEQUENCE**, add or subtract the same number between terms. In a **GEOMETRIC SEQUENCE**, multiply or divide by the same number between terms. For example, 2, 6, 10, 14, 18 and 11, 4, –3, –10, –17 are arithmetic sequences because you add 4 to each term in the first example and you subtract 7 from each term in the second example. The sequence 5, 15, 45, 135 is a geometric sequence because you multiply each term by 3. In arithmetic sequences, the number by which you add or subtract is called the **COMMON DIFFERENCE**. In geometric sequences, the number by which you multiply or divide is called the **COMMON RATIO**.

In an arithmetic sequence, the nth term (a_n) can be found by calculating $a_n = a_1 + (n - 1)d$, where d is the common difference and a_1 is the first term in the sequence. In a geometric sequence, $a_n = a_1(r^n)$, where r is the common ratio.

EXAMPLES

32. Find the common difference and the next term of the following sequence: 5, –1, –7, –13

33. Find the twelfth term of the following sequence: 2, 6, 18, 54

34. The fourth term of a sequence is 9. The common difference is 11. What is the tenth term?

Absolute Value

The **ABSOLUTE VALUE** of a number (represented by the symbol $||$) is its distance from zero, not its value. For example, $|3| = 3$, and $|-3| = 3$ because both 3 and –3 are three units from zero. The absolute value of a number is always positive.

Equations with absolute values will have two answers, so you need to set up two equations. The first is simply the equation with the absolute value symbol removed. For the second equation, isolate the absolute value on one side of the equation and multiply the other side of the equation by –1.

EXAMPLES

35. Solve for x: $|2x - 3| = x + 1$

36. Solve for y: $2|y + 4| = 10$

Solving Word Problems

Any of the math concepts discussed here can be turned into a word problem, and you'll likely see word problems in various formats throughout the test. (In fact, you may have noticed that several examples in the ratio and proportion sections were word problems.)

Be sure to read the entire problem before beginning to solve it: a common mistake is to provide an answer to a question that wasn't actually asked. Also, remember that not all of the information provided in a problem is necessarily needed to solve it.

When working multiple-choice word problems like those on the PSAT, it's important to check your work. Many of the incorrect answer choices will be answers that result from common mistakes. So even if a solution you calculated is listed as an answer choice, that doesn't necessarily mean you've done the problem correctly—you have to check your own answer to be sure.

Some general steps for word-problem solving are:

1. Read the entire problem and determine what the question is asking.

2. List all of the given data and define the variables.

3. Determine the formula(s) needed or set up equations from the information in the problem.

4. Solve.

5. Check your answer. (Is the amount too large or small? Is the answer in the correct unit of measure?)

Word problems generally contain **KEY WORDS** that can help you determine what math processes may be required in order to solve them.

- **Addition**: *added, combined, increased by, in all, total, perimeter, sum*, and *more than*

- **Subtraction**: *how much more, less than, fewer than, exceeds, difference*, and *decreased*

- **Multiplication**: *of, times, area*, and *product*

- **Division**: *distribute, share, average, per, out of, percent*, and *quotient*

- **Equals**: *is, was, are, amounts to*, and *were*

BASIC WORD PROBLEMS

A word problem in algebra is just an equation or a set of equations described using words. Your task when solving these problems is to turn the *story* of the problem into mathematical equations. Converting units can often help you avoid operations with fractions when dealing with time.

EXAMPLES

37. A store owner bought a case of 48 backpacks for $476.00. He sold 17 of the backpacks in his store for $18 each, and the rest were sold to a school for $15 each. What was the store owner's profit?

38. Thirty students in Mr. Joyce's room are working on projects over 2 days. The first day, he gave them $\frac{3}{5}$ hour to work. On the second day, he gave them $\frac{1}{2}$ as much time as the first day. How much time did each student have to work on the project?

DISTANCE WORD PROBLEMS

Distance word problems involve something traveling at a constant or average speed. Whenever you read a problem that involves *how fast*, *how far*, or *for how long*, you should think of the distance equation, where d stands for distance, r for rate (speed), and t for time.

These problems can be solved by setting up a grid with d, r, and t along the top and each moving object on the left. When setting up the grid, make sure the units are consistent. For example, if the distance is in meters and the time is in seconds, the rate should be meters per second.

EXAMPLES

39. Will drove from his home to the airport at an average speed of 30 mph. He then boarded a helicopter and flew to the hospital at an average speed of 60 mph. The entire distance was 150 miles, and the trip took 3 hours. Find the distance from the airport to the hospital.

40. Two riders on horseback start at the same time from opposite ends of a field that is 45 miles long. One horse is moving at 14 mph and the second horse is moving at 16 mph. How long after they begin will they meet?

WORK PROBLEMS

WORK PROBLEMS involve situations where several people or machines are doing work at different rates. Your task is usually to figure out how long it will take these people or machines to complete a task while working together. The trick to doing work problems is to figure out how much of the project each person or machine completes in the same unit of time. For example, you might calculate how much of a wall a person can paint in 1 hour, or how many boxes an assembly line can pack in 1 minute.

DID YOU KNOW?

The PSAT will give you most formulas you need to work problems, but they won't give you the formulas for percent change or work problems.

The next step is to set up an equation to solve for the total time. This equation is usually similar to the equation for distance, but here *work = rate × time*.

EXAMPLES

41. Bridget can clean an entire house in 12 hours while her brother Tom takes 8 hours. How long would it take for Bridget and Tom to clean 2 houses together?

42. Farmer Dan needs to water his cornfield. One hose can water a field 1.25 times faster than a second hose. When both hoses are running, they water the field together in 5 hours. How long would it take to water the field if only the slower hose is used?

43. Ben takes 2 hours to pick 500 apples, and Frank takes 3 hours to pick 450 apples. How long will they take, working together, to pick 1000 apples?

Answer Key

1. Plug in each number for the correct variable and simplify:

$2x + 6y - 3z = 2(2) + 6(4) - 3(-3) = 4 + 24 + 9 = \mathbf{37}$

2. Start by grouping together like terms:

$(5xy + 11xy) + (2yz - 5yz) + 7y$

Now you can add together each set of like terms:

$\mathbf{16xy + 7y - 3yz}$

3. Multiply the coefficients and variables together:

$3 \times 2 = 6$

$y^2 \times y^4 = y^6$

$z \times z^5 = z^6$

Now put all the terms back together:

$\mathbf{6x^4y^6z^6}$

4. Multiply each term inside the parentheses by the term $2y^2$:

$(2y^2)(y^3 + 2xy^2z + 4z) =$

$(2y^2 \times y^3) + (2y^2 \times 2xy^2z) + (2y^2 \times 4z) =$

$\mathbf{2y^5 + 4xy^4z + 8y^2z}$

5. Use the acronym FOIL—first, outer, inner, last—to multiply the terms:

first: $5x \times 3x = 15x^2$

outer: $5x \times 3 = 15x$

inner: $2 \times 3x = 6x$

last: $2 \times 3 = 6$

Now combine like terms:

$\mathbf{15x^2 + 21x + 6}$

6. Simplify by looking at each variable and checking for those that appear in the numerator and denominator:

$\frac{2}{8} = \frac{1}{4}$

$\frac{x^4}{x^2} = \frac{x^2}{1}$

$\frac{z}{z^2} = \frac{1}{z}$

$\mathbf{\frac{2x^4y^3z}{8x^2z^2} = \frac{x^2y^3}{4z}}$

7. First, find the highest common factor. Both terms are divisible by 9:

$\frac{27x^2}{9} = 3x^2$ and $\frac{9x}{9} = x$.

Now the expression is $9(3x^2 - x)$. But wait, you're not done! Both terms can be divided by x:

$\frac{3x^2}{x} = 3x$ and $\frac{x}{x} = 1$.

The final factored expression is $\mathbf{9x(3x - 1)}$.

8. Since there is no obvious factor by which you can divide terms, you should consider whether this expression fits one of your polynomial identities. This expression is a difference of squares: $a^2 - b^2$, where $a^2 = 25x^2$ and $b^2 = 16$.

Recall that $a^2 - b^2 = (a + b)(a - b)$. Now solve for a and b:

$a = \sqrt{25x^2} = 5x$

$b = \sqrt{16} = 4$

$(a + b)(a - b) = \mathbf{(5x + 4)(5x - 4)}$

You can check your work by using the FOIL acronym to expand your answer back to the original expression:

first: $5x \times 5x = 25x^2$

outer: $5x \times -4 = -20x$

inner: $4 \times 5x = 20x$

last: $4 \times -4 = -16$

$25x^2 - 20x + 20x - 16 = 25x^2 - 16$

9. This is another polynomial identity, $a^2 + 2ab + b^2$. (The more you practice these problems, the faster you will recognize polynomial identities.)

$a^2 = 100x^2$, $2ab = 60x$, and $b^2 = 9$

Recall that $a^2 + 2ab + b^2 = (a + b)^2$. Now solve for a and b:

$a = \sqrt{100x^2} = 10x$

$b = \sqrt{9} = 3$

(Double check your work by confirming that $2ab = 2 \times 10x \times 3 = 60x$)

$(a + b)^2 = \mathbf{(10x + 3)^2}$

10. This equation has no parentheses, fractions, or like terms on the same side, so you can start by subtracting 12 from both sides of the equation:

$25x + 12 = 62$

$(25x + 12) - 12 = 62 - 12$

$25x = 50$

Now, divide by 25 to isolate the variable:

$\frac{25x}{25} = \frac{50}{25}$

$\mathbf{x = 2}$

11. Start by distributing to get rid of the parentheses (don't forget to distribute the negative):

$2x - 4(2x + 3) = 24 \rightarrow$

$2x - 8x - 12 = 24$

There are no fractions, so now you can join like terms:

$2x - 8x - 12 = 24 \rightarrow -6x - 12 = 24$

Now add 12 to both sides and divide by −6.

$-6x - 12 = 24 \rightarrow$

$(-6x - 12) + 12 = 24 + 12 \rightarrow$

$-6x = 36 \rightarrow \frac{-6x}{-6} = \frac{36}{-6}$

$\mathbf{x = -6}$

12. Start by multiplying by the least common denominator to get rid of the fractions:

$\frac{x}{3} + \frac{1}{2} = \frac{x}{6} - \frac{5}{12} \rightarrow$

$12\left(\frac{x}{3} + \frac{1}{2}\right) = 12\left(\frac{x}{6} - \frac{5}{12}\right) \rightarrow$

$4x + 6 = 2x - 5$

Now you can isolate the x:

$(4x + 6) - 6 = (2x - 5) - 6 \rightarrow$

$4x = 2x - 11 \rightarrow$

$(4x) - 2x = (2x - 11) - 2x \rightarrow$

$2x = -11$

$\mathbf{x = -\frac{11}{2}}$

13. This equation looks more difficult because it has 2 variables, but you can use the same steps to solve for x. First, distribute to get rid of the parentheses and combine like terms:

$2(x + y) - 7x = 14x + 3 \rightarrow$

$2x + 2y - 7x = 14x + 3 \rightarrow$

$-5x + 2y = 14x + 3$

Now you can move the x terms to one side and everything else to the other, and then divide to isolate x:

$-5x + 2y = 14x + 3 \rightarrow$

$-19x = -2y + 3 \rightarrow$

$\mathbf{x = \frac{2y - 3}{19}}$

14. Slope is easiest to find when the equation is in point-slope form: ($y = mx + b$). Rearrange the equation to isolate y:

$\frac{3y}{2} + 3 = x$

$3y + 6 = 2x$

$y + 2 = \frac{2x}{3}$

$y = \frac{2x}{3} - 2$

Finally, identify the term m to find the slope of the line:

$\mathbf{m = \frac{2}{3}}$

15. First, rearrange the linear equation to point-slope form

$(y = mx + b)$:

$2y - 4x = 6$

$y = 2x + 3$

Next, identify the y-intercept (b) and the slope (m):

$b = 3$, $m = 2$

Now, plot the y-intercept $(0,b) = (0,3)$:

Next, plug in values for x and solve for y:

$y = 2(1) + 3 = 5 \rightarrow (1,5)$

$y = 2(-1) + 3 = 1 \rightarrow (-1,1)$

Plot these points on the graph, and connect the points with a straight line:

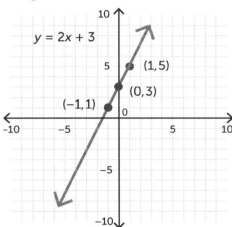

16. To solve this system using substitution, first solve one equation for a single variable:

$3y - 4 + x = 0$

$3y + x = 4$

$x = 4 - 3y$

Next, substitute the expression to the right of the equal sign for x in the second equation:

$5x + 6y = 11$

$5(4 - 3y) + 6y = 11$

$20 - 15y + 6y = 11$

$20 - 9y = 11$

$-9y = -9$

$y = 1$

Finally, plug the value for y back into the first equation to find the value of x:

$3y - 4 + x = 0$

$3(1) - 4 + x = 0$

$-1 + x = 0$

$x = 1$

The solution is **$x = 1$ and $y = 1$**, or the point **(1,1)**.

17. To solve this system using elimination, start by manipulating one equation so that a variable (in this case x) will cancel when the equations are added together:

$2x + 4y = 8$

$-2(2x + 4y = 8)$

$-4x - 8y = -16$

Now you can add the two equations together, and the x variable will drop out:

$-4x - 8y = -16$

$\underline{4x + 2y = 10}$

$-6y = -6$

$y = 1$

Lastly, plug the y value into one of the equations to find the value of x:

$2x + 4y = 8$

$2x + 4(1) = 8$

$2x + 4 = 8$

$2x = 4$

$x = 2$

The solution is **$x = 2$ and $y = 1$**, or the point **(2,1)**.

18. Start by building an equation. David's amount will be d, Jesse's amount will be j, and Mark's amount will be m. All three must add up to $100:

$$d + j + m = 100$$

It may seem like there are three unknowns in this situation, but you can express j and m in terms of d:

Jesse gets $10 less than David, so $j = d - 10$. Mark gets $15 less than Jesse, so $m = j - 15$.

Substitute the previous expression for j to solve for m in terms of d:

$$m = (d - 10) - 15 = d - 25$$

Now back to our original equation, substituting for j and m:

$$d + (d - 10) + (d - 25) = 100$$

$$3d - 35 = 100$$

$$3d = 135$$

$$d = 45$$

David will get **$45.**

19. Start by building an equation. One of the numbers in question will be x. The three numbers are consecutive, so if x is the smallest number then the other two numbers must be $(x + 1)$ and $(x + 2)$. You know that the sum of the three numbers is 54:

$$x + (x + 1) + (x + 2) = 54$$

Now solve for the equation to find x:

$$3x + 3 = 54$$

$$3x = 51$$

$$x = 17$$

The question asks about the middle number $(x + 1)$, so the answer is **18**.

Notice that you could have picked any number to be x. If you picked the middle number as x, your equation would be $(x - 1) + x + (x + 1) = 54$. Solve for x to get 18.

20. This word problem might seem complicated at first, but as long as you keep your variables straight and translate the words into mathematical operations you can easily build an equation. The quantity you want to solve is the number of girls on the swim team, so this will be x.

The number of boys on the swim team will be y. There are 6 fewer boys than girls so $y = x - 6$.

The total number of boys and girls on the swim team is $x + y$.

42 is 8 more than half this number, so $42 = 8 + (x + y) \div 2$

Now substitute for y to solve for x:

$$42 = 8 + (x + x - 6) \div 2$$

$$34 = (2x - 6) \div 2$$

$$68 = 2x - 6$$

$$74 = 2x$$

$$x = 37$$

There are 37 girls on the swim team.

21. Collect like terms on each side as you would for a regular equation:

$$-7x + 2 < 6 - 5x \rightarrow$$

$$-2x < 4$$

When you divide by a negative number, the direction of the sign switches:

$$-2x < 4 = \boldsymbol{x > -2}$$

22. To rearrange the inequality into $y = mx + b$ form, first subtract 4 from both sides:

$$-3x - 4 \geq -y$$

Next divide both sides by −1 to get positive y; remember to switch the direction of the inequality symbol:

$$3x + 4 \leq y$$

Now plot the line $y = 3x + 4$, making a solid line:

Finally, shade the side above the line:

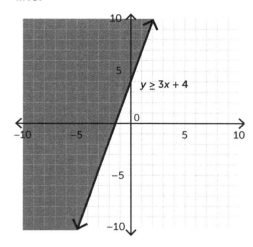

$y \geq 3x + 4$

23. Not every quadratic equation you see will be presented in the standard form. Rearrange terms to set one side equal to 0:

$2x^2 + 14x = 0$

Note that $a = 2$, $b = 14$, and $c = 0$ because there is no third term.

Now divide the expression on the left by the common factor:

$(2x)(x + 7) = 0$

To find the roots, set each of the factors equal to 0:

$2x = 0 \rightarrow x = \mathbf{0}$

$x + 7 = 0 \rightarrow x = \mathbf{-7}$

24. First rearrange the equation to set one side equal to 0:

$3x^2 - 7x + 2 = 0$

Next identify the terms a, b, and c:

$a = 3$, $b = -7$, $c = 2$

Now plug those terms into the quadratic formula:

$x = \dfrac{-b \pm \sqrt{b^2 - 4ac}}{2a}$

$x = \dfrac{7 \pm \sqrt{(-7)^2 - 4(3)(2)}}{2(3)}$

$x = \dfrac{7 \pm \sqrt{25}}{6}$

$x = \dfrac{7 \pm 5}{6}$

Since the determinant is positive, you can expect two real numbers for x. Solve for the two possible answers:

$x = \dfrac{7 + 5}{6} \rightarrow \mathbf{x = 2}$

$x = \dfrac{7 - 5}{6} \rightarrow \mathbf{x = \dfrac{1}{3}}$

25. First, find the axis of symmetry. The equation for the line of symmetry is $x = \dfrac{-b}{2a}$.

$x = \dfrac{-4}{2(1)} = -2$

Next, plug in −2 for x to find the y coordinate of the vertex:

$y = (-2)^2 + 4(-2) + 1 = -3$

The vertex is (−2, −3).

Now, make a table of points on either side of the vertex by plugging in numbers for x and solving for y:

x	$y = x^2 + 4x + 1$	(x, y)
−3	$y = (-3)^2 + 4(-3) + 1 = -2$	(−3,−2)
−1	$y = (-1)^2 + 4(-1) + 1 = -2$	(−1,−2)
−4	$y = (-4)^2 + 4(-4) + 1 = 1$	(−4,1)
0	$y = 0^2 + 4(0) + 1 = 1$	(0,1)

Finally, draw the axis of symmetry, plot the vertex and your table of points, and trace the parabola:

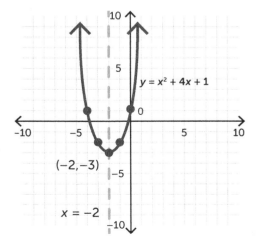

$y = x^2 + 4x + 1$

(−2,−3)

$x = -2$

26. Plug in 9 for x:

$f(9) = 2(9) - 10$

$f(9) = 8$

27. The function $f(x)$ has a range of only positive numbers, since x cannot be negative. The function $g(x)$ has a range of positive and negative numbers, since x can be either positive or negative.

The number −2, therefore, must be in the range for $g(x)$ but not for $f(x)$.

28. First, estimate the shape and direction of the graph based on the value of a. Since $a > 1$, you know that $f(x)$ will approach infinity as x increases and there will be a horizontal asymptote along the negative x-axis.

Next, plot the points (0, 1) and (1, a).

Finally, plug in one or two more values for x, plot those points and trace the graph:

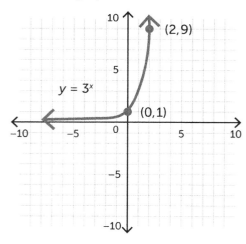

$f(2) = 3^2 = 9 \rightarrow (2, 9)$

29. $64 = 2^x$

The inverse of an exponent is a log. Take the log of both sides to solve for x:

$\log_2 64 = x$

$x = 6$

30. First, estimate the shape and direction of the graph based on the value of a. Since $a > 1$, you know that $f(x)$ will approach infinity as x increases and there will be a vertical asymptote along the negative y-axis.

Next, plot the points (1,0) and (a,1).

Finally, it is easier to plug in a value for $f(x)$ and solve for x rather than attempting to solve for $f(x)$. Plug in one or two values for $f(x)$, plot those points and trace the graph:

$2 = \log_4 x$

$4^2 = x$

$16 = x \rightarrow (16,2)$

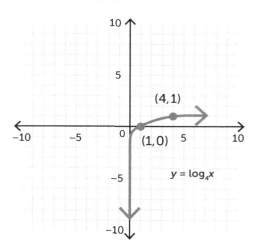

31. Rewrite the function in exponent form:

$x = \dfrac{1}{3}^{f(x)}$

$81 = \dfrac{1}{3}^{f(x)}$

The question is asking: to what power must you raise $\frac{1}{3}$ to get 81?

Recognize that $3^4 = 81$,

so $\dfrac{1}{3}^4 = \dfrac{1}{81}$

Switch the sign of the exponent to flip the numerator and denominator:

$$\frac{1}{3}^{-4} = \frac{81}{1}$$

$f(81) = -4$

32. Find the difference between two terms that are next to each other:

    $$5 - (-1) = -6$$

    The common difference is −6. (It must be negative to show the difference is subtracted, not added.)

    Now subtract 6 from the last term to find the next term:

    $$-13 - 6 = -19$$

    The next term is −19.

33. First, decide whether this is an arithmetic or geometric sequence. Since the numbers are getting farther and farther apart, you know this must be a geometric sequence.

    Divide one term by the term before it to find the common ratio:

    $$18 \div 6 = 3$$

    Next, plug in the common ratio and the first term to the equation $a_n = a_1(r^n)$:

    $$a_{12} = 2(3^{12})$$

    $a_{12} = 1{,}062{,}882$

    Notice that it would have taken a very long time to multiply each term by 3 until you got the 12th term – this is where that equation comes in handy!

34. To answer this question, you can simply add 9 + 11 = 20 to get the 5th term, 20 + 11 = 31 to get the 6th term, and so on until you get the 10th term. Or you can plug the information you know into your equation $a_n = a_1 + (n - 1)d$. In this

case, you do not know the first term. If you use the fourth term instead, you must replace $(n - 1)$ with $(n - 4)$:

$$a_{10} = 9 + (10 - 4)11$$

$a_{10} = 75$

35. Set up the first equation by removing the absolute value symbol then solve for x:

    $$|2x - 3| = x + 1$$
    $$2x - 3 = x + 1$$
    $$x = 4$$

    For the second equation, remove the absolute value and multiply by −1:

    $$|2x - 3| = x + 1 \rightarrow$$
    $$2x - 3 = -(x + 1) \rightarrow$$
    $$2x - 3 = -x - 1 \rightarrow$$
    $$3x = 2$$
    $$x = \frac{2}{3}$$

    Both answers are correct, so the complete answer is **$x = 4$ or $\frac{2}{3}$.**

36. Set up the first equation:

    $$2(y + 4) = 10$$
    $$y + 4 = 5$$
    $$y = 1$$

    Set up the second equation. Remember to isolate the absolute value before multiplying by −1:

    $$2|y + 4| = 10 \rightarrow$$
    $$|y + 4| = 5 \rightarrow$$
    $$y + 4 = -5$$
    $$y = -9$$

    $y = 1$ or −9

37. Start by listing all the data and defining the variable:

    total number of backpacks = 48

    cost of backpacks = $476.00

backpacks sold in store at price of $18 = 17

backpacks sold to school at a price of $15 = 48 − 17 = 31

total profit = x

Now set up an equation:

income − cost = total profit

(306 + 465) − 476 = 295

The store owner made a profit of **$295**.

38. Start by listing all the data and defining your variables. Note that the number of students, while given in the problem, is not needed to find the answer:

time on 1st day = $\frac{3}{5}$ hr. = 36 min.

time on 2nd day = $\frac{1}{2}(36)$ = 18 min.

total time = x

Now set up the equation and solve:

total time = time on 1st day + time on 2nd day

$x = 36 + 18 = 54$

The students had **54 minutes** to work on the projects.

39. The first step is to set up a table and fill in a value for each variable:

	d	r	t
driving	d	30	t
flying	150 − d	60	3 − t

You can now set up equations for driving and flying. The first row gives the equation $d = 30t$ and the second row gives the equation 150 − d = 60(3 − t).

Next, solve this system of equations. Start by substituting for d in the second equation:

$d = 30t$

150 − d = 60(3 − t) → 150 − 30t = 60(3 − t)

Now solve for t:

150 − 30t = 180 − 60t

−30 = −30t

1 = t

Although you've solved for t, you're not done yet. Notice that the problem asks for distance. So, you need to solve for d: what the problem asked for. It does not ask for time, but you need to calculate it to solve the problem.

Driving: 30t = 30 miles

Flying: 150 − d = 120 miles

The distance from the airport to the hospital is 120 miles.

40. First, set up the table. The variable for time will be the same for each, because they will have been on the field for the same amount of time when they meet:

	d	r	t
horse #1	d	14	t
horse #2	45 − d	16	t

Next set up two equations:

Horse #1: $d = 14t$

Horse #2: 45 − d = 16t

Now substitute and solve:

$d = 14t$

45 − d = 16t → 45 − 14t = 16t

45 = 30t

$t = 1.5$

They will meet 1.5 hr. after they begin.

41. Start by figuring out how much of a house each sibling can clean on his or her own. Bridget can clean the house in 12 hours, so she can clean $\frac{1}{12}$ of the house in an hour.

Using the same logic, Tom can clean $\frac{1}{8}$ of a house in an hour.

By adding these values together, you get the fraction of the house they can clean together in an hour:

$\frac{1}{12} + \frac{1}{8} = \frac{5}{24}$

They can do $\frac{5}{24}$ of the job per hour.

Now set up variables and an equation to solve:

t = time spent cleaning (in hours)

h = number of houses cleaned = 2

work = rate × time

$h = \frac{5}{24}t \rightarrow$

$2 = \frac{5}{24}t \rightarrow$

$t = \frac{48}{5} = \mathbf{9\frac{3}{5}}$ **hr.**

42. In this problem you don't know the exact time, but you can still find the hourly rate as a variable:

The first hose completes the job in f hours, so it waters $\frac{1}{f}$ field per hour. The slow hose waters the field in $1.25f$, so it waters the field in $\frac{1}{1.25f}$ hours. Together, they take 5 hours to water the field, so they water $\frac{1}{5}$ of the field per hour.

Now you can set up the equations and solve:

$\frac{1}{f} + \frac{1}{1.25f} = \frac{1}{5} \rightarrow$

$1.25f(\frac{1}{f} + \frac{1}{1.25f}) = 1.25f(\frac{1}{5}) \rightarrow$

$1.25 + 1 = 0.25f$

$2.25 = 0.25f$

$f = 9$

The fast hose takes 9 hours to water the field. The slow hose takes 1.25(9) = **11.25 hours**.

43. Calculate how many apples each person can pick per hour:

Ben: $\frac{500 \text{ apples}}{2 \text{ hr.}} = \frac{250 \text{ apples}}{\text{hr.}}$

Frank: $\frac{450 \text{ apples}}{3 \text{ hr.}} = \frac{150 \text{ apples}}{\text{hr.}}$

Together: $\frac{250 + 150 \text{ apples}}{\text{hr.}} = \frac{400 \text{ apples}}{\text{hr.}}$

Now set up an equation to find the time it takes to pick 1000 apples:

total time = $\frac{1 \text{ hr.}}{400 \text{ apples}} \times 1000$

apples = $\frac{1000}{400 \text{ hr.}} = \mathbf{2.5 \text{ hours}}$

CHAPTER FIVE
Geometry

Properties of Shapes
AREA and PERIMETER

AREA and PERIMETER problems require you to use the equations shown in the table below to find either the area inside a shape or the distance around it (the perimeter). These equations will not be given on the test, so you need to have them memorized on test day.

Table 5.1. Area and Perimeter Equations

SHAPE	AREA	PERIMETER
circle	$A = \pi r^2$	$C = 2\pi r = \pi d$
triangle	$A = \dfrac{b \times h}{2}$	$P = s_1 + s_2 + s_3$
square	$A = s^2$	$P = 4s$
rectangle	$A = l \times w$	$P = 2l + 2w$

EXAMPLES

1. A farmer has purchased 100 meters of fencing to enclose his rectangular garden. If one side of the garden is 20 meters long and the other is 28 meters long, how much fencing will the farmer have left over?

2. Taylor is going to paint a square wall that is 3.5 meters high. How much paint will he need?

VOLUME

Volume is the amount of space taken up by a three-dimensional object. Different formulas are used to find the volumes of different shapes.

Table 5.2. Volume Formulas

Shape	Volume
cylinder	$V = \pi r^2 h$
pyramid	$V = \frac{l \times w \times h}{3}$
cone	$V = \frac{\pi r^2 h}{3}$
sphere	$V = \frac{4}{3}\pi r3$

EXAMPLES

3. Charlotte wants to fill her circular swimming pool with water. The pool has a diameter of 6 meters and is 1 meter deep. How many cubic meters of water will she need to fill the pool?

4. Danny has a fishbowl that is filled to the brim with water, and purchased some spherical glass marbles to line the bottom of it. He dropped in four marbles, and water spilled out of the fishbowl. If the radius of each marble is 1 centimeter, how much water spilled?

CIRCLES

The definition of a circle is the set of points that are equal distance from a center point. The distance from the center to any given point on the circle is the **RADIUS**. If you draw a straight line segment across the circle going through the center, the distance along the line segment from one side of the circle to the other is called the **DIAMETER**. The radius is always equal to half the diameter: $d = 2r$.

DID YOU KNOW?
The equation for a circle on the coordinate plane is $(x - h)^2 + (y - k)^2 = r^2$ where (h,k) is the center of the circle and r is the radius.

A **CENTRAL ANGLE** is formed by drawing radii out from the center to two points A and B along the circle. The **INTERCEPTED ARC** is the portion of the circle (the arc length) between points A and B. You can find the intercepted arc length l if you know the central angle θ and vice versa:

$$l = 2\pi r \frac{\theta}{360°}$$

A **CHORD** is a line segment that connects two points on a circle. Unlike the diameter, a chord does not have to go through the center. You can find the chord length if you know either the central angle θ or the radius of the circle r and the distance from the center of the circle to the chord d (d must be at a right angle to the chord):

If you know the central angle, chord length = $2r\sin\frac{\theta}{2}$

If you know the radius and distance, chord length = $2\sqrt{r^2 - d^2}$

A SECANT is similar to a chord; it connects two points on a circle. The difference is that a secant is a line, not a line segment, so it extends outside of the circle on either side.

A TANGENT is a straight line that touches a circle at only one point.

A SECTOR is the area within a circle that is enclosed by a central angle; if a circle is a pie, a sector is the piece of pie cut by two radii. You can find the AREA OF A SECTOR if you know either the central angle θ or the arc length s.

If you know the central angle, the area of the sector = $\pi r^2\frac{\theta}{360°}$

If you know the arc length, the area of a sector = $\frac{1}{2}rl$

There are two other types of angles you can create in or around a circle. INSCRIBED ANGLES are *inside* the circle: the vertex is a point P on the circle and the rays extend to two other points on the circle (A and B). As long as A and B remain constant, you can move the vertex P anywhere along the circle and the inscribed angle will be the same. CIRCUMSCRIBED ANGLES are *outside* of the circle: the rays are formed by two tangent lines that touch the circle at points A and B.

You can find the inscribed angle if you know the radius of the circle r and the arc length l between A and B:

$$\text{inscribed angle} = \frac{90°l}{\pi r}$$

To find the circumscribed angle, find the central angle formed by the same points A and B and subtract that angle from 180°.

EXAMPLES

5. A circle has a diameter of 10 centimeters. What is the intercepted arc length between points A and B if the central angle between those points measures 46°?

6. A chord is formed by line segment $\overline{QP}$. The radius of the circle is 5 cm and the chord length is 6 cm. Find the distance from center C to the chord.

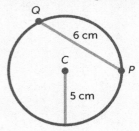

Congruence

CONGRUENCE means having the same size and shape. Two shapes are congruent if you can turn (rotate), flip (reflect), and/or slide (translate) one to fit perfectly on top of the other. Two angles are congruent if they measure the same number of degrees; they do not have to face the same direction nor must they necessarily have rays of equal length. If two triangles have one of the combinations of congruent sides and/or angles listed below, then those triangles are congruent:

- ▶ **SSS** – side, side, side
- ▶ **ASA** – angle, side, angle
- ▶ **SAS** – side, angle, side
- ▶ **AAS** – angle, angle, side

There are a number of common sets of congruent angles in geometry. An ISOSCELES TRIANGLE has two sides of equal length (called the legs) and two congruent angles. If you bisect an isosceles triangle by drawing a line perpendicular to the third side (called the base), you will form two congruent right triangles.

Where two lines cross and form an *X*, the opposite angles are congruent and are called VERTICAL ANGLES. PARALLEL LINES are lines that never cross; if you cut two parallel lines by a transversal, you will form four pairs of congruent CORRESPONDING ANGLES.

A PARALLELOGRAM is a quadrilateral in which both pairs of opposite sides are parallel and congruent (of equal length). In a parallelogram, the two pairs of opposite angles are also congruent. If you divide a parallelogram by either of the diagonals, you will form two congruent triangles.

EXAMPLES

7. Kate and Emily set out for a bike ride together from their house. They ride 6 miles north, then Kate turns 30° to the west and Emily turns 30° to the east. They both ride another 8 miles. If Kate rides 12 miles to return home, how far must Emily ride to get home?

8. Angle *A* measures 53°. Find angle *H*.

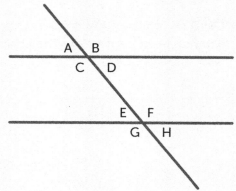

Right Triangles and Trigonometry
PYTHAGOREAN THEOREM

Shapes with 3 sides are known as TRIANGLES. In addition to knowing the formulas for their area and perimeter, you should also know the Pythagorean Theorem, which describes the relationship between the three sides (*a*, *b*, and *c*) of a triangle:

$$a^2 + b^2 = c^2$$

EXAMPLE

9. Erica is going to run a race in which she'll run 3 miles due north and 4 miles due east. She'll then run back to the starting line. How far will she run during this race?

TRIGONOMETRY

Using TRIGONOMETRY, you can calculate an angle in a right triangle based on the ratio of two sides of that triangle. You can also calculate one of the side lengths using the measure of an angle and another side. SINE (SIN), COSINE (COS), and TANGENT (TAN) correspond to the three possible ratios of side lengths. They are defined below:

$$\sin \theta = \frac{opposite}{hypotenuse} \qquad \cos \theta = \frac{adjacent}{hypotenuse} \qquad \tan \theta = \frac{opposite}{adjacent}$$

Opposite is the side opposite from the angle θ, *adjacent* is the side adjacent to the angle θ, and *hypotenuse* is the longest side of the triangle, opposite from the right angle. SOH-CAH-TOA is an acronym to help you remember which ratio goes with which function.

When solving for a side or an angle in a right triangle, first identify which function to use based on the known lengths or angle.

EXAMPLES

10. Phil is hanging holiday lights. To do so safely, he must lean his 20-foot ladder against the outside of his house at an angle of 15° or less. How far from the house can he safely place the base of the ladder?

11. Grace is practicing shooting hoops. She is 5 feet 4 inches tall; her basketball hoop is 10 feet high. From 8 feet away, at what angle does she have to look up to see the hoop? Assume that her eyes are 4 inches lower than the top of her head.

Coordinate Geometry

Coordinate geometry is the study of points, lines, and shapes that have been graphed on a set of axes.

POINTS, LINES, and PLANES

In coordinate geometry, points are plotted on a **COORDINATE PLANE**, a two-dimensional plane in which the **x-AXIS** indicates horizontal direction and the **y-AXIS** indicates vertical direction. The intersection of these two axes is the **ORIGIN**. Points are defined by their location in relation to the horizontal and vertical axes. The coordinates of a point are written (x, y). The coordinates of the origin are $(0, 0)$. The x-coordinates to the right of the origin and the y-coordinates above it are positive; the x-coordinates to the left of the origin and the y-coordinates below it are negative.

A **LINE** is formed by connecting any two points on a coordinate plane; lines are continuous in both directions. Lines can be defined by their **SLOPE**, or steepness, and their **y-INTERCEPT**, or the point at which they intersect the y-axis. A line is represented by the equation $y = mx + b$. The constant m represents slope and the constant b represents the y-intercept.

EXAMPLES

12. Matt parks his car near a forest where he goes hiking. From his car he hikes 1 mile north, 2 miles east, then 3 miles west. If his car represents the origin, find the coordinates of Matt's current location.

13. A square is drawn on a coordinate plane. The bottom corners are located at (−2,3) and (4,3). What are the coordinates for the top right corner?

THE DISTANCE and MIDPOINT FORMULAS

To determine the distance between the points (x_1, y_1) and (x_2, y_2) from a grid use the formula:

$$d = \sqrt{(x_2 - x_1)^2 + (y_2 - y_1)^2}$$

The midpoint, which is halfway between the 2 points, is the point:

$$\left(\frac{x_1 + x_2}{2}, \frac{y_1 + y_2}{2} \right)$$

EXAMPLES

14. What is the distance between points (3,−6) and (−5,2)?

15. What is the midpoint between points (3,−6) and (−5,2)?

Answer Key

1. The perimeter of a rectangle is equal to twice its length plus twice its width:

$P = 2(20) + 2(28) = 96$ m

The farmer has 100 meters of fencing, so he'll have $100 - 96 =$ **4 meters** left.

2. Each side of the square wall is 3.5 meters:

$A = 3.5^2 =$ **12.25m²**

3. This question is asking about the volume of Charlotte's pool. The circular pool is actually a cylinder, so use the formula for a cylinder: $V = \pi r^2 h$.

The diameter is 6 meters. The radius is half the diameter so $r = 6 \div 2 = 3$ meters.

Now solve for the volume:

$V = \pi r^2 h$

$V = \pi (3 \text{ m})^2 (1 \text{ m})$

$V = 28.3 \text{ m}^3$

Charlotte will need approximately **28.3 cubic meters** of water to fill her pool.

4. Since the fishbowl was filled to the brim, the volume of the water that spilled out of it is equal to the volume of the marbles that Danny dropped into it. First, find the volume of one marble using the equation for a sphere:

$V = \frac{4}{3}\pi r^3$

$V = \frac{4}{3}\pi (1 \text{ cm})^3$

$V = 4.2 \text{ cm}^3$

Since Danny dropped in 4 marbles, multiply this volume by 4 to find the total volume:

$4.2 \text{ cm}^3 \times 4 = 16.8 \text{ cm}^3$

Approximately **16.8 cubic centimeters** of water spilled out of the fishbowl.

5. First divide the diameter by two to find the radius:

$r = 10 \text{ cm} \div 2 = 5 \text{ cm}$

Now use the formula for intercepted arc length:

$l = 2\pi r \frac{\theta}{360°}$

$l = 2\pi (5 \text{ cm}) \frac{46°}{360°}$

$l =$ **4.0 cm**

6. Use the formula for chord length:

chord length $= 2\sqrt{r^2 - d^2}$

In this example, we are told the chord length and the radius, and we need to solve for d:

$6 \text{ cm} = 2\sqrt{(5 \text{ cm})^2 - d^2}$

$3 \text{ cm} = \sqrt{(5 \text{ cm})^2 - d^2}$

$9 \text{ cm}^2 = 25 \text{ cm}^2 - d^2$

$d^2 = 16 \text{ cm}^2$

$d =$ **4 cm**

7. Draw out Kate's and Emily's trips to see that their routes form two triangles. The triangles have corresponding sides with lengths of 6 miles and 8 miles, and a corresponding angle in between of 150°. This fits the "SAS" rule so the triangles must be congruent. The length Kate has to ride home corresponds to the length Emily has to ride home, so **Emily must ride 12 miles.**

8. For parallel lines cut by a transversal, look for vertical and corresponding angles.

Angles *A* and *D* are vertical angles, so angle *D* must be congruent to angle *A*. Angle *D* = 53°.

Angles *D* and *H* are corresponding angles, so angle *H* must be congruent to angle *D*. **Angle H = 53°.**

9. Start by drawing a picture of Erica's route. You'll see it forms a triangle:

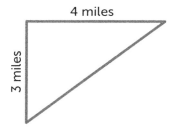

One leg of the triangle is missing, but you can find its length using the Pythagorean Theorem:

$a^2 + b^2 = c^2$

$3^2 + 4^2 = c^2$

$25 = c^2$

$c = 5$

Adding all 3 sides gives the length of the whole race:

$3 + 4 + 5 =$ **12 miles**

10. Draw a triangle with the known length and angle labeled.

The known side (the length of the ladder) is the hypotenuse of the triangle, and the unknown distance is the side opposite the angle. Therefore, you can use sine:

$\sin\theta = \frac{opposite}{hypotenuse}$

$\sin15° = \frac{opposite}{20 \text{ feet}}$

Now solve for the opposite side:

$opposite = \sin15°(20 \text{ feet})$

$opposite =$ **5.2 feet**

11. Draw a diagram and notice that the line from Grace's eyes to the hoop of the basket forms the hypotenuse of a right triangle. The side adjacent to the angle of her eyes is the distance from the basket: 8 feet. The side opposite to Grace's eyes is the difference between the height of her eyes and the height of the basket: 10 feet − 5 feet = 5 feet.

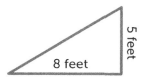

Next, use the formula for tangent to solve for the angle:

$\tan\theta = \frac{opposite}{adjacent}$

$\tan\theta = \frac{5 \text{ ft}}{8 \text{ ft}}$

Now take the inverse tangent of both sides to solve for the angle:

$\theta = \tan^{-1}\frac{5}{8}$

$\theta = 32°$

12. To find the coordinates, you must find Matt's displacement along the *x*- and *y*-axes. Matt hiked 1 mile north and zero miles south, so his displacement along the *y*-axis is +1 mile. Matt hiked 2

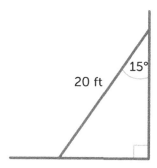

miles east and 3 miles west, so his displacement along the *x*-axis is + 2 miles − 3 miles = −1 mile.

Matt's coordinates are (−1,1).

13. Draw the coordinate plane and plot the given points. If you connect these points you will see that the bottom side is 6 units long. Since it is a square, all sides must be 6 units long. Count 6 units up from the point (4,3) to find the top right corner.

The coordinates for the top right corner are (4,9).

14. Plug the values for x_1, x_2, y_1, and y_2 into the distance formula and simplify:

$d = \sqrt{(-5-3)^2 + (2-(-6))^2} =$

$\sqrt{64+64} = \sqrt{64 \times 2} = \mathbf{8\sqrt{2}}$

15. Plug the values for x_1, x_2, y_1, and y_2 into the midpoint formula and simplify:

$midpoint = \left(\frac{3+(-5)}{2}, \frac{(-6)+2}{2} \right)$

$= \left(\frac{-2}{2}, \frac{-4}{2} \right) = \mathbf{(-1,-2)}$

CHAPTER SIX
Statistics and Probability

Describing Sets of Data

STATISTICS is the study of sets of data. The goal of statistics is to take a group of values—numerical answers from a survey, for example—and look for patterns in how that data is distributed.

When looking at a set of data, it's helpful to consider the **MEASURES OF CENTRAL TENDENCY**, a group of values that describe the central or typical data point from the set. The PSAT covers three measures of central tendency: mean, median, and mode.

MEAN is the mathematical term for *average*. To find the mean, total all the terms and divide by the number of terms. The **MEDIAN** is the middle number of a given set. To find the median, put the terms in numerical order; the middle number will be the median. In the case of a set of even numbers, the middle two numbers are averaged. **MODE** is the number which occurs most frequently within a given set. If two different numbers both appear with the highest frequency, they are both the mode.

When examining a data set, also consider **MEASURES OF VARIABILITY**, which describe how the data is dispersed around the central data point. The PSAT covers two measures of variability: range and standard deviation. **RANGE** is simply the difference between the largest and smallest values in the set. **STANDARD DEVIATION** is a measure of how dispersed the data is, or how far it reaches from the mean.

EXAMPLES

1. Find the mean of 24, 27, and 18.

2. The mean of three numbers is 45. If two of the numbers are 38 and 43, what is the third number?

3. What is the median of 24, 27, and 18?

4. What is the median of 24, 27, 18, and 19?

5. What is the mode of 2, 5, 4, 4, 3, 2, 8, 9, 2, 7, 2, and 2?

6. What is the standard deviation of 62, 63, 61, and 66?

Graphs and Charts

These questions require you to interpret information from graphs and charts; they are pretty straightforward as long as you pay careful attention to detail. There are several different graph and chart types that may appear on the PSAT.

BAR GRAPHS

BAR GRAPHS present the numbers of an item that exist in different categories. The categories are shown on the x-axis, and the number of items is shown on the y-axis. Bar graphs are usually used to easily compare amounts.

EXAMPLES

7. The chart below shows rainfall in inches per month. Which month had the least amount of rainfall? Which had the most?

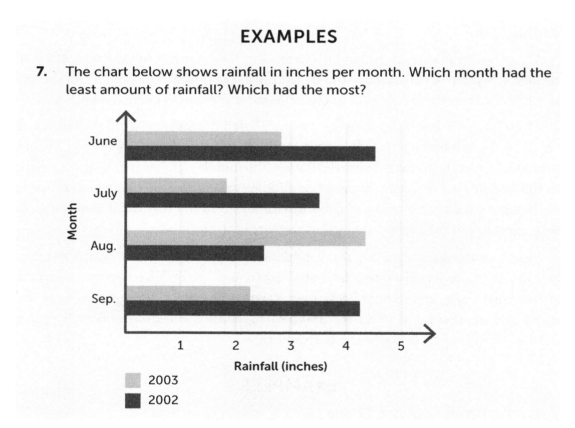

8. Using the chart below, how many more ice cream cones were sold in July than in September?

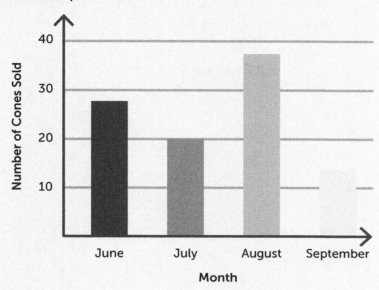

PIE CHARTS

PIE CHARTS present parts of a whole, and are often used with percentages. Together, all the slices of the pie add up to the total number of items, or 100%.

EXAMPLES

9. The pie chart below shows the distribution of birthdays in a class of students. How many students have birthdays in the spring or summer?

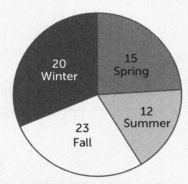

Distribution of Students' Birthdays

10. Using the same graph above, what percentage of students have birthdays in winter?

LINE GRAPHS

LINE GRAPHS show trends over time. The number of each item represented by the graph will be on the *y*-axis, and time will be on the *x*-axis.

EXAMPLES

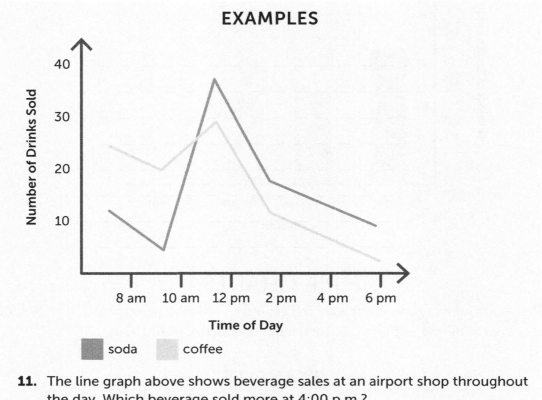

11. The line graph above shows beverage sales at an airport shop throughout the day. Which beverage sold more at 4:00 p.m.?

12. At what time of day were the most beverages sold?

HISTOGRAMS

A **HISTOGRAM** shows a distribution of types within a whole in bar chart form. While they look like bar graphs, they are more similar to pie charts: they show you parts of a whole.

EXAMPLE

13. The chart on the following page shows the number of cars that traveled through a toll plaza throughout the day. How many cars passed through the toll plaza between 8:00 a.m. and 5:00 p.m.?

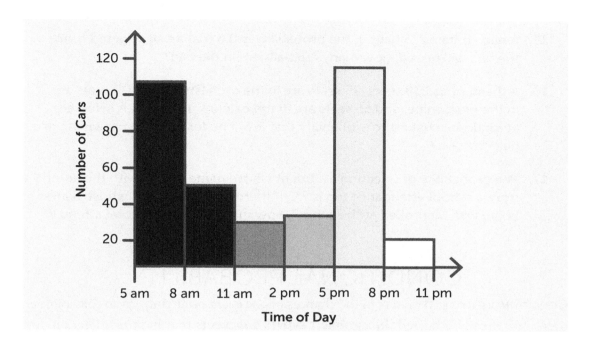

Probability

PROBABILITY is the likelihood that an event will take place. This likelihood is expressed as a value between 0 and 1. The closer the probability is to zero, the less likely the event is to occur; the closer the probability is to 1, the more likely it is to occur.

PROBABILITY of a SINGLE EVENT

The probability of an outcome occurring is found by dividing the number of desired outcomes by the number of total possible outcomes. As with percentages, a probability is the ratio of a part to a whole, with the whole being the total number of possibilities, and the part being the number of desired results. Probabilities can be written using percentages (40%), decimals (0.4), fractions, or in words (the probability of an outcome is 2 in 5).

$$\text{probability} = \frac{\text{desired outcomes}}{\text{total possible outcomes}}$$

EXAMPLES

14. A bag holds 3 blue marbles, 5 green marbles, and 7 red marbles. If you pick one marble from the bag, what is the probability it will be blue?

15. A bag contains 75 balls. If the probability is 0.6 that a ball selected from the bag will be red, how many red balls are in the bag?

16. A theater has 230 seats: 75 seats are in the orchestra area, 100 seats are in the mezzanine, and 55 seats are in the balcony. If a ticket is selected at random, what is the probability that it will be for either a mezzanine or balcony seat?

17. The probability of selecting a student whose name begins with the letter *S* from a school attendance log is 7%. If there are 42 students whose names begin with *S* enrolled at the school, how many students in total attend it?

CONDITIONAL PROBABILITY

CONDITIONAL PROBABILITY refers to the chances of one event occurring, given that another event has already occurred. INDEPENDENT EVENTS are events that have no effect on one another. The classic example is flipping a coin: whether you flip heads or tails one time has no bearing on how you might flip the next time. Your chance of flipping heads is always 50/50. DEPENDENT EVENTS, on the other hand, have an effect on the next event's probability. If you have a bag full of red and blue marbles, removing a red marble the first time will decrease the probability of picking a red marble the second time, since now there are fewer red marbles in the bag. The probability of event *B* occurring, given that event *A* has occurred, is written $P(B|A)$.

The probability of either event *A* or event *B* occurring is called the UNION of events *A* and *B*, written $A \cup B$. The probability of $A \cup B$ is equal to the <u>sum</u> of the probability of *A* occurring and the probability of *B* occurring, <u>minus</u> the probability of both *A* and *B* occurring. The probability of both *A* and *B* occurring is called the INTERSECTION of events *A* and *B*, written $A \cap B$. The probability of $A \cap B$ is equal to the <u>product</u> of the probability of *A* and the probability of *B*, given *A*. Review the equations for the probabilities of unions and intersections below:

$$P(A \cup B) = P(A) + P(B) - P(A \cap B)$$
$$P(A \cap B) = P(A) \times P(B|A)$$

The COMPLEMENT of an event is when the event <u>does not</u> occur. The probability of the complement of event *A*, written $P(A')$, is equal to $1 - P(A)$.

EXAMPLES

18. A bag contains 5 red marbles and 11 blue marbles. What is the probability of pulling out a blue marble, followed by a red marble?

19. Caroline randomly draws a playing card from a full deck. What is the chance she will select either a queen or a diamond?

Answer Key

1. Add the terms, then divide by the number of terms:

   mean $= \frac{24 + 27 + 18}{3} = $ **23**

2. Set up the equation for mean with x representing the third number, then solve:

   $mean = \frac{38 + 43 + x}{3} = 45$

   $\frac{38 + 43 + x}{3} = 45$

   $38 + 43 + x = 135$

   $x = $ **54**

3. Place the terms in order, then pick the middle term:

   18, 24, 27

   The median is **24**.

4. Place the terms in order. Because there is an even number of terms, the median will be the average of the middle 2 terms:

   18, 19, 24, 27

   $median = \frac{19 + 24}{2} = $ **21.5**

5. The mode is **2** because it appears the most within the set.

6. To find the standard deviation, first find the mean:

   $mean = \frac{62 + 63 + 61 + 66}{4} = 63$

   Next, find the difference between each term and the mean, and square that number:

   $63 - 62 = 1 \rightarrow 1^2 = 1$

   $63 - 63 = 0 \rightarrow 0^2 = 0$

   $63 - 61 = 2 \rightarrow 2^2 = 4$

   $63 - 66 = -3 \rightarrow (-3)^2 = 9$

   Now, find the mean of the squares:

   mean $= \frac{1 + 0 + 4 + 9}{4} = 3.5$

   Finally, find the square root of the mean:

   $\sqrt{3.5} = 1.87$

   The standard deviation is **1.87**.

7. The shortest bar will be the month that had the least rain, and the longest bar will correspond to the month with the greatest amount: **July 2003 had the least**, and **June 2002 had the most**.

8. Tracing from the top of each bar to the scale on the left shows that sales in July were 20 and September sales were 15. So, **5 more cones were sold in July**.

9. 15 students have birthdays in the spring and 12 in winter, so there are **27 students** with birthdays in spring or summer.

10. Use the equation for percent:

    percent $= \frac{part}{whole} = \frac{winter\ birthdays}{total\ birthdays} \rightarrow$

    $\frac{20}{20 + 15 + 23 + 12} = \frac{20}{70} = \frac{2}{7} = .286$

    or **28.6%**

11. At 4:00 p.m., approximately 12 sodas and 5 coffees were sold, so more **soda** was sold.

12. This question is asking for the time of day with the most sales of coffee and soda combined. It is not necessary to add up sales at each time of day to find the answer. Just from looking at the graph, you can see that sales for both beverages were highest at noon, so the answer must be **12:00 p.m.**

13. To find the total number, we need to add the number of cars for each relevant time period (note that all number are approximations):

8:00 a.m. – 11:00 a.m.: 50 cars

11:00 a.m. – 2:00 p.m.: 30 cars

2:00 p.m. – 5:00 p.m.: 35 cars

50 + 30 + 35 = **115 cars**

14. Because there are 15 marbles in the bag (3 + 5 + 7), the total number of possible outcomes is 15. Of those outcomes, 3 would be blue marbles, which is the desired outcome. Using that information, you can set up an equation:

$probability = \frac{desired\ outcomes}{total\ possible\ outcomes}$
$= \frac{3}{15} = \frac{1}{5}$

The probability is **1 in 5 or 0.2** that a blue marble is picked.

15. Because you're solving for desired outcomes (the number of red balls), first you need to rearrange the equation:

$probability = \frac{desired\ outcomes}{total\ possible\ outcomes}$
$desired\ outcomes = probability \times total\ possible\ outcomes$

Here, choosing a red ball is the desired outcome; the total possible outcomes are represented by the 75 total balls.

There are **45 red balls** in the bag.

16. In this problem, the desired outcome is a seat in either the mezzanine or balcony area, and the total possible outcomes are represented by the 230 total seats. So you can write this equation:

$probability = \frac{desired\ outcomes}{total\ possible\ outcomes}$
$= \frac{100 + 55}{230} = \mathbf{0.67}$

17. Because you're solving for total possible outcomes (total number of students), first you need to rearrange the equation:

$total\ possible\ outcomes$
$= \frac{desired\ outcomes}{probability}$

In this problem, you are given a probability (7% or 0.07) and the number of desired outcomes (42). Plug these numbers into the equation to solve:

total possible outcomes = $\frac{42}{0.07}$ = **600 students**

18. This question is asking about an intersection of events. The equation for an intersection of events is

$P(A \cap B) = P(A) \times P(B|A)$.

The first event, event A, is picking out a blue marble. Find $P(A)$:

$P(A) = \frac{11\ blue\ marbles}{16\ total\ marbles} = \frac{11}{16}$

The second event, event B, is picking out a red marble, now that there are 15 marbles left. Find $P(B|A)$:

$P(B|A) = \frac{5\ red\ marbles}{15\ total\ marbles} = \frac{5}{15} = \frac{1}{3}$

$P(A \cap B) = P(A) \times P(B|A)$
$= \frac{11}{16} \times \frac{1}{3} = \mathbf{\frac{11}{48}}$

19. This question is asking about a union of events. The equation for a union of events is

$P(A \cup B) = P(A) + P(B) - P(A \cap B)$.

The first event, event A, is selecting a queen. Find $P(A)$:

$P(A) = \frac{4\ queens}{52\ total\ cards} = \frac{4}{52}$

The second event, event B, is selecting a diamond. Find $P(B)$:

$P(B) = \frac{13\ diamonds}{52\ total\ cards} = \frac{13}{52}$

Now, find the probability of selecting a queen that is also a diamond:

$$P(A \cap B) = \frac{1 \text{ diamond queen}}{52 \text{ total cards}} = \frac{1}{52}$$

$$P(A \cup B) = P(A) + P(B) - P(A \cap B)$$
$$= \frac{4}{52} + \frac{13}{52} - \frac{1}{52} = \frac{16}{52} = \mathbf{\frac{4}{13}}$$

PART III
Test Your Knowledge
139 questions ¦ 2 hours and 45 minutes

CHAPTER SEVEN
Practice Test

Reading

There are several passages in this test and each passage is accompanied by several questions. After reading a passage, choose the best answer to each question and fill in the corresponding oval on your answer document. You may refer to the passages as often as necessary.

Questions 1 – 10 are based on the following passage, adapted from Nathaniel Hawthorne's short story "The Artist of the Beautiful," originally published in 1844. Owen Warland is a young watchmaker, who studied his trade as an apprentice under retired watchmaker Peter Hovenden.

From the time that his little fingers could grasp a penknife, Owen had been remarkable for a delicate ingenuity, which sometimes produced pretty shapes in wood, principally figures of flowers and birds, and sometimes seemed to aim at the hidden mysteries of mechanism. But it was always for purposes of grace, and never with any mockery of
(5) the useful. He did not, like the crowd of school-boy artisans, construct little windmills on the angle of a barn or watermills across the neighboring brook. Those who discovered such peculiarity in the boy as to think it worth their while to observe him closely, sometimes saw reason to suppose that he was attempting to imitate the beautiful movements of Nature as exemplified in the flight of birds or the activity of little animals.
(10) It seemed, in fact, a new development of the love of the beautiful, such as might have made him a poet, a painter, or a sculptor, and which was as completely refined from all utilitarian coarseness as it could have been in either of the fine arts. He looked with singular distaste at the stiff and regular processes of ordinary machinery. Being once carried to see a steam-engine, in the expectation that his intuitive comprehension of
(15) mechanical principles would be gratified, he turned pale and grew sick, as if something monstrous and unnatural had been presented to him. This horror was partly owing to

the size and terrible energy of the iron laborer; for the character of Owen's mind was microscopic, and tended naturally to the minute, in accordance with his diminutive frame and the marvelous smallness and delicate power of his fingers. Not that his sense (20) of beauty was thereby diminished into a sense of prettiness. The beautiful idea has no relation to size, and may be as perfectly developed in a space too minute for any but microscopic investigation as within the ample verge that is measured by the arc of the rainbow. But, at all events, this characteristic minuteness in his objects and accomplishments made the world even more incapable than it might otherwise have been (25) of appreciating Owen Warland's genius. The boy's relatives saw nothing better to be done—as perhaps there was not—than to bind him apprentice to a watchmaker, hoping that his strange ingenuity might thus be regulated and put to utilitarian purposes.

Peter Hovenden's opinion of his apprentice has already been expressed. He could make nothing of the lad. Owen's apprehension of the professional mysteries, it is true, (30) was inconceivably quick; but he altogether forgot or despised the grand object of a watchmaker's business, and cared no more for the measurement of time than if it had been merged into eternity. So long, however, as he remained under his old master's care, Owen's lack of sturdiness made it possible, by strict injunctions and sharp oversight, to restrain his creative eccentricity within bounds; but when his apprenticeship was served (35) out, and he had taken the little shop which Peter Hovenden's failing eyesight compelled him to relinquish, then did people recognize how unfit a person was Owen Warland to lead old blind Father Time along his daily course. One of his most rational projects was to connect a musical operation with the machinery of his watches, so that all the harsh dissonances of life might be rendered tuneful, and each flitting moment fall (40) into the abyss of the past in golden drops of harmony. If a family clock was entrusted to him for repair,—one of those tall, ancient clocks that have grown nearly allied to human nature by measuring out the lifetime of many generations,—he would take upon himself to arrange a dance or funeral procession of figures across its venerable face, representing twelve mirthful or melancholy hours. Several freaks of this kind quite (45) destroyed the young watchmaker's credit with that steady and matter-of-fact class of people who hold the opinion that time is not to be trifled with, whether considered as the medium of advancement and prosperity in this world or preparation for the next. His custom rapidly diminished—a misfortune, however, that was probably reckoned among his better accidents by Owen Warland, who was becoming more and more (50) absorbed in a secret occupation which drew all his science and manual dexterity into itself, and likewise gave full employment to the characteristic tendencies of his genius.

1. The main purpose of the first paragraph is—
   A) to characterize Owen as an unconventional genius
   B) to explain how Owen came to be apprenticed at the watch shop
   C) to recall a significant event in Owen's life
   D) to describe Owen's most recent project

2. The narrator implies that Owen is—
- **A)** incompetent as a watchmaker
- **B)** overwhelmed by the details of life
- **C)** an outsider in his community
- **D)** a highly rational thinker

3. In line 12, *utilitarian* most nearly means—
- **A)** noble
- **B)** creative
- **C)** practical
- **D)** artistic

4. The description of Owen's response to the train in lines 13 through 16 primarily serves to—
- **A)** describe a significant, formative event in Owen's life
- **B)** illustrate Owen's interest in mechanical systems
- **C)** define Owen's unique definition of beauty
- **D)** further characterize Owen's peculiar affinity for the minute

5. Which choice provides the best evidence for the answer to the previous question?
- **A)** *But, at all events, this characteristic minuteness in his objects and accomplishments made the world even more incapable than it might otherwise have been of appreciating Owen Warland's genius.*
- **B)** *Peter Hovenden's opinion of his apprentice has already been expressed. He could make nothing of the lad.*
- **C)** *So long, however, as he remained under his old master's care, Owen's lack of sturdiness made it possible, by strict injunctions and sharp oversight, to restrain his creative eccentricity within bounds.*
- **D)** *One of his most rational projects was to connect a musical operation with the machinery of his watches, so that all the harsh dissonances of life might be rendered tuneful, and each flitting moment fall into the abyss of the past in golden drops of harmony.*

6. Which statement best characterizes the relationship between Owen Warland and Peter Hovenden?
- **A)** Owen is disinterested in Peter Hovenden's artistic endeavors.
- **B)** Owen is flattered to apprentice under such an accomplished watchmaker as Peter Hovenden.
- **C)** Peter Hovenden is perplexed by Owen's unique brilliance.
- **D)** Peter Hovenden resents Owen for the negative attention he has received from the community.

7. Which choice provides the best evidence for the answer to the previous question?

   A) *But, at all events, this characteristic minuteness in his objects and accomplishments made the world even more incapable than it might otherwise have been of appreciating Owen Warland's genius.*

   B) *Peter Hovenden's opinion of his apprentice has already been expressed. He could make nothing of the lad.*

   C) *So long, however, as he remained under his old master's care, Owen's lack of sturdiness made it possible, by strict injunctions and sharp oversight, to restrain his creative eccentricity within bounds.*

   D) *One of his most rational projects was to connect a musical operation with the machinery of his watches, so that all the harsh dissonances of life might be rendered tuneful, and each flitting moment fall into the abyss of the past in golden drops of harmony.*

8. As used in line 34, *eccentricity* most nearly means—

   A) brilliance.
   B) peculiarity.
   C) energy.
   D) fickleness.

9. According to the passage, Peter Hovenden turned his shop over to Owen Warland because—

   A) Failing eyesight prevented him from continuing the work himself.
   B) Owen had become an accomplished watchmaker and no longer needed Peter.
   C) He did not understand Owen and no longer felt they could work together.
   D) He was embarrassed by the reputation Owen had earned in the community.

10. The description of the *steady and matter-of-fact class of people* in lines 40 through 42 primarily serves to—

    A) illustrate the open-mindedness of the community in which Owen lives
    B) characterize Owen's community as responsible and reliable
    C) distinguish between those who value time and those who do not
    D) draw a contrast between Owen and the other members of the community

Questions 11 – 21 are based on the following passages, which address the topic of America's involvement in foreign affairs. Passage 1 is adapted from George Washington's farewell address, published in American newspapers in 1796 at the end of the president's third term. In his letter, Washington offers his advice on America's future involvement with foreign nations. Passage 2 is adapted from an address given by Harry S. Truman, the 33rd American president, before a joint session of Congress in 1947. In his speech, Truman urges Congress to provide assistance to countries at risk of Communist takeover.

Passage 1

The great rule of conduct for us, in regard to foreign nations, is, in extending our commercial relations, to have with them as little political connection as possible. So far as we have already formed engagements, let them be fulfilled with perfect good faith. Here let us stop.

(5)   Europe has a set of primary interests, which to us have none, or a very remote relation. Hence she must be engaged in frequent controversies, the causes of which are essentially foreign to our concerns. Hence, therefore, it must be unwise in us to implicate ourselves, by artificial ties, in the ordinary vicissitudes of her politics, or the ordinary combinations and collisions of her friendships or enmities.

(10)   Our detached and distant situation invites and enables us to pursue a different course. If we remain one people, under an efficient government, the period is not far off, when we may defy material injury from external annoyance; when we may take such an attitude as will cause the neutrality, we may at any time resolve upon, to be scrupulously respected; when belligerent nations, under the impossibility of making

(15)   acquisitions upon us, will not lightly hazard the giving us provocation; when we may choose peace or war, as our interest, guided by justice, shall counsel.

Why forego the advantages of so peculiar a situation? Why quit our own to stand upon foreign ground? Why, by interweaving our destiny with that of any part of Europe, entangle our peace and prosperity in the toils of European ambition, rivalship, interest,

(20)   humor, or caprice?

It is our true policy to steer clear of permanent alliances with any portion of the foreign world; so far, I mean, as we are now at liberty to do it; for let me not be understood as capable of patronizing infidelity to existing engagements. I hold the maxim no less applicable to public than to private affairs, that honesty is always the best policy. I

(25)   repeat it, therefore, let those engagements be observed in their genuine sense. But, in my opinion, it is unnecessary and would be unwise to extend them.

Passage 2

One of the primary objectives of the foreign policy of the United States is the creation of conditions in which we and other nations will be able to work out a way of life free from coercion. This was a fundamental issue in the war with Germany and Japan. Our

(30)   victory was won over countries which sought to impose their will, and their way of life, upon other nations.

To ensure the peaceful development of nations, free from coercion, the United States has taken a leading part in establishing the United Nations. The United Nations is designed to make possible lasting freedom and independence for all its members.

(35)   We shall not realize our objectives, however, unless we are willing to help free peoples

to maintain their free institutions and their national integrity against aggressive movements that seek to impose upon them totalitarian regimes. This is no more than a frank recognition that totalitarian regimes imposed on free peoples, by direct or indirect aggression, undermine the foundations of international peace and hence the *(40)* security of the United States.

The peoples of a number of countries of the world have recently had totalitarian regimes forced upon them against their will. The Government of the United States has made frequent protests against coercion and intimidation, in violation of the Yalta agreement, in Poland, Romania, and Bulgaria. I must also state that in a number of *(45)* other countries there have been similar developments.

At the present moment in world history nearly every nation must choose between alternative ways of life. The choice is too often not a free one.

One way of life is based upon the will of the majority, and is distinguished by free institutions, representative government, free elections, guarantees of individual liberty, *(50)* freedom of speech and religion, and freedom from political oppression.

The second way of life is based upon the will of a minority forcibly imposed upon the majority. It relies upon terror and oppression, a controlled press and radio, fixed elections, and the suppression of personal freedoms.

I believe that it must be the policy of the United States to support free peoples who *(55)* are resisting attempted subjugation by armed minorities or by outside pressures.

I believe that we must assist free peoples to work out their own destinies in their own way.

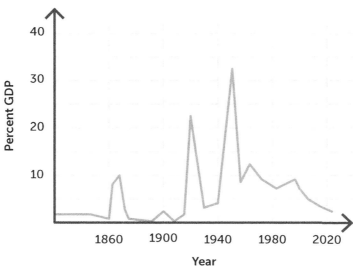

11. As used in line 8, *vicissitudes* most nearly means—
    A) fluctuations
    B) ideals
    C) mutations
    D) stagnation

12. Washington's central argument in Passage 1 is that—
    A) America should back out of the alliances it has made with other countries.
    B) America should increase its involvement with foreign nations.
    C) America should attempt to intervene in European conflicts whenever international safety is a concern.
    D) America should avoid foreign entanglements whenever it is able to do so.

13. Which choice provides the best evidence for the answer to the previous question?
    A) *It is our true policy to steer clear of permanent alliances with any portion of the foreign world; so far, I mean, as we are now at liberty to do it...*
    B) *So far as we have already formed engagements, let them be fulfilled with perfect good faith.*
    C) *Europe has a set of primary interests, which to us have none, or a very remote relation.*
    D) *If we remain one people, under an efficient government, the period is not far off, when we may defy material injury from external annoyance...*

14. Washington most likely employs a series of questions in the fourth paragraph in order to—
    A) challenge the reader to consider his own entanglements with others
    B) question the assumption that neutrality is the best course of action
    C) emphasize the absurdity of giving up a position of safe, passive neutrality
    D) minimize the impact of his opponent's counterargument

15. As used in line 43, *coercion* most nearly means—
    A) intimidation
    B) brutality
    C) cruelty
    D) authority

16. Which choice provides the best evidence for the answer to the previous question?
    A) *This was a fundamental issue in the war with Germany and Japan.*
    B) *The United Nations is designed to make possible lasting freedom and independence for all its members.*
    C) *We shall not realize our objectives, however, unless we are willing to help free peoples to maintain their free institutions and their national integrity against aggressive movements that seek to impose upon them totalitarian regimes.*
    D) *At the present moment in world history nearly every nation must choose between alternative ways of life.*

17. In Passage 2, President Truman most likely references *the war with Germany and Japan* in order to—

   A) remind Americans of the nation's stance on foreign intervention

   B) reassure Americans that they can win another war

   C) suggest a comparison between the current situation and the one that led to the war

   D) distinguish between the current situation and the one that led to America's intervention in the war

18. In lines 39 through 44, Truman most likely contrasts two ways of life in order to _____

   A) illustrate some of the benefits of a democratic government

   B) challenge the tyrannical leaders of oppressed nations to reconsider their approach to government

   C) describe the reasons that America might consider intervening in a foreign nation

   D) suggest that free people have a responsibility to fight on behalf of those who are not free

19. Which statement best describes the relationship between the passages?

   A) The two presidents take similar perspectives on foreign intervention.

   B) The two presidents take opposing perspectives on foreign intervention.

   C) The two presidents agree on most items related to foreign intervention but disagree on some key points.

   D) The two presidents agree on a few items related to foreign intervention but disagree of most key points.

20. President Truman (Passage 2) would most likely respond to Washington's claim in lines 6 through 14 by asserting that—

   A) *Our victory [in the war with Germany and Japan] was won over countries which sought to impose their will, and their way of life, upon other nations.*

   B) *To ensure the peaceful development of nations, free from coercion, the United States has taken a leading part in establishing the United Nations.*

   C) *...totalitarian regimes imposed on free peoples, by direct or indirect aggression, undermine the foundations of international peace and hence the security of the United States.*

   D) *The peoples of a number of countries of the world have recently had totalitarian regimes forced upon them against their will.*

21. Based on the passages and the graph, what conclusion can be drawn about the relationship between foreign policy and government spending in the 20th century?

A) Government spending on national defense significantly decreased as a result of the new foreign policy approach.

B) There was a correlation between the new foreign policy approach and increased government spending on defense.

C) Government spending on national defense remained stagnant despite the new approach to foreign policy.

D) There was no recognizable correlation between the new foreign policy approach and government spending on defense.

Questions 22 – 31 are based on the following passage, which provides an overview of the purpose and applications of social psychology. Information was drawn from Dr. Eliot Aronson's acclaimed book The Social Animal.

In his treatise *Politics*, Aristotle wrote, "Man is by nature a social animal; an individual who is unsocial naturally and not accidentally is either beneath our notice or more than human. Society is something in nature that precedes the individual. Anyone who either cannot lead the common life or is so self-sufficient as not to need to, and therefore does

(5) not partake of society, is either a beast or a god." For centuries, philosophers have been examining the relationship between man and his social world. It is no wonder, then, that a field of study has arisen to examine just that; the field is referred to as social psychology.

Social psychologists have been studying the effect of societal influences on human

(10) behavior for decades, and a number of fascinating findings have been the result. Together, these discoveries have shed light on one clear truth—that human behavior cannot be understood in a vacuum; that is, our daily behaviors are inextricably linked with the social context in which they occur.

Why is this important? According to social psychologist Eliot Aronson, it's

(15) important because it helps us to understand that the behaviors we witness in others may be as much a result of social influence as they are of the individual's disposition. For example, if you have ever been cut off in the middle of bad city traffic, you may have immediately assumed that the offender was inconsiderate or incompetent. While this may be true, it may be equally likely that the person is dealing with an emergency

(20) situation or that they simply did not see you. According to Aronson, this tendency to attribute behaviors, especially negative behaviors, to disposition is risky and can ultimately be detrimental to us and to the other person.

Take, for example, Philip Zimbardo's famous prison experiment, conducted at Stanford University in 1971. At the beginning of the experiment, the participants, all

(25) healthy, stable, intelligent male Stanford University students, were classified as either guards or prisoners and told they would be acting their parts in a simulated prison environment for two weeks. However, after just six days, Zimbardo had to terminate

the experiment because of the extreme behaviors he was witnessing in both groups: prisoners had become entirely submissive to and resentful of the guards, while the (30) guards had become cruel and unrelenting in their treatment of the prisoners. The otherwise healthy, well-adjusted students had experienced dramatic transformations as a result of their assigned roles. Zimbardo's conclusion? Even giving individuals temporary power over others was enough to completely alter the way they viewed and behaved toward each other; indeed, the behaviors he witnessed in each of the groups (35) were not a result of the dispositions of the participants but of the situation in which they had been placed.

Today, social psychologists study the effect of social influence on a number of different behaviors: conformity, obedience, aggression, prejudice, and even attraction and love. The insights these researchers have gained have laid the foundation for further (40) examination of human social behavior and, ultimately, for a refined approach to legal and social policy.

22. The author most likely uses the Aristotle quote in lines 1 through 5 in order to—

A) illustrate the seriousness with which social psychology should be treated

B) support his/her claim that curiosity about man's relationship with the social world is not a quality unique to modern thinking

C) encourage introverts to build stronger relationships with those around them

D) compare the social environment of beasts with the social environment of man

23. Which choice provides the best evidence for the answer to the previous question?

A) *For centuries, philosophers have been examining the relationship between man and his social world.*

B) *Social psychologists have been studying the effect of societal influences on human behavior for decades, and a number of fascinating findings have been the result.*

C) *According to social psychologist Eliot Aronson, it's important because it helps us to understand that the behaviors we witness in others may be as much a result of social influence as they are of the individual's disposition.*

D) *The insights these researchers have gained have laid the foundation for further examination of human social behavior and, ultimately, for a refined approach to legal and social policy.*

24. As used in line 12, the phrase *in a vacuum* most nearly means—

A) without evidence of intention

B) in conjunction with other behaviors

C) without consideration of the individual's needs

D) in isolation

25. The author indicates that making assumptions about people based on isolated actions is—

A) a prudent way to draw conclusions about one's social world

B) recommended when no other information is available

C) the most accurate way to assess various personality strengths

D) unwise and potentially harmful to all involved

26. In lines 24 and 25, the author most likely includes the description of the Stanford students in order to—

A) provide a contrast between their normal dispositions and the behavior they displayed during the experiment

B) engage the reader through characterization

C) illustrate the importance of quality education

D) shed light on the characteristics that made them susceptible to social influence

27. The author most likely includes the example of the Stanford Prison Experiment in order to—

A) encourage the reader to participate in social psychology studies

B) challenge the reader to question how he or she would behave in the same situation

C) illustrate the extent to which social context can influence behavior

D) undermine the reader's assumption that the quality of one's education can influence his or her behavior

28. As used in line 30, the term *unrelenting* most nearly means—

A) insistent

B) forgetful

C) remorseless

D) persistent

29. Which choice provides the best evidence for the answer to the previous question?

A) *According to Aronson, this tendency to attribute behaviors, especially negative behaviors, to disposition is risky and can ultimately be detrimental to us and to the other person.*

B) *At the beginning of the experiment, the participants, all healthy, stable, intelligent male Stanford University students, were classified as either guards or prisoners and told they would be acting their parts in a simulated prison environment for two weeks.*

C) *Even giving individuals temporary power over others was enough to completely alter the way they viewed and behaved toward each other...*

D) *Today, social psychologists study the effect of social influence on a number of different behaviors: conformity, obedience, aggression, prejudice, and even attraction and love.*

30. The author most likely includes *attraction and love* in the list in lines 38 and 39 in order to—

A) suggest that individuals who are struggling with relationship issues should contact a social psychologist

B) discount the assumption that social psychologists are only interested in negative human behaviors

C) illustrate the diversity of topics that social psychologists study

D) dispel any doubts about the qualifications of social psychologists to study human behavior

31. The author most likely includes the statement in lines 40 and 41 about legal and social policy in order to—

A) mention one possible application for the findings of social psychologists.

B) advocate for prison reform.

C) criticize the work of social psychologists.

D) dispel doubts regarding the reliability of the research of social psychologists.

Questions 32 – 41 are based on the following passage, which is adapted from an article entitled "NASA Finds Good News on Forests and Carbon Dioxide," published online by the National Aeronautics and Space Administration in December 2014.

A new NASA-led study shows that tropical forests may be absorbing far more carbon dioxide than many scientists thought, in response to rising atmospheric levels of the greenhouse gas. The study estimates that tropical forests absorb 1.4 billion metric tons of carbon dioxide out of a total global absorption of 2.5 billion—more than is absorbed
(5) by forests in Canada, Siberia and other northern regions, called boreal forests.

"This is good news, because uptake in boreal forests is already slowing, while tropical forests may continue to take up carbon for many years," said David Schimel of NASA's Jet Propulsion Laboratory, Pasadena, California. Schimel is lead author of a paper on the new research, appearing online today in the *Proceedings of National Academy of*
(10) *Sciences*.

Forests and other land vegetation currently remove up to 30 percent of human carbon dioxide emissions from the atmosphere during photosynthesis. If the rate of absorption were to slow down, the rate of global warming would speed up in return.

The new study is the first to devise a way to make apples-to-apples comparisons
(15) of carbon dioxide estimates from many sources at different scales: computer models of ecosystem processes, atmospheric models run backward in time to deduce the sources of today's concentrations (called inverse models), satellite images, data from experimental forest plots and more. The researchers reconciled all types of analyses and assessed the accuracy of the results based on how well they reproduced independent, ground-based
(20) measurements. They obtained their new estimate of the tropical carbon absorption from the models they determined to be the most trusted and verified.

"Until our analysis, no one had successfully completed a global reconciliation of information about carbon dioxide effects from the atmospheric, forestry and modeling communities," said co-author Joshua Fisher of JPL. "It is incredible that all these
(25) different types of independent data sources start to converge on an answer."

The question of which type of forest is the bigger carbon absorber "is not just an accounting curiosity," said co-author Britton Stephens of the National Center for Atmospheric Research, Boulder, Colorado. "It has big implications for our understanding of whether global terrestrial ecosystems might continue to offset our carbon dioxide
(30) emissions or might begin to exacerbate climate change."

As human-caused emissions add more carbon dioxide to the atmosphere, forests worldwide are using it to grow faster, reducing the amount that stays airborne. This effect is called carbon fertilization. "All else being equal, the effect is stronger at higher temperatures, meaning it will be higher in the tropics than in the boreal forests,"
(35) Schimel said.

But climate change also decreases water availability in some regions and makes Earth warmer, leading to more frequent and larger wildfires. In the tropics, humans compound the problem by burning wood during deforestation. Fires don't just stop carbon absorption by killing trees, they also spew huge amounts of carbon into the atmosphere as the
(40) wood burns.

For about 25 years, most computer climate models have been showing that mid-latitude forests in the Northern Hemisphere absorb more carbon than tropical forests. That result was initially based on the then-current understanding of global air flows and limited data suggesting that deforestation was causing tropical forests to release
(45) more carbon dioxide than they were absorbing.

In the mid-2000s, Stephens used measurements of carbon dioxide made from aircraft to show that many climate models were not correctly representing flows of carbon above ground level. Models that matched the aircraft measurements better showed more carbon absorption in the tropical forests. However, there were still not
(50) enough global data sets to validate the idea of a large tropical-forest absorption. Schimel said that their new study took advantage of a great deal of work other scientists have done since Stephens' paper to pull together national and regional data of various kinds into robust, global data sets.

Schimel noted that their paper reconciles results at every scale from the pores of a
(55) single leaf, where photosynthesis takes place, to the whole Earth, as air moves carbon dioxide around the globe. "What we've had up till this paper was a theory of carbon dioxide fertilization based on phenomena at the microscopic scale and observations at the global scale that appeared to contradict those phenomena. Here, at least, is a hypothesis that provides a consistent explanation that includes both how we know
(60) photosynthesis works and what's happening at the planetary scale."

32. As it is used in line 18, the term *reconciled* most nearly means—
   A) forgave.
   B) studied.
   C) integrated.
   D) gathered.

33. Which choice provides the best evidence for the answer to the previous question?
   A) *They obtained their new estimate of the tropical carbon absorption from the models they determined to be the most trusted and verified.*
   B) *"It is incredible that all these different types of independent data sources start to converge on an answer."*
   C) *That result was initially based on the then-current understanding of global air flows and limited data suggesting that deforestation was causing tropical forests to release more carbon dioxide than they were absorbing.*
   D) *Models that matched the aircraft measurements better showed more carbon absorption in the tropical forests. However, there were still not enough global data sets to validate the idea of a large tropical-forest absorption.*

34. According to the passage, what is the relationship between photosynthesis and global warming?
   A) Photosynthesis allows carbon dioxide gas to be released into the atmosphere, exacerbating the issue of global warming.
   B) Carbon dioxide prevents trees from flourishing, thus increasing the amount of greenhouse gas and exacerbating the issue of global warming.
   C) Trees absorb carbon dioxide during photosynthesis, removing much of the carbon dioxide from the atmosphere and slowing the effects of global warming.
   D) Greenhouse gases like carbon dioxide slow the effects of global warming by prevent trees from completing the cycle of photosynthesis.

35. The passage indicates that research into carbon dioxide absorption is significant because—
   A) It challenges us to question our own opinions on global warming and climate change.
   B) It forces us to recognize that global warming poses a significant threat to our vegetation.
   C) It encourages us to consider whether forests are effective alternatives to carbon dioxide emissions.
   D) It allows us to understand the impact of the earth's forests on climate change.

36. The passage indicates that wildfires—

   A) both result from and contribute to climate change

   B) are the most significant contributor to climate change

   C) occur when temperature and humidity are both high

   D) have little to no effect on carbon dioxide emissions

37. According to the passage, increased carbon dioxide emissions may result in—

   A) increased water availability.

   B) smaller, less frequent wildfires.

   C) faster-growing forests.

   D) decreased oxygen availability.

38. A student claims that preserving the earth's forests is an essential step in slowing climate change. Which of the following statements from the passage supports this student's claim?

   A) *"This is good news, because uptake in boreal forests is already slowing, while tropical forests may continue to take up carbon for many years," said David Schimel of NASA's Jet Propulsion Laboratory, Pasadena, California.*

   B) *If the rate of absorption [of carbon dioxide] were to slow down, the rate of global warming would speed up in return.*

   C) *But climate change also decreases water availability in some regions and makes Earth warmer, leading to more frequent and larger wildfires.*

   D) *That result was initially based on the then-current understanding of global air flows and limited data suggesting that deforestation was causing tropical forests to release more carbon dioxide than they were absorbing.*

39. As used in line 53, the term *robust* most nearly means—

   A) round

   B) comprehensive

   C) sturdy

   D) prosperous

40. The author mostly likely mentions the Stephens study in lines 46 through 49 in order to—

   A) criticize the work of environmental scientists before Stephens

   B) demonstrate the effect that a limited data set can have on the results of an experiment

   C) question the findings of Stephens and his colleagues

   D) emphasize the need for thorough data sets in drawing conclusions about climate change

41. According to the final paragraph (lines 54 through 60), NASA's recent study into carbon dioxide absorption was significant because—

 A) it provided insight into the absorption speeds of two different kinds of forests.

 B) it offered a hypothesis on how to predict and prevent wildfires.

 C) it demonstrated the power of collaborative research methods.

 D) it resulted in a theory of climate change that accommodated both large and small-scale considerations.

Questions 42 – 52 are based on the following passage, which is adapted from an article entitled "NASA Contributes to First Global Review of Arctic Marine Mammals," published online by the National Aeronautics and Space Administration in April 2015. The accompanying graphic was initially published to NASA's Cryosphere Science Research Portal, alongside an article entitled "Current State of the Sea Ice Cover."

Many human communities want answers about the current status and future of Arctic marine mammals, including scientists who dedicate their lives to studying them and indigenous people whose traditional ways of subsistence are intertwined with the fate of species such as ice seals, narwhals, walruses and polar bears.

(5)   But there are many unknowns about the current status of eleven species of marine mammals who depend on Arctic sea ice to live, feed and breed, and about how their fragile habitat will evolve in a warming world.

  A recently published multinational study attempted to gauge the population trends of Arctic marine mammals and changes in their habitat, identify missing scientific *(10)* information, and provide recommendations for the conservation of Arctic marine mammals over the next decades.

  The Arctic sea ice cover, made of frozen seawater floating on top of the Arctic Ocean and its neighboring seas, naturally grows in the fall and winter and melts during the spring and summer every year. But over the past decades, the melt season has grown *(15)* longer and the average extent of Arctic sea ice has diminished, changing the game for many Arctic marine mammals—namely beluga, narwhal and bowhead whales; ringed, bearded, spotted, ribbon, harp and hooded seals; walruses; and polar bears.

  "This research would not have been possible without support from NASA," said Kristin Laidre, lead author of the new study and a polar scientist with University of *(20)* Washington in Seattle. "NASA backed us on research related to the biodiversity and ecology of Arctic marine mammals, as well as the development of metrics for the loss of sea ice, their habitat."

Laidre's team used the Arctic sea ice record derived from microwave measurements taken by NASA and Department of Defense satellites. This record began in late 1978,
(25) is uninterrupted, and relies on NASA-developed methods for processing the microwave data.

"It's really our best global view of the Arctic sea ice," said Harry Stern, author of the paper with Laidre and a mathematician specializing in sea ice and climate at University of Washington.

(30) Stern divided the Arctic Ocean into twelve regions. Using daily sea ice concentration data from the satellite record, he calculated changes in the dates of the beginning of the melt season in spring and the start of the fall freeze-up from 1979 to 2013. He found that, in all regions but one, the melt season had grown longer (mostly by five to ten weeks, and by twenty weeks in one region).

(35) "Sea ice is critical for Arctic marine mammals because events such as feeding, giving birth, molting, and resting are closely timed with the availability of their ice platform," Laidre said. "It is especially critical for the ice-dependent species—seals and polar bears. Ice seals use the sea ice platform to give birth and nurse pups during very specific weeks of the spring, and polar bears use sea ice for feeding, starting in late winter and
(40) continuing until the ice breaks up."

Pacific walrus use the floating pack ice both as a platform on which to rest between feeding bouts and as a passive transport around their habitat.

"Loss of sea ice has resulted in walrus hauling out on land in Alaska and Russia in massive numbers—these land haul outs result in trampling of their young," Laidre
(45) said. "Also, now walrus must travel a longer way to reach their feeding areas, which is energetically costly."

In the case of Arctic whales, the changes in sea ice might benefit their populations, at least in the short term: the loss and earlier retreat of sea ice opens up new habitats and, in some areas of the Arctic, has also led to an increase in food production and the
(50) length of their feeding season.

In the future, Stern said higher-resolution satellite microwave data might come in handy when studying the interactions of Arctic marine mammals with their icy habitat.

"For example, we know that narwhals congregate in specific areas of the Arctic in the wintertime, so maybe a higher spatial resolution in these areas might help us better
(55) understand their relationship with the ice," Stern said. "But mainly, just continuing daily coverage is what's important for the long-term monitoring of habitat changes."

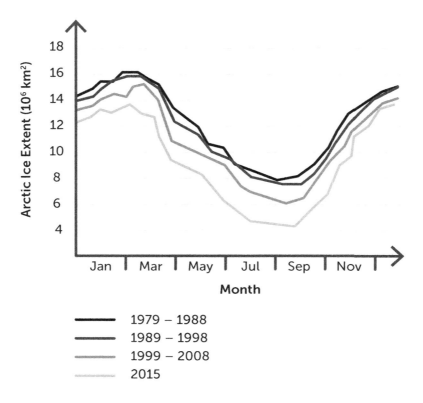

Arctic Ice Extent (10^6 km^2) vs. Month

1979 – 1988
1989 – 1998
1999 – 2008
2015

42. In the first paragraph, the author includes a detail about indigenous people of the Arctic in order to—

   A) provide readers with a relatable story to consider as they read the article

   B) emphasize the importance of protecting the habitats of Arctic marine mammals

   C) challenge readers to make Arctic preservation efforts their top priority

   D) illustrate a contrast between the indigenous people and the scientists mentioned in the first part of the sentence

43. In lines 12 through 17, the author indicates that while fluctuation in sea ice extent is expected throughout the year—

   A) variability from year to year is a recent phenomenon.

   B) the fluctuation is usually minute.

   C) daily changes in sea ice extent are becoming more typical.

   D) changes in the populations of Arctic mammals are not.

44. The author most likely includes the list of Arctic marine mammals in lines 16 through 17 in order to—

   A) illustrate a discrepancy between the number of Arctic species and the number of species that depend on sea ice for survival

   B) challenge the assertion that the recession of sea ice is significant

   C) articulate a general truth about life in the Arctic

   D) highlight the number of species that depend on sea ice for their survival

45. The passage indicates that when it comes to research about sea ice and the animals who rely on it—

A) Scientists know everything they need to know.

B) Data collection is rarely a simple process.

C) Very few answers currently exist.

D) Vigilant observation is an essential tool in gaining insight.

46. As used in line 7, the term *fragile* most nearly means—

A) brittle

B) flimsy

C) breakable

D) unstable

47. Which choice provides the best evidence for the answer to the previous question?

A) *Using daily sea ice concentration data from the satellite record, he calculated changes in the dates of the beginning of the melt season in spring and the start of the fall freeze-up from 1979 to 2013.*

B) *"Sea ice is critical for Arctic marine mammals because events such as feeding, giving birth, molting, and resting are closely timed with the availability of their ice platform[.]"*

C) *The Arctic sea ice cover, made of frozen seawater floating on top of the Arctic Ocean and its neighboring seas, naturally grows in the fall and winter and melts during the spring and summer every year.*

D) *But over the past decades, the melt season has grown longer and the average extent of Arctic sea ice has diminished, changing the game for many Arctic marine mammals...*

Writing and Language

In the following passages, there are numbered and underlined words and phrases that correspond with the questions. You are to choose the answer that best completes the statement grammatically, stylistically, and/or logically. If you think the original version is best, select "NO CHANGE."

AEROSPACE ENGINEERING

In the 21st century, the growing population and the public interest in space exploration will undoubtedly call for increased investment in air and space travel. (1)Therefore, individuals who excel at maths and sciences and are interested in a full-time career with high salaries and job security ought to consider a career in aerospace engineering.

1. Which of the following choices most effectively frames the main argument of the passage?

A) NO CHANGE

B) As such, individuals who enjoy a good challenge ought to consider a career in aerospace engineering.

C) Accordingly, individuals who want to start a career should consider pursuing aerospace engineering.

D) Consequently, individuals who like space should consider starting a career in aerospace engineering.

Aerospace engineers typically get to choose from one of two (2)concentrations such as aeronautical engineering or astronautical engineering—and as a result are able to focus their efforts in the field that most interests them. Aeronautical engineers work on designing and constructing aircraft for travel within the earth's

2. **A)** NO CHANGE

B) concentrations, aeronautical engineering

C) concentrations—aeronautical engineering

D) concentrations. Aeronautical engineering

(3)atmosphere, astronautical engineers, on the other hand, build spacecraft for use both inside and outside of earth's atmosphere. Though the two specialties have their own

(4)unique challenges and demands, both require a strong grasp of physics and higher-level mathematics, so individuals who excel at logical reasoning are well-suited for these fields.

Aerospace engineers typically work full time schedules and, when in leadership positions, may work as much as fifty or sixty hours per week. The bulk of those hours occurs in an office setting, where these engineers use advanced software programs to design models and run simulations. Most of these individuals work for firms that are contracted out to the federal government; they may contribute to the design and construction of aircraft, missiles, or systems for national defense. As a result, many aerospace engineering jobs require advanced security clearance. Citizenship in the U.S. may even be a requirement for many positions.

Like other kinds of engineers, aerospace engineers must have a bachelor's degree in their field. While in school, (5)they studied advanced calculus, trigonometry, general engineering, and physics (including propulsion, mechanics, structures, and aerodynamics). As a result, the degree is typically more rigorous than degrees in other areas of engineering.

3. **A)** NO CHANGE
   B) atmosphere and astronautical engineers
   C) atmosphere, however, astronautical engineers
   D) atmosphere; astronautical engineers

4. **A)** NO CHANGE
   B) challenging demands
   C) challenges
   D) demand that are challenging

5. **A)** NO CHANGE
   B) they must study
   C) they would study
   D) they will study

(6)However, aerospace engineers usually see a much bigger payoff in terms of salary than do other engineers: <u>the median salary for aerospace engineers is quite a bit larger than the median salary for other engineering professions.</u>

6. Which of the following completes this sentence with accurate information from the graph at the conclusion of the passage?

A) NO CHANGE

B) the median salary for aerospace engineers is almost twenty thousand dollars more than the median salary for other engineering professions.

C) the median salary for aerospace engineers is almost fifty thousand dollars more than the median salary for other engineering professions.

D) the median salary for aerospace engineers is about the same as the median salary for other engineering professions.

<u>(7)</u>

7. For the sake of logical coherence, the preceding sentence should be placed—

A) where it is now

B) at the beginning of the paragraph

C) after the first sentence

D) after the second sentence

(8) In 2012, the United States Bureau of Labor Statistics projected that the profession of aerospace engineering would expand by seven percent before 2022, creating over six thousand new jobs over the next decade. Further, opportunities for advancement

8. Which of the following provides the most effective transition from the previous paragraph to this one?
   A) The Bureau of Labor Statistics researches various professions to gather information about the changing job market.
   B) The field of aerospace engineering is not shrinking.
   C) In addition to earning a high salary, aerospace engineers can expect a high level of job security.
   D) Aerospace engineering is clearly a great option for those entering the workforce.

(9)is plentiful. Aerospace engineers

9. A) NO CHANGE
   B) are
   C) were
   D) was

(10)which excel in their field can work their way toward careers as technical specialists, supervisors, or even engineering or program

10. A) NO CHANGE
    B) whom
    C) that
    D) who

managers. (11)

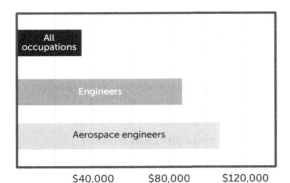

Salary (USD)

11. At this point, the writer is considering adding the following sentence:

By taking advantage of apprenticeships or advanced educational opportunities, aerospace engineers can increase their chances of advancement in their field.

Should the writer make this addition?

A) Yes, because it emphasizes the possibility of career advancement for aerospace engineers and provides some insight into how that advancement is earned.

B) Yes, because it provides important information about additional requirements that an entry-level aerospace engineer might have to complete.

C) No, because advancement is most likely not a significant factor for graduates entering the field of aerospace engineering.

D) No, because individuals who are interested in aerospace engineering should not be worried about advancement so early in their career.

YOUNG ABRAHAM

A young Abraham Lincoln awoke with a (12)jolt, excited to pick up where he had left off with his reading. He had chores to complete in the morning, of course, but he loved those days when he could fit in a couple hours of studying before he had to begin with his work.

12. A) NO CHANGE

B) jolt, being excited

C) jolt and excited

D) jolt; excited

<u>(13)</u>

13. At this point, the writer is considering adding the following sentence:

He was especially looking forward to the quiet time on this particular morning: he was reading a book about his hero, George Washington.

Should he/she make this addition?

A) Yes, because it gives the reader insight into who Lincoln admired as a young boy.

B) Yes, because it provides information about the events that are about to unfold.

C) No, because it distracts the reader from the main point of the paragraph.

D) No, because the detail is irrelevant to the narrative.

Young Abe <u>(14)rolled over, stretches his arms, and reaches toward the wall,</u> where he had lodged his book between two of the logs that constructed his family's cabin. *Oh no*, he thought as he felt the book's binding.

14. A) NO CHANGE

B) rolls over, stretching his arms, and reaches toward the wall,

C) rolling over, stretching his arms, and reaching toward the wall,

D) rolled over, stretched his arms, and reached toward the wall,

It was noticeably <u>(15)sopping</u> and had been warped

15. A) NO CHANGE

B) drenched

C) damp

D) soaking

by the moisture: (16)evidently it had rained most of the previous night. He pulled the book from its slot in the wall and set it down in front of him.

Oh no, he repeated to himself. Young Abe was a dedicated and diligent reader, but because of his family's financial situation, he could not afford to buy his own books. He read only when he could find a book to borrow, (17)which unfortunately was not often.

(18)This book, *The Life of Washington*, was one of his favorites. He had borrowed this wonderful book from his teacher, Andrew Crawford, by whom he had been instructed in manners and composition. He knew he had to tell Crawford the truth about his book, but he was petrified by the thought of admitting his mistake. Still, Abe decided, it was the right thing to do. He attempted to dry the book's pages as best he could and set it aside.

16. Which choice provides the most relevant detail at this point in the narrative?
- **A)** NO CHANGE
- **B)** Evidently the pages were thinner than Lincoln had realized.
- **C)** Evidently the book was a popular one.
- **D)** Evidently the book had not budged at all while young Lincoln slept.

17. Which choice most effectively illustrates the young Abe Lincoln's commitment to learning?
- **A)** NO CHANGE
- **B)** and he had a fine reputation for being cautious with the books he borrowed
- **C)** so he had only read a handful of books
- **D)** sometimes walking miles to retrieve it

18. The writer is considering deleting the underlined sentence. Should he/she make this deletion?
- **A)** Yes, because it gives away the ending of the narrative.
- **B)** Yes, because it attributes undue importance to the book itself.
- **C)** No, because it provides important insight into why the incident was so disappointing.
- **D)** No, because it sheds light on who Lincoln was as a child.

(19)

Later that afternoon, young Abe stepped out into the crisp autumn air to make the journey to the Crawford home, (20)wear he would have to deliver the news about the ruined book. He took a deep breath and began to walk.

Before long, he found himself at the door of the Crawford home, talking to the man himself. "So you see," Young Abe stammered, "I intended to take good care of your book, but it seems I made an error in judgment. I hope you will allow me to repay you for my blunder." Crawford and Abe both knew that (21)he had no money and that the only way he could pay was through work.

"Give me three (22)day's work on the harvest," said Crawford, "and the manuscript is yours."

Young Abraham Lincoln was jubilant. Of course the three days of harvesting corn in the Crawford's field would not be ideal, but at the end of it, he would be the proud owner of a shabby—but readable—copy of *The Life of Washington*.

19. For the sake of logic and coherence, the preceding paragraph should be placed—
   A) where it is now
   B) at the beginning of the narrative
   C) after the first paragraph
   D) after the second paragraph

20. A) NO CHANGE
    B) where
    C) were
    D) whir

21. A) NO CHANGE
    B) they
    C) the boy
    D) him

22. A) NO CHANGE
    B) days
    C) daze
    D) days'

GLOBAL FOOD PRODUCTION

Environmental concerns have been at the center of ongoing debate in the 21st century: we are going green in both our homes and our offices, and discourse around renewable energy sources, responsible recycling, and threatening pollution (23)are commonplace. Still, according to acclaimed environmental scientist Dr. Jonathon Foley, for all of our concern about the environment, we often

23.
A) NO CHANGE
B) were
C) is
D) was

(24)overlook one of the most significant threats to our planet: global food production.

24.
A) NO CHANGE
B) oversee
C) disregard
D) overview

(25)Though we must make food in order to survive as a species, we do not have to do it irresponsibly.

25.
A) NO CHANGE
B) Incidentally
C) Until
D) When

The threat of global food production is manifest in many forms. Greenhouse gases such as methane, nitrous oxide, and carbon dioxide are released in larger amounts by farming and agricultural practices (26) than all the world's transportation vehicles combined. Additionally, the world's limited water supply is both depleted and polluted by farming and agricultural techniques.

26.
A) NO CHANGE
B) than are all the
C) than by all the
D) than do all the

(27) The further clearing of land for crops poses a threat to indigenous wildlife in some areas and has, in some cases substantially, contributed to species extinction.

27. **A)** NO CHANGE

B) Further, the clearing of land for crops in some areas poses a threat to indigenous wildlife and has contributed, in some cases substantially, to species extinction.

C) In some cases substantially, the clearing of land for crops poses a threat in some areas to indigenous wildlife and has contributed to species extinction.

D) In some areas, the clearing of further land for crops has contributed, in some cases substantially, to species extinction and poses a threat to indigenous wildlife.

(28)

28. At this point, the writer is considering adding the following sentence:

Altogether, the threat that is posed to our planet by our own food production practices is one that we can no longer afford to ignore.

Should the writer make this addition?

A) Yes, because it ties together the author's ideas about sustainability and affordability.

B) Yes, because it provides a brief summary of the previous paragraph and an effective transition into the next paragraph.

C) No, because it distracts the reader from the main point of the paragraph.

D) No, because the tone does not align with the author's purpose.

Fortunately, researchers like Dr. Foley have committed (29)his career to finding solutions to these challenges. In fact, Foley has refined a clear, five-step system that he believes will lead to significant positive change.

First, says Foley, we must halt agricultural expansion. Globally, (30)land devoted to food productions accounts for an area as large as South America and Africa combined. Moving forward, we must commit to preserving natural habits where they currently exist. Second, we must seek to expand production on the lands we have already committed to farming.

(31)Especially in those areas where crop yields are low, new technologies have the potential to significantly increase yields and improve efficiency. Third, we must learn to make better use of our precious, non-renewable resources like water. By borrowing techniques from commercial and organic farming,

29. **A)** NO CHANGE
    B) there careers
    C) their careers
    D) they're careers

30. **A)** NO CHANGE
    B) land devoted to food production account
    C) lands devoted to food production account
    D) lands devoted to food production accounts

31. **A)** NO CHANGE
    B) Significantly, in those areas where crop yields are low, new technologies especially have the potential to increase yields and improve efficiency.
    C) New technologies have the potential where crop yields are significantly low to improve efficiency and increase yields.
    D) Where crop yields are significantly low, new technologies especially have the potential to improve efficiency and increase yields.

(32)farmers around the world can begin to make more conscious choices about efficient water use and protect water sources from contamination.

Fourth, we must reconsider the structures of our diets. Today, more than thirty-five percent of the world's crops are used to feed livestock, but only a small percent of the calories consumed by these animals make it into human diets. By designing diets that are less reliant on meat proteins, we can return some of those crop yields, and calories, to the global food bank. Finally, we must work to minimize food waste worldwide by buying and using food products more consciously.

32. **A)** NO CHANGE
   B) farmers around the world can begin to make more conscious choices about using water efficiently and protecting water sources from contamination.
   C) farmers around the world can begin to make more conscious choices about efficient water use and protecting water sources from contamination.
   D) farmers around the world can begin to make more conscious choices about efficient water use and protect water sources from contamination.

(33)

33. At this point the writer wants to add a concluding statement. Which of the following provides a conclusion that is appropriate to both the tone and purpose of the passage?

A) These changes will be especially challenging in developed countries, where food production costs are high and meals are easier to come by.

B) By following these simple steps in countries all around the globe, we can begin to make positive changes that will feed our population while protecting our environment.

C) While these changes will no doubt be challenging for us as a population, we can definitely make them work for us.

D) By taking these simple steps in countries around the globe, we can ensure that there will be enough food to feed the entire human population.

The Origins of Humanity?

(34)Charles Darwin wrote *The Origin of Species* over one hundred years ago, in 1859. However, musings on the beginnings of human existence are by no means unique to our modern

34. Which of the following most effectively introduces the topic of the article by relating to the modern reader?

A) NO CHANGE

B) There is currently no way for us to know where our species came from or how we were when we first appeared.

C) Philosophers have, for centuries, pondered the meaning and origins of human life on Earth.

D) In today's technologically advanced world, scientists are spending more time than ever asking questions about the origins of our planet and our species.

mind. (35) Indeed, creation myths are numerous and varied. Despite their differences, however, the universal theme of

35. At this point, the writer wants to add additional support for the paragraph's main point. Which choice most effectively accomplishes this goal?

A) Even centuries ago, the earliest human civilizations sought to understand where they came from.

B) In fact, modern sciences also seek to understand how our universe itself came to be.

C) Scientists have never been clearer about where the human species came from.

D) Still, it is important to be content with one's own understanding, so as not to become dependent on others for one's ideas.

(36)this story highlights the instinctive desire that exists in all cultures to understand how our species came to be.

Some early civilizations subscribed to beliefs about man's evolution from nature. According to Sanchuniathon, an ancient Phoenician mythographer, all things on Earth, including humanity, evolved from the winds themselves. The winds swirled around each other to produce Desire, which eventually took form as a slimy substance called Mot. From Mot (37)was born simple creatures that eventually evolved into conscious human beings.

(38)However, the early peoples of southern California believed humanity evolved from animals—coyotes in particular. According to the legend, coyotes began their evolution when they started sitting up

to bury their dead. (39)Over time, their tails were worn down, their paws lengthened, and their snouts shortened into human noses.

36. **A)** NO CHANGE
     B) these stories highlights
     C) this story highlight
     D) these stories highlight

37. **A)** NO CHANGE
     B) were born simple creatures
     C) was born a simple creature
     D) were born a simple creature

38. **A)** NO CHANGE
     B) Consequently,
     C) Regardless,
     D) In a similar manner,

39. At this point, the writer is considering deleting the underlined sentence. Should he/she make this deletion?
     A) Yes, because it distracts the reader from the main point of the paragraph.
     B) Yes, because the reader already understands that humans evolved from coyotes.
     C) No, because it provides further detail about how the early tribes of southern California believed humans evolved from coyotes.
     D) No, because it provides a humorous detail that helps readers to relate to the people who believed this myth.

The early Borneo people had their own myth about (40)humanities beginning: they believed that humanity was born out of a

40. **A)** NO CHANGE
B) humanity's
C) humanity
D) the human

rock, which one day opened (41)her mouth to let the first humans walk out. Those humans, through their hard work and sacrifices, grew the rest of the earth and its inhabitants.

41. **A)** NO CHANGE
B) his
C) it's
D) its

(42)Still, not all ancient peoples believed humans evolved from nature. Some mythologies included stories of humanity's creation by deities. According to Mesopotamian myth, for example, Marduk, the fierce god of the sun, created humanity out of the body of another god, Tiamat,

42. Which choice provides the most effective, appropriate transition from the previous paragraph to this one?
A) NO CHANGE
B) Regardless of their location, many primitive populations used these kinds of myths to make sense of their world.
C) If humanity's evolution from nature was not crazy enough, other cultures believed even crazier myths.
D) In spite of information to the contrary, myths about humanity's evolution from nature were not especially popular.

(43)who he had defeated in an epic battle.

According to the mythology of the Hopi Indians, Tawa, the Sun Spirit, was responsible for the creation of humanity. Their legend stated that Tawa created the first world, which to his disappointment was inhabited only by insects that could not understand the meaning of life. To elevate his creation, he formed a second world and forced the insects to climb to it. Over the course of this challenging journey, they

43. **A)** NO CHANGE
B) who it had defeated
C) whom he had defeated
D) whom it had defeated

evolved into more complex creatures and eventually into humans.

Other civilizations believed humanity was (44)neither a descendant of the earth or a creation of the gods: these peoples believed that humanity descended directly from the gods themselves. According to the Hindu creation myth, for example, the deity Purusha, who was both man and woman, was split in half. The two halves of the deity united and continued to reunite in different forms until all of the creatures on Earth had been created.

44. **A)** NO CHANGE

   B) neither a descendant of the earth nor a creation of the gods

   C) either a descendant of the earth or a creation of the gods

   D) both a descendant of the earth and a creation of the gods

Mathematics

For questions 1 – 13, work the problem and choose the most correct answer. For questions 14 – 17, work the problem and write in the correct answer in the space provided.

FORMULA CHART

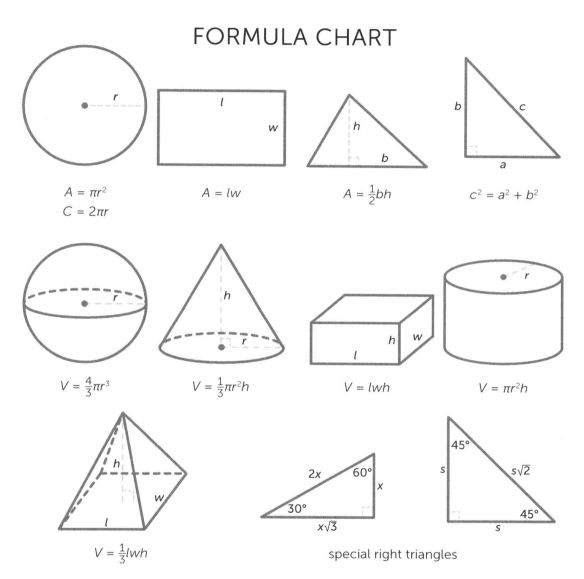

$A = \pi r^2$
$C = 2\pi r$

$A = lw$

$A = \frac{1}{2}bh$

$c^2 = a^2 + b^2$

$V = \frac{4}{3}\pi r^3$

$V = \frac{1}{3}\pi r^2 h$

$V = lwh$

$V = \pi r^2 h$

$V = \frac{1}{3}lwh$

special right triangles

▶ The number of degrees of arc in a circle is 360.

▶ The number of radians of arc in a circle is 2π.

▶ The sum of the measures in degrees of the angles of a triangle is 180.

NO CALCULATOR
Multiple-Choice

1. What is the axis of symmetry for the given parabola?

   $y = -2(x + 3)^2 + 5$

   A) $y = 3$

   B) $x = -3$

   C) $y = -3$

   D) $x = 3$

2. Which of the following is equivalent to $z^3(z + 2)^2 - 4z^3 + 2$?

   A) 2

   B) $z^5 + 4z^4 + 4z^3 + 2$

   C) $z^6 + 4z^3 + 2$

   D) $z^5 + 4z^4 + 2$

3. Which of the following is an equation of the line that passes through the points $(4,-3)$ and $(-2,9)$ in the xy-plane?

   A) $y = -2x + 5$

   B) $y = -\frac{1}{2}x - 1$

   C) $y = \frac{1}{2}x - 5$

   D) $y = 2x - 11$

4. What is the domain of the inequality $\left|\frac{x}{8}\right| \geq 1$?

   A) $(-\infty,\infty)$

   B) $[8,\infty)$

   C) $(-\infty,-8]$

   D) $(-\infty,-8] \cup [8,\infty)$

5. What is the greatest number of complex roots a 17th degree polynomial can have?

   A) 8

   B) 17

   C) 16

   D) $16i$

6. In the xy-plane, the line given by which of the following equations is parallel to the line $3x + 2y = 10$?

   A) $y = -3x + 2$

   B) $y = -\frac{3}{2}x + 5$

   C) $y = \frac{1}{3}x + 5$

   D) $y = \frac{2}{3}x - 10$

7. Which of the following represents a linear equation?

   A) $\sqrt[3]{y} = x$

   B) $\sqrt[3]{x} = y$

   C) $\sqrt[3]{y} = x^2$

   D) $y = \sqrt[3]{x^3}$

8. Justin has a summer lawn care business and earns $40 for each lawn he mows. He also pays $35 per week in business expenses. Which of the following expressions represents Justin's profit after x weeks if he mows m number of lawns?

   A) $40m - 35x$

   B) $40m + 35x$

   C) $35x(40 + m)$

   D) $35(40m + x)$

9. What are the real zero(s) of the following polynomial?

   $2n^2 + 2n - 12 = 0$

   A) (2)

   B) $(-3,2)$

   C) $(2,4)$

   D) There are no real zeros of n.

10. Which graph shows the solution to $y = 2x + 1$?

A)

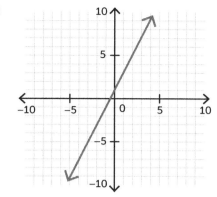

B)

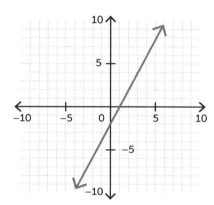

C)

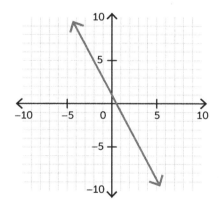

D)

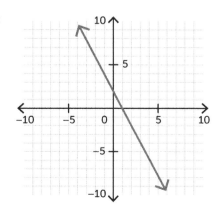

11. A cube with volume 27 cubic meters is inscribed within a sphere such that all of the cube's vertices touch the sphere. What is the length of the sphere's radius?

A) 2.6 meters

B) 3 meters

C) 5.2 meters

D) 9 meters

12. Which of the following defines y as a function of x?

I. $y^2 + x = 3$

II.

x	y
0	4
1	5
2	8
3	13
4	20

III.

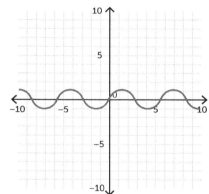

A) II only

B) I and II only

C) II and III only

D) I, II, III only

Go On

13. What is the domain of the piece-wise function shown in the graph?

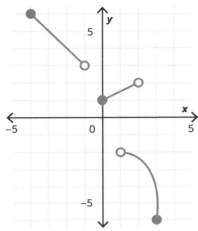

A) D: [−4,−1) ∪ [0,3]
B) D: (−4,3)
C) D: [−4,1] ∪ (0,3)
D) D: (−4,−1) ∪ [0,1) ∪ [1,3]

NO CALCULATOR
Grid-In

14. What is the slope of the graph below?

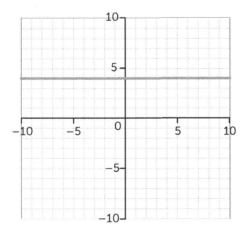

——————————————————

15. Solve the equation: $\sqrt{2x-5} + 4 = x$

——————————————————

16. Given the diagram, if $XZ = 100$, $WZ = 80$, and $XU = 70$, then $WY = ?$

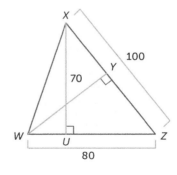

——————————————————

17. What is the y-intercept of the given equation?

$7y - 42x + 7 = 0$

——————————————————

CALCULATOR
Multiple Choice

For questions 1 – 27, work the problem and choose the most correct answer. For questions 28 – 31, work the problem and write in the correct answer in the space provided.

1. If a student answers 42 out of 48 questions correctly on a quiz, what percentage of questions did she answer correctly?
   A) 82.5%
   B) 85%
   C) 87.5%
   D) 90%

2. The population of a town was 7,250 in 2014 and 7,375 in 2015. What was the percent increase from 2014 to 2015 to the nearest tenth of a percent?
   A) 1.5%
   B) 1.6%
   C) 1.7%
   D) 1.8%

3. What are the roots of the equation $y = 16x^3 - 48x^2$?
   A) $\left(\frac{3 + i\sqrt{5}}{2}, \frac{3 - i\sqrt{5}}{2} \right)$
   B) $(0, 3, -3)$
   C) $(0, 3i, -3i)$
   D) $(0, 3)$

4. Bryce has 34 coins worth a total of $6.25. If all the coins are dimes or quarters, how many of each coin does he have?
   A) 9 dimes and 15 quarters
   B) 10 dimes and 24 quarters
   C) 15 dimes and 19 quarters
   D) 19 dimes and 15 quarters

5. Which of the following is a solution to the inequality $2x + y \leq -10$?
   A) $(0,0)$
   B) $(10,2)$
   C) $(10,10)$
   D) $(-10,-10)$

6. An ice chest contains 24 sodas, some regular and some diet. The ratio of diet soda to regular soda is 1:3. How many regular sodas are there in the ice chest?
   A) 1
   B) 4
   C) 18
   D) 24

7. In the circle below with center O, the minor arc ACB measures 5 feet. What is the measurement of $m\angle AOB$?

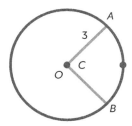

   A) 90
   B) 90.5
   C) 95
   D) 95.5

8. In the fall, 425 students pass the math benchmark. In the spring, 680 students pass the same benchmark. What is the percentage increase in passing scores from fall to spring?

A) 37.5%

B) 55%

C) 60%

D) 62.5%

9. A baby weighed 7.5 pounds at birth and gained weight at a rate of 6 ounces per month for the first six months. Which equation describes the baby's weight in ounces, y, after t months?

A) $y = 6t - 7.5$

B) $y = 6t + 120$

C) $y = 7.5t + 120$

D) $y = 6t + 7.5$

10. A fruit stand sells apples, bananas, and oranges at a ratio of 3:2:1. If the fruit stand sells 20 bananas, how many total pieces of fruit does the fruit stand sell?

A) 10

B) 30

C) 40

D) 60

11. A person earning a salary between $75,000 and $100,000 per year will pay $10,620 in taxes plus 20% of any amount over $75,000. What would a person earning $80,000 per year pay in taxes?

A) $10,620

B) $11,620

C) $12,120

D) $12,744

12. The given equation represents which type of conic section?

$x^2 + 2xy + 4y^2 + 6x + 14y = 86$

A) circle

B) ellipse

C) hyperbola

D) parabola

13. A bike store is having a 30%-off sale, and one of the bikes is on sale for $385. What was the original price of this bike?

A) $253.00

B) $450.00

C) $500.50

D) $550.00

14. Which expression is equivalent to $5^2 \times (-5)^{-2} - (2 + 3)^{-1}$?

A) 0

B) 1

C) $\frac{5}{4}$

D) $\frac{4}{5}$

15. Tiles are $12.51 per square yard. What will it cost to cover the floor of a room with tiles if the room is 10 feet wide and 12 feet long?

A) $166.80

B) $178.70

C) $184.60

D) $190.90

16. Jane earns $15 per hour babysitting. If she starts with $275 in her bank account, which equation represents how many hours (h) she will have to babysit for her account to reach $400?

A) $400 = 275 + 15h$

B) $400 = 15h$

C) $400 = \frac{15}{h} + 275$

D) $400 = -275 - 15h$

17. Using the information in the table, which equation demonstrates the linear relationship between x and y?

x	y
3	3
7	15
10	24

- **A)** $y = 6x - 6$
- **B)** $y = 5x - 6$
- **C)** $y = 4x - 6$
- **D)** $y = 3x - 6$

18. A chemical experiment requires that a solute be diluted with 4 parts (by mass) water for every 1 part (by mass) solute. If the desired mass for the solution is 90 grams, how many grams of solute should be used?

- **A)** 15 grams
- **B)** 16.5 grams
- **C)** 18 grams
- **D)** 22.5 grams

19. Which of the following is equivalent to $\frac{\sin x}{1 - \cos x}$?

- **A)** $\frac{1 + \cos x}{\sin x}$
- **B)** $\frac{\sin x}{\cos x}$
- **C)** $\tan x$
- **D)** 1

20. If an employee who makes $37,500 per year receives a 5.5% raise, what is the employee's new salary?

- **A)** $35,437.50
- **B)** $35,625
- **C)** $39,375
- **D)** $39,562.50

21. Which expression is equivalent to $6x + 5 \geq -15 + 8x$?

- **A)** $x \leq -5$
- **B)** $x \leq 5$
- **C)** $x \leq 10$
- **D)** $x \leq 20$

22. Juan plans to spend 25% of his workday writing a report. If he is at work for 9 hours, how many hours will he spend writing the report?

- **A)** 2.25
- **B)** 2.50
- **C)** 2.75
- **D)** 4.00

23. If a car uses 8 gallons of gas to travel 650 miles, how many miles can it travel using 12 gallons of gas?

- **A)** 870 miles
- **B)** 895 miles
- **C)** 915 miles
- **D)** 975 miles

24. If $y = 2x^2 + 12x - 3$ is written in the form $y = a(x - h)^2 + k$, what is the value of k?

- **A)** -3
- **B)** -15
- **C)** -18
- **D)** -21

25. A theater has 180 rows of seats. The first row has 10 seats. Each row has 4 seats more than the row in front of it. How many seats are in the entire theater?

- **A)** 18,000
- **B)** 36,200
- **C)** 42,500
- **D)** 66,240

26. Which of the following graphs reflects the inequality: $3x + 6y \leq 12$?

A)

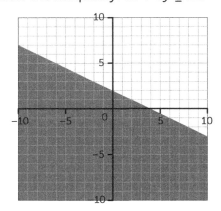

B)

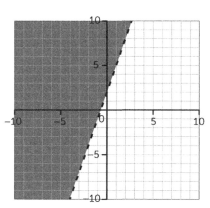

C)

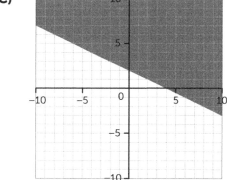

D)

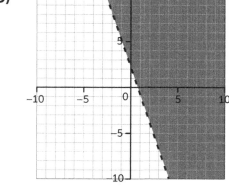

27. What is the equation of the following line?

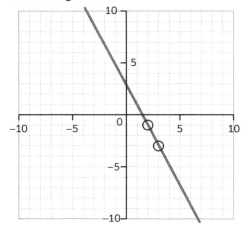

A) $y = 3x - 2$

B) $y = -3x + 2$

C) $y = 2x - 3$

D) $y = -2x + 3$

GRID-IN
Calculator

28. The graph below shows Company X's profits for the years 2010 to 2013. How much more profit did Company X make in 2013 than in 2012?

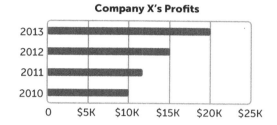

Company X's Profits

----

29. In 2016, LeBron James averaged 26.4 points per game over 74 games. How many points did James score that year? (Round to the nearest whole number.)

----

30. Kim and Chris are writing a book together. Kim wrote twice as many pages as Chris, and together they wrote 240 pages. How many pages did Chris write?

----

31. Fifty shares of a financial stock and 10 shares of an auto stock are valued at $1,300. If 10 shares of the financial stock and 10 shares of the auto stock are valued at $500, what is the value of 50 shares of the auto stock?

Answer Key
READING

1. **A)** The author writes that "Owen had been remarkable for a delicate ingenuity" and that the "characteristic minuteness in his objects and accomplishments made the world even more incapable than it might otherwise have been of appreciating Owen Warland's genius."

2. **C)** In the second paragraph the author writes, "Several freaks of this kind quite destroyed the young watchmaker's credit with that steady and matter-of-fact class of people who hold the opinion that time is not to be trifled with, whether considered as the medium of advancement and prosperity in this world or preparation for the next."

3. **C)** In this sentence, "utilitarian coarseness" is contrasted with Owen's "love of the beautiful," implying that Owen has an affinity for things that are artistic and beautiful and has little interest in practical things.

4. **D)** The author writes that "the character of Owen's mind was microscopic, and tended naturally to the minute, in accordance with his diminutive frame and the marvelous smallness and delicate power of his fingers."

5. **A)** This quotation established Owen's peculiar affinity for the minute, which is reinforced by the story of his visit to the steam-engine.

6. **C)** The author writes, "Peter Hovenden's opinion of his apprentice has already been expressed. He could make nothing of the lad. Owen's apprehension of the professional mysteries, it is true, was inconceivably quick; but he altogether forgot or despised the grand object of a watchmaker's business, and cared no more for the measurement of time than if it had been merged into eternity." This implies that Peter Hovenden did not understand Owen's peculiar genius or his indifference to the measurement of time.

7. **B)** This quotation describes Peter Hovenden's opinion of Owen.

8. **B)** The author writes that "Owen's lack of sturdiness made it possible, by strict injunctions and sharp oversight, to restrain his creative eccentricity within bounds." This implies that Owen's eccentricity was unusual.

9. **A)** The author writes that "when his [Owen's] apprenticeship was served out, and he had taken the little shop which Peter Hovenden's failing eyesight compelled him to relinquish, then did people recognize how unfit a person was Owen Warland to lead old blind Father Time along his daily course."

10. **D)** The author writes that Owen's reputation in his community was "quite destroyed" as a result of his

disregard for the seriousness of time.

11. **A)** Washington states that Europe is "engaged in frequent controversies" and that it would be "unwise to implicate ourselves... in the ordinary vicissitudes of her politics, or the ordinary combinations and collisions of her friendships and enmities."

12. **D)** The author writes, "It is our true policy to steer clear of permanent alliances with any portion of the foreign world; so far, I mean, as we are now at liberty to do it."

13. **A)** In this quote, Washington asserts that America should avoid foreign entanglements whenever it is possible to do so.

14. **C)** Washington asks, "Why forego the advantages of so peculiar a situation? Why quit our own to stand upon foreign ground? Why, by interweaving our destiny with that of any part of Europe, entangle our peace and prosperity in the toils of European ambition, rivalship, interest, humor, or caprice?"

15. **A)** Truman says, "To ensure the peaceful development of nations, free from coercion, the United States has taken a leading part in establishing the United Nations... We shall not realize our objectives, however, unless we are willing to help free peoples to maintain their free institutions and their national integrity against aggressive movements that seek to impose upon them totalitarian regimes."

16. **C)** The author indicates that establishing freedom from

coercion means defending "free peoples...against aggressive movements that seek to impose upon them totalitarian regimes."

17. **C)** Truman states, "This was a fundamental issue in the war with Germany and Japan. Our victory was won over countries which sought to impose their will, and their way of life, upon other nations." Later, he says, "At the present moment in world history nearly every nation must choose between alternative ways of life. The choice is too often not a free one."

18. **D)** Truman states that "every nation must choose between alternative ways of life" and that "the choice is too often not a free one." He then goes on to say that "it must be the policy of the United States to support free people who are resisting attempted subjugation by armed minorities or by outside pressures."

19. **B)** Washington advocates for a policy of isolationism: "It is our true policy to steer clear of permanent alliances with any portion of the foreign world; so far, I mean, as we are now at liberty to do it." On the other hand, Truman advocates for intervention on behalf of oppressed foreign nations:"I believe that it must be the policy of the United States to support free peoples who are resisting attempted subjugation by armed minorities or by outside pressures."

20. **C)** While Washington argues that America should avoid entanglements that are "foreign to our [America's] concerns," Truman

argues that any presence of "totalitarian regimes" in the world poses a threat to America's own freedom.

21. **B)** The graph indicates that there was a correlation between the new foreign policy approach and increased government spending in the twentieth century.

22. **B)** The author writes, "For centuries, philosophers have been examining the relationship between man and his social world. It is no wonder, then, that a field of study has arisen to examine just that."

23. **A)** This quote suggests that the author included Aristotle's quote in order to highlight the long-term interest in the relationship between man and his social environment.

24. **D)** The author writes that "our daily behaviors are inextricably linked with the social context in which they occur."

25. **D)** The author writes that "the behaviors we witness in others may be as much a result of social influence as they are of the individual's disposition" and that the "tendency to attribute behaviors, especially negative behaviors, to disposition is risky and can ultimately be detrimental to us and to the other person."

26. **A)** The author describes the participants as "healthy, stable, intelligent male Stanford University students" in order to provide a contrast to the "cruel and unrelenting...treatment of the prisoners."

27. **C)** The author writes, "Even giving individuals temporary power over others was enough to completely alter the way they viewed and behaved toward each other; indeed, the behaviors he witnessed in each of the groups were not a result of the dispositions of the participants but of the situation in which they had been placed."

28. **C)** The author writes that "the guards had become cruel and unrelenting in their treatment of the prisoners."

29. **C)** This quote highlights the change from the "healthy, stable, intelligent" personalities of the Stanford students and the "cruel and unrelenting" behaviors they displayed after being named guards.

30. **C)** The author writes, "Today, social psychologists study the effect of social influence on a number of different behaviors."

31. **A)** The author implies that the findings of social psychologists have practical, meaningful applications.

32. **C)** The use of the word *reconciled* indicates that scientists gathered, compared, contrasted, and integrated data into a comprehensive, global data set.

33. **B)** This quote suggests that the data was integrated into a global data set that pointed to a single conclusion about carbon fertilization.

34. **C)** The author writes, "Forests and other land vegetation currently

remove up to 30 percent of human carbon dioxide emissions from the atmosphere during photosynthesis. If the rate of absorption were to slow down, the rate of global warming would speed up in return."

35. **D)** The author indicates that the research into carbon dioxide absorption "'has big implications for our understanding of whether global terrestrial ecosystems might continue to offset our carbon dioxide emissions or might begin to exacerbate climate change.'"

36. **A)** The author writes that climate change "decreases water availability in some regions and makes Earth warmer, leading to more frequent and larger wildfires." At the same time, those fires "stop carbon absorption by killing trees" and "spew huge amount of carbon into the atmosphere as the wood burns," contributing to the warming of Earth's atmosphere.

37. **C)** The author writes, "As human-caused emissions add more carbon dioxide to the atmosphere, forests worldwide are using it to grow faster, reducing the amount that stays airborne."

38. **B)** The author indicates that an inverse relationship exists between the rate of absorption of global forests and the rate of global warming; therefore, saving forests and increasing the rate of carbon dioxide absorption would slow the effects of climate change.

39. **B)** The author writes that researchers "pull[ed] together national and regional data of

various kinds" to create "global data sets" that allowed them to examine carbon dioxide fertilization at many different levels.

40. **D)** The author writes that "Stephens used measurements of carbon dioxide made from aircraft to show that many climate models were not correctly representing flows of carbon above ground level. Models that matched the aircraft measurements better showed more carbon absorption in the tropical forests. However, there were still not enough global data sets to validate the idea of a large tropical-forest absorption."

41. **D)** The author writes, "Schimel noted that their paper reconciles results at every scale from the pores of a single leaf, where photosynthesis takes place, to the whole Earth, as air moves carbon dioxide around the globe."

42. **B)** The author writes that "many human communities want answers about the current status and future of Arctic marine mammals, including...indigenous people whose traditional ways of subsistence are intertwined with the fate of species such as ice seals, narwhals, walruses and polar bears." This implies that the survival of these groups depends on the survival of these animal species.

43. **A)** The author writes, "The Arctic sea ice cover...naturally grows in the fall and winter and melts during the spring and summer every year. But over the past decades, the melt season has grown longer and the average

extent of Arctic sea ice has diminished."

44. D) The author writes that "the melt season has grown longer and the average extent of Arctic sea ice has diminished, changing the game for many Arctic marine mammals."

45. D) The author quotes one scientist as saying, "Mainly, just continuing daily coverage is what's important for the long-term monitoring of habitat changes."

46. D) The author writes that "there are many unknowns...about how their fragile habitat will evolve in a warming world." This implies that the habitat is at risk due to the changes in the earth's temperature.

47. D) This implies that the survival of Arctic species is in jeopardy as a result of longer melting seasons and decreased sea ice extent.

WRITING and LANGUAGE

1. A) This sentence effectively frames the passage's main argument: that anyone who has the required skills should consider an aerospace engineering career.

2. C) This choice contains an opening dash to go with the closing one following *astronautical engineering*. Also, *such as* is ungrammatical here; it is correct to delete this phrase.

3. D) This choice is both succinct and correctly punctuated with a semicolon. A semicolon correctly connects two related complete sentences.

4. C) This choice is not redundant.

5. B) The present-tense verb *study* agrees with the phrase *while in school*, which indicates the present tense. The modal verb *must* shows that students who want to be aerospace engineers are required to study the following topics.

6. B) According to the graph, the median salary for all occupations is just over eighty thousand dollars, whereas the median salary for aerospace engineers is just over one hundred thousand dollars. The difference is approximately twenty thousand dollars.

7. A) This sentence makes sense where it is now. The author is saying that, while aerospace engineering students must work harder in school than other engineering students must, aerospace engineers are compensated by receiving higher salaries than other engineers receive.

8. C) This sentence provides an effective transition between the two paragraphs. It mentions content from the fourth paragraph and then ties that in to the fifth paragraph's content.

9. B) The plural noun *opportunities* agrees with the plural verb *are*.

10. **D)** The relative pronoun *who* agrees with its referent, *engineers*.

11. **A)** Most people are interested in career advancement.

12. **A)** This choice is grammatical and correctly punctuated.

13. **B)** The sentence provides background information for the rest of the narrative.

14. **D)** All three verbs are in past-tense form. This agrees with most of the other verb tenses in the narrative.

15. **C)** It makes more sense that the book would be damp rather than sopping wet.

16. **A)** This detail explains why the book is damp and warped.

17. **D)** This choice shows how much effort Lincoln would put into borrowing a book.

18. **C)** Since Lincoln loves the book, he probably feels very disappointed that he will not be able to finish it. He also probably feels very guilty for ruining the borrowed book.

19. **A)** The paragraph makes good sense where it is now. It explains why Lincoln goes to the Crawford home next.

20. **B)** The relative pronoun *where* should be used to introduce the relative clause here.

21. **C)** This choice is specific enough to show that the author is referring to young Lincoln, not to Crawford.

22. **D)** Crawford asks Lincoln to work for three days; he asks that Lincoln "give [him] three days' work."

23. **C)** The singular verb *is* agrees with the singular subject *discourse*.

24. **A)** Here, *overlook* means "fail to see or take seriously."

25. **A)** The subordinating conjunction *though* correctly connects the subordinate clause to the main clause of the sentence.

26. **C)** Adding the preposition *by* creates parallel structure with the phrase *by farming and agricultural practices*.

27. **B)** Although this sentence is long, it is well constructed and properly punctuated. The reader is able to clearly understand its meaning.

28. **B)** The sentence sums up the main topic of the second paragraph, "the threat...posed...by...food production," and effectively introduces the main topic of the third paragraph, solutions to this threat.

29. **C)** The plural possessive pronoun *their* and the plural noun *careers* agree with the plural noun *researchers*, which is the sentence's subject.

30. **C)** The plural noun *lands* agrees with the plural verb *account*.

31. **A)** This sentence is well constructed and makes sense here.

32. **B)** The writer used parallel construction to write this clause; the clause includes two

progressive verbs, *using* and *protecting*.

33. **B)** This sentence effectively summarizes and concludes the passage.

34. **D)** This sentence relates to the modern reader and effectively introduces the article's topic.

35. **A)** This sentence adds support for the paragraph's main point: that "creation myths are numerous and varied."

36. **B)** The plural phrase *these stories* agrees with its plural antecedent, *creation myths*. The singular verb *highlights* agrees with the singular noun phrase *the universal theme*.

37. **B)** The plural verb *were born* agrees with the plural noun *creatures*.

38. **D)** The phrase *in a similar manner* correctly likens man's evolution from nature to man's evolution from animals.

39. **C)** The sentence provides further details on early people's belief that humans evolved from coyotes.

40. **B)** Using a singular noun in possessive form, *humanity's*, correctly shows that the "beginning" mentioned in the sentence belongs to humanity.

41. **D)** The writer should use the neutral possessive pronoun *its* in this context. A rock is a thing; it is gender neutral.

42. **A)** This sentence mentions ancient people who "believed humans evolved from nature," the topic of the previous paragraph. It also mentions peoples who did *not* share this belief; this leads smoothly into the topic of the fifth paragraph: "stories of humanity's creation by deities."

43. **C)** The writer should use the object pronoun *whom* to refer to Tiamat, the god whom Marduk defeats.

44. **B)** The conjunction *neither* must be paired with *nor*.

MATHEMATICS: NO CALCULATOR

1. **B)** The axis of symmetry will be a vertical line that runs through the vertex, which is the point $(-3,5)$. The line of symmetry is $x = -3$.

2. **D)** Simplify using PEMDAS.

$$z^3(z + 2)^2 - 4z^3 + 2$$
$$z^3(z^2 + 4z + 4) - 4z^3 + 2$$
$$z^5 + 4z^4 + 4z^3 - 4z^3 + 2$$
$$\mathbf{z^5 + 4z^4 + 2}$$

3. **A)** Use the points to find the slope.

$$m = \frac{y_2 - y_1}{x_2 - x_1} = \frac{-3 - 9}{4 - (-2)} = -2$$

Use the point-slope equation to find the equation of the line.

$$(y - y_1) = m(x - x_1)$$
$$y - (-3) = -2(x - 4)$$
$$\mathbf{y = -2x + 5}$$

4. **D)** Split the absolute value inequality into two inequalities and simplify. Switch the inequality when making one side negative.

$$\frac{x}{8} \geq 1$$

$$x \geq 8$$

$$-\frac{x}{8} \geq 1$$

$$\frac{x}{8} \leq -1$$

$$x \leq -8$$

$x \leq -8$ or $x \geq 8 \rightarrow$ **(−∞,−8] ∪ [8,∞)**

5. **C)** Complex solutions always come in pairs. Therefore, the number of possible complex solutions is the greatest even number equal to or less than the power of the polynomial. A 17th degree polynomial can have at most **16 complex roots**.

6. **B)** Find the slope of the given line. Any parallel lines will have the same slope.

$$3x + 2y = 10$$

$$2y = -3x + 10$$

$$y = -\frac{3}{2}x + 5$$

7. **D)** Solve each equation for y and find the equation with a power of 1.

$$\sqrt[3]{y} = x \rightarrow y = x^3$$

$$\sqrt[3]{x} = y \rightarrow y = \sqrt[3]{x}$$

$$\sqrt[3]{y} = x^2 \rightarrow y = x^6$$

$$y = \sqrt[3]{x^3} \rightarrow y = x$$

8. **A)** His profit will be his income minus his expenses. He will earn $40 for each lawn, or 40$m$. He pays $35 is expenses each week, or 35w.

profit = 40m − 35x

9. **B)** Factor the trinomial and set each factor equal to 0.

$$2n^2 + 2n - 12 = 0$$

$$2(n^2 + n - 6) = 0$$

$$2(n + 3)(n - 2) = 0$$

$n = -3$ and $n = 2$

10. **A)** The line $y = 2x + 1$ will have a slope of 2 and y-intercept of 1. The lines shown in graphs C and D have negative slopes. The line in graph B has a y-intercept of −2.

Alternatively, use a table to find some coordinates, and identify the graph that contains those coordinates.

x	y
0	1
1	3
2	5

11. **A)** Since the cube's volume is 27, each side length is equal to $\sqrt[3]{27}$ = 3. The long diagonal distance from one of the cube's vertices to its opposite vertex will provide the sphere's diameter:

$$d = \sqrt{3^2 + 3^2 + 3^2} = \sqrt{27} = 5.2$$

Half of this length is the radius, which is **2.6 meters**.

12. **B)** Only I and II define y as a function of x.

I. This is not a function: the equation represents a horizontal parabola, which fails the vertical line test.

II. This is a function: each x-value corresponds to only one y-value.

III. This is a function: the graph passes the vertical line test.

13. **A)** The domain is the possible values of x from left to right. Here, the domain starts at −4, inclusive,

and stops at −1, exclusive. It starts again at 0, inclusive, and goes to 3, inclusive. The two line segments from 0 to 3 cross over each other, so the domain includes this whole interval. Note that closed circles represent inclusion (square bracket), and open circles represent exclusions (round bracket).

14. The slope of a horizontal line is always **0**.

15. Isolate the $\sqrt{2x - 5}$ by subtracting 4:

$\sqrt{2x - 5} = x - 4$

Square both sides to clear the radical:

$2x - 5 = x^2 - 8x + 16$

Collect all variables to one side:

$x^2 - 10x + 21 = 0$

Factor and solve.

$(x - 7)(x - 3) = 0$

$x = 7$ or $x = 3$

Check solutions by plugging into the original, as squaring both sides can cause extraneous solutions:

$\sqrt{2(3) - 5} + 4 = 3$

$\sqrt{1} + 4 = 3$

False, 3 is NOT a solution.

$\sqrt{2(7) - 5} + 4 = 7$

$\sqrt{9} + 4 = 7$

True, 7 is a solution.

$X = 7$

16. The given values can be used to write two equations for the area of $\triangle WXZ$ with two sets of bases and heights. First, determine the quantities known and the quantity needed:

$WZ = b_1 = 80$

$XU = h_1 = 70$

$XZ = b_2 = 100$

$WY = h_2 = ?$

Next, use the formula for the area of a triangle to find the unknown quantity:

$A = \frac{1}{2}bh$

$A_1 = \frac{1}{2}(80)(70) = 2800$

$A_2 = \frac{1}{2}(100)(h_2)$

Set the two equations equal to each other, and solve for WY.

$2800 = \frac{1}{2}(100)(h_2)$

$h_2 = 56$

$WY = 56$

17. Plug 0 in for x and solve for y.

$7y - 42x + 7 = 0$

$7y - 42(0) + 7 = 0$

$y = -1$

The y-intercept is at (0,−1).

MATHEMATICS: CALCULATOR

1. **C)** Use the formula for percentages.

percent $= \frac{\text{part}}{\text{whole}}$

$= \frac{42}{48}$

$= 0.875 = \textbf{87.5\%}$

2. **C)** Use the formula for percent change.

percent change $= \frac{\text{amount of change}}{\text{original amount}}$

$= \frac{7,375 - 7,250}{7,250} = 0.017 = \textbf{1.7\%}$

3. **D)** Factor the equation and set each factor equal to 0.

$y = 16x^3 - 48x^2$

$16x^2(x - 3) = 0$

$x = 0$ and $x = 3$

4. **C)** Set up a system of equations where d equals the number of dimes and q equals number of quarters.

$d + q = 34$

$0.1d + 0.25q = 6.25$

$0.1d + 0.25(34 - d) = 6.25$

$d = $ **15**

$q = 34 - 15 = $ **19**

5. **D)** Plug in each set of values and determine if the inequality is true.

$2(0) + 0 \leq -10$ FALSE

$2(10) + 2 \leq -10$ FALSE

$2(10) + 10 \leq -10$ FALSE

$2(-10) + (-10) \leq -10$ TRUE

6. **C)** One way to find the answer is to draw a picture.

Put 24 cans into groups of 4. One out of every 4 cans is diet (light gray) so there is 1 light gray can for every 3 dark gray cans. That leaves 18 dark gray cans (regular soda).

Alternatively, solve the problem using ratios.

$\frac{\text{regular}}{\text{total}} = \frac{3}{4} = \frac{x}{24}$

$4x = 72$

$x = 18$

7. **D)** Identify the important parts of the circle.

$r = 3$

length of $\overline{ACB} = 5$

Plug these values into the formula for the length of an arc and solve for θ.

$s = \frac{\theta}{360°} \times 2\pi r$

$5 = \frac{\theta}{360} \times 2\pi(3)$

$\frac{5}{6\pi} = \frac{\theta}{360}$

$\theta = 95.5°$

m$\angle AOB = $ **95.5°**

8. **C)** Use the formula for percent change.

percent change $= \frac{\text{amount of change}}{\text{original amount}}$

$= \frac{(680 - 425)}{425}$

$= \frac{255}{425} = 0.60 = $ **60%**

9. **B)** There are 16 ounces in a pound, so the baby's starting weight is 120 ounces. He gained 6 ounces per month, or $6t$. So, the baby's weight will be his initial weight plus the amount gained for each month:

$y = 6t + 120$

10. **D)** Assign variables and write the ratios as fractions. Then, cross multiply to solve for the number of apples and oranges sold.

$x = $ apples

$\frac{\text{apples}}{\text{bananas}} = \frac{3}{2} = \frac{x}{20}$

$60 = 2x$

$x = 30$ apples

$y = $ oranges

$\frac{\text{oranges}}{\text{bananas}} = \frac{1}{2} = \frac{y}{20}$

$2y = 20$

$y = 10$ oranges

To find the total, add the number of apples, oranges, and bananas together. $30 + 20 + 10 = $ **60 pieces of fruit**.

11. **B)** Add the base amount and the tax on the extra percentage of the person's income.

$10,620 + 0.2(80,000 - 75,000)$

$= $ **$11,620**

12. **B)** Calculate the discriminant.

$B^2 - 4AC = 2^2 - 4(1)(4) = -12$

The discriminant is negative and A ≠ C, so **it is an ellipse**.

13. **D)** Set up an equation. The original price (p) minus 30% of the original price is $385.

$p - 0.3p = 385$

$p = \frac{385}{0.7} = $ **$550**

14. **D)** Simplify using PEMDAS.

$5^2 \times (-5)^{-2} - 5^{-1}$

$= 25 \times \frac{1}{25} - \frac{1}{5}$

$= 1 - \frac{1}{5} = \mathbf{\frac{4}{5}}$

15. **A)** Find the area of the room in square feet and convert it to square yards (1 square yard = 9 square feet). Then multiply by the cost per square yard.

area = 10 × 12 = 120 square feet

$\frac{120}{9} = \frac{40}{3}$ square yards

$\frac{40}{3} \times $12.51 = \frac{$500.40}{3}$

=**$166.80**

16. **A)** The amount of money in Jane's bank account can be represented by the expression 275 + 15h ($275 plus $15 for every hour she works). Therefore, the equation **400 = 275 + 15h** describes how many hours she needs to babysit to have $400.

17. **D)** Substitute one (x,y) pair into each answer choice to find the correct equation.

A) $y = 6x - 6$; (3,3)

$y = 6(3) - 6$

$y = 18 - 6$

$y = 12 \neq 3$

B) $y = 5x - 6$; (3,3)

$y = 5(3) - 6$

$y = 15 - 6$

$y = 9 \neq 3$

C) $y = 4x - 6$; (3,3)

$y = 4(3) - 6$

$y = 12 - 6$

$y = 6 \neq 3$

D) $y = 3x - 6$; (3,3)

$y = 3(3) - 6$

$y = 9 - 6$

$\mathbf{y = 3}$

18. **C)** The ratio of solute to solution is 1:5. Write a proportion and solve.

$\frac{1}{5} = \frac{x}{90}$

$1(90) = x(5)$

18 = x

19. **A)** Use trigonometric identities.

$\frac{\sin x}{1 - \cos x} \times \frac{1 + \cos x}{1 + \cos x}$

$\frac{(\sin x)(1 + \cos x)}{1 - \cos^2 x}$

$\frac{(\sin x)(1 + \cos x)}{\sin^2 x}$

$\mathbf{\frac{1 + \cos x}{\sin x}}$

20. **D)** Find the amount of change and add to the original amount.

amount of change = original amount × percent change

= 37,500 × 0.055 = 2,062.50

37,500 + 2,062.50 = **$39,562.50**

21. **C)** Isolate the variable on the left side of the inequality. Reverse the direction of the inequality when dividing by a negative number.

$6x + 5 \geq -15 + 8x$

$-2x + 5 \geq -15$

$-2x \geq -20$

$\mathbf{x \leq 10}$

22. **A)** Use the equation for percentages.

part = whole × percentage =

9 × 0.25 = **2.25**

23. **D)** Set up a proportion and solve.

$$\frac{8}{650} = \frac{12}{x}$$

$12(650) = 8x$

x = 975 miles

24. **D)** Complete the square to put the quadratic equation in vertex form.

$y = 2x^2 + 12x - 3$

$y = 2(x^2 + 6x +$ _____$) - 3 +$ _____

$y = 2(x^2 + 6x + 9) - 3 - 18$

$y = 2(x + 3)^2 - 21$

25. **D)** Use the formula for the sum of an arithmetic series.

$$S_n = \frac{n}{2}(a_1 + a_n)$$

$$= \frac{n}{2}[2a_1 + (n - 1)d]$$

$$= \frac{180}{2}[2(10) + (180 - 1)4]$$

= **66,240 seats**

26. **A)** The x- and y-intercepts are (4,0) and (0,2). Because of the inequality, the graph must be shaded below the line, making A) the correct choice.

$3x + 6y \leq 12$

$3(0) + 6y = 12$

$y = 2$

y-intercept: (0,2)

$3x + 6(0) \leq 12$

$x = 4$

x-intercept: (4,0)

27. **D)** The y-intercept can be identified on the graph as (0,3), so $b = 3$. To find the slope, choose any two points and plug the values into the slope equation. The two points chosen here are (2,−1) and (3,−3):

$$m = \frac{(-3)-(-1)}{3 - 2} = \frac{-2}{1} = -2$$

Replace m with −2 and b with 3 in $y = mx + b$.

$y = -2x + 3$

28. **$5,000**

Find Company X's profits for 2012 and 2013 from the bar graph:

2012 profit ≈ $15,000

2013 profit ≈ $20,000

Subtract to find the change in profit:

$20,000 − $15,000 = **$5,000**

29. Multiply the average number of points per game by the number of games he played:

26.4 × 74 = 1953.6 ≈ **1954 points**

30. Write a formula to find the answer.

p = number of pages written by Chris

$2p$ = number of pages written by Kim

$p + 2p = 240$

$p = 80$

Chris wrote 80 pages.

31. Set up a system of equations and solve using elimination.

f = the cost of a financial stock

a = the cost of an auto stock

$50f + 10a = 1300$

$10f + 10a = 500$

$$\begin{aligned} 50f + 10a &= 1300 \\ + -50f - 50a &= -2500 \\ \hline -40a &= -1,200 \\ a &= 30 \end{aligned}$$

50(30) = **1,500**

To take your SECOND PSAT practice test, follow the link below:

https://www.acceptedinc.com/psat-online-resources

Made in the USA
Las Vegas, NV
05 October 2021

ASPIRE
SUCCEED
PROGRESS

Complete Chemistry for Cambridge Secondary 1

Philippa Gardom Hulme

Contents

Stage 9

How to use your Student Book

Welcome to your **Complete Chemistry for Cambridge Secondary 1** Student Book. This book has been written to help you study Chemistry at all three stages of Cambridge Secondary 1.

Most of the pages in this book work like this:

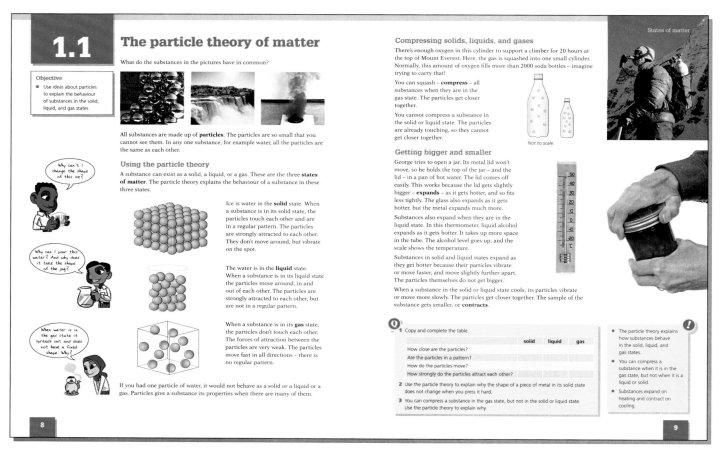

- Every page starts with the learning objectives for the lesson. The learning objectives match the Cambridge Secondary 1 Science curriculum framework.

- New vocabulary is marked in bold. You can check the meaning of these words in the glossary at the back of the book.

- At the end of each page there are questions to test that you understand what you have learned.

- The key points to remember from the page are also summarised here.

These pages cover the Chemistry topics in the Cambridge Secondary 1 Science curriculum framework. In addition, in every chapter there are also pages that help you think like a scientist, prepare for the next level, and test your knowledge. Find out more on the next page.

Scientific enquiry

These pages help you to practise the skills that you need to be a good scientist. They cover all the scientific enquiry learning objectives from the curriculum framework.

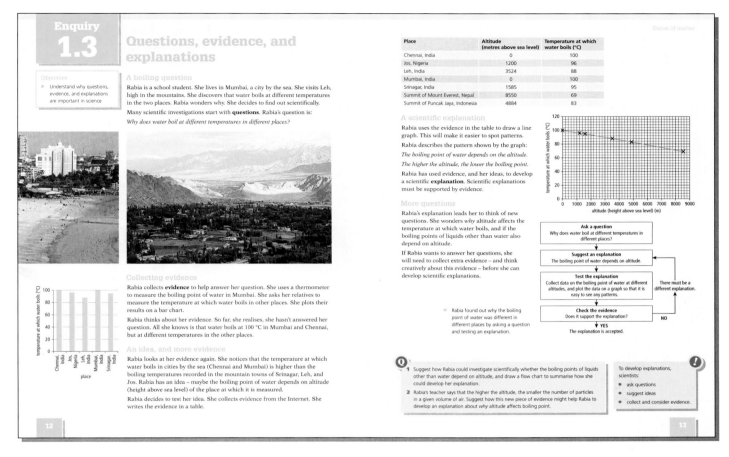

You will learn how to:

- consider ideas
- plan investigations and experiments
- record and analyse data
- evaluate evidence to draw scientific conclusions.

You will also learn how scientists throughout history and from around the globe created theories, carried out research, and drew conclusions about the world around them.

Extension

Throughout this book there are lots of opportunities to learn even more about chemistry beyond the Cambridge Secondary 1 Science curriculum framework. These topics are called *Extension* because they extend and develop your science skills even further.

You can tell when a topic is extension because it is marked with a dashed line, like the one on the left. Or when the page has a purple background, like below.

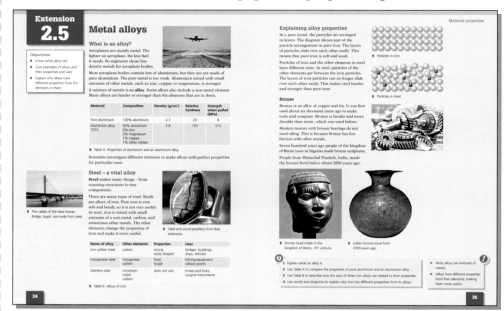

Extension topics will not be in your Cambridge Checkpoint test, but they will help you prepare for moving onto the next stage of the curriculum and eventually for Cambridge IGCSE® Chemistry.

Review

At the end of every chapter and every stage there are review questions.

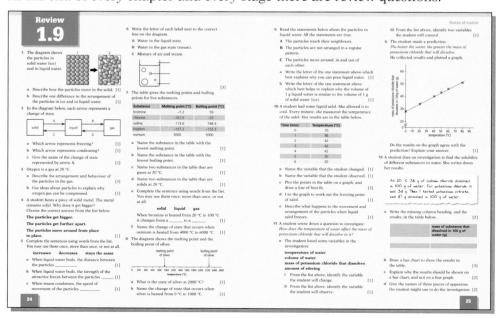

These questions are written in the style of Cambridge Checkpoint test. They are there to help you review what you have learned in that chapter or stage.

®IGCSE is the registered trademark of Cambridge International Examinations

Reference

At the back of this book there are reference pages. These pages will be useful throughout every stage of Cambridge Secondary 1 Science.

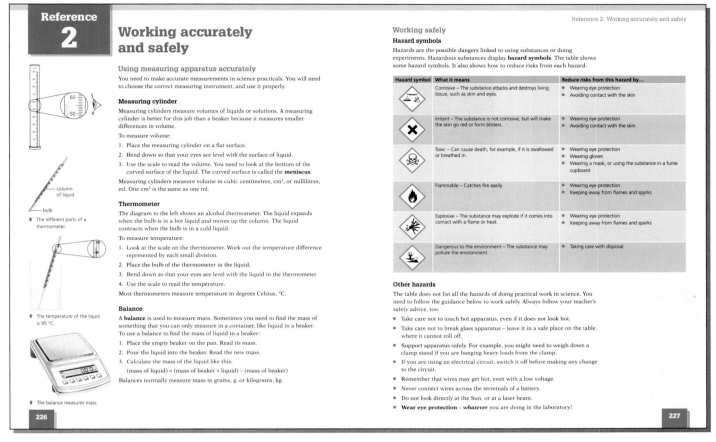

They include information on:

- how to choose suitable apparatus
- how to work accurately and safely
- how to detect gases
- how to record, display, and analyse results
- and a periodic table.

The particle theory of matter

What do the substances in the pictures have in common?

All substances are made up of **particles**. The particles are so small that you cannot see them. In any one substance, for example water, all the particles are the same as each other.

Using the particle theory

A substance can exist as a solid, a liquid, or a gas. These are the three **states of matter**. The particle theory explains the behaviour of a substance in these three states.

Why can't I change the shape of this ice?

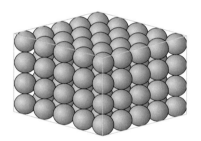

Ice is water in the **solid** state. When a substance is in its solid state, the particles touch each other and are in a regular pattern. The particles are strongly attracted to each other. They don't move around, but vibrate on the spot.

Why can I pour this water? And why does it take the shape of the jug?

The water is in the **liquid** state. When a substance is in its liquid state the particles move around, in and out of each other. The particles are strongly attracted to each other, but are not in a regular pattern.

When water is in the gas state it spreads out and does not have a fixed shape. Why?

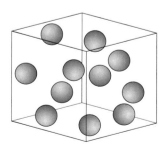

When a substance is in its **gas** state, the particles don't touch each other. The forces of attraction between the particles are very weak. The particles move fast in all directions – there is no regular pattern.

If you had one particle of water, it would not behave as a solid or a liquid or a gas. Particles give a substance its properties when there are many of them.

Compressing solids, liquids, and gases

There's enough oxygen in this cylinder to support a climber for 20 hours at the top of Mount Everest. Here, the gas is squashed into one small cylinder. Normally, this amount of oxygen fills more than 2000 soda bottles – imagine trying to carry that!

You can squash – **compress** – all substances when they are in the gas state. The particles get closer together.

You cannot compress a substance in the solid or liquid state. The particles are already touching, so they cannot get closer together.

Not to scale.

Getting bigger and smaller

George tries to open a jar. Its metal lid won't move, so he holds the top of the jar – and the lid – in a pan of hot water. The lid comes off easily. This works because the lid gets slightly bigger – **expands** – as it gets hotter, and so fits less tightly. The glass also expands as it gets hotter, but the metal expands much more.

Substances also expand when they are in the liquid state. In this thermometer, liquid alcohol expands as it gets hotter. It takes up more space in the tube. The alcohol level goes up, and the scale shows the temperature.

Substances in solid and liquid states expand as they get hotter because their particles vibrate or move faster, and move slightly further apart. The particles themselves do not get bigger.

When a substance in the solid or liquid state cools, its particles vibrate or move more slowly. The particles get closer together. The sample of the substance gets smaller, or **contracts**.

Q

1 Copy and complete the table.

	solid	liquid	gas
How close are the particles?			
Are the particles in a pattern?			
How do the particles move?			
How strongly do the particles attract each other?			

2 Use the particle theory to explain why the shape of a piece of metal in its solid state does not change when you press it hard.

3 You can compress a substance in the gas state, but not in the solid or liquid state. Use the particle theory to explain why.

- The particle theory explains how substances behave in the solid, liquid, and gas states.

- You can compress a substance when it is in the gas state, but not when it is a liquid or solid.

- Substances expand on heating and contract on cooling.

1.2 Boiling, evaporating, and condensing

Objectives

- Name the changes of state involving liquids and gases
- Explain changes of state using ideas about particles

Changing state

Chahaya lights a candle. Some of the solid wax changes to the liquid state. Some of the liquid wax becomes wax gas. The wax gas burns.

When a substance changes from one state to another, its particles don't change. All that changes is the distance between the particles, their speed, and the attraction between them.

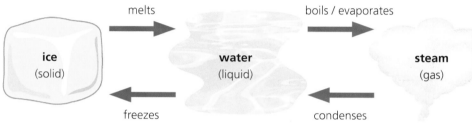

↑ Melting, boiling, evaporating, condensing, and freezing are all **changes of state**.

Liquid to gas

When a liquid becomes a gas, the particles move faster and spread out. The attractive forces between the particles become very weak.

A substance in the liquid state becomes a gas by **evaporation** or by **boiling**.

Evaporation

Evaporation happens when particles leave the surface of a liquid. The particles spread out to form a gas. Evaporation can happen at any temperature.

↑ Clothes dry when water evaporates from them.

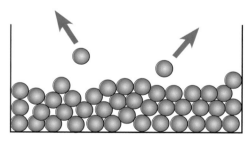

↑ During evaporation, particles leave the liquid surface. *Not to scale.*

Boiling

Boiling occurs throughout the whole of a liquid. When you heat a beaker of liquid water, bubbles of water in the gas state form throughout the liquid. The bubbles rise to the surface and escape. The water is boiling. Boiling can only happen when a liquid is hot enough.

↑ Water is constantly evaporating from lakes and the sea.

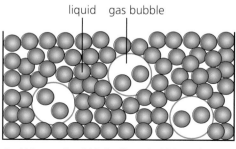

↑ When a liquid is boiling, bubbles of gas form throughout. *Not to scale.*

Boiling point

Different substances boil at different temperatures. The temperature at which a substance boils is its **boiling point**. Every substance has its own boiling point.

Substance	Boiling point (°C)
nitrogen	−196
ethanol	78
water	100
mercury	357
copper	2595
diamond	5100

Nitrogen has the lowest boiling point of the substances in the table. Diamond and copper have very high boiling points.

Measuring boiling point

Mbizi has a colourless liquid. He knows that the liquid is either ethanol or water, but does not know which. To find out, Mbizi uses an electric heater to heat the liquid. Ethanol is very flammable and so Mbizi is very careful; he wears safety goggles and a lab coat. He measures its temperature every minute. He plots the data on a graph.

The graph shows that the temperature of the liquid increased for the first five minutes. Then the temperature stayed at 78 °C for three minutes while the liquid boiled. The boiling point of the liquid is 78 °C. Data from the table show that the liquid is ethanol.

Gas to liquid

When a substance changes state from gas to liquid, the particles move more slowly. They get closer until they touch each other. The forces of attraction between the particles are much stronger in the liquid.

A gas becomes a liquid by **condensation**. A substance in the gas state condenses when it is cooled to its boiling point or below.

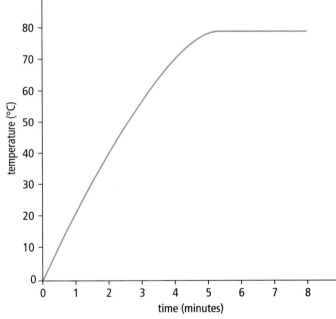

⬆ The graph shows how the temperature of the liquid changed.

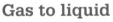
1 Name the change of state when a substance in the gas state becomes a liquid.

2 Describe how the movement of the particles change when a substance boils.

3 Use data from the table at the top of the page to name one substance which is in the gas state at 20 °C.

4 Suggest how a scientist could measure the boiling point of a piece of metal.

● A liquid evaporates or boils to form a gas.

● A gas condenses to form a liquid.

● Every substance has its own boiling point.

Questions, evidence, and explanations

A boiling question

Rabia is a school student. She lives in Mumbai, a city by the sea. She visits Leh, high in the mountains. She discovers that water boils at different temperatures in the two places. Rabia wonders why. She decides to find out scientifically.

Many scientific investigations start with **questions**. Rabia's question is:

Why does water boil at different temperatures in different places?

Collecting evidence

Rabia collects **evidence** to help answer her question. She uses a thermometer to measure the boiling point of water in Mumbai. She asks her relatives to measure the temperature at which water boils in other places. She plots their results on a bar chart.

Rabia thinks about her evidence. So far, she realises, she hasn't answered her question. All she knows is that water boils at 100 °C in Mumbai and Chennai, but at different temperatures in the other places.

An idea, and more evidence

Rabia looks at her evidence again. She notices that the temperature at which water boils in cities by the sea (Chennai and Mumbai) is higher than the boiling temperatures recorded in the mountain towns of Srinagar, Leh, and Jos. Rabia has an idea – maybe the boiling point of water depends on altitude (height above sea level) of the place at which it is measured.

Rabia decides to test her idea. She collects evidence from the Internet. She writes the evidence in a table.

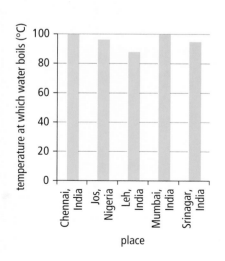

Place	Altitude (metres above sea level)	Temperature at which water boils (°C)
Chennai, India	0	100
Jos, Nigeria	1200	96
Leh, India	3524	88
Mumbai, India	0	100
Srinagar, India	1585	95
Summit of Mount Everest, Nepal	8550	69
Summit of Puncak Jaya, Indonesia	4884	83

A scientific explanation

Rabia uses the evidence in the table to draw a line graph. This will make it easier to spot patterns.

Rabia describes the pattern shown by the graph:

The boiling point of water depends on the altitude.

The higher the altitude, the lower the boiling point.

Rabia has used evidence, and her ideas, to develop a scientific **explanation**. Scientific explanations must be supported by evidence.

More questions

Rabia's explanation leads her to think of new questions. She wonders *why* altitude affects the temperature at which water boils, and if the boiling points of liquids other than water also depend on altitude.

If Rabia wants to answer her questions, she will need to collect extra evidence – and think creatively about this evidence – before she can develop scientific explanations.

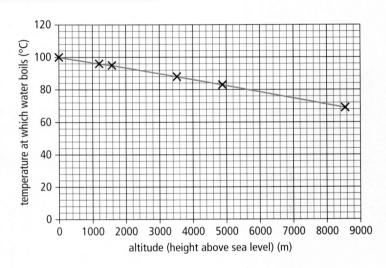

➡ Rabia found out why the boiling point of water was different in different places by asking a question and testing an explanation.

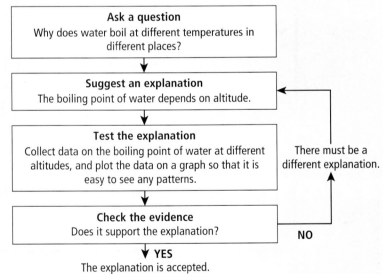

Ask a question
Why does water boil at different temperatures in different places?

Suggest an explanation
The boiling point of water depends on altitude.

Test the explanation
Collect data on the boiling point of water at different altitudes, and plot the data on a graph so that it is easy to see any patterns.

Check the evidence
Does it support the explanation?

There must be a different explanation.

NO

YES
The explanation is accepted.

Q

1 Suggest how Rabia could investigate scientifically whether the boiling points of liquids other than water depend on altitude, and draw a flow chart to summarise how she could develop her explanation.

2 Rabia's teacher says that the higher the altitude, the smaller the number of particles in a given volume of air. Suggest how this new piece of evidence might help Rabia to develop an explanation about *why* altitude affects boiling point.

To develop explanations, scientists:

- ask questions
- suggest ideas
- collect and consider evidence.

1.4 Melting, freezing, and subliming

Objectives

- Name and explain changes of state involving solids
- Describe how melting points help identify substances

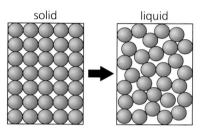

↑ When a substance melts, the movement and arrangement of its particles change.

Solid to liquid

The change of state from solid to liquid is called **melting**. When a solid melts, its particles move out of their regular pattern. The particles start to move around, in and out of each other. This means that the particle arrangement changes all the time.

The particles touch each other when a substance is in both its solid and liquid states.

Melting point

Different substances melt at different temperatures. The temperature at which a substance melts is its **melting point**. Every substance has its own melting point.

Substance	Melting point (°C)
nitrogen	−210
mercury	−39
water	0
gold	1063
copper	1083

↑ Gallium melts on your hand. Its melting point is 30 °C.

↑ Gold melts at a very high temperature.

Using melting points

Scientists use melting point to help identify substances. Sarah has a white solid. She heats the solid until it melts. Its melting point is 561 °C. She uses a data book to find that one substance with this melting point is calcium nitrate. Sarah concludes that her white solid might be calcium nitrate. She decides to do further tests to make sure.

Melting temperatures also tell you about the purity of a substance. If a substance has a sharp melting point, it is not mixed with anything else – it is a **pure substance**. If a substance melts over a range of temperatures, it is a mixture of substances.

↑ This apparatus measures melting point accurately.

Liquid to solid

The change of state from liquid to solid is called **freezing**. Freezing is the opposite of melting. When a liquid freezes, its particles stop moving around from place to place. They arrange themselves in a regular pattern, and vibrate on the spot.

The temperature at which a substance freezes is its **freezing point**. Every substance has its own freezing point. The freezing point of a pure substance is the same as its melting point. For example:

- Freezing point of water = 0 °C
- Melting point of water = 0 °C

⬆ Butter and ghee are mixtures of substances, so they melt over a range of temperatures. They do not have sharp melting points.

⬆ This photograph shows ice crystals forming from liquid water. The photograph was taken in polarised light.

Sublimation

Most solids melt to form liquids when you heat them. But some solids do not change state to become liquids. Instead, they become gases. The process is called **sublimation**. A solid **sublimes** when it changes directly into a gas, without first becoming a liquid.

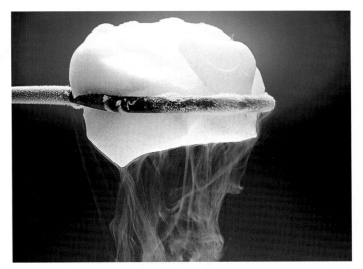

⬆ Solid carbon dioxide – also called dry ice – sublimes to make carbon dioxide gas. It is used in stage shows, such as rock concerts.

⬆ Solid grey iodine sublimes on heating to make a purple gas. When it cools, it forms solid iodine again.

Q

1 Name the change of state when a substance in the solid state becomes a liquid.

2 Describe how the movement and arrangement of particles change when a substance freezes.

3 Jati has a sample of a solid. Suggest how he could find out whether the solid is a pure substance or a mixture of substances.

- A solid melts to become a liquid.
- A liquid freezes to become a solid.
- Some solids sublime to form gases.
- Every substance has its own melting / freezing point.

Energy and changes of state

Forces between particles

When a substance is in its solid or liquid state, strong forces hold the particles together. The forces between particles are much weaker when a substance is in its gas state.

Energy for boiling and evaporation

In a liquid, the particles touch each other. Strong forces of attraction between the particles stop them escaping from the liquid.

Particles in liquids move around. Some particles move faster than others. The faster moving particles have more energy.

Evaporation happens when some faster-moving particles have enough energy to overcome the forces that hold the particles together. These particles escape from the surface of the liquid.

Boiling happens when, overall, the particles in a liquid move quickly enough to overcome the forces holding them together. A liquid needs energy from heating to make its particles move quickly enough. This is why a substance can only boil when it is at its boiling point.

⬆ Water particles in sweat take heat energy from your skin. They use this energy to evaporate. This is why sweating cools you down.

➡ Liquid nitrogen takes in energy from the surroundings. The temperature increases to its boiling point. Bubbles form throughout the liquid nitrogen. It boils and changes to the gas state.

Explaining boiling points

The boiling point of a substance depends on the strength of the forces between the particles in the liquid state. The stronger the forces, the more energy is needed to separate the particles, and the higher the boiling point.

Explaining melting

When a substance is in its solid state, strong forces hold the particles in a pattern. Energy is needed to overcome these forces to make the solid melt.

Your hand can supply enough energy to melt a small piece of gallium metal or an ice cube. Much more energy is needed to melt a small piece of copper.

⬆ Melting copper.

The melting point of a substance depends on the strength of the forces that hold the particles in a pattern. The stronger these forces, the more energy is needed to make the solid melt, and the higher the melting point.

Explaining freezing

Obi investigates how stearic acid cools. He pours hot liquid stearic acid into a test tube and lets it cool. He records the temperature every minute. His results are in the table.

Obi plots his data on a graph, and draws a smooth curve.

Time (min)	Temperature (°C)
0	96
1	77
2	70
3	70
4	70
5	70
6	70
7	66
8	63
9	61
10	58

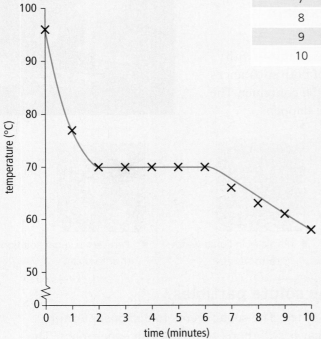

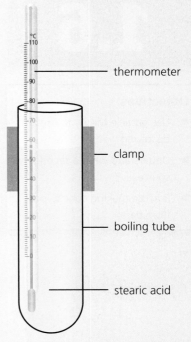

↑ Apparatus to investigate cooling.

The graph shows that stearic acid freezes at 70 °C. At this temperature, the particles transfer energy to the surroundings. They stop moving around from place to place, and arrange themselves in a pattern.

↑ The liquid water in food freezes in a freezer. The water does not freeze instantly. It takes time for energy to leave the water, and for the water particles to arrange themselves in a pattern.

Q

1 Describe how the strength of the forces between particles change when a liquid becomes a gas.

2 Describe and explain what happens to the particles when a liquid evaporates.

3 The boiling point of copper is 2595 °C. The boiling point of gold is 2970 °C. Predict which substance has stronger forces between the particles in the liquid state. Explain your answer.

- Boiling and melting need energy.
- Energy leaves a substance when it freezes.

Using particle theory to explain dissolving

Objectives

- Use particle theory to explain dissolving
- Understand what a secondary source is
- Practise making conclusions from data

Making a solution

Kasarna makes coffee. She pours hot water over coffee powder, then she adds sugar and stirs. The sugar and coffee powder **dissolve**. Kasarna has made a **solution**. Water is the **solvent**. Sugar and the substances from the coffee powder are **solutes**.

Using particles to explain dissolving

When a substance dissolves, it mixes with the solvent. The particles of both substances are randomly arranged in the container. The diagrams below show what happens.

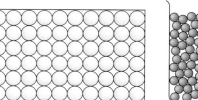 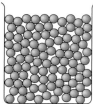 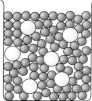

⬆ Particles in solid sugar (not to scale). ⬆ Particles in liquid water (not to scale). ⬆ Particles in sugar solution (not to scale).

What happens to the solute particles?

Amun adds sugar to a cup of tea. The sugar seems to disappear. Amun wants to check that the sugar is still there, so he does an experiment. The experiment involves:

1. Finding the mass of a glass of water.
2. Weighing out 10 g of sugar.
3. Adding the sugar to the water, with stirring.
4. Finding the mass of the solution.

The mass of the solution is the same as the masses of the water and sugar added together. The sugar particles have not disappeared!

How much solute can dissolve in a solvent?

Sunanda likes sweet tea. One day, for an experiment, she puts 60 spoons of sugar in a glass of tea and stirs the mixture. Some sugar stays in the bottom. It doesn't dissolve. Sunanda has made a **saturated solution**.

There is a limit to the mass of a substance that dissolves in 100 g of water. This is the **solubility** of the substance. Every substance has a different solubility. The greater the mass of a substance that will dissolve in water, the more **soluble** the substance.

Collecting information from secondary sources

Sunanda wants to compare the solubility of different substances. She cannot do an experiment to measure solubilities, since she does not have a balance to measure mass.

Sunanda collects data from a chemistry data book. The book is a **secondary source**. Secondary sources provide evidence that you have not collected by doing an investigation yourself. They include books, scientific journals, and the Internet. If another student gives you evidence from his investigation, the student is a secondary source.

You can trust some secondary sources more than others. **Scientific journals** are collections of papers written by scientists, which describe their work. Other scientists check the papers carefully. This means that evidence from scientific journals is usually trustworthy. You can also trust evidence in data books and text books. However the quality of evidence from the Internet varies.

Making conclusions from data

Sunanda uses her data to draw a bar chart. The bar chart shows the masses of different substances that dissolve in 100 g of water.

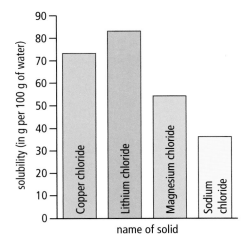

Practise making conclusions from bar charts by answering question 4.

1 Define these words: dissolve, solution, solvent, solute, solubility.

2 Describe how to do an experiment to show that when you dissolve salt in water the salt is still there.

3 Suggest how to do an experiment to find the solubility of salt.

4 Use the bar chart above to identify:

a The most soluble substance shown on the bar chart.

b The least soluble substance shown on the bar chart.

c The solubility of copper chloride.

- A solution is a mixture of solute and solvent particles.

- Solubility is the mass of a solid that dissolves in 100 g of water.

- Secondary sources give evidence collected by others.

Planning an investigation

Suggesting ideas to test

Zahra notices that she can dissolve more sugar in hot tea than in cold tea. She wonders if this is true for other solids, such as sodium carbonate.

She decides to investigate the question:

How does water temperature affect the mass of sodium carbonate that dissolves?

Making a prediction

Zahra knows that more sugar dissolves in hot tea than in cold tea. She does a quick experiment with sugar and water, instead of tea. She finds that more sugar dissolves in hot water than in cold water.

Zahra uses her scientific knowledge to make a **prediction**. She thinks that sodium carbonate might behave in the same way as sugar.

She predicts that:

As the temperature of water increases, the mass of sodium carbonate that dissolves will increase.

Considering variables

Zahra lists all the possible **variables** in her investigation. A variable is a quantity or characteristic that can change. Here is her list:

● *water temperature*
● *water volume*
● *mass of sodium carbonate that dissolves*
● *size of pieces of sodium carbonate*
● *speed of stirring*

Zahra makes decisions about the variables:

> *Variable to change – water temperature*
>
> *Variable to observe – mass of sodium carbonate that dissolves*

Zahra wants her investigation to be a **fair test**, so she must control the other variables. She will use the same volume of water for each test, and pieces of sodium carbonate of the same size. She will stir at the same speed.

Identifying evidence to collect

Zahra thinks about the evidence she will need to help her answer her question:

How does water temperature affect the mass of sodium carbonate that dissolves?

She decides to measure out 100 cm³ of water and cool it to 0 °C. She will add sodium carbonate, 1 g at a time, and stir the mixture until no more dissolves. She will repeat this procedure at different temperatures.

Choosing and using apparatus

Zahra needs to choose suitable apparatus for her investigation.

Zahra could use a **measuring cylinder** or a **beaker** to measure the volume of water. She chooses a measuring cylinder because it measures smaller differences in volume.

Zahra has a choice of two **thermometers**. The clinical thermometer measures temperatures between 35 °C and 42 °C. Zahra wants to measure over a wider range of temperatures, so she chooses a thermometer with a measurement range of 0 °C to 110 °C.

Zahra's school has two instruments to measure mass. She can use the **balance** with balance weights, to measure mass changes as small as 1 g. The balance works without electricity. The **electric balance** measures smaller differences in mass. Zahra decides to use the balance with balance weights since her electricity supply is unreliable.

Zahra uses a **Bunsen burner** to heat the water, and a **stirring rod** to stir the mixtures.

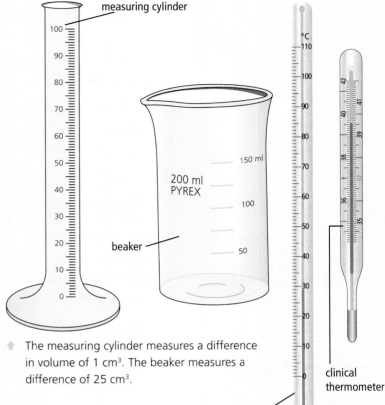

↟ The measuring cylinder measures a difference in volume of 1 cm³. The beaker measures a difference of 25 cm³.

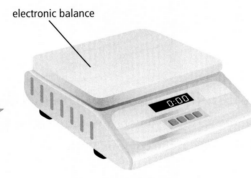

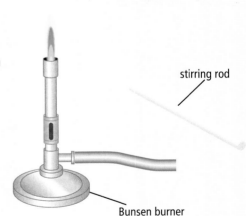

Making observations

Zahra uses her apparatus to find the mass of sodium carbonate that dissolves in water at five different temperatures. She makes measurements and observations. Her results are on the next page.

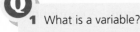

Q

1 What is a variable?

2 Explain why Zahra kept some variables constant in her investigation.

3 Suggest how Zahra could investigate the question: how does the speed of stirring affect the time for salt to dissolve in water? Include a list of variables and apparatus choices in your answer.

!

Planning an investigation involves:

● asking questions

● making predictions

● considering variables

● identifying evidence to collect

● choosing apparatus.

Presenting evidence

Presenting evidence in a table

Zahra is investigating the question:

How does water temperature affect the mass of sodium carbonate that dissolves?

She begins to collect evidence, and notes her observations and measurements on a scrap of paper.

At 0 °C 7 g of solid dissolved when I stirred it, and at 10 °C about 12 g dissolved.

Zahra knows she will need to look for patterns in her evidence. She decides to organise the data in a table. If the data are organised, it will be easier to spot patterns.

Water temperature (°C)	Mass of sodium carbonate that dissolves (g)
0	7
10	12
20	22
30	39
40	49

When you draw tables:

- write the variable you change in the left column
- write the variable you observe or measure in the right column
- include units in the column headings.

Bar chart or line graph?

Zahra looks carefully at the data in the table. She notices that, as the water temperature increases, so does the mass of sodium carbonate that dissolves. Her prediction is correct.

Zahra decides to examine the pattern more closely. She wants to draw a bar chart or line graph. But which is more suitable?

- Draw a bar chart when the variable you change is **discrete**. A discrete variable is a variable whose values are words, or whose values can have only certain numerical values.
- Draw a line graph when the variable you change is **continuous**. A continuous variable can have any value.

The variable Zahra changes – temperature – is continuous. It can have any value. A line graph will show changes in the mass that dissolves as temperature increases.

Drawing a line graph

Zahra plots her data on a graph.

When you draw a line graph:

- label the *x*-axis with the name and units of the variable you change
- label the *y*-axis with the name and units of the variable you observe
- choose a scale for each axis
- write values on the lines on the *x*-axis – use evenly spaced numbers
- write values on the lines on the *y*-axis – use evenly spaced numbers.

Then draw a line of best fit to show the pattern. The line of best fit can be a curve or a straight line. Zahra decides to draw a straight line on her graph.

Choosing scales

To choose scales for the axes on a line graph:

1. Find the difference between the biggest *y*-value and the smallest *y*-value. This is the **range**.
2. Divide the range by the number of squares on the *y*-axis.
3. Round up your answer to choose the interval that each square represents.
4. Repeat steps 1–3 for the *x*-axis.

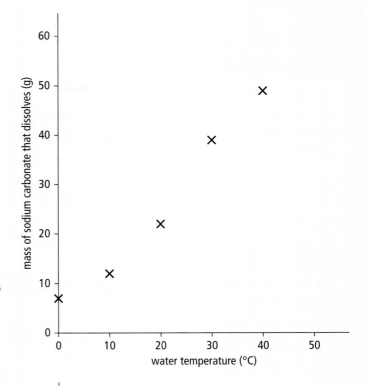

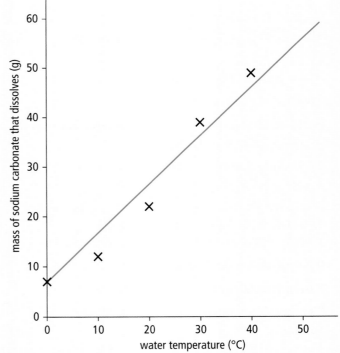

1 What is a discrete variable?

2 Explain why Zahra recorded her results in a table.

3 Explain why Zahra decided to present her results in a line graph, not a bar chart.

4 Another student collected boiling point data for 10 different substances. Should he display his results in a line graph or a bar chart? Explain your answer.

- Use tables to organise data as you collect it.
- Draw a bar chart if the variable you change is discrete.
- Draw a line graph if the variable you change is continuous.

1 The diagram shows the particles in solid water (ice) and in liquid water.

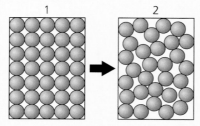

   a Describe how the particles move in the solid. [1]

   b Describe one difference in the arrangement of the particles in ice and in liquid water. [1]

2 In the diagram below, each arrow represents a change of state.

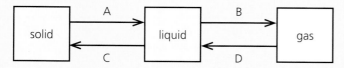

   a Which arrow represents freezing? [1]

   b Which arrow represents condensing? [1]

   c Give the name of the change of state represented by arrow A. [1]

3 Oxygen is a gas at 20 °C.

   a Describe the arrangement and behaviour of the particles in the gas. [3]

   b Use ideas about particles to explain why oxygen gas can be compressed. [1]

4 A student heats a piece of solid metal. The metal remains solid. Why does it get bigger?
   Choose the correct answer from the list below.

   The particles get bigger.

   The particles get further apart.

   The particles move around from place to place. [1]

5 Complete the sentences using words from the list. You may use them once, more than once, or not at all.

   increases   decreases   stays the same

   a When liquid water boils, the distance between the particles _____. [1]

   b When liquid water boils, the strength of the attractive forces between the particles _____. [1]

   c When steam condenses, the speed of movement of the particles _____. [1]

6 Write the letter of each label next to the correct line on the diagram.

   A Water in the liquid state.

   B Water in the gas state (steam).

   C Mixture of air and steam.

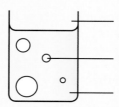

   [3]

7 The table gives the melting points and boiling points for five substances.

Substance	Melting point (°C)	Boiling point (°C)
bromine	−7.2	59
chlorine	−101.5	−35
iodine	113.6	184.4
krypton	−157.2	−152.3
osmium	3000	5000

   a Name the substance in the table with the lowest melting point. [1]

   b Name the substance in the table with the lowest boiling point. [1]

   c Name two substances in the table that are gases at 20 °C. [1]

   d Name two substances in the table that are solids at 20 °C. [1]

   e Complete the sentence using words from the list. You may use them once, more than once, or not at all.

   solid   liquid   gas

   When bromine is heated from 20 °C to 100 °C it changes from a _____ to a _____. [1]

   f Name the change of state that occurs when osmium is heated from 4000 °C to 6000 °C. [1]

8 The diagram shows the melting point and the boiling point of silver.

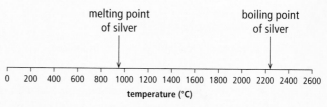

   a What is the state of silver at 2000 °C? [1]

   b Name the change of state that occurs when silver is heated from 0 °C to 1000 °C. [1]

9 Read the statements below about the particles in liquid water. All the statements are true.

   A The particles touch their neighbours.

   B The particles are not arranged in a regular pattern.

   C The particles move around, in and out of each other.

   a Write the letter of the one statement above which best explains why you can pour liquid water. [1]

   b Write the letter of the one statement above which best helps to explain why the volume of 1 g liquid water is similar to the volume of 1 g of solid water (ice). [1]

10 A student had some liquid salol. She allowed it to cool. Every minute, she measured the temperature of the salol. Her results are in the table below.

Time (min)	Temperature (°C)
0	70
1	56
2	42
3	42
4	42
5	30
6	20

   a Name the variable that the student changed. [1]

   b Name the variable that the student observed. [1]

   c Plot the points in the table on a graph, and draw a line of best fit. [3]

   d Use the graph to work out the freezing point of salol. [1]

   e Describe what happens to the movement and arrangement of the particles when liquid salol freezes. [1]

11 A student wrote down a question to investigate: *How does the temperature of water affect the mass of potassium chloride that will dissolve in it?*

   a The student listed some variables in the investigation:

   temperature of water
   volume of water
   mass of potassium chloride that dissolves
   amount of stirring

   i From the list above, identify the variable the student will change. [1]

   ii From the list above, identify the variable the student will observe. [1]

   iii From the list above, identify two variables the student will control. [1]

   b The student made a prediction:
   The hotter the water, the greater the mass of potassium chloride that will dissolve.
   He collected results and plotted a graph.

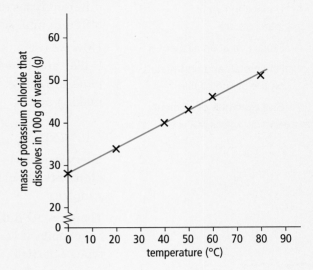

   Do the results on the graph agree with the prediction? Explain your answer. [1]

12 A student does an investigation to find the solubility of different substances in water. She writes down her results.

   > At 20 °C 36 g of sodium chloride dissolved in 100 g of water. For potassium chloride it was 34 g. Then I tested potassium nitrate, and 47 g dissolved in 100 g of water.

   a Write the missing column heading, and the results, in the table below. [2]

	mass of substance that dissolved in 100 g of water (g)

   b Draw a bar chart to show the results in the table. [3]

   c Explain why the results should be shown on a bar chart, and not on a line graph. [2]

   d Give the names of three pieces of apparatus the student might use to do the investigation. [2]

Introducing elements

What are things made of?

Look around you. Can you see anything made of wood, plastic, or cotton? Wood, plastic, and cotton are example of **materials**. Materials are the different types of matter that things are made of. There are millions of different materials. They do an amazing variety of things.

How we use a material depends on its **properties** – what the material is like, and how it behaves. For example, wood is stiff and strong, and it looks attractive. These properties mean that wood is a good material for making tables.

Elements

Every material – and everything in the Universe – is made from one or more **elements**. An element is a substance that cannot be split into anything simpler.

There are 92 different types of element found naturally on Earth. Scientists have made at least another 25 elements. Each element is made of its own type of particle, which is unique to that element. And every element has its own properties.

The periodic table

The **periodic table** lists all the elements, and groups together elements with similar properties.

The periodic table opposite shows a stepped line. The elements on the left of the line are **metals**. The elements on the right of the line are **non-metals**.

Q

1 What is an element?

2 Identify two types of element that are shown on the periodic table.

3 Use the periodic table to list six metal elements and six non-metal elements.

4 Suggest two properties of a typical metal.

- Materials are the different types of matter things are made of.

- Everything is made up of one or more elements.

- The elements are listed on the periodic table, with metals on the left of the stepped line and non-metals on the right.

Potassium is vital to life – it keeps your heart, kidneys, and nerves working. You cannot eat pure potassium, but foods like peanuts and bananas contain potassium joined to other elements.

Hydrogen is a colourless gas at 20 °C. It is the most common element in the Universe.

All living things contain carbon – including you!

Nitrogen is a non-metal. It is the most common element in the Earth's atmosphere.

Helium is the second most common element in the Universe.

Hydrogen																	Helium
Lithium	Beryllium											Boron	Carbon	Nitrogen	Oxygen	Fluorine	Neon
Sodium	Magnesium											Aluminium	Silicon	Phosphorus	Sulfur	Chlorine	Argon
Potassium	Calcium	Scandium	Titanium	Vanadium	Chromium	Manganese	Iron	Cobalt	Nickel	Copper	Zinc	Gallium	Germanium	Arsenic	Selenium	Bromine	Krypton
Rubidium	Strontium	Yttrium	Zirconium	Niobium	Molybdenum	Technetium	Ruthenium	Rhodium	Palladium	Silver	Cadmium	Indium	Tin	Antimony	Tellurium	Iodine	Xenon
Caesium	Barium	Lanthanum	Hafnium	Tantalum	Tungsten	Rhenium	Osmium	Iridium	Platinum	Gold	Mercury	Thallium	Lead	Bismuth	Polonium	Astatine	Radon
Francium	Radium	Actinium	Rutherfordium	Dubnium	Seaborgium	Bohrium	Hassium	Meitnerium	Darmstadtium								

The periodic table of the elements. Some elements have been omitted.

Most of the metal objects that we use contain the element iron. Worldwide, more iron is produced than any other element.

Silver makes attractive jewellery.

Copper is a metal. It is an excellent conductor of electricity.

Mercury is a metal. It is the only metal that is liquid at room temperature (20 °C).

Oxygen and silicon are the two most common elements in the Earth's crust (the outer layer of the Earth). These elements are often found joined to each other or other elements.

Metal elements

Metal elements

Do you use a phone? Travel by bus or bicycle? Wear jewellery? All of these contain metals. About three-quarters of the 92 elements that are found naturally on Earth are metals.

Metals have similar physical properties to each other. Their properties make them useful.

Physical properties of metals

State and appearance

Most metals have high melting and boiling points. All metals, except mercury, are in the solid state at 20 °C.

All metals are shiny when you first cut them, or if you rub them with sandpaper. After a while most metals go dull on the outside, but gold and platinum are always shiny – that's why they make such good jewellery.

Sonority

When you hit a metal it makes a ringing sound. Scientists say that metals are **sonorous**.

Conduction of heat and electricity

Metals are good conductors of heat and electricity. This means that heat and electricity travel through metals easily.

Some metals conduct electricity better than others – the best are copper and silver. The best conductors of heat are copper and gold.

⬆ Metals are sonorous, so they are used to make bells.

Other properties

Most metals are **strong**. Big forces are needed to break or squash them.

Many metals are **hard**. It is not easy to scratch them.

Most metals have a high **density**. They feel heavy for their size.

Thin metal sheets are bendy. So when a car crashes its metal body doesn't break into lots of little pieces – it just bends.

⬆ The metal in this car bent when it crashed.

Metals are also:

● **malleable** – they can be hammered into shape without cracking.

● **ductile** – they can be pulled out to make wires.

Using metals

Metal elements do not have exactly the same properties as each other. The properties of a particular metal explain how we use it. Read on to learn about the properties and uses of two important metals.

Gold

Gold is a shiny, yellow metal. It is malleable and ductile, and stays shiny in air and water. These properties mean that gold makes excellent jewellery and coins.

Today, gold is also used to make electrical connectors in audio equipment such as speakers. It is also used in printed circuit boards. Gold is perfect for this job because it conducts electricity well and it is not damaged by air.

⬆ Skilled craftspeople made this jewellery in Egypt 3500 years ago.

⬆ Mansa Musa, a king in Mali, traded gold in the 1300s.

Iron

Iron is a shiny, grey metal. Worldwide, we use more iron than any other metal. Iron is the main metal in ships, cars, and tools. Iron is used because, when mixed with small amounts of other elements, it is strong and malleable. It is also cheap compared to other metals.

⬆ Gold jewellery is still valued.

⬆ Shipping containers are mainly iron.

⬆ Iron usually goes rusty, but this iron pillar has stood in Delhi, India, for 1500 years. The climate prevents rust forming.

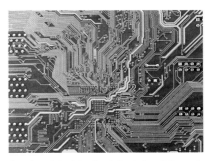

⬆ A gold-plated printed circuit board.

Q

1 List six physical properties of a typical metal.

2 Platinum is a typical metal. Identify two properties of platinum which mean it makes good jewellery.

3 Suggest two metal properties that explain why they are used for making buses.

- Most metals are shiny and sonorous.
- Metals are good conductors of heat and electricity.
- A typical metal is strong, hard, malleable, ductile, and has a high density.

Non-metal elements

The elements of life

Only about twenty elements are not metals, but they are very important.

Every living thing is made mostly from non-metal elements, joined together to make substances with particular physical properties. Your muscles are mainly made of carbon, hydrogen, oxygen, nitrogen, and sulfur. The picture shows the elements that make up the body of a 50 kg person.

The non-metal elements are shown on the right of the stepped line on the periodic table (see p. 27).

32.5 kg oxygen

9 kg carbon

5 kg hydrogen

1.5 kg nitrogen

1.5 kg metals

0.5 kg phosphorus

Physical properties of non-metals

The properties of a typical non-metal are different from the properties of a typical metal.

Boiling and melting points

Compared to metals, most non-metals have low melting and boiling points. This means that some non-metal elements exist as gases at 20 °C.

⬆ This balloon is filled with helium gas.

⬆ Neon gas makes these signs glow brightly.

⬆ Hospitals use oxygen gas to help treat patients.

Solid non-metal elements

A few non-metals – like sulfur, carbon, and phosphorus – exist as solids at 20 °C. Most are not shiny. They are usually **brittle,** which means that they break easily if you hit them with a hammer. You cannot bend solid non-metals. Most non-metals do not conduct electricity.

⬆ Sulfur is a typical non-metal. As a solid, it is dull, brittle, and does not conduct electricity.

⬆ There are three types of phosphorus. White phosphorus quickly catches fire in air, and is a deadly poison. Phosphorus fire bombs were used in World War II.

Carbon

Carbon is a very special non-metal. There are several types of solid carbon. In each type of carbon the particles have a different arrangement. This means that each type of carbon has its own physical properties.

↑ This drill has a hard diamond tip.

↑ The softness of graphite makes it useful for pencils.

Diamond

The pattern of particles in one form of carbon, diamond, forms beautiful crystals. The crystals are incredibly hard – diamond drills and cutting tools cut through almost anything. Like most non-metals, diamond does not conduct electricity.

Graphite

In another form of carbon, graphite, the particles are arranged in layers. This makes graphite soft, like most other non-metals. But graphite is unlike other non-metals in one way – it is a good conductor of electricity.

Metalloids

Computers and cell phones rely on microchips. These are electronic circuits made with tiny pieces of the element silicon. Silicon is a **semiconductor**. It conducts electricity less well than metals, but better than non-metals.

Silicon exists as a shiny, grey solid at 20 °C. It is not bendy, but brittle – it smashes easily if you hit it with a hammer. Its brittleness makes it more like a non-metal than a metal. But silicon conducts electricity, which is what metals do. Scientists classify silicon as a **metalloid** or **semi-metal**.

There are other elements with properties similar to silicon, including germanium, boron, arsenic, and antimony. They are all metalloids, and are close to the stepped line on the periodic table.

1 List three physical properties of a typical non-metal element.

2 Explain what makes sulfur a typical non-metal.

3 Extension: Draw a table to compare the physical properties of two forms of carbon: diamond and graphite.

- Most non-metals have low boiling and melting points.
- Some non-metals exist as gases at 20 °C.
- Most non-metals are brittle and dull when in the solid state.

Making conclusions from data

Making conclusions from data in tables

Comparing how well metals conduct heat

Catherine is investigating the question:

Which of the metals aluminium, copper, iron, and zinc is the best conductor of heat?

She sets up the apparatus below. The size of each rod is the same. She measures the time for the pin to fall off each metal rod.

Catherine collects the data in Table A below.

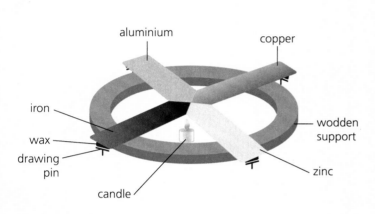

Metal	Time from start of heating until pin drops off (s)
aluminium	18
copper	10
iron	39
zinc	35

⬆ Table A. Catherine's results.

She examines the data in the table. She notices that the pin on the copper rod dropped off most quickly. Heat must have travelled along the copper rod more quickly than along the other rods.

Catherine makes a conclusion:

Of the four metals tested, copper was the best conductor of heat.

Metal or non-metal?

Ketan collects data from a text book to test his friend Darshan on the differences between metal and non-metal elements. The data is in Table B below.

Element	Appearance	Does the element conduct electricity?	Melting point (°C)	Boiling point (°C)
W	shiny grey	yes	3410	5930
X	orange-brown	no	−7	59
Y	shiny silver-coloured	yes	−39	357
Z	shiny silver-coloured	yes	1890	2482

⬆ Table B. Properties of elements.

Darshan looks at the data for element W. The element is shiny and it conducts electricity. The melting point and boiling point data show that element W is in the solid state at room temperature.

Darshan makes a conclusion:

Element W has the properties of a typical metal, so element W is a metal.

Observations that do not fit a pattern

Bar charts

Peni collects data from the Internet on the melting point of different metals. She wants to identify metals that have melting points that are not typical of metals.

Peni examines the data on the bar chart. She notices that two metals have melting points that are much lower than those of the other metals.

Peni makes a conclusion:

Lithium and sodium have melting points that are lower than those of the other metals on the bar chart.

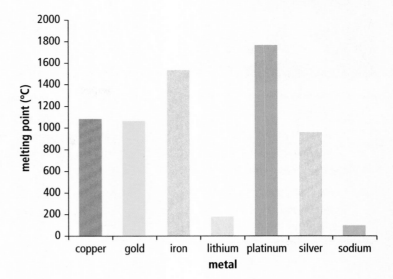

Line graphs

Grace investigates a metal spring. She hangs weights on the spring. She measures the **extension** of the spring (its increase in length) when she hangs different weights from it. Grace plots her results and draws a line of best fit.

Grace examines the graph, and notices that one result does not fit the pattern. She decides to measure the extension at this weight again, to see if she might have made a mistake in her investigation.

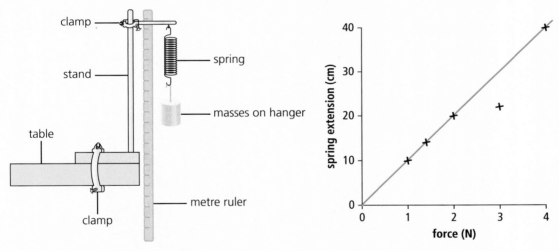

Grace repeats the test for the weight that gave the odd result. The value for extension is higher than before. It now fits the pattern. Grace decides she must have made a mistake the first time she did this test, and decides not to use the data she collected at first.

Q

1 Use the data in Table A to identify the metal in the table that is the least good conductor of heat.

2 Use the data in Table B to decide whether elements X, Y, and Z are metals or non-metals. Give reasons for your decisions.

3 Describe the pattern shown on the line graph above.

4 Write a second conclusion for the data on the bar chart that is different from the one written by Peni at the top of the page.

- You can make conclusions from results presented in different ways.
- If a result does not fit the pattern, repeat the test to see if you have made a mistake.

Metal alloys

What is an alloy?

Aeroplanes are mainly metal. The lighter an aeroplane, the less fuel it needs. So engineers chose low density metals for aeroplane bodies.

Most aeroplane bodies contain lots of aluminium, but they are not made of pure aluminium. The pure metal is too weak. Aluminium mixed with small amounts of other metals, such as zinc, copper, or magnesium, is stronger.

A mixture of metals is an **alloy**. Some alloys also include a non-metal element. Many alloys are harder or stronger than the elements that are in them.

Material	Composition	Density (g/cm³)	Relative hardness	Strength when pulled (MPa)
Pure aluminium	100% aluminium	2.7	23	8
Aluminium alloy 7075	90% aluminium 6% zinc 2% magnesium 1% copper 1% other metals	2.8	150	572

⬆ Table A. Properties of aluminium and an aluminium alloy.

Scientists investigate different mixtures to make alloys with perfect properties for particular uses.

Steel – a vital alloy

Steel makes many things – from stunning structures to tiny components.

There are many types of steel. Steels are alloys of iron. Pure iron is very soft and bendy, so it is not very useful. In steel, iron is mixed with small amounts of a non-metal, carbon, and sometimes other metals. The other elements change the properties of iron and make it more useful.

⬆ The cables of the New Aswan Bridge, Egypt, are made from steel.

⬆ Steel and wood jewellery from Bali, Indonesia.

Name of alloy	Other elements	Properties	Uses
low carbon steel	carbon	strong easily shaped	bridges, buildings, ships, vehicles
manganese steel	manganese carbon	hard tough	mining equipment, railway points
stainless steel	chromium nickel carbon	does not rust	knives and forks, surgical instruments

⬆ Table B. Alloys of iron.

Explaining alloy properties

In a pure metal, the particles are arranged in layers. The diagram shows part of the particle arrangement in pure iron. The layers of particles slide over each other easily. This means that pure iron is soft and weak.

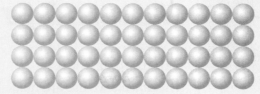
⬆ Particles in iron.

Particles of iron and the other elements in steel have different sizes. In steel, particles of the other elements get between the iron particles. The layers of iron particles can no longer slide over each other easily. This makes steel harder and stronger than pure iron.

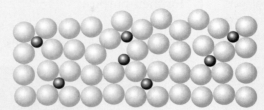
⬆ Particles in steel.

Bronze

Bronze is an alloy of copper and tin. It was first used about six thousand years ago to make tools and weapons. Bronze is harder and more durable than stone, which was used before.

Modern motors with bronze bearings do not need oiling. This is because bronze has low friction with other metals.

Seven hundred years ago people of the kingdom of Benin (now in Nigeria) made bronze sculptures.

People from Himachal Pradesh, India, made the bronze bowl below about 2000 years ago.

⬆ Bronze head made in the kingdom of Benin, 16ᵗʰ century.

⬆ Indian bronze bowl from 2000 years ago.

 Q

1 Explain what an alloy is.

2 Use Table A to compare the properties of pure aluminium and an aluminium alloy.

3 Use Table B to describe how the uses of three iron alloys are related to their properties.

4 Use words and diagrams to explain why iron has different properties from its alloys.

 !

- Most alloys are mixtures of metals.
- Alloys have different properties from their elements, making them more useful.

Material properties

Fit for purpose

The objects we use are made from many different materials, including wood, glass, and polythene. The materials chosen to make an object must be suitable for their purpose.

For example, a desk must be stiff and strong. Its surface must be hard. Wood has these physical properties. It makes excellent tables.

⬆ This water container is made from clay. A small amount of water is absorbed by the container. This evaporates from the surface, which helps to keep the water inside the container cool.

⬆ This woman is wearing clothes made from cotton. Cotton fabric is soft and flexible. Water and air can pass through its small holes, helping to keep the wearer cool.

⬆ The nurse is wearing gloves made from rubber. Rubber is flexible and waterproof. It has no holes. Water, blood, and germs cannot pass through it.

⬆ Sisal is strong when pulled. It makes useful ropes.

⬆ Most windows are made from glass. Glass is transparent, so you can see through it. Unfortunately glass is also brittle – it breaks easily.

⬆ This bottle is made from plastic. The plastic is flexible, transparent, and tough.

Material properties

Scientists consider many physical properties when choosing materials for particular purposes. They choose materials which are suitable for their purpose and which are not too expensive.

Strength

Scientists ask questions about strength:

- With what size force can you pull a material before it breaks?
- What size force will squash the material?

Stiffness, flexibility, and brittleness

A stiff material is one that is difficult to bend. A thick piece of wood is stiff.

Flexible materials bend easily. Thin pieces of aluminium are flexible, so are thin pieces of wood from some tree species.

A **brittle** material breaks easily when you bend or hit it. Glass is brittle.

↑ This fence is made from flexible willow wood.

Hardness

You can scratch a soft material, such as leather, with your fingernail. Diamond is a very hard material. You cannot scratch it – even with a steel knife. This means that diamonds in jewellery cannot be damaged by scratching.

↑ Diamonds are hard and cannot be damaged by scratching.

Conducting heat

Metals like copper and aluminium are good conductors of heat. They are used to transfer heat away from processing units in computers, to stop them overheating.

Materials that do not allow heat to pass through them are heat insulators. Wool and fur are good heat insulators.

↑ Copper heat sinks stop computers overheating.

↑ Fur prevents this yak from losing too much heat.

Conducting electricity

Electricity passes easily through good conductors of electricity, such as copper and aluminium. These materials are used for electric cables.

Electricity cannot pass through plastics. Plastics are insulators.

Water absorption

A waterproof material, such as polythene, does not allow water through it. A substance is absorbent if it has tiny holes that water can seep into.

Q
1 Explain why cotton is a suitable material for making clothes.
2 Identify a material used to make rope, and explain why it is suitable for this purpose.
3 Suggest the physical properties a material for making a football needs to have.

- The physical properties of a material determine its uses.

Polymers

Plastics everywhere

Look around you. How many things are made of plastics? Imagine life without plastics. Your great-great-grandparents probably did live without most of them – plastics only started to be widely used in the 1930s.

↑ These buckets, baskets, and trays are all made from plastics.

Most of the materials we call plastics are made from polymers. **Polymers** are substances that have very long particles.

Inside poly(ethene)

Poly(ethene), also known as polythene, is an important polymer. Its physical properties make it useful. It is strong, tough, and waterproof. It is an electrical insulator. Poly(ethene) can be flexible, too.

Poly(ethene) particles are very long. They are made by joining up particles of two elements – carbon and hydrogen.

The long particles explain the physical properties of poly(ethene):

- It is strong because it is difficult to break up its particles.
- It is flexible because its particles can slide over each other easily.

More polymers

There are thousands of polymers, each with their own properties and uses.

Poly(propene)

Poly(propene) is strong. It is not damaged by high temperatures. It is flexible, and you can bend it many times without it breaking. This means that poly(propene) is useful for making many things, including:

- ropes
- underground water pipes
- hinges for flip-top bottles.

↑ The properties of poly(ethene) make it perfect for bags and bottles.

↑ Poly(propene) rope.

↑ A flip-top plastic bottle.

Poly(chloroethene)

Poly(chloroethene) is better known as poly(vinyl chloride) or PVC. It is another polymer with useful physical properties. PVC is flexible and waterproof. It does not conduct electricity.

PVC is used to make:

- underground water pipes
- the insulation on electric cables
- waterproof clothes.

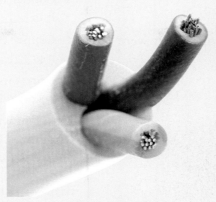

↑ PVC is an electrical insulator.　↑ PVC is waterproof.

Natural polymers

Poly(ethene), poly(propene), and PVC are **synthetic polymers**. They are made by people and machines in factories and science laboratories.

We also use **natural polymers**. Fibres like cotton, silk, and wool are made up of polymers. So is wood. Natural polymers are made by plants and animals.

↑ Cotton plants produce cotton fibre.

↑ Silk worms produce silk.

Q

1　Explain what a polymer is.

2　Name six polymers.

3　Explain why poly(ethene) is strong.

4　Give three uses of PVC, and explain why its properties make it suitable for these uses.

- The physical properties of a polymer determine its uses.

1 The photograph shows some gold coins. They were made about 800 years ago in India.

The list gives some physical properties of gold.
It is a good conductor of electricity.
It melts at 1063 °C.
It is always shiny.
It is a good conductor of heat.
It is yellow.

a Which one of the properties in the list best shows that gold is solid at 20 °C? [1]

b Identify two properties in the list that are typical of all metals. [1]

c Which one of the properties in the list best explains why gold was used to make coins? [1]

d Which two of the properties in the list best explain why gold is used to make connectors in some electrical devices? [1]

2 The table shows the physical properties of four elements. Each element is represented by a letter.

Element	Appearance at 25 °C	Does it conduct electricity?	Melting point (°C)
A	green	no	−101
B	shiny silver-coloured	yes	961
C	shiny grey	yes	1535
D	dull yellow	no	113

a Give the letter of the element in the table that has the highest melting point. [1]

b Give the letters of the elements in the table that are non-metals. Explain your choices. [1]

3 Copy and complete the following sentences using words from the list. You may use them once, more than once, or not at all.

a good conductor of heat　　　　　**strong**
a good conductor of electricity　　　**sonorous**

a Aluminium is used to make cooking pans because it is _____. [1]

b Copper is used in the cable of a lamp because it is _____. [1]

c Copper can be used to make bells because it is _____. [1]

d Iron is used to make cars because it is _____. [1]

4 A student wants to compare the strength of four substances. She sets up the apparatus below. She adds weights until the wires break.

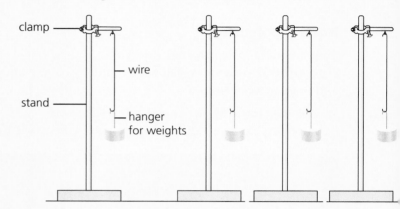

clamp — wire
stand — hanger for weights

a Identify the variable the student changes. [1]

b Suggest two variables the student should control to make the test fair. [2]

c The student's results are in the table.

Substance	Mass at which wire broke (kg)
copper	11
tungsten	8
stainless steel	5
aluminium alloy	3

i Which substance makes the strongest wires? [1]

ii Display the results on a bar chart. [3]

5 The list gives some properties materials can have.

waterproof	**flexible**	**low density**
transparent	**rusts easily**	**strong**
brittle	**absorbent**	

a Which two physical properties in the list make glass suitable for windows? [2]

b Which two physical properties in the list make rubber suitable for nurses' gloves? [2]

c Which three physical properties in the list make plastics such as poly(propene) suitable for making buckets? [3]

d Which two physical properties in the list make iron suitable for making buckets? [2]

e Which one property in the list is vital for a material used to make a baby's nappy? [1]

6 The table shows the physical properties of two materials that are used to make ropes. Manila fibre is obtained from a plant. Poly(propene) is made from substances obtained from oil.

Material	Durability	Breaking strength for 10 mm rope (N)	Flexibility
manila fibre	rots slowly	5400	very flexible
poly-(propene)	does not rot	10 800	very flexible

a Identify two advantages of poly(propene) ropes compared to manila ropes. [2]

b Suggest one advantage of making ropes from manila. [1]

c The graph below shows how the strengths of manila and poly(propene) ropes change as rope diameter increases.

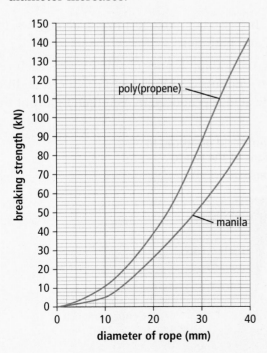

i Use the graph to find the strength of manila rope of diameter 30 mm. [1]

ii Use the graph to predict the diameter of poly(propene) rope that has a strength of 120 kN. [1]

iii Use the graph to describe how the strength of manila rope changes as its diameter increases. [1]

iv Use the graph to work out which is stronger – 30 mm manila rope or 20 mm poly(propene) rope. [1]

7 The table gives data about three materials that can be used to build houses.

Material	Strength when compressed (MPa)	Conductivity of heat (W/mK)
limestone	60	1.3
concrete	60	1.7
wood	15	0.1

a Which of the materials in the table is the weakest when compressed? [1]

b Which of the materials in the table is the best conductor of heat? [1]

c A person wants to build a house which will feel cool inside. He chooses to build his house from wood. Explain why. [1]

d Use the data in the table to suggest one advantage of building a house from limestone compared to wood. [1]

8 The bar chart below compares how well different metals conduct electricity.

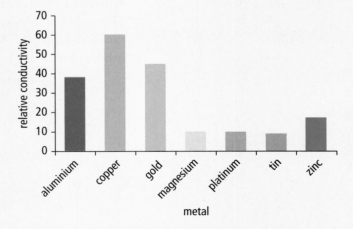

a Explain why the data is presented in a bar chart, not in a line graph. [1]

b List the metals in the bar chart in order of increasing conductivity (lowest conductivity first). [2]

Acids and alkalis

Objectives

- Give examples of acids and alkalis
- Compare the properties of acids and alkalis
- Make conclusions from data

⬆ Vinegar preserves fruit and vegetables in pickles.

Everyday acids

Lemons, limes, and vinegar taste sour. Why? They all contain **acids**.

Acids are vital to life. Hydrochloric acid in your stomach helps digest food. Ascorbic acid – vitamin C – in fruit keeps your skin healthy and helps to make bones. You need omega-3 fatty acids from oily fish or soya beans to help defend your body against disease.

Acids have other uses. Vinegar is a solution of ethanoic acid in water. It is used to preserve fruit and vegetables in pickles. Fizzy drinks contain acids to flavour and preserve them.

Natural acids can also be a nuisance. Methanoic acid helps to make bee and ant stings painful. Acids make sweat smelly, too.

Laboratory acids

At school you might use sulfuric acid, hydrochloric acid, and nitric acid. These acids are **corrosive**, even when mixed with lots of water. This means they destroy living tissue, so they will burn your skin and eyes.

You must wear eye protection when using acids in the lab and make sure they do not get on your skin.

⬆ This symbol shows that a chemical is corrosive. Wear eye protection and take care not to get the chemical on your skin.

Making conclusions from data in charts

Sulfuric acid is very important. It is used to make fertilizers, detergents, dyes, medicines, insecticides, paints, and batteries.

Worldwide, factories make over 180 million tonnes of sulfuric acid each year. This pie chart shows the relative amounts of sulfuric acid produced in different areas of the world. More sulfuric acid is produced in Asia than in any of the other areas.

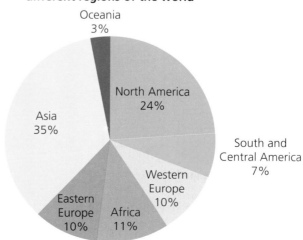

Percentage of sulfuric acid produced in different regions of the world

Oceania 3%
North America 24%
South and Central America 7%
Western Europe 10%
Africa 11%
Eastern Europe 10%
Asia 35%

Alkalis

Alkalis are the chemical opposite of acids. They often feel soapy, although you should never touch an alkali unless you have been told it is safe to do so. Toothpaste and washing powder make alkaline solutions when mixed with water. Seawater is also slightly alkaline.

Sodium hydroxide solution is an important alkali. It is used to make paper and detergents. It also used to produce aluminium metal.

Many alkaline solutions are extremely corrosive. A small splash of sodium hydroxide on your skin gives a nasty blister. If sodium hydroxide gets in your eye, it may cause blindness. You must always wear eye protection when using alkalis or acids in the lab.

⬆ Sodium hydroxide is an important alkali.

 Some cleaning fluids contain alkaline substances.

Discovering acids and alkalis

Jabir Ibn Hayyan was an important scientist. He worked in the area now known as Iraq around 1200 years ago.

Jabir Ibn Hayyan discovered how to make sulfuric acid, nitric acid, and hydrochloric acid. He was probably the first person to use the word 'alkali'. Jabir wrote more than 100 books about his findings, which scientists found useful for hundreds of years.

⬆ Jabir Ibn Hayyan

Q
1 Name six acids.
2 Give one hazard of using sodium hydroxide, and state how to reduce the risks from this hazard.
3 Give one property that is typical of acids, and one property that is typical of alkalis.
4 Use data from the pie chart opposite to answer this question:
  a Name the area that produces the least sulfuric acid.
  b Give the total percentage of sulfuric acid produced in Africa, Asia, and South and Central America.

- Acids include sulfuric acid, hydrochloric acid, and nitric acid.
- Alkalis include sodium hydroxide.
- Acids and alkalis have many uses.
- Acids and alkalis can be corrosive.

The pH scale and indicators

The pH scale

The pH scale shows how acidic or alkaline a solution is:

- The pH of an acid is less than 7. The lower the pH, the more acidic the solution.
- The pH of an alkali is more than 7. The higher the pH, the more alkaline the solution.
- Some solutions are neither acidic nor alkaline. They are neutral. Their pH is 7. Pure water has a pH of 7.

Using indicators

Litmus indicator shows whether a solution is acidic or alkaline. You can use it as a solution, or soaked into paper.

You can use **Universal Indicator** to find the pH of a solution. When you add it to a solution it changes to one of the colours on the pH scale shown below. The colour shows the pH of the solution.

⬆ Litmus indicator is red in acidic solution and blue in alkaline solution.

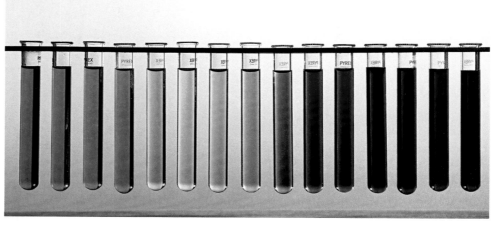

⬆ The colours of Universal Indicator solution from pH 0 (left) to pH 14 (right).

Choosing and using apparatus

Some plants, like hibiscus flowers and red cabbage, contain chemicals that change colour when they are added to solutions of different pH. This means you can make your own indicators.

Making an indicator

Femi makes a hibiscus flower indicator at home. She adds hibiscus flowers to warm water in a cooking pot. She then pours the mixture through a colander and collects the solution in a glass.

Adamma makes a hibiscus flower indicator in a science laboratory. She adds hibiscus flowers to water in a beaker and heats the mixture with a Bunsen burner. She pours the mixture through filter paper and collects the solution in a conical flask.

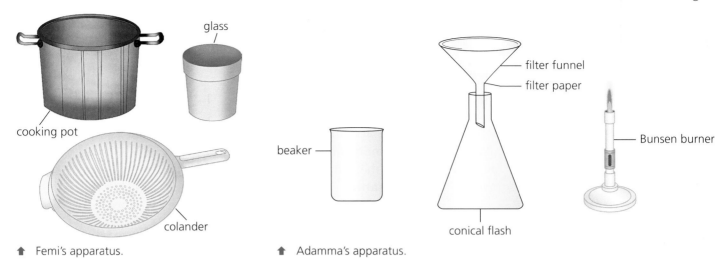

↑ Femi's apparatus.   ↑ Adamma's apparatus.

Both Femi and Adamma have chosen suitable apparatus, since both made a usable indicator.

Testing the indicator

Femi placed some acid on a green plate and added hibiscus indicator. She repeated the test with an alkali instead of the acid. She wrote down the colours she saw.

Adamma poured some acid into a test tube and added hibiscus indicator. She repeated the test with an alkali. She wrote down the colours she saw.

In this part of the experiment, Femi's apparatus was not suitable. She could not see the colours properly on the green plate. Adamma made a better choice of apparatus.

Concentrated or dilute?

The lorry is carrying ethanoic acid. The acid could give you terrible burns. But ethanoic acid in vinegar is safe to eat in pickles and chutneys. What's the difference?

In vinegar, ethanoic acid is mixed with a large amount of water. This is a **dilute** solution. But the ethanoic acid in the lorry is mixed with very little water, so it is a **concentrated** solution.

Concentrated acids and alkalis are more corrosive than dilute ones.

Q

1 Give the colours of litmus indicator in acidic and alkaline solutions.

2 A solution has a pH of 8. Is it acidic or alkaline?

3 Which is more acidic, a solution of pH 6 or a solution of pH 4?

4 Look at the section above on *Testing the indicator*. Suggest some apparatus that Femi could use at home to test her indicator. Explain why Adamma's apparatus is better than a green plate.

!

- An acid has a pH of less than 7.
- An alkali has a pH of more than 7.
- A neutral solution has a pH of 7.
- The colour of Universal Indicator can be used to estimate the pH of a solution.

Neutralisation

⬆ Bee stings are acidic.

Neutralisation

A bee stings Sudi. It hurts! Sudi rubs toothpaste on the sting. It feels a bit better. Toothpaste is alkaline. The alkali cancels out – **neutralises** – some of the acid in the sting. This process is **neutralisation**.

Neutralisation in the laboratory

You can do neutralisation reactions in the laboratory. Hasina has 100 cm³ of hydrochloric acid. She wants to find the volume of sodium hydroxide solution needed to neutralise the acid.

⬆ The Universal Indicator is red. This shows that the solution is acidic.

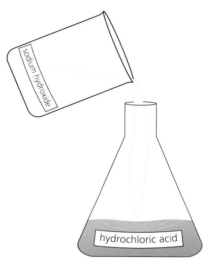

⬆ The Universal Indicator is orange. This shows that the pH of the solution has increased. The sodium hydroxide has neutralised some of the hydrochloric acid.

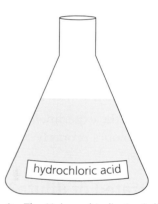

⬆ The Universal Indicator is light green. This shows that the pH of the solution is 7. The solution is neutral. The sodium hydroxide has neutralised all the hydrochloric acid.

To neutralise an acid you need to add the correct volume of alkali. The volume depends on how dilute or concentrated the solutions are.

Using neutralisation reactions

Soil pH

Some soils are more acidic or alkaline than others. Every plant has its favourite soil pH. Carrots grow well in soil of pH 6.0. Tea grows best in soil of pH 4.0 to 5.5. Date palms prefer pH 6.5 to 8.0.

The table shows the preferred soil pH of some vegetables.

Vegetable	Preferred soil pH
cabbage	6.0–7.0
onion	6.0–6.5
maize	5.5–7.0
sweet potato	5.0–6.0
tomato	5.5–6.8

Zainab takes some soil from her garden. She mixes it with pure water. She adds Universal Indicator. The indicator shows that the soil is acidic – its pH is 5.0. The soil is suitable for sweet potatoes.

Zainab also wants to grow cabbage and onions. But they grow best on soils of higher pH. Zainab adds an alkali to the soil in one part of the garden. This neutralises some of the acid. The soil pH increases. Zainab can now grow cabbage and onions.

⬆ Sweet potatoes grow best in soil of pH 5.0 – 6.0.

Acid rain

Scientists were worried about the Taj Mahal in India. The magnificent marble monument was being damaged by **acid rain**. Local factories polluted the air with acidic gases. The gases dissolved in rainwater, making the rain acidic.

⬆ Acid rain damaged the Taj Mahal.

The government has taken action. Now, nearby factories must neutralise any acidic gases they produce, or move away.

In the last century gases from burning coal in Europe made acid rain. The acidic rain fell over Europe and ran into rivers and lakes. Rivers and lakes became more acidic. Some animal and plant species could not survive.

Substances were added to lakes to neutralise the extra acid. Some power stations stopped releasing acidic gases into the air. By 2000 the water pH in many lakes had returned to normal.

Q

1 Explain what neutralisation is.

2 Ola has a solution of pH 9. Should he add acid or alkali to neutralise the solution?

3 Use the table on the opposite page to help you answer this question. Cabar measures the soil pH on her farm. Its pH is 8.0. Cabar wants to grow onions. What type of substance should she add to the soil so that its pH is suitable for growing onions?

- Neutralisation is the 'cancelling out' of an acid by an alkali, or of an alkali by an acid.
- Neutralisation changes soil pH.
- Acid rain damages some buildings and harms plants and animals that live in lakes.

Planning investigations and collecting evidence

Neutralisation

Kali has stomach ache. He takes an indigestion tablet. The tablet contains a substance that neutralises the extra acid in his stomach. Kali feels better.

Kali saw three different types of indigestion tablet in the pharmacy. He wants to find out which type of tablet is best. He decides to investigate.

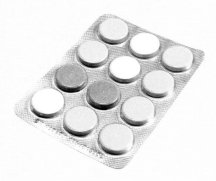

Read on to find out how Kali plans his investigation.

Suggesting ideas to test

Kali thinks of possible questions to investigate:

● *Which type of tablet is best?*

● *Which type of tablet causes the greatest increase in pH when added to stomach acid?*

● *Which type of tablet neutralises the most acid?*

Kali decides to answer the second question. He does not make a prediction since he has no scientific evidence to base it on.

Choosing variables

Kali identifies the variables in his investigation. He decides which to change, observe, and control.

● *Variable to change – type of tablet.*

● *Variable to observe and measure – pH change of stomach acid when I add a tablet to it.*

● *Variables to control to make the test fair:*

  ▶ *type of acid to represent stomach acid*

  ▶ *volume of acid*

  ▶ *how concentrated or dilute the acid is.*

Collecting evidence

Kali chooses hydrochloric acid to represent stomach acid. He uses a measuring cylinder to measure equal volumes of acid for the three tests. A measuring cylinder measures smaller differences in volume than a beaker.

Kali pours the acid into a conical flask. He adds Universal Indicator. He uses a colour chart to find the acid pH.

Next, Kali adds a tablet to the acid. He measures the pH of the mixture, and records his results in a table.

Finally, Kali repeats the procedure for the other two types of tablet.

Considering evidence

Kali records his data.

Type of tablet	pH before adding tablet	pH after adding tablet	Change in pH
A	1	4	3
B	1	1	0
C	1	5	4

Kali looks at his results and thinks about his question. He writes a conclusion which includes a scientific explanation:

Tablet C caused the greatest increase in pH. This means that tablet C neutralised the most acid.

Observations that do not fit a pattern

Kali was surprised the pH did not change when he added tablet B to the acid. He thought he might have made a mistake. He repeated the test for tablet B three more times. His results are in the table.

Tablet B test number	pH before adding tablet	pH after adding tablet	Change in pH
1	1	1	0
2	1	4	3
3	1	4	3
4	1	4	3

Kali noticed that the result for test 1 was different from the others. He decided to ignore this result.

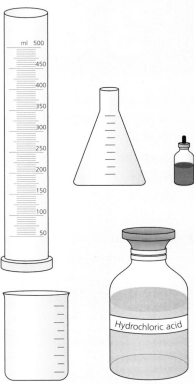

↑ Apparatus for measuring the pH change when an indigestion tablet is added to an acid.

1 Explain why Kali kept some variables constant in his investigation.

2 Why did Kali use a measuring cylinder to measure out equal volumes of acid, and not a beaker?

3 Suggest why Kali chose to answer the second question in the section *Suggesting ideas to test*.

- Planning an investigation can involve asking questions, considering variables, and choosing apparatus.
- If a result does not fit the pattern, repeat the test.

1 Copy and complete the sentences using phrases from the list. You may use them once, more than once, or not at all.

more than   **equal to**   **less than**

The pH of an acid is _____ 7. The pH of an alkali is _____ 7. The pH of a neutral solution is _____7.   [3]

2 a Copy and complete the table to show whether each mixture is acidic, alkaline, or neutral.

Mixture	pH	Acidic, alkaline, or neutral?
orange juice	3	
cola drink	2	
sweat	5	
indigestion medicine	9	

[4]

b Name one substance in the table above that could be used to neutralise orange juice.   [1]

c Name one substance in the table that could be used to neutralise the indigestion medicine.   [1]

3 This question is about litmus indicator.

a Copy and complete the table below.

Type of solution	Colour of litmus indicator
acidic	
alkaline	

[2]

b A student has 100 cm³ of an acid. She adds a few drops of litmus indicator. The student then adds 500 cm³ of an alkaline solution of the same concentration as the acid. Describe the colour changes he would observe.   [2]

4 Read the information in the box. Then answer the questions below.

> Your blood is slightly alkaline. Its pH is always 7.4. You would be very ill if your blood pH was higher than 7.6 or lower than 7.2.
>
> The pH of your urine changes to help adjust blood pH:
>
> ~ If your blood gets too acidic, extra acid comes out in your urine. You urine pH gets lower.
>
> ~ If your blood gets too alkaline, extra alkali comes out in your urine. You urine pH gets higher.

a Explain why your urine pH gets lower when your blood is too acidic.   [1]

b What happens to your urine pH if your blood is too alkaline? Explain why.   [1]

c A hospital patient has a blood pH of 7.5. Explain how her body tried to get the blood pH back to normal.   [1]

5 The table gives the preferred soil pH of some plants.

Plant	Preferred soil pH
pineapple	4.5 to 5.5
banana	5.5 to 6.5
sugar cane	5.5 to 6.5
maize	5.5 to 7.0
cassava	4.5 to 7.5

a Name the one crop in the table that can grow well in a slightly alkaline soil.   [1]

b A farmer tests the soil pH on her farm. Its pH is 5.0. Suggest two crops she could try growing.   [2]

c A farmer knows her soil is acidic, but does not know the soil pH. Suggest one crop she could try growing.   [1]

d The soil pH on another farm is 7.0.

   i Suggest two crops that might grow well on this soil.   [2]

   ii The farmer on this farm wants to grow bananas. What type of substance should he add to his soil?   [1]

6 A student wants to make an indicator from red cabbage. The apparatus available to the student is listed and pictured below.

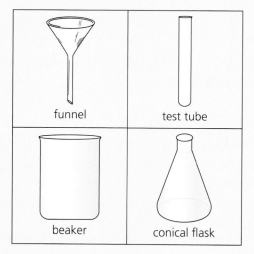

funnel   test tube

beaker   conical flask

a The student first heats a mixture of pure water and chopped cabbage. Name the best apparatus in which to do this. [1]

b Next the student filters the mixture. She wants to keep the solution. Name the best two pieces of apparatus for this stage. [2]

c The student adds her indicator to small amounts of acid and alkali to observe its colours in the two solutions. Name the best apparatus in which to do this. [1]

7 Table A shows the pH that some animals can live in. The animals can only survive at pH that are shaded grey. Table B shows how the pH of two lakes changed over time.

Table A

Animal	Water pH the animal can live in							
	4.0	4.5	5.0	5.5	6.0	6.5	7.0	7.5
trout								
salmon								
eel								
frog								
snail								
mayfly								

Table B

Name of lake	pH of lake water			
	1960	1970	1990	2001
Lake X	-	-	5.0	6.0
Lake Y	6.0	4.5	-	-

a What was the pH of Lake Y in 1960? [1]

b What happened to the acidity of Lake Y between 1960 and 1970? [1]

c Name two animals that might have lived in Lake Y in 1960. [2]

d Name one animal that might have lived in Lake Y in 1970. [1]

e A biologist found a large number of snails in Lake Y in 2010. Suggest what might have happened to the lake pH to make this possible. [1]

f i A biologist found no mayflies in Lake X in 1990. Suggest one possible reason for this. [1]

ii The biologist looked for mayflies in Lake X in 2001. Do you think she found any? Explain your answer. [1]

8 A student investigates the question below:
How does the volume of acid needed to neutralise an alkali depend on the concentration of the alkali?
The concentration of a solution is the mass of substance dissolved in 1 litre of the solution.
The student writes down what she plans to do.
~ Take 50 cm³ of alkaline solution.
~ Add Universal Indicator.
~ Add acid until the indicator shows the solution is neutral.
~ Write down the volume of acid used.
~ Repeat with alkaline solution of different concentrations.

a The student uses a measuring cylinder, not a beaker, to measure the volume of acid added. Suggest why. [1]

b Copy and complete the table. Use the phrases below.

volume of acid	concentration of acid
concentration of alkali	volume of alkali
type of indicator	

Variable to change	
Variable to observe	
Control variables	1. 2. 3.
[5]

c The student's results are in the table below.

Concentration of alkali (g/dm³)	Volume of acid (cm³)
0.1	10
0.2	20
0.3	30
0.4	50
0.5	50

i Plot the results on a graph. [3]

ii Draw a line of best fit. [1]

iii Draw a circle around the one odd result on your graph. [1]

The structure of the Earth

The ground beneath your feet

Imagine you could dig a hole more than 6000 km deep, to the centre of the Earth. What would you find?

Scientists have been curious about the structure of the Earth for many years. They made observations and collected data, and thought carefully about them. They created **scientific models** to explain their observations.

A scientific model is an idea that explains observations. It can be used to make predictions.

Objectives

■ Describe a model for the Earth's structure

■ Explain how we know about the Earth's structure

Early models of the structure of the Earth

Flat Earth model

For many years, people thought the Earth was flat. They based this idea on their observations.

Gradually, observations made people think that the flat Earth model might be wrong. Sailors noticed that ships appear to sink as they go over the horizon.

Aristotle lived more than 2000 years ago. He saw that the shadow of the Earth on the Moon is round. These observations led to a new model of the Earth, as a sphere.

⬆ Observations from space give further evidence that the Earth is a sphere.

⬆ Ships appear to sink as they go over the horizon.

The hollow Earth model

About 300 years ago Edmond Halley suggested a new model of the Earth. He said the Earth consisted of three hollow shells separated by air. Halley created his model to explain some unusual compass readings.

The modern model of the structure of the Earth

Scientists used many observations and data to create the modern model of the structure of the Earth.

The model states that the Earth is made up of several layers:

● a solid **crust** made of different types of rock

● the **mantle**, which goes down almost halfway to the centre of the Earth. It is solid but can flow very slowly.

● the liquid **outer core**, made up mainly of iron and nickel

● the solid **inner core**, also mainly iron and nickel.

crust

mantle

outer core

inner core

⬆ The modern model for the structure of the Earth.

How do we know about the structure of the Earth?

Observations and data from many scientists have contributed to our understanding of the Earth. Scientists studied rocks on the surface and under oceans. They examined rocks brought to the surface by volcanoes.

Shock waves from earthquakes also provided evidence. In the 1930s Inge Lehmann examined shock wave patterns. She couldn't explain them using the model of the time – that the Earth's core was the same all the way through. She created a new model – that the core consists of two parts. Inge Lehmann had discovered the solid inner core.

Hotter and hotter

Temperatures increase from crust to core. The core, 6000 km below the surface, is very hot. It may be hotter than the surface of the Sun.

Some of the deepest mines in the world are in South Africa. They are nearly 4 km deep. At these depths the rock temperature is about 60 °C. The air is cooled so that miners can do their work.

⬆ Inge Lehmann discovered the inner core.

⬆ Deep South African gold mines are very hot.

Q

1 Name the layers of the Earth, starting from the inside.
2 Identify two pieces of evidence that suggest the Earth is spherical.
3 Outline the evidence suggesting that the Earth has a solid inner core.

- The Earth consists of the crust, mantle, outer core, and inner core.
- Temperature increases from the crust towards the core.

Igneous rock

Objectives

- Describe the properties of igneous rocks
- Give examples of igneous rocks
- Explain how igneous rocks formed
- Link igneous rock properties to their uses

The Earth's crust

Think about the things you've used today. Where did they all come from? The answer is the Earth's crust, the air, and the oceans.

The Earth's crust is made up of different types of rock. We use some types of rock just as they are. We extract metals from other rock types. We process some rock types to make cement and other building materials.

Grouping rocks

The pictures show three types of rock. They have very different properties.

↑ Basalt, an igneous rock.

↑ Limestone, a sedimentary rock.

↑ Marble, a metamorphic rock.

There are many different types of rock. Scientists classify rocks into three groups:

- igneous rocks
- sedimentary rocks
- metamorphic rocks.

Igneous rocks

What do the structures below have in common?

↑ The Giant's Causeway in Northern Ireland was formed from basalt.

↑ The Pakistan Monument in Islamabad, completed in 2007.

↑ This statue of an Egyptian queen, Hatshepsut, is 3500 years old.

Both structures are made from **granite**. Granite is an example of an **igneous rock**. Igneous rocks are made when **magma** (liquid rock) cools and solidifies.

Granite consists of interlocking **crystals**, strongly joined together. The crystals are quite big – you can see them easily. Each crystal is made of one substance.

Another igneous rock is **basalt**, which makes up much of the seabed.

Properties of igneous rocks

Igneous rocks are hard and durable. The rocks that originally surrounded these granite boulders on Belitung Island have been worn away, but the granite remains.

Most igneous rocks are also **non-porous** – water does not soak into them. This is because there are no gaps between their interlocking crystals.

Using igneous rocks

The properties of igneous rocks explain their uses.

⬆ Granite boulders on Belitung Island, Indonesia.

⬆ Basalt is hard and durable. It is used as railway ballast.

⬆ This sculpture is made from an igneous rock called gabbro. It is hard, durable, and attractive.

⬆ Quartz consists of a single mineral, silicon dioxide.

Minerals

Substances that exist naturally as crystals are called **minerals**. Most rocks are a mixture of minerals. Minerals also occur on their own.

Explaining crystal size

Basalt forms when runny liquid rock pours out of volcanoes and cools quickly, often under the sea. As the liquid cools, crystals grow as the particles arrange themselves in patterns. When all the particles are arranged in crystals, there is no liquid rock left. It has all become solid basalt.

Basalt's crystals are tiny. You need a magnifying glass to see them. The crystals are small because the liquid rock cooled and solidified in just a few weeks.

Granite forms when liquid rock cools underground. The cooling takes longer, so its particles have more time to arrange themselves. The crystals grow bigger.

⬆ Granite is a mixture of minerals. This sample includes quartz (grey crystals), calcium feldspar (white crystals), biotite (black crystals), and potassium feldspar (pink crystals).

Q

1 Describe the properties of a typical igneous rock.
2 What is a mineral?
3 Explain why you can often see different colours in a lump of granite.
4 Basalt has smaller crystals than granite. Explain why.

- There are three types of rock: igneous, sedimentary, and metamorphic.
- Igneous rocks are hard, durable, and non-porous.
- Igneous rocks formed from liquid rocks.
- Rocks that cooled quickly have small crystals.

Sedimentary rocks

Sedimentary rock properties

Limestone is a typical sedimentary rock. Sedimentary rocks are less hard than most igneous rocks. This means it is easier to scratch them.

Most sedimentary rocks are **porous**. You can find out if a rock is porous by dropping water onto it. If the water soaks in, the rock is porous. If the water does not soak in, the rock is non-porous.

The structure of a sedimentary rock explains its properties. They are made of **grains**. The grains are held together less strongly than the crystals in igneous rocks. There are small spaces between the grains. Gases (like air) or liquids (like water) fill the spaces.

Identifying sedimentary rocks

You can identify sedimentary rocks by doing these tests:

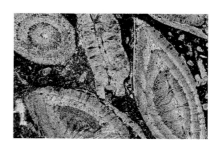

- Look at the rock through a hand lens or magnifying glass. Sedimentary rocks have separate grains with spaces between them.

- Place a few drops of water on the rock. Sedimentary rocks are porous, so the water will soak in.

- Place the rock in a beaker of water. If you see bubbles, the rock must include air spaces. It is probably a sedimentary rock.

- Try scratching the rock. If you can scratch it with your fingernail or an iron nail it is quite soft. It is likely to be a sedimentary rock.

⬆ India Gate, in New Delhi, India, is made of granite and sandstone.

Different sedimentary rocks

Different types of sediment make different types of rock. Each rock type has its own properties and uses.

Sandstone

Sandstone is a hard sedimentary rock. This means it makes a good building material. Its medium-sized grains are made of the mineral quartz. Other minerals cement the grains together.

Claystone and mudstone

Claystone and mudstone have tiny grains. They were squashed together by the weight of the layers above them.

It is easy to mould wet clay into different shapes. Bricks and pottery are moulded from wet clay. They are then fired to make them hard.

⬆ Brick making in Rwanda.

Limestone

Limestone is a useful building material. It was made from the remains of living things. Billions of dead shellfish piled up on the seabed. Their shells and skeletons broke into small pieces. Over millions of years, the sediments stuck together to form limestone. The process is still happening in the sea around the islands of the Bahamas.

⬆ Limestone often contains fossils.

⬆ Cement is made from limestone.

Making sedimentary rocks – an introduction

It takes millions of year to make sedimentary rocks. The process happens in stages. The diagram below summarises these stages.

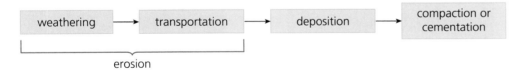

Q

1 Name three sedimentary rocks.

2 Explain why claystone is used to make bricks, and why sandstone is used to make buildings.

3 Sundara has a rock. Suggest how she could find out if the rock is a sedimentary one.

4 Describe two properties of sedimentary rocks. Explain why sedimentary rocks have one of these properties.

!

- Use a hand lens and water to identify sedimentary rocks.
- Sandstone, claystone, mudstone, and limestone are sedimentary rocks.
- Rock uses are linked to their properties.

Sedimentary rock formation

Weathering

Weathering breaks up all types of rock into smaller pieces, called **sediments**. Sediments can be huge boulders or tiny pieces of clay. The sediments may end up in new sedimentary rocks, or they may end up as part of the soil.

There are three types of weathering: physical, chemical, and biological.

Physical weathering

Physical weathering is caused by the effects of changing temperature on rocks. It makes rocks break apart.

One type of physical weathering is freeze-thaw weathering. It happens when water gets into rock cracks:

● On cold nights, water freezes to form ice.

● As the water freezes, it expands.

● The ice pushes against the sides of the crack. The crack gets bigger.

● This happens again and again. The rock breaks.

Water freezes in a crack in the rock.

Months later

CRASH!

↑ Freeze-thaw weathering.

↑ This limestone carving was made about 1000 years ago at El Tajin, Mexico. Acid rain is breaking up its surface by chemical weathering.

Chemical weathering

When rainwater falls on some rocks minerals, new substances are formed. This is **chemical weathering**. Chemical weathering happens more in acidic rain.

Biological weathering

Plants and animals break up rocks in many ways. For example:

- Tree roots grow through rock cracks to find water. As the tree grows, its roots gradually break the rock.
- Lichens make chemicals which break down rocks so that the lichens can get the nutrients they need.

⬆ Tree roots break up rocks as they grow.

Transportation

Weathering breaks up rock into smaller sediments. These sediments are moved away from their original rock by **transportation**.

Transportation can happen by gravity, or by wind, water, or ice.

⬆ Water carries pebbles along the river bed.

⬆ The wind carries sand grains from place to place.

⬆ Gravity moves sediments in rock falls and landslides.

The processes of weathering and transportation together make up **erosion**. Erosion is different from weathering:

- Weathering is the breakdown of rock into sediments.
- In erosion, a rock is broken into sediments, *and* the sediments are moved away.

New rocks are formed!

Eventually sediments stop moving away from their original rock. They settle in layers. This is **deposition**.

Then the sediments form new rocks. This happens by one of two processes:

- In **compaction** the weight of the layers above squash the sediments together tightly. The sediments are the grains of the new rock.
- In **cementation** new minerals stick the sediments together.

⬆ Sediments were laid down in layers to form this sedimentary rock.

 Q

1 Describe two ways that a grain of rock could be transported from one place to another.

2 Explain what is meant by *weathering*.

3 **Extension:** Describe three ways in which weathering occurs.

!

- Weathering breaks up all types of rock to make sediments.
- Sediments can be transported by gravity, wind, water, or ice.
- New rocks are formed when sediments settle and are squashed together, or stuck together by new minerals.

Metamorphic rocks

The same but different

Objectives

- Explain how metamorphic rocks are made
- Identify metamorphic rocks
- Give examples of metamorphic rocks

Skilled craftspeople carved these beautiful sculptures from natural rock. The rocks of the two sculptures look and feel very different.

⬆ This sculpture is made from limestone.

⬆ This sculpture is made from marble.

Both types of rock are mainly one mineral – calcite. The table shows the properties of the two rocks.

Rock	Colour	Texture
Limestone	White, grey, or cream.	Surface often rough. Tiny rounded grains. Gaps between the grains. Fossils often visible.
Marble	Usually white. Often has whirling streaks or spots of brown, red, blue, or yellow.	Surface usually smooth. Interlocking, evenly sized crystals. No gaps. No fossils.

Marble from limestone

Conditions are hostile beneath your feet. Just 15 km below the Earth's surface the temperature is 400 °C. The pressure at that depth is 4000 times greater than the surface pressure.

In some places, hot magma comes close to the surface. It heats up the rocks around it. The heat makes rocks change.

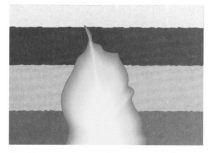

⬆ Hot magma makes surrounding rocks change.

When limestone gets hot, its atoms arrange themselves in a new pattern. This makes big crystals which interlock tightly. A new rock has been made – its name is marble.

Both marble and limestone consist mainly of one mineral – calcite. White marble is pure calcite. Coloured marble has tiny amounts of other minerals mixed with the calcite.

Metamorphic rocks

Marble is a **metamorphic rock**. Metamorphic rocks form when heat, or high pressure, or both, change igneous or sedimentary rocks. The rocks remain solid during the process. They do not get hot enough to melt. The changes happen in the Earth's crust.

All igneous and sedimentary rocks can be changed into metamorphic rocks. So there are many different metamorphic rocks.

Recognising metamorphic rocks

Metamorphic rocks are made up of crystals. This means that:

- metamorphic rocks are not porous
- you cannot see separate grains when you look at the rock through a hand lens.

Metamorphic rocks often look squashed or stripy. Some types are made up of thin layers.

More examples of metamorphic rocks

Slate splits into smooth flat sheets. This means it makes good roofing tiles.

⬆ Slate is made up of layers.

⬆ This fossil formed in mudstone. Its shape changed when high pressures converted the mudstone into slate.

Slate was formed from mudstone. Mudstone is a sedimentary rock. It is a mixture of minerals. High pressures underground squash mudstone. Water is squeezed out. New crystals form and arrange themselves in layers. If the mudstone contains fossils, so will the slate, but they will be squashed out of shape.

Gneiss is another metamorphic rock. It is hard, and often stripy. It is made up of big, interlocking crystals. It was formed at high temperatures and pressures deep within the Earth's crust.

⬆ A piece of gneiss.

Q

1 Name three metamorphic rocks.

2 Explain how metamorphic rocks are formed.

3 Explain why metamorphic rocks are not porous.

4 Raj has a piece of rock. Suggest how he could find out whether it is sedimentary or metamorphic.

!

- Metamorphic rocks form when rocks are changed by high temperatures or pressures.
- Metamorphic rocks have interlocking crystals.
- Marble, slate, and gneiss are metamorphic rocks.

Questions, evidence, and explanations: the rock cycle

Objectives

- To understand why questions, evidence, and explanations are important in science

- To interpret the rock cycle

Asking questions

This picture shows some **geologists** at work. Geologists don't just collect rocks. They ask questions about the Earth. How was the Earth formed? What is it made from? How and why does it change?

Early evidence and explanations

For many years, people have wondered about this question:

What makes mountains?

Scientists worked hard to answer this question. They made careful observations. They thought about their evidence, and used it to create explanations. For example:

One thousand years ago Ibn Sina of Kazakhstan observed layers of rock in mountains.

He described his evidence:

We see that mountains appear to be piled up layer by layer.

Ibn Sina considered the evidence.

He wrote an explanation:

It is therefore likely that the clay from which mountains were formed was itself at one time arranged in layers. One layer was formed first and then at a different period a further layer was formed and piled upon the first, and so on.

Eight hundred years ago Chinese thinker Chu Hsi found fossilised seashells on a mountain top. He considered this evidence, and realised that the shellfish once lived in the sea.

He created an explanation:

Everything at the bottom came to be at the top.

⬆ Ibn Sina

Piecing together the evidence

Geologists continued to collect evidence about mountain making, and about how rocks are made. In the 1700s James Hutton thought about the evidence. Could he create an explanation to link it all together?

Eventually James Hutton came up with an explanation. He called it the **rock cycle**. The rock cycle explains how rocks change and are recycled into new rocks over millions of years. It also answers our original question:

What makes mountains?

The rock cycle

Erosion wears down mountains. The sediments make sedimentary rocks. Under the Earth's surface, high temperatures and pressures may turn sedimentary or igneous rocks into metamorphic rocks.

Some rocks sink deep under the surface. They get hot enough to melt and make magma. The magma is pushed upwards. Some of the magma cools and solidifies underground. Some magma comes out of volcanoes, and solidifies on the surface. Igneous rocks are made.

At any time, huge forces from inside the Earth may push rocks upwards to make mountains. This is called **uplift**. This means that any type of rock – sedimentary, igneous, or metamorphic – may end up on a mountain top.

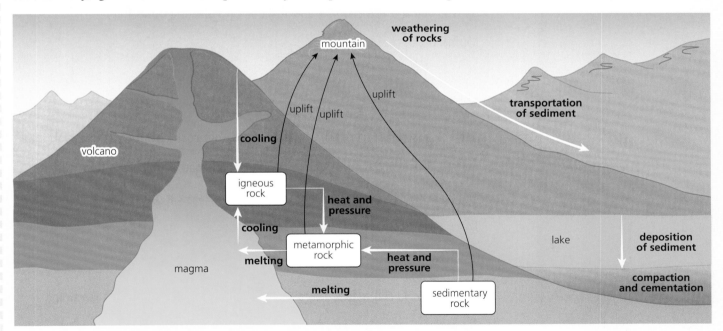

⬆ The rock cycle.

 Q

1 Outline how a scientist may develop an explanation.

2 Use the rock cycle to outline how mountains are made.

3 Use the rock cycle to describe one way in which matter is recycled in rocks.

 !

● To develop explanations, scientists ask questions, suggest ideas, and collect evidence.

● The rock cycle shows how matter is constantly recycled in rocks.

Using science to explain predictions: volcanoes

Eruption!

Pertiwi lives in Java, Indonesia. She writes a diary.

23 October 2010

There were more earthquakes today.

They say it's the volcano getting ready to erupt.

It's scary!

Mount Merapi, Indonesia, erupted in October 2010.

25 October 2010

My grandparents have been evacuated – now they are staying with us. The volcano has erupted and there is lava spewing down the southern slopes.

26 October 2010

The volcano refuses to rest. Showers of red-hot rock have been flung high into the sky. There are flames, smoke and poisonous gases, which are hotter than boiling water, erupting from the volcano. The gases can move faster than cars. There have been several deaths – it's a tragedy!

30 October 2010

The volcano is still active. There's black soot everywhere and sand is raining down. There was a massive fire ball. Thousands of people are travelling to safety, including us...

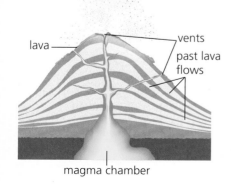

lava

vents

past lava flows

magma chamber

⬆ Inside a volcano.

What comes out of volcanoes?

The rock underneath a volcano is very hot. It melts to make **magma**. Magma collects under and inside volcanoes. It comes out of a volcano as liquid **lava**. Volcanoes also fling out solid materials (like volcanic 'bombs' and ash) and gases (including sulfur dioxide, carbon dioxide, and water vapour).

Explaining predictions

It's impossible to know exactly when – or how – a volcano will erupt. But vulcanologists work hard to predict what a volcano will do next. They tell people when to evacuate their homes and get out of the way.

Vulcanologists make observations and measurements. They look for patterns in their data. They use these patterns to help them make predictions. Vulcanologists support their predictions with scientific explanations.

    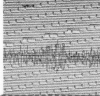

My tilt meter measures the steepness of the volcano slope. I predict that, when the steepness changes, the volcano is more likely to erupt.

I measure the amount of sulfur dioxide gas coming out of the volcano. I predict that, if the amount of sulfur dioxide increases suddenly, the volcano will erupt.

I monitor earth movements near the volcano. I predict that, if earth movements increase, the volcano will soon erupt.

Explanation:

Changes in the shape of a volcano show that magma is moving inside the volcano. Moving magma means an eruption is likely.

Explanation:

Magma contains dissolved sulfur dioxide gas. The gas escapes when magma rises to the surface. Extra sulfur dioxide shows that magma is near the surface. An eruption is likely.

Explanation:

Earth movements may be caused by magma pushing up against the surface rock. If magma is moving, an eruption is likely.

Benefits of volcanoes

Since 1500, volcanoes have killed around 200 000 people. But volcanoes are not all bad. Soils formed from volcanic rock are very fertile, so plants grow well. Water pumped underground gets very hot in volcanic areas. Steam from hot underground rocks generates electricity in many countries, including Indonesia and the Philippines.

1 State why vulcanologists make predictions about when a volcano will erupt.

2 Explain why scientists monitor earth movements around volcanoes.

3 Explain why extra gas coming out of a volcano is evidence that a volcano might soon erupt.

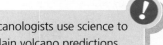

- Vulcanologists use science to explain volcano predictions.

Soil

Objectives

- List soil components
- Name soil types
- Describe soil properties

Vital soil

Soil is vital. It holds plant roots in place, and provides plants with essential nutrients. Without soil, there would be few plants. Without plants, there would be few animals.

What is soil?

Soil is a mixture. The pie chart shows its main components. Read on to find out more about these components.

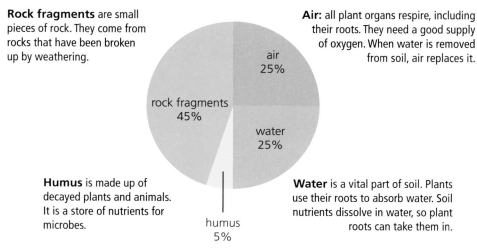

Rock fragments are small pieces of rock. They come from rocks that have been broken up by weathering.

Air: all plant organs respire, including their roots. They need a good supply of oxygen. When water is removed from soil, air replaces it.

Humus is made up of decayed plants and animals. It is a store of nutrients for microbes.

Water is a vital part of soil. Plants use their roots to absorb water. Soil nutrients dissolve in water, so plant roots can take them in.

⬆ The components of a typical soil.

Soil is also home to lots of living things, like earthworms, insects, and other small animals. These help with decay processes and change soil structure.

Soil types

Rock fragments in soil have different sizes. Their sizes help determine the properties of a soil, and how well plants grow in it.

Scientists have classified the size of rock fragments.

Name of rock fragment	Fragment diameter (mm)
small stones	more than 2.00
sand	0.05 – 2.00
silt	0.002 – 0.05
clay	less than 0.002

You can separate the different types of rock fragment by adding water to soil in a measuring cylinder. Shake, and leave to settle.

⬆ You can separate soil components by adding water to soil and shaking.

- humus
- water
- clay
- sand
- stones

The main types of soil are:

- **Clay soil** – At least 40% of the rock fragments are clay.
- **Sandy soil** – Most of the rock fragments are sand.
- **Loam** – The rock fragments in this soil are 40% sand, 40% silt, and 20% clay.

Soil properties

The properties of a soil determine how well things grow in it. You can compare several important soil properties in the laboratory – or outside.

Soil texture

To find out about the texture of a soil, rub it between your thumb and fingers.

- Sandy soil feels gritty.
- Dry silty soils feel floury.
- Clay soils feel sticky when wet and hard when dry.

Soil drainage

Water drains quickly through some soils, and slowly through others. You can use the apparatus on the right to test soil drainage.

Salama takes three soil samples of the same mass. She pours 100 cm³ water onto each sample. She measures the volume of water in the measuring cylinder after 30 minutes. Her results are in the table.

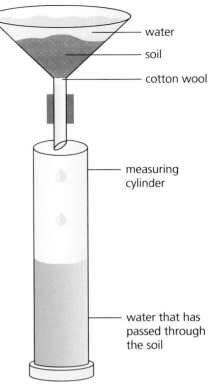

↑ Apparatus to test soil drainage.

Type of soil	Volume of water collected in 30 minutes (cm³)
clay	19
sand	91
loam	52

The results show that water drains most quickly through sandy soil. This means that, in sandy soil, water is available to plant roots for just a short time. Soluble nutrients leave the soil quickly.

Turn over to read more about testing soil properties.

1 Name the four main components of soil.
2 Describe how to separate soil components.
3 Describe and explain three differences between a sandy soil and a clay soil.
4 Predict which will drain more quickly – sandy soil or clay soil. Explain why.

- Soil is made up of rock fragments, humus, living things, air, and water.
- The main types of soil are clay, loam, and sand.
- You can test soils for texture and drainage.

More about soil

Soil water content

Different types of soil can hold different amounts of water in their **pores** (spaces between the solid matter). Sandy soil holds very little water. Clay soils hold more water. The table shows the percentage of soil that is water for three different soil samples.

Type of soil	Percentage of soil that is water when the smallest pores are filled with water and the biggest pores are filled with air and water
sand	7
loam	18
clay	23

Soil air content

The amount of air in a sample of soil depends on how wet the soil is. Soil pores can be filled with air or water. The more water in a soil, the less space there is for air.

Pavan and Badal take soil samples to school. They want to compare the amounts of air in the two soils. This is what they do:

- Place 100 cm³ soil in a measuring cylinder.
- Add water to the 200 cm³ mark.
- Stir until there are no more air bubbles leaving the soil.
- Read the new water level on the measuring cylinder.
- Calculate the volume of air in the soil. This is:
  the original water level (200 cm³) – new water level after stirring.

Measuring the volume of air in a soil sample.

The students' results are in the table below.

Soil sample	First reading of water level (cm³)	Final water level reading (cm³)	Volume of air in soil sample (cm³)
Pavan	200	190	10
Badal	200	170	30

Soil pH

Cassava grows in soils of pH 4 to 8.

Ayu and Dian are at the same school. Ayu's family grow cassava and sweet potatoes on their farm. They tried growing peanuts, but the crop was poor. Dian's family grow peanuts and soya beans.

Ayu and Dian ask a question:

Why do different crops grow well on the two farms?

The students wonder if soil pH is the reason. They collect evidence to test their idea.

Ayu and Dian each take a sample of soil. They shake it up with Universal Indicator in a test tube. They record their soil pH values.

Farm	Soil pH
Ayu	7.5
Dian	6.0

Ayu and Dian also collect evidence from secondary sources on the Internet. They find out the preferred soil pH for four crops.

Crop	Preferred soil pH
Cassava	4.5 to 7.5 (tolerates 4 to 8)
Sweet potatoes	5.5 to 6.5 (tolerates 4.5 to 7.5)
Peanuts	best is 6.0
Soya beans	best is 6.0

Ayu and Dian write an explanation to answer their question:

Soil pH explains why different crops grow well on our farms. Dian's crops grow well on soil of pH 6.0. Ayu's crops grow in soil of higher pH.

If Ayu's family want to grow peanuts or soya beans they will need to lower their soil pH by adding acid.

Soil colour

Soil colour provides evidence for the minerals in soil. Red soils may be rich in iron minerals. Humus-rich soils are black or dark brown.

⬆ Red soils are rich in iron minerals.

1 Name the element present in red soil minerals.

2 Describe how to measure the amount of air in a soil sample.

3 A third student measured soil air content, like Pavan and Badal. The first water level reading was 200 cm³. The final water level reading was 180 cm³. Calculate the volume of air in the soil.

- You can measure soil air content, and pH.
- Different crops grow best in soils of different pH.

4.10 Fossils

Objectives

- State what a fossil is
- Describe how fossils form
- Give examples showing what we can learn from the fossil record

Learning from fossils

The pictures show three **fossils**. What can fossils tell us about our human past? The history of life on Earth? The origin of the Earth itself? Read on to find out.

What are fossils, and how are they made?

Fossils are the remains or traces of a plant or animal that lived many years ago. They have been preserved by natural processes. Usually only the hard parts of living things are fossilised.

Fossils form very rarely. Normally a dead animal is eaten, or it rots away. But occasionally one is buried quickly by sand or mud – perhaps on a river bed or under the sea. Here the dead body is safe from animals that might eat it.

A fossil may then form. This can happen in several ways. The pictures below show one method of fossil formation.

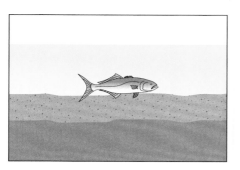

⬆ An animal dies. It falls onto mud or sand.

⬆ More mud or sand quickly buries the body.

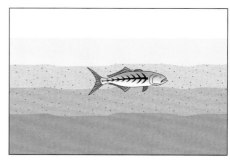

⬆ Bacteria slowly break down the soft parts of the body. Its skeleton remains.

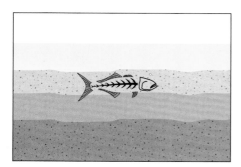

⬆ The mud or sand above and around the skeleton starts to become rock.

⬆ As rock forms, underground water that is rich in dissolved minerals seeps into tiny spaces in the skeleton. These minerals gradually replace the original minerals of the skeleton. A hard copy of the original skeleton is formed.

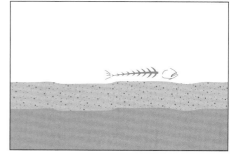

⬆ Many years later, soft rock around the fossil is eroded. The fossil is exposed.

What do fossils tell us about the history of life on Earth?

Palaeontologists collect and study fossils. They use evidence from fossils to help piece together the history of life on Earth. Fossils tell us about the features of animals and plants that lived at different times, and about their changing environments. All the evidence from fossils, taken together, is the **fossil record**.

Oldest plants

In 2010 Claudia Rubinstein and her team found fossils from the earliest known land plants in Argentina. The plants lived more than 470 million years ago. The plants were a type of liverwort, which have no roots or stems. This new find suggests that all land plants may have evolved from liverworts.

⬆ A modern liverwort.

Oldest animals

In 2012 a team of palaeontologists discovered sponge-like fossils in Namibia. The fossils are the oldest record of animal life ever found. Scientists previously thought that animal life began between 600 and 650 million years ago. These fossils could be up to 760 million years old.

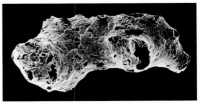
⬆ Fossils of *Otavia antiqua* are the earliest record of animal life ever found.

Dinosaurs

Without fossils, we would not know about dinosaurs.

⬆ This dinosaur embryo, found in South Africa, is about 190 million years old. It was close to hatching when it was buried.

⬆ Fossilised dinosaur faeces tell us what dinosaurs ate, and about the environments they lived in.

1 Explain why only very few plants and animals form fossils.

2 Describe the stages by which a fossil forms.

3 Choose an example of a fossil find, and describe what scientists have learnt as a result of it.

- Conditions must be perfect for fossils to form.
- The fossil record tells us about the history of life on Earth.

Estimating the age of the Earth

The story of our Earth

Many years ago, a great swirl of dust and gas came together in space. It formed our Solar System. Most of the dust and gas ended up in the Sun, but some was left over. Gravity pulled this dust and gas into clumps. The clumps became planets. Our Earth was born.

When did this happen? How old is the Earth? Read on to find out.

Cooling calculations

Scientist William Thomson examined evidence showing that the temperature of the Earth's crust increases with depth. He assumed the Earth formed as a liquid.

Thomson calculated the time needed for the Earth to cool to its current surface temperature. He worked out that the Earth formed between 20 and 400 million years ago.

We now know that Thomson did not realise that heat is produced inside the Earth. His assumption – that the Earth formed as a liquid – is also wrong. The Earth is older than Thomson thought.

Relative dating from rock strata

Sedimentary rocks are built up layer by layer, over millions of years. The layers are called **strata**. Where rock is undisturbed, the oldest rock layer is on the bottom. Younger layers are deposited above.

↑ Our Solar System formed from clouds of dust and gas.

Fossils and strata

William Smith worked in coal mines. Around 1800, he noticed that different rock strata contained different fossils. He realised that, in his coal mine, a certain rock layer always contained the same fossils. Smith asked a question:

Would rock strata of the same age always contain fossils of the same living organisms, even in different places?

Smith travelled to collect evidence to help answer his question. He published his findings so that other scientists could also look for evidence.

He used the evidence to devise an explanation:

Rock strata of the same age contain fossils of the same living organisms.

Certain fossils are only found in rock strata of certain ages.

Evidence from fossils in strata is useful in working out the order of events.

↑ Older strata are found beneath younger ones.

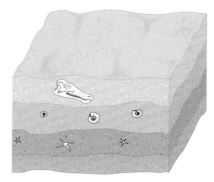

↑ A fossil in a lower rock layer is probably older than one in a layer above it.

Geological time scale

Scientists used Smith's explanation to classify rock strata by the fossils they contained. By the 1850s they had divided the Earth's history into geological time periods. At the time, they did not know when the rocks in each time period were formed.

The names of the geological time periods are shown in the table on the right. Each time period has its own **index fossil** to help identify it.

Radioactive dating

Evidence from strata and index fossils is useful in working out the order of events. But simply looking at strata cannot tell us how old they are.

In the twentieth century scientists used a new technique to measure the ages of rocks – **radiometric dating**. This uses the natural decay of the particles in a rock to measure its age. Radiometric dating tells us when rocks in different geological time periods were formed.

The oldest rocks on Earth are 4 600 000 000 years old. This is the best estimate for the age of the Earth.

Geological time period	Index fossil	Approximate date for start of time period (million years ago)
Quaternary		2.6
Tertiary		66
Cretaceous		146
Jurassic		200
Triassic		251
Permian		299
Carboniferous		359
Devonian		416
Silurian		444
Ordovician		488
Cambrian		542

⬆ Geological time periods and their index fossils.

Q

1 Give the best estimate for the age of the Earth.

2 William Thomson estimated the age of the Earth. Explain why his answer was incorrect.

3 Explain how index fossils are useful.

!

- Rock strata tell us about the order of events.
- Index fossils identify geological time periods.
- Radiometric dating measures the ages of rocks.

Human fossils

Selam

It's the end of a hot day in Dikika, Ethiopia. Scientist Zeresenay Alemseged and his team have spent weeks looking for human fossils. They've found fossilised bones of otters and elephants. Could humans have lived here too?

⬆ Zeresenay at work.

⬆ Zeresenay pieced together Selam's skull.

Suddenly, someone spots a small fossil face. It has a smooth brow and short canine teeth. The face looks human.

For five years Zeresenay studies the evidence. He works out that the skull, and other nearby bones, probably belonged to a three-year-old girl. He names her Selam. She almost certainly walked upright, like modern humans.

Geologists examine the rocks around Selam. The evidence shows that she lived by a river. Fossilised snails in nearby sandstone show that the river flowed into a lake with sandy beaches.

Many of Selam's fossilised bones were in a big lump of rock made from sand and pebbles. This shows that Selam probably died in a river flood. Fast-flowing water carried pebbles and sand that quickly covered her body and stopped animals from eating it.

Radiometric dating of the surrounding rock shows that Selam died about 3 300 000 years ago.

More fossil finds

Selam's fossilised bones, and their surrounding rocks, tell us when she lived and what her environment was like. Scientists have found many other human fossils. These finds help to piece together our human past.

Toumaï – ape or human?

In 2001 scientists discovered fossilised skull bones in Chad. They named their find Toumaï. The fossils were found in 7 million-year-old sand. If the fossils are the same age as the sand, they are older than any human remains in the fossil record.

Scientists examined Toumaï. They compared the skull bones to those of modern chimpanzees and humans. They decided that Toumaï belonged to an extinct species.

Animal	Number of teeth	Canine teeth	Average skull volume (cm³)
Toumaï	32	small	325
chimpanzee	32	big	390
gorilla	32	big	350
modern human	32	small	1500

 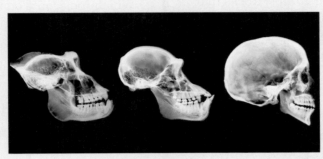

⬆ Skulls of Toumaï, a gorilla, a chimpanzee, and a modern human.

Scientists disagree about whether the extinct species is an ancestor of modern humans. Some believe the evidence shows that it is an ancestor of both chimpanzees and humans. Other scientists think that Toumaï is more closely related to the modern gorilla. The debate continues.

Footprints in Laetoli

More than three million years ago, early humans made these footprints in what is now Tanzania. Soon after, they were covered in volcanic ash. Scientists discovered the ancient footprints in 1978.

Scientists have compared the footprints to those of modern humans. They provide some of the earliest evidence of humans walking on two legs. They were probably made by an early species of humans called *Australopithecus afarensis*.

Tiny humans

Scientists discovered the remains and tools of an extinct human-like animal in a cave on the island of Flores, Indonesia. They measured the bones, and worked out that the animal was just one metre tall.

The scientists believe they had discovered an extinct human species. They named it *Homo floresiensis*. Other scientists think that the remains are from modern humans.

⬆ Footprints at Laetoli.

⬆ The *Homo floresiensis* fossils were found in this cave in Indonesia.

Q

1 Explain how scientists worked out that Selam lived near a lake with sandy beaches.

2 Explain how scientists know when Selam died.

3 Explain why scientists are not sure which species Toumaï belongs to.

● Fossils tell us about our human past.

!

1 Complete these sentences using words from the list. You may use each word once, more than once, or not at all.

igneous   metamorphic   sedimentary

Scientists classify rocks in three groups. Rocks that were formed when magma cooled and solidified are _____ rocks. Rocks formed from fragments of rock are _____ rocks. Rocks formed by the action of heat and pressure on existing rock are _____ rocks. [3]

2 Copy and complete the table using the words below.

sandstone   granite   marble

Type of rock	Example
igneous	
sedimentary	
metamorphic	

[3]

3 This question is about the four types of rock shown in the diagrams below.

(A) 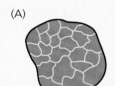   (B)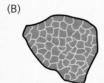

(C) 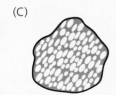   (D)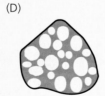

a Give the letters of two igneous rocks. [1]

b Give the letter of the igneous rock that cooled more slowly. [1]

c Give the letters of two porous rocks. [1]

d Give the letters of two rocks that formed when magma cooled and solidified. [1]

e Give the letter of two rocks which could contain fossils. [1]

f Give the letters of two rocks that are made up of crystals. [1]

4 The diagram shows the rocks in the wall of a mine.

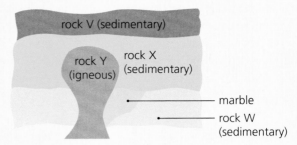

a Which rock could contain fossils (V, W, X, or Y)? [1]

b Which is the youngest sedimentary rock? [1]

c Which is most likely to be limestone? Explain your choice. [2]

d Suggest how the marble formed. [1]

e Which is most likely to be granite? Explain your choice. [2]

5 The photograph shows a piece of pumice.

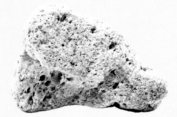

A student investigated the properties of pumice. He also found out about pumice from secondary sources. He wrote down the notes below.

1 I put it on water and it floated, so it must have a low density.

2 When I pushed the pumice into a beaker of water, bubbles rose to the surface.

3 My text book says pumice is formed from hot lava when it is thrown high into the air by a volcano. The gases that were dissolved in the lava come out of solution, forming the 'bubbles' you can see.

a Give the number of the note which shows that pumice is an igneous rock. [1]

b Use evidence from the notes to describe two ways in which the properties of pumice are not typical of igneous rocks. [2]

c Which note(s) refer to a secondary source? [1]

d i Copy the part of the sentence in note 1 which is an observation. [1]

   ii Copy the part of the sentence in note 1 which is an explanation. [1]

6 Two students investigate some rocks. They write their results in the table below.

Rock	Is it made up of crystals or grains?	Is it porous?	Does the piece of rock contain fossils?
A	grains	yes	no fossils
B	crystals	no	yes, but its shape looks squashed
C	crystals	no	no

a Name a piece of equipment the student could use to help her decide whether a rock is made up of crystals or grains. [1]

b Which rock is probably a metamorphic rock? [1]

c Which rock might be basalt? [1]

d One of the students, Junaid, says that rock A is a sedimentary rock. The other student, Farooq, says that rock A cannot be a sedimentary rock because it contains no fossils.
Write the name of the student you think is correct. Give a reason for your decision. [2]

7 A student compares the drainage of three soil samples. She uses the apparatus below.

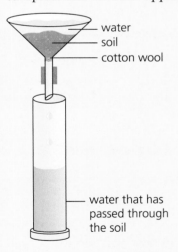
water
soil
cotton wool
water that has passed through the soil

The student writes her results in a table.

Soil sample	Volume of water collected in 1 hour (cm³)
L	15
M	89
N	48

a Give the letter of the soil which drains water most quickly. [1]

b Give the letter of the soil from which nutrients are removed most quickly. [1]

c Give the letter of the soil which remains wet for the longest time after heavy rain. [1]

d Give the letter of the soil which is most likely to be a clay soil. [1]

8 A student wants to compare the amounts of air in soil samples from two fields. She uses the apparatus below.

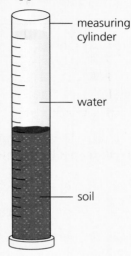
measuring cylinder
water
soil

She observes the level of water in the measuring cylinder after shaking the mixture of soil and water. The lower the water level, the greater the volume of air that was in the soil.

a Name the variable that the student changes. [1]

b Name the variable that the student observes. [1]

c Suggest two variables that the student should keep constant. [2]

9 The diagram shows the structure of the Earth.

a Use the words below to label a copy of the diagram.

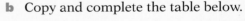

outer core   **crust**
mantle   **inner core**

b Copy and complete the table below.

Layer	Solid, liquid, or gas?
crust	
inner core	
mantle	
outer core	

10 The statements below explain how a fossil was formed. They are in the wrong order. Write the letters in the correct order. [4]

a The soft parts of the body slowly break down. Only the bones are left.

b More sand quickly buries the body.

c An animal dies. It falls onto sand at the bottom of a lake.

d Underground water that is rich in minerals seeps into the gaps in the bones. The minerals replace the original minerals of the skeleton.

e The sand above the bones is compressed, and begins to form rock.

1 Bromine can exist as a solid, liquid, or gas. The diagrams show the arrangements of particles in each of these states.

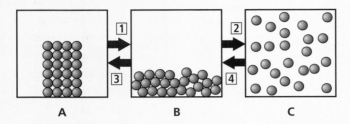

a Give the name of the state represented by diagram A. [1]

b Give the name of the change of state that is represented by arrow 1. [1]

c Describe how the movement of the particles changes during the change of state represented by arrow 3. [1]

d A student collects data about bromine.
melting point of bromine = –7 °C
boiling point of bromine = 59 °C

  i Give the letter of the diagram that best represents the particles in bromine at 20 °C. [1]

  ii Give the letter of the diagram that best represents the particles in bromine at –10 °C. [1]

  iii At what temperature does the change represented by arrow 3 occur? [1]

2 A student investigated the variables that affect the time taken for 20 g of sugar to dissolve in water.

a The student changed one variable in the first part of her investigation. Her results are in the table.
Investigation 1

Temperature (°C)	Time to dissolve (s)
0	400
20	100
40	25
60	12
80	3

  i Name the variable the student changed in Investigation 1. [1]

  ii Plot the points in the table on a graph. Draw a line of best fit. [4]

  iii Write a conclusion for Investigation 1. [1]

b The student changed a different variable in the second part of her investigation. Her results are in the table.

Investigation 2

Size of pieces of sugar	Time to dissolve (s)
big crystals	100
small crystals	70
very fine powder	50

  i List three variables the student should have kept constant in Investigation 2. [3]

  ii Write a conclusion for Investigation 2. [1]

c The student did Investigation 2 at 20 °C. Use the data in both tables to suggest what size sugar pieces she used in Investigation 1. [1]

3 From the list below, write the properties that are typical of metals.

high melting point	**shiny**
dull appearance	**malleable**
poor conductor of heat	**sonorous**
low boiling point	**brittle**
good conductor of electricity	[5]

4 This question is about the pH of the water in three East African lakes.

The pH range of the water in each lake is given in the table below.

Name of lake	pH range of lake water
Lake Malawi	7.8–8.6
Lake Tanganyika	7.2–8.6
Lake Victoria	8.6–9.5

a In which lake can the most alkaline water be found? [1]

b A student collected a sample of water from Lake Victoria. She added a few drops of Universal Indicator to the water. Use data from the table, and the diagram below, to predict the colour of this mixture. [1]

	acidic			neutral	alkaline		
colour of indicator	red	orange	yellow	green	blue	dark blue	purple

c Read the paragraph in the box. It is from a book about Lake Malawi.

> The pH of Lake Malawi water is different in different parts of the lake. In calm bays, more carbon dioxide dissolves in the water. Carbon dioxide gas is acidic, so the water in calm bays is more acidic.
>
> Where the water is not calm, the water is more alkaline. This is because less carbon dioxide is dissolved in the water.

Use the information in the box, and data from the table, to predict the pH in a calm bay of Lake Malawi. [2]

d Predict how the pH of the lakes might change if the rain in the region became more acidic. [1]

e The picture shows one species of tilapia fish. [1]

Tilapia prefer to live in water of pH 6 to 9. However, many can survive in water of pH 5 to 10. Predict which of the lakes in the table are suitable for tilapia.

5 This question is about igneous rocks.

a Explain how igneous rocks were formed. [1]

b Explain why igneous rocks never contain fossils. [1]

c Give the names of two igneous rocks.

6 The diagrams below shows the sides of two quarries. The quarries are on different continents. The rocks shown are sedimentary rocks. They were built up in layers. Each layer took millions of years to form.

Fossils have been found in some of the layers. They are also shown in the diagram.

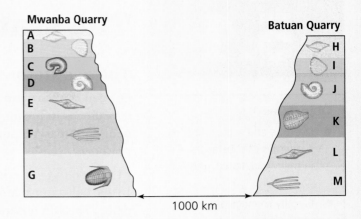

Mwanba Quarry

Batuan Quarry

1000 km

a Explain how the diagrams show that all the rocks in both quarries are sedimentary. [1]

b Give the letter of the youngest rock in Mwamba Quarry. [1]

c In which of the quarries is the oldest rock found? Explain your answer. [2]

d Which rock in Batuan Quarry was formed in the same period as rock D in Mwamba Quarry? [1]

e Suggest why the number of rock layers in each quarry is different. [1]

f The fossils shown are index fossils.

i Explain what an index fossil is. [1]

ii The table below gives the index fossils for some geological time periods.

Geological time period	Index fossil
Quaternary	
Tertiary	
Devonian	
Cambrian	

Write the letters of the rocks in both quarries that were formed in the Devonian period. [1]

The states of matter revisited

The gas state

Oxygen is all around us, mixed with other substances in the air. Without oxygen, we could not live. Without oxygen, fuels would not burn.

In the air, oxygen exists in the gas state. Its particles move around from place to place. They do not touch each other, and spread out to fill the whole container. There are very weak forces of attraction between the particles.

The arrangement and behaviour of the particles in the gas state explain each of the properties below:

- gases fill the whole container – their volume is the same as the volume of the container
- gases take the shape of their container
- gases can flow
- gases can be compressed.

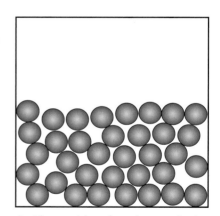

↑ Particles of a substance in the gas state.

The liquid state

If oxygen is cooled to –183 °C it changes state from gas to liquid. This change of state is called condensation.

In any change of state, the particles themselves do not change. Their mass, for example, remains the same. It is only the arrangement and behaviour of the particles that change.

In the liquid state, there are strong forces holding the particles together. The particles touch each other, and there is very little empty space between them. The particles are not arranged in a regular pattern. They move around from place to place, in and out of each other.

The arrangement and behaviour of the particles in the liquid state explain each of the properties below:

- liquids have a fixed volume
- liquids take the shape of their container
- liquids can flow
- liquids can be slightly compressed.

↑ This Indian satellite launch vehicle uses liquid oxygen to help propel it into space.

↑ The particles of a substance in the liquid state.

The solid state

At –218 °C, oxygen changes from the liquid state to the solid state. This change of state is called freezing.

Solid oxygen behaves differently from oxygen in the gas and liquid states. Like all solids, it has the properties below:

- solids have a fixed shape and volume
- solids cannot be compressed
- solids cannot flow.

The particle theory explains the properties of substances in the solid state. The particles are arranged in a regular pattern, and cannot be any closer together. Strong attractive forces hold the particles in their pattern. The particles do not move around from place to place – they vibrate on the spot.

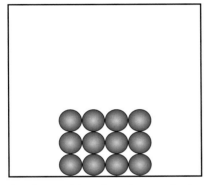

↑ The particles of a substance in the solid state.

↑ Solid oxygen is pale blue.

More changes of state

Solid oxygen changes to the liquid state when it is warmed to –218 °C. This is melting.

At higher temperatures, particles escape from the surface of liquid oxygen. Some of the liquid oxygen has changed state to form oxygen gas. This is evaporation.

At –183 °C liquid oxygen boils. In boiling, bubbles of oxygen gas form throughout the liquid. The bubbles rise to the surface and escape. Eventually, all the liquid oxygen changes state to become a gas.

Q

1 Draw circles to represent particles of oxygen in the liquid state.

2 Describe the behaviour of oxygen particles in the gas state.

3 Explain why you cannot compress oxygen in the solid state, but why you can compress oxygen in the gas state.

4 Describe how the behaviour of the particles changes when a substance changes from its solid state to its liquid state.

5 Use the information below to give the state of nitrogen at -200 °C.

	Temperature
melting point of nitrogen	-210 °C
boiling point of nitrogen	-196 °C

!

- The arrangement and behaviour of particles explains the different properties of the substance in the gas, liquid, and solid states.

5.2 Explaining diffusion

Diffusion

Objectives
- Use the particle theory to explain diffusion
- Describe evidence for diffusion

Rebekah is cooking dinner for her family. Very soon, everyone in the house can smell the food. Why?

air particle

food particle

Food particles evaporate as Rebekah is cooking. They move around randomly in the air, and spread out. The food particles mix with air particles. Soon there are food particles all over the house. Some of the food particles enter your nose, which detects the smell.

The random movement and mixing of particles is called **diffusion**. Particles move because they have energy. You do not need to move or stir to make diffusion happen.

The speed of mixing by diffusion depends on three factors:

- temperature
- size and mass of the particles
- the states of the substances that are diffusing.

Diffusion and temperature

Particles from warm food diffuse more quickly than those from cool food. The warmer particles have more energy, so they move faster.

Diffusion and particle size and mass

A teacher sets up the apparatus below.

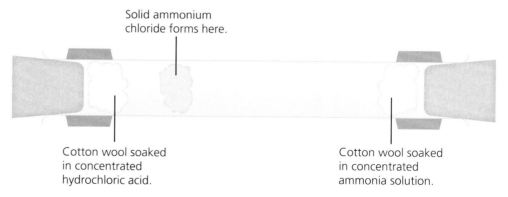

Solid ammonium chloride forms here.

Cotton wool soaked in concentrated hydrochloric acid.

Cotton wool soaked in concentrated ammonia solution.

Particles of hydrogen chloride and ammonia evaporate from the cotton wool. They diffuse along the tube. When the two types of particle meet they react. This forms a new substance, which is a white solid. You can see the solid in the tube.

The solid forms closer to the cotton wool soaked in hydrochloric acid. This shows that hydrogen chloride particles diffuse more slowly than ammonia particles. A hydrogen chloride particle has a greater mass than an ammonia particle.

Big, heavy particles diffuse more slowly than smaller, lighter particles.

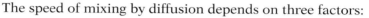

Diffusion in gases, liquids, and solids

Diffusion through gases

Diffusion happens quickly in a gas. This is because a particle can travel a long distance before it hits another particle.

Diffusion through liquids

Mo puts a crystal of potassium manganate(VII) in a Petri dish of water. He watches carefully. The purple colour starts to spread through the water.

The next day Mo looks at the mixture again. The purple colour has spread all through the water. Purple particles have moved away from the crystal and mixed with the water particles.

Diffusion happens more slowly in liquids than in gases. This is because particles are closer in liquids, and there are stronger forces between them.

⬆ Purple potassium manganate(VII) crystals start to diffuse through liquid water.

Diffusion in solids

Diffusion happens very slowly – if at all – in solids. This is because very strong forces hold the particles in position. However, solid diffusion can happen enough to be useful.

Solar cells generate electricity from sunlight. One type of solar cell is made from thin slices of pure silicon. When the cell is being made, phosphorus particles diffuse into the silicon. The process happens at a high temperature, just below the melting point of silicon.

Evidence for moving particles

In 1828, Robert Brown suspended pollen grains in water. He looked at them through a microscope. The pollen grains moved around quickly. Why?

The pollen grains were pushed around by the random movements of the water particles around them. But how? Water particles are tiny compared to pollen grains. The answer lies in the speed of the water particles – on average, a water particle moves faster than 1600 km/h at 20 °C.

⬆ Solid diffusion is used in making solar cells.

1 Explain the meaning of the word *diffusion*.

2 List three factors that affect the speed of diffusion.

3 Explain why diffusion happens more quickly at higher temperatures.

- Diffusion is the random movement and mixing of particles.
- Diffusion happens faster at higher temperatures.
- Big, heavy particles diffuse slower than smaller, lighter particles.
- Diffusion is quicker in gases than in liquids. Solid diffusion is very slow.

Explaining density

What is density?

Ravi is a weightlifter. His dumbbells are made from iron. Why not make dumbbells from aluminium or wood?

Substance	Density (g/cm³)
iron	7.9
aluminium	2.7
wood	about 0.5

⬆ Ravi lifts iron dumbbells. Bikram's are made from aluminium.

Iron dumbbells are heavier than aluminium dumbbells of the same size. This is because iron has a greater **density** than aluminium. Density is how heavy something is for its size. A 1 cm³ cube of iron is heavier than a 1 cm³ cube of aluminium.

Calculating density

Katrina has a block of lead. She wants to calculate its density. She measures:

- the mass of the block of lead
- the volume of the block of lead.

Katrina writes down her data.

Mass of block of lead = 44 g

Volume of block of lead = 4 cm³

She uses this equation to calculate density:

$$\text{density} = \frac{\text{mass}}{\text{volume}}$$

$$\text{density} = \frac{44 \text{ g}}{4 \text{ cm}^3}$$

$$= 11 \text{ g/cm}^3$$

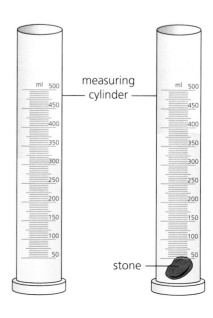

measuring cylinder

stone

You can work out the volume of a sample of solid in two ways.

- If your sample is a cube or cuboid, measure the lengths of its sides. Then calculate height × width × depth.
- If your sample is of any other shape, take a known volume of water. Place the sample in the water. The volume increase is the volume of the sample.

height

depth

width

Explaining density

The density of a substance depends on two things:

- the mass of its particles
- how closely packed its particles are.

Particle mass

In the solid state, the metals with the heaviest particles have the highest densities.

Metal	Relative mass of particles	Density (g/cm³)
cobalt	59	9
nickel	59	9
copper	63.5	9
iridium	192	23
platinum	195	21
gold	197	19

Closeness of particles

The particles of a substance in the liquid state are more closely packed than the particles in the gas state. The liquid has a greater density than the gas.

The pictures show the mass of 500 cm³ of liquid water compared to 500 cm³ of steam. The mass of the bottle is 20 g.

For most substances, the solid density is greater than the liquid density. This is because the solid particles are packed more closely.

Water is different. At 0 °C the particles in ice are packed less closely than the particles in liquid water. Ice has a lower density than liquid water. This explains why ice floats on water.

Using density

About 1000 years ago, al-Biruni of Persia studied gemstones. He collected data on their colour and hardness. He calculated their densities, and used density values to identify gems. Al-Biruni used the apparatus shown here to measure the volume of gemstones. He found their mass and calculated their density.

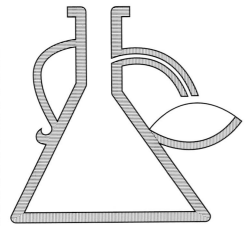

⬆ Al-Biruni used this apparatus to measure the volume of gemstones. He found their mass and calculated their density.

⬆ Ice floats on liquid water because ice has a lower density at 0 °C.

1 Give the meaning of the word *density*.

2 A block of silver has a mass of 20 g and a volume of 2 cm³. Calculate its density.

3 The mass of a particle of chromium is 52. The mass of a particle of tungsten is 184. Predict which of the two metals has the higher density. Explain your prediction.

- density $= \dfrac{\text{mass}}{\text{volume}}$
- The density of a substance depends on the mass of its particles and how closely packed its particles are.

Explaining gas pressure

Explaining gas pressure

Raj blows up a balloon. The balloon gets bigger and bigger. Why?

When Raj starts blowing, air particles enter the balloon. The particles move quickly in all directions. They bump into, or **collide** with, the rubber. The colliding particles exert a force on the rubber, and push it outwards. The force per unit area is called **pressure**.

As Raj continues blowing, more air particles enter the balloon. The balloon gets bigger.

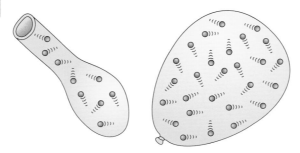

⬆ The more Raj blows into the balloon, the greater the number of air particles inside it.

How does temperature affect gas pressure?

Raj ties up his balloon. He leaves it in a warm room. The balloon gets even bigger. Why?

The air particles inside the balloon warm up. They move faster. They hit each other, and the sides of the container, more often. The air pressure inside the balloon has increased. In the warm balloon, the faster moving particles are further apart. This is why the balloon gets bigger.

Saniyah puts a plastic bottle in a freezer. The air in the bottle cools down. The particles move more slowly. They hit each other, and the inside of the bottle, less often. The pressure inside the bottle has decreased. The bottle collapses.

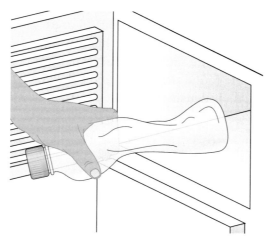

⬆ The bottle collapses as the air pressure inside it decreases.

Air pressure

Tirto lives in Padang, a city by the sea. He visits the mountains. He feels breathless. Why?

Air particles collide with you all the time. The force exerted by these particles per unit area is **air pressure**. The pressure does not squash you because you have air inside your body too.

Air pressure depends on how high up you are. At the top of a mountain there is less air pressing down on you than there is at sea level. The air pressure is less at the top of the mountain.

At the top of the mountain, air particles are further apart than they are at sea level. You need to breathe more often to take in enough oxygen.

People who live in the mountains all the time don't breathe more often than people who live at sea level. Their bodies have adapted to the lower air pressure.

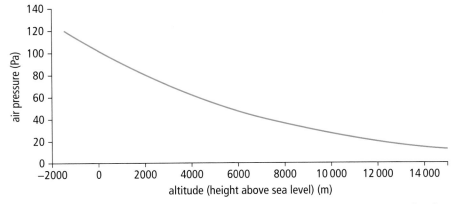

↑ The graph shows how air pressure changes with altitude (height above sea level).

Air pressure and boiling point

Bubu heats liquid water. Water particles leave the surface of the liquid. These particles form a vapour above the liquid.

Water boils when the pressure of the vapour above the liquid is the same as the air pressure around the liquid.

This explains why boiling point changes with altitude (height above sea level). The higher the altitude, the lower the air pressure. The lower the air pressure, the lower the temperature at which the vapour pressure is equal to the air pressure.

Q

1 Gases exert pressure on the walls of a container. Explain why.

2 Shahid pumps up a bicycle tyre. Describe how the air pressure inside the tyre changes as he pumps.

3 Nadeem places a plastic bottle of air in a pan of hot water. Predict and explain how the pressure inside the bottle changes.

4 **Extension:** Use the graph to estimate the air pressure in Nairobi, altitude 1660 m.

5 **Extension:** In Asmara, a city by the sea, water boils at 100 °C. In Addis Ababa, a city 2300 m above sea level, water boils at 92 °C. Explain this difference.

- Gas pressure is caused by particles colliding with the walls of a container.

- The higher the temperature, the greater the gas pressure.

Ideas and evidence

Scientific questions

Scientists ask questions. What is matter made of? How old is the Earth? Which malaria medicine is best?

A question is scientific if doing an experiment, or making observations, will help to answer it. Scientific questions are also called **empirical questions**.

Not all questions can be answered by science. A scientist could investigate which malaria medicines work best. But she could not use science to answer the question:

Should the government provide free malaria treatment for everyone?

Many scientific discoveries start with questions. But others begin when scientists respond creatively to an accident or mistake. Teflon, a material used in space vehicles and artificial heart valves, was first made accidentally.

A question of pressure

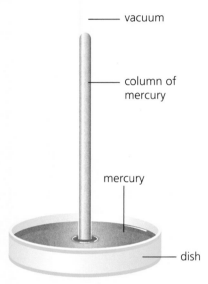

Robert Boyle had a barometer. Sometimes the mercury was high in the tube. At other times it was lower. But the mercury level in the tube never fell below a certain minimum level. Boyle wondered why. He asked an empirical question:

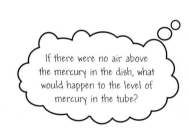

If there were no air above the mercury in the dish, what would happen to the level of mercury in the tube?

⬆ Boyle's barometer. This type of barometer was first made by Torricelli.

Suggesting an explanation

Boyle knew that another scientist, Torricelli, had explained that air pressure on the mercury in the dish supported the mercury in the tube (see diagram). Torricelli had used **creative thinking**, and experimental evidence, to come up with his explanation.

Boyle used this knowledge, and his own creative thinking, to suggest an explanation to answer his question.

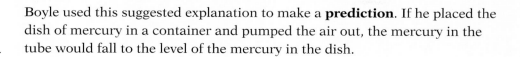

Suggested explanation

If there is no air above the mercury in the dish, there will be no air pressure on the surface of this mercury. The mercury in the tube will not be supported.

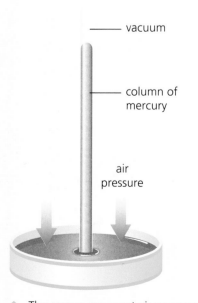

⬆ The arrows represent air pressure.

Boyle used this suggested explanation to make a **prediction**. If he placed the dish of mercury in a container and pumped the air out, the mercury in the tube would fall to the level of the mercury in the dish.

Testing the explanation

Boyle did an investigation to test his explanation. First, he and another scientist, Robert Hooke, designed and made an air pump. This took many weeks.

Next, the scientists placed the dish of mercury in the pump. The tube stuck out of the top. The scientists sealed the gap round the tube.

Then Boyle and Hooke began to pump out air. The level of mercury in the tube fell. They pumped harder. In the end, the height of the mercury column fell to 2.5 cm.

Checking the evidence

Boyle discussed the investigation results with Hooke and other scientists. Was his prediction correct? Did the evidence support his suggested explanation?

Boyle concluded that the evidence supported his suggested explanation. The height of mercury in the tube did not quite fall to the level of mercury in the dish, but it came close. Small air leaks into the pump, said Boyle, meant that the mercury in the dish always experienced some air pressure.

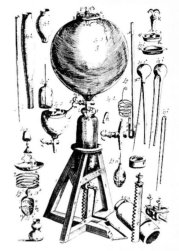
⬆ Boyle and Hooke's air pump.

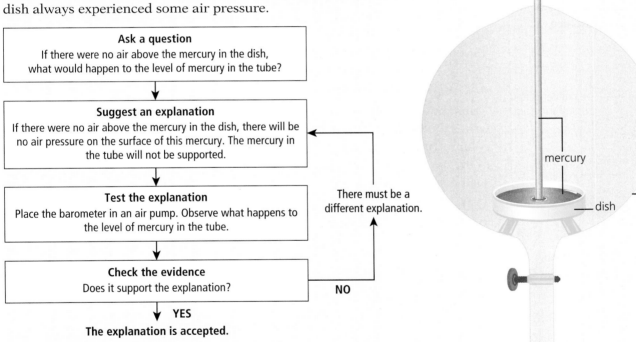

⬆ The diagram summarises the steps in developing a scientific explanation.

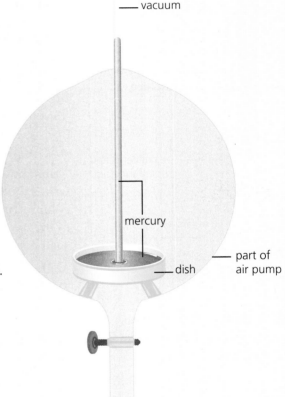
⬆ A simplified diagram of Boyle and Hooke's apparatus

Q

1 What is an empirical question?

2 Scientists collect evidence and make observations to help answer a scientific question. What else do they do?

3 Explain why scientists collect evidence and make observations.

4 A scientist collects evidence. It does not support his suggested explanation. Suggest what the scientist might do next.

!

To develop explanations, scientists:

- ask empirical questions
- think creatively to suggest an explanation
- collect evidence and make observations.

Doing an investigation

Planning an investigation

Objectives

Understand how to:

- plan an investigation
- obtain and present evidence
- consider evidence

Azibo wants to find out if there is a relationship between the temperature of air and its volume. He plans an investigation.

First, Azibo identifies important variables. He decides which to change and measure:

- variable to change – temperature
- variable to measure – volume of air.

Azibo wants his investigation to be a fair test. He keeps the other important variable – air pressure – constant.

Azibo chooses his apparatus, because the experiment uses concentrated sulfuric acid Azibo's teacher will perform the experiment for him. Concentrated sulfuric acid is very corrosive and dangerous to use. Azibo's plan is to measure the height of the air column at six different temperatures. He will then calculate the volume of air at each temperature.

Before the experiment starts, Azibo makes a prediction. He knows that heating a gas makes its particles move faster and get further apart. He uses this scientific knowledge to predict that heating the gas in the tube will make its volume increase. Cooling the gas, predicts Azibo, will reduce its volume.

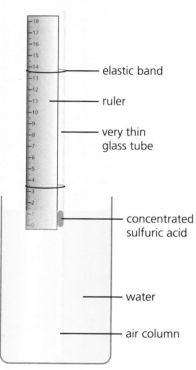

- elastic band
- ruler
- very thin glass tube
- concentrated sulfuric acid
- water
- air column

↑ Apparatus to investigate how the volume of air varies with temperature.

Presenting evidence

Azibo draws a table for the results. He writes the variable he changes in the left column, and the variable he measures in the next column. He includes units in each column heading.

Azibo collects his data whilst his teacher is carrying out the experiment. He writes them in the table.

Temperature (°C)	Height of column (mm)
2	1
17	18
20	24
26	33
30	46
37	60

Considering evidence

Doing calculations

Azibo needs to calculate the volume of air at each temperature. He uses the equation below:

volume = 80 mm³ + [height (mm) × cross sectional area of tube (mm²)]

volume = 80 mm³ + [height (mm) × 0.8 mm²]

He adds a column to his table.

Temperature (°C)	Height of column (mm)	Volume of air (mm³)
2	1	80.8
17	18	94.4
20	24	99.2
26	33	106.4
30	46	104.0
37	60	128.0

Identifying trends and patterns

Azibo can see from his table that his results show a pattern – as temperature increases, gas volume increases. But Azibo wants to look more closely at the pattern. He plots the points on a graph, and draws a line of best fit.

The graph shows that as temperature increases, gas volume increases steadily. This relationship is an example of a **correlation** between two variables.

Azibo looks back at his prediction. It was correct! This makes him more confident that the science explanation on which he based his prediction is correct.

Identifying anomalous results

Azibo looks at his results again. One of the points on the graph is not near the line of best fit. The result for 30 °C is **anomalous**.

Azibo wants to find out why this result is anomalous. He repeats the experiment at 30 °C. The height of the column is 46 mm. Azibo has not made a mistake when collecting data.

Azibo checks his calculation. He has made a mistake. For a height of 46 mm, the volume should be 116.8 mm³. He plots this point on his graph. It is close to the line of best fit.

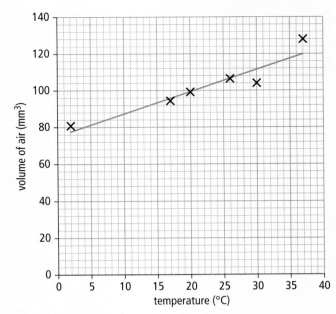

⬆ Graph showing how the volume of a gas varies with temperature at constant pressure.

Another correlation

Graph A, below, shows a correlation between two variables.

Graph B does not show a correlation.

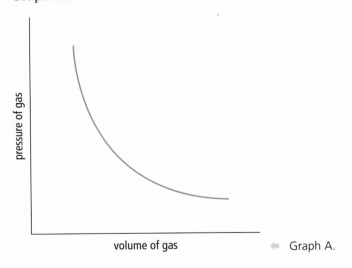

⬅ Graph A.

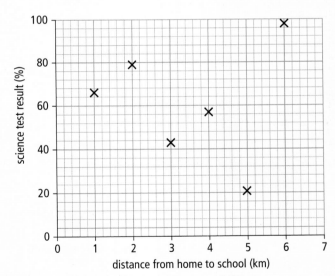

⬆ Graph B. There is no correlation between the distance a student lives from school, and their science test results.

1 Why does Azibo keep the air pressure constant in his investigation?

2 Describe the correlation shown on graph A.

3 Marcos does a similar investigation to Azibo. He measures the volume at 6 temperatures between 0 °C and 60 °C. Explain how Marcos's investigation is better than Azibo's.

Doing an investigation involves:

- planning
- obtaining and presenting evidence
- considering the evidence.

1 Copy and complete the table to show the properties of a substance in the solid, liquid, and gas states. [8]

property	solid	liquid	gas
volume		fixed volume	
shape			same as container
can it flow?		yes	
can it be compressed?			yes

2 A student heated some liquid water. He recorded the temperature of the water every minute. He plotted a graph of his results.

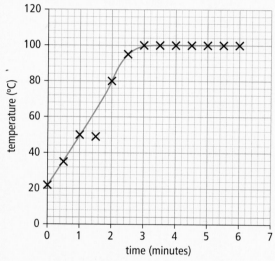

a Name the change of state that is happening between the third and sixth minutes. [1]

b Identify the anomalous result shown on the graph. [1]

c Suggest one mistake the student might have made to get this anomalous result. [1]

3 The diagram shows the particles of a substance in its liquid state.

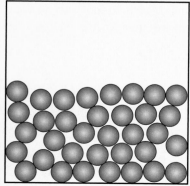

a What could you do to make the particles in the liquid move more quickly? [1]

b Draw a diagram to show the same particles after the liquid has evaporated. [1]

c Describe the movement of the particles after the liquid has evaporated. [1]

4 Copy and complete the sentences below using words from the list. You may use the words once, more than once, or not at all.

bigger than   smaller than   the same as

a The size of one particle in liquid mercury is _____ the size of one particle in solid mercury. [1]

b In liquid mercury the distance between the particles is _____ the distance between the particles in mercury gas. [1]

c The forces between the particles in liquid mercury are _____ the forces between the particles in solid mercury. [1]

5 Copy these and draw lines to match each property with the best explanation.

Property	Explanation
You cannot compress a solid.	The particles move around, in and out of each other.
If a gas is in a container with no lid, it escapes from the container.	There is no empty space between the particles.
A liquid takes the shape of the bottom of its container.	Its particles are in fixed positions.
A solid cannot be poured.	The particles move around in all directions.

[3]

6 A teacher sets up the apparatus below. She leaves it in a hot room, at 30 °C.

gas jar of air

gas jar of bromine vapour

a One hour later, the teacher observes an orange vapour in both gas jars. Explain why. [1]

b The teacher sets up exactly the same apparatus again. She leaves the jars in a cooler room, at 15 °C.

   i Predict one difference in her observations at the two temperatures. [1]

   ii Use ideas about particles to explain this difference. [2]

7 Pawel has a stone. He wants to find its density.

a He pours water into a measuring cylinder until it is half full. The diagram shows the surface of the water. Write down the water volume in cm³.

62 cm³

[1]

b Pawel places the stone in the water. The water surface of the water moves up. The diagram shows the new surface of the water.

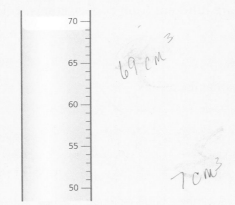

69 cm³

7 cm³

Use the diagram, and your answer to part (a) to work out the volume of the stone. [1]

c The mass of the stone is 11.5 g. Use the equation below to calculate the density of the stone. Include units in your answer.

$$\text{density} = \frac{\text{mass}}{\text{volume}}$$

[2]

11.5

8 Pippa investigates the speed of diffusion of four coloured substances in agar gel. She plans to set up the apparatus below.

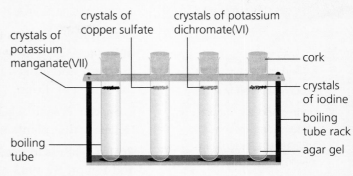

a Pippa lists the important variables in her investigation.

type of agar gel
temperature of agar gel
substance that diffuses
distance from top of agar gel to
    bottom of colour
time for which the solids are left to diffuse

   i Choose the variable in the list above that Pippa should change. [1]

   ii Choose the variable in the list above that Pippa should measure. [1]

   iii Pippa must control the other variables in the list. Explain why. [1]

b Potassium dichromate(VI) is very toxic if swallowed. It can also cause skin ulcers. Suggest how Pippa can reduce the risk from each of these hazards. [2]

c Draw a table for Pippa's results. Include units in the column headings, if necessary. [2]

d Pippa decides to do the whole investigation twice more. She writes down the distance from the top of the agar to the bottom of the iodine colour in each investigation.

First time – 0.5 cm
Second time – 0.6 cm
Third time – 0.4 cm

Pippa then calculates the average distance for iodine.

   i Suggest why Pippa repeated the investigation three times, and calculated an average. [1]

   ii Suggest why the distance was different in each investigation. [1]

6.1 Atoms

Objectives

- Explain what an element is
- Explain what an atom is
- Understand the importance of questions, evidence, and creative thought in developing explanations

Zinc – a vital element

In the late 1950s, Professor Ananda Prasad moved to Iran from his home in India. A 21-year-old man visited Professor Prasad. He had not grown properly, and looked like an eight-year-old boy. Many other Iranians had the same condition.

Professor Prasad asked a question. What was the cause of the condition? He knew that plants needed zinc to grow. Did humans need zinc too?

Professor Prasad decided to test his idea. He collected evidence in Iran and Egypt. By 1963 he had an answer. A shortage of zinc causes growth problems.

People who eat mainly cereals and beans, or cassava and potatoes, risk zinc deficiency. In Indonesia, Mexico, and Peru, zinc chemicals are added to flour.

Atoms and elements

Zinc is an element. Like all elements, it cannot be split into anything simpler. There are 92 elements found naturally on Earth. Scientists have made at least 25 more.

Elements are made up of particles called **atoms**. An atom is the smallest part of an element that can exist. Atoms are tiny. The diameter of one atom is about 0.000 000 01 cm. If you could place one hundred million atoms side by side, they would stretch one centimetre.

Every element has its own type of atom. The atoms of each element are different from the atoms of every other element. So all zinc atoms are alike, but zinc atoms are different from copper atoms, gold atoms, and iron atoms.

Imagining atoms

Toy bricks can help us imagine atoms.

⬆ If these bricks represent oxygen atoms...

⬆ ...then these represent atoms of another element, like nitrogen.

⬆ If these bricks represent gold atoms...

⬆ ...then this shows a piece of gold.

Of course the toy brick model is not perfect. Atoms do not have straight edges. And atoms are much, much, much smaller than the toy bricks.

Atoms – ideas and evidence

Ideas about atoms are not new. More than 2500 years ago, Greek thinkers asked a question. Could you go on cutting a piece of matter into smaller and smaller pieces for ever?

Zeno answered 'yes'. He said that matter completely fills its space. So you can keep cutting it into smaller pieces for ever.

Leucippus and Democritus thought differently. They said that matter is divided into tiny separate bits – atoms – with empty space between. They believed that atoms are the smallest pieces of matter that exist.

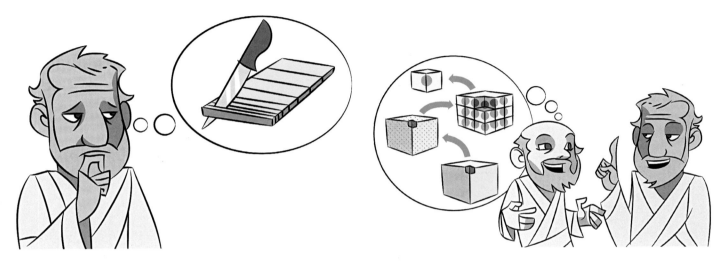

At least a thousand years ago, Indian thinkers developed ideas about atoms. They described four elements. Each element had its own type of atom. Atoms, they said, could not be split up.

As far as we know, the Greek and Indian thinkers did not do practical experiments. They used creative thought to answer their questions.

Evidence for atoms came later. In the 1660s, Robert Boyle used ideas about atoms to explain experimental observations. Around the year 1800, John Dalton collected evidence from his own investigations, and from other scientists. He thought about the evidence. It supported the explanation that matter is made up of atoms.

Q

1 What is an atom?

2 What is an element?

3 Are the atoms in a piece of gold the same as, or different from, each other?

4 Are oxygen atoms the same as, or different from, gold atoms?

- An element is a substance that cannot be split into anything simpler.
- An atom is the smallest part of an element that can exist.
- Scientists ask questions, collect evidence, and think creatively to develop explanations.

Elements and their symbols

Symbols for the elements

Some elements have long names. So each element has its own **chemical symbol**. It's much easier to write Pr than praseodymium!

Often, the chemical symbol is the first one or two letters of an element's name in English. The table gives some examples:

Element	Chemical symbol
carbon	C
calcium	Ca
cobalt	Co
nitrogen	N
neon	Ne
nickel	Ni

Sometimes the chemical symbol is made up from the first and third letters of the English name of an element. For example:

Element	Chemical symbol
magnesium	Mg
manganese	Mn
chromium	Cr
chlorine	Cl

The chemical symbols for some elements come from other languages:

- the chemical symbol for iron, Fe, comes from the Latin name for iron, *ferrum*.
- the chemical symbol for tungsten, W, comes from the German name for tungsten, *wolfram*.

Scientists all over the world use the same chemical symbols. All scientists recognise S as the chemical symbol for sulfur, even though it's called *belerang* in Indonesian, كبريت (kibrit) in Arabic, *soufre* in French and *azufre* in Spanish.

Writing chemical symbols

Follow these rules to write chemical symbols correctly:

- Write a capital letter for a one-letter symbol. For example, the chemical symbol for nitrogen is N, not n.
- Write a capital letter followed by a lower-case letter for a two-letter symbol. For example, the chemical symbol for magnesium is Mg, not mg or MG.

Chemical symbols in the periodic table

The periodic table lists all the elements. The periodic table on the next page gives their names and chemical symbols. You need to learn the chemical symbols of the first 20 elements, from hydrogen to calcium.

																	H hydrogen																He helium

Periodic table:

										H hydrogen							He helium
Li lithium	Be beryllium											B boron	C carbon	N nitrogen	O oxygen	F fluorine	Ne neon
Na sodium	Mg magnesium											Al aluminium	Si silicon	P phosphorus	S sulfur	Cl chlorine	Ar argon
K potassium	Ca calcium	Sc scandium	Ti titanium	V vanadium	Cr chromium	Mn manganese	Fe iron	Co cobalt	Ni nickel	Cu copper	Zn zinc	Ga gallium	Ge germanium	As arsenic	Se selenium	Br bromine	Kr krypton
Rb rubidium	Sr strontium	Y yttrium	Zr zirconium	Nb niobium	Mo molybdenum	Tc technetium	Ru ruthenium	Rh rhodium	Pd palladium	Ag silver	Cd cadmium	In indium	Sn tin	Sb antimony	Te tellurium	I iodine	Xe xenon
Cs caesium	Ba barium	La lanthanum	Hf hafnium	Ta tantalum	W tungsten	Re rhenium	Os osmium	Ir iridium	Pt platinum	Au gold	Hg mercury	Tl thallium	Pb lead	Bi bismuth	Po polonium	At astatine	Rn radon
Fr francium	Ra radium																

Note: This periodic table does not include all the elements.

Two interesting elements

Platinum

Platinum is a silvery-white element. Its chemical symbol is Pt. Platinum is a metal, so it conducts electricity well. It is shiny, and is not damaged by air or water.

Platinum jewellery is very attractive. South Americans made platinum jewellery about 2000 years ago. The Egyptians also made jewellery and decorative boxes out of platinum. Princess Shepenupet was buried with a platinum box about 2700 years ago.

Now, computer hard disks store information in layers of platinum and cobalt. Platinum in catalytic converters reduces pollution from cars.

⬆ Ancient South American gold and platinum jewellery.

Tantalum

Tantalum has the chemical symbol Ta. It is shiny. Acids do not damage it. Tantalum is a good conductor of electricity.

Tantalum capacitors store electrical energy in cell phones and computers.

Q

1 Give the chemical symbols of these elements: hydrogen, helium, lithium, beryllium, boron, carbon, nitrogen, oxygen, fluorine, neon.

2 Give the names of the elements with these chemical symbols: Na, Mg, Al, Si, P, S, Cl, Ar, K, Ca.

3 **Extension:** Describe the properties of platinum, and list three uses of the metal.

- Each element has its own chemical symbol.

Discovering the elements

Early ideas about elements

For thousands of years, thinkers thought about elements. They wanted to know about the simple substances that make up everything else.

More than 2000 years ago, a Greek thinker created an explanation. He said there were four elements – air, water, fire, and earth. This idea was popular for hundreds of years. Scientists in India used the explanation to help develop their ideas about atoms.

From about 1700, scientists realised that the idea of four elements was wrong. They looked for substances that did not break down into simpler substances. They already knew about some of them…

The first discoveries

Some elements exist naturally on their own. Early humans saw sulfur near volcanoes. They made charcoal by burning wood. They found gold in stream beds.

↑ This gold headdress was made over 4000 years ago. It was found in a grave in Ur, modern Iraq.

↑ Sulfur on Ijen volcano in East Java, Indonesia.

↑ Charcoal is a type of carbon. It forms when wood burns.

↑ The people of the Indus Valley started using bronze about 5000 years ago.

Copper can also exist on its own, but most copper is found joined to other elements in rocks. People started extracting copper from its rock 7000 years ago. They used copper to make weapons, tools, and jewellery.

Later, people mixed copper with tin to make bronze. The properties of bronze mean that it makes excellent swords and knives.

People first extracted iron from rock about 3500 years ago. They made tools and weapons from the iron.

↑ Most early copper was extracted from malachite.

1200–1700 – zinc and phosphorus

It is not easy to get zinc from its rock. However, when it is heated to high temperatures zinc evaporates easily, and escapes to the air. Indian scientists solved this problem 800 years ago. They heated zinc-containing rock with waste wool in closed containers.

Hennig Brandt made the first phosphorus. He evaporated water from urine. He heated the solid that remained until it was red hot. Phosphorus vapour evaporated.

↑ These iron tools are from around Europe.

The 1700s – elements from the air, and more metals

Scientists discovered 17 new elements in the 1700s. They isolated nickel from rocks and magnesium from pond water. They separated oxygen and nitrogen from the air.

Henry Cavendish and Joseph Priestley removed oxygen from the air. They put a mouse in the remaining air. It died. Another scientist, Daniel Rutherford, explained the evidence. He said that air is mainly nitrogen.

The 1800s – technology drives discoveries

The 1880s saw the discovery of more than 50 elements. A new piece of equipment, the spectroscope, helped scientists to discover caesium and rubidium.

Aluminium was also found in the 1800s. It wasn't found earlier because it is strongly joined to oxygen in its rock.

The twentieth and twenty-first centuries

The last gaps in the periodic table were filled in the 1920s. Ida Tacke and her colleagues discovered the elements rhenium and technetium.

Scientists made more than 25 artificial elements in the twentieth century. Russian and American scientists created element 117 in the early 2000s.

elements discovered before 1200
elements discovered between 1200 and 1700
elements discovered in the 1700s
elements discovered in the 1800s
elements discovered in the 1900s

H hydrogen																	He helium
Li lithium	Be beryllium											B boron	C carbon	N nitrogen	O oxygen	F fluorine	Ne neon
Na sodium	Mg magnesium											Al aluminium	Si silicon	P phosphorus	S sulfur	Cl chlorine	Ar argon
K potassium	Ca calcium	Sc scandium	Ti titanium	V vanadium	Cr chromium	Mn manganese	Fe iron	Co cobalt	Ni nickel	Cu copper	Zn zinc	Ga gallium	Ge germanium	As arsenic	Se selenium	Br bromine	Kr krypton
Rb rubidium	Sr strontium	Y yttrium	Zr zirconium	Nb niobium	Mo molybdenum	Tc technetium	Ru ruthenium	Rh rhodium	Pd palladium	Ag silver	Cd cadmium	In indium	Sn tin	Sb antimony	Te tellurium	I iodine	Xe xenon
Cs caesium	Ba barium	La lanthanum	Hf hafnium	Ta tantalum	W tungsten	Re rhenium	Os osmium	Ir iridium	Pt platinum	Au gold	Hg mercury	Tl thallium	Pb lead	Bi bismuth	Po polonium	At astatine	Rn radon
Fr francium	Ra radium																

Note: This periodic table does not include all the elements.

↑ The colours in this periodic table show when the elements were discovered.

Q

1 Explain why people have known of sulfur, gold, and carbon for hundreds of years.

2 Use the periodic table to list five elements discovered between 1200 and 1700.

3 Name the two naturally-occurring elements that were discovered in the 1900s.

- Elements that are found on their own, not joined to other elements, were discovered first.
- Other elements were discovered as technology developed.

Organising the elements

Asking empirical questions

By 1860 scientists had found about 60 elements. They asked questions about the elements:

● What are the patterns in the properties of elements?

● How many more elements are there?

● Can we use patterns in properties to help find new elements?

These questions are empirical questions. Scientists could do experiments and make observations to help answer them.

But scientific evidence alone would not be enough to answer the questions. Creative thinking would be vital too.

Scientists hoped to develop an explanation to answer the questions. They wanted to use their explanation to make predictions, too.

iodine

copper

copper sulfate

sulfur

⬆ Some of the 60 elements that had been discovered by 1860.

Collecting evidence and suggesting an explanation

For many years, scientists did experiments and made observations to collect evidence about the properties of elements.

In the early 1800s, John Dalton studied evidence from experiments. He suggested that elements are made from atoms. Atoms of each element have a different mass, he said. Later, another scientist worked out these masses.

Many scientists worked on finding patterns in the elements. It was the Russian scientist Dmitri Mendeleev who, in 1869, first grouped the elements in the way we still use today.

Mendeleev made lots of small cards. On each card he wrote the name of an element, its properties, and the mass of one of its atoms. He started arranging the cards in different ways.

Eventually Mendeleev came up with an arrangement that worked. He put the elements in order of the mass of their atoms, from smallest to largest. He also grouped together elements with similar properties.

Mendeleev wrote the arrangement on the back of an envelope. This was the first periodic table.

Mendeleev was confident in his explanation. It explained what scientists knew about elements. He could also use it to make predictions. Mendeleev left gaps in his table where he was sure that an element should exist, even if it hadn't been discovered. He also used his table to predict the properties of these missing elements.

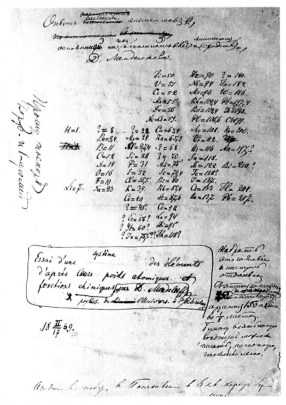

⬆ Mendeleev's first periodic table.

Testing the explanation and checking the evidence

Other scientists tested the explanation. They tried to find the elements that Mendeleev had predicted.

In 1874 a French scientist found one of the missing elements. He discovered the element under aluminium, and called it gallium. The properties of gallium were those predicted by Mendeleev.

Swedish and German scientists soon discovered two more of Mendeleev's missing elements – scandium and germanium.

The evidence showed that Mendeleev's predictions were correct. Scientists were confident in his great explanation. The periodic table is the foundation of modern chemistry.

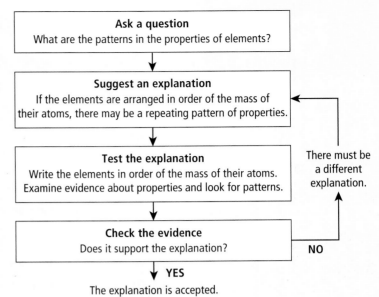

Ask a question
What are the patterns in the properties of elements?

Suggest an explanation
If the elements are arranged in order of the mass of their atoms, there may be a repeating pattern of properties.

Test the explanation
Write the elements in order of the mass of their atoms. Examine evidence about properties and look for patterns.

Check the evidence
Does it support the explanation?

There must be a different explanation.

NO

YES
The explanation is accepted.

⬆ This diagram summarises how Mendeleev and other scientists developed the periodic table.

⬆ Scientists all over the world use the periodic table. This one is from a Chinese text book.

Q
1 Mendeleev used evidence to help develop the periodic table. What else did he use?
2 List three types of evidence that Mendeleev used to help develop the periodic table.
3 Write down one question that Mendeleev's periodic table helped to answer.
4 Suggest why other scientists accepted Mendeleev's periodic table as an explanation of the patterns of the properties of the elements.

!
● Scientists asked questions, collected evidence, and used creative thought to develop of the periodic table.

Interpreting data from secondary sources

Patterns in the properties of elements

Yara and Mallana are looking for patterns in the properties of elements in the periodic table.

They do not do experiments themselves. They collect data from a data book. The data book is a secondary source.

Element	Melting point (°C)
fluorine	−220
chlorine	−101
bromine	−7
iodine	114

⬆ Data for Group 7.

Element	Melting point (°C)
lithium	180
sodium	98
potassium	64
rubidium	39
caesium	29

⬆ Data for Group 1.

Melting point patterns

The vertical columns in the periodic table are called **groups**. The students collect data about the elements in Groups 1 and 7.

The students present the data in bar charts. They choose bar charts because the variable they change (the element) is discrete – its values are words.

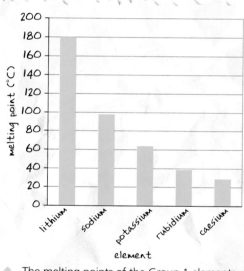

⬆ The melting points of the Group 1 elements.

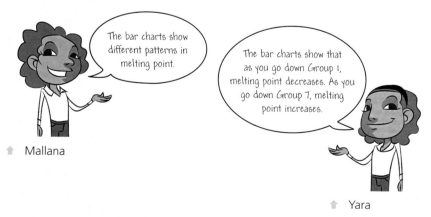

⬆ This outline periodic table shows the positions of Groups 1 and 7.

The students interpret the data. Whose interpretation is better?

Mallana: The bar charts show different patterns in melting point.

Yara: The bar charts show that as you go down Group 1, melting point decreases. As you go down Group 7, melting point increases.

⬆ Mallana

⬆ Yara

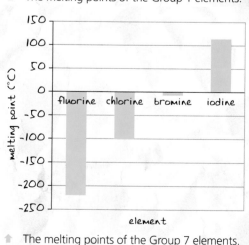

⬆ The melting points of the Group 7 elements.

Both students give correct interpretations. Yara's is better because she interprets each bar chart separately. Yara also gives more detail.

Density patterns

Mendeleev developed the periodic table. He predicted the density of an element that had not been discovered. The element is below silicon in the periodic table.

Yara and Mallana write down the densities of the other elements in the same group.

Element	Density (g/cm³)
carbon (graphite)	2.3
silicon	2.3
undiscovered element	5.5 (predicted by Mendeleev)
tin	7.3
lead	11.3

The students interpret the data. Whose interpretation is better?

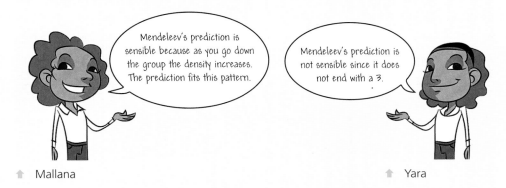

Mendeleev's prediction is sensible because as you go down the group the density increases. The prediction fits this pattern.

Mendeleev's prediction is not sensible since it does not end with a 3.

⬆ Mallana ⬆ Yara

Mallana's interpretation is better. She thinks about the complete density values, not just the number to the right of the decimal point.

The elements of the Earth's crust

Haki uses a secondary source – his text book – to find out the percentages of the elements in the Earth's crust. He displays his findings in a pie chart.

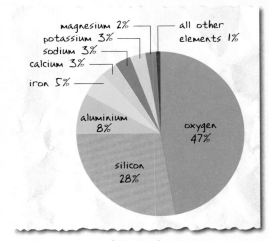

⬆ The elements of the Earth's crust.

Q

1 Use the pie chart to name the three elements that are most abundant in the Earth's crust.

2 Haki makes a conclusion from his pie chart. He says there is no tin in the Earth's crust. Do you think he is correct? Give a reason for your decision.

3 Use the bar charts on the opposite page to compare the melting points of the Group 1 elements with the melting points of the Group 7 elements.

- When interpreting data, describe patterns and trends in as much detail as possible.

6.6 Explaining differences between metals and non-metals

Objectives

- Describe differences between metals and non-metals
- Explain differences between metals and non-metals

Metals and non-metals in the periodic table

Most elements are metals. Some are non-metals. In the periodic table:

- the elements to the left of the stepped line are metals
- the elements to the right of the stepped line are non-metals.

																	He helium
H hydrogen																	
Li lithium	Be beryllium											B boron	C carbon	N nitrogen	O oxygen	F fluorine	Ne neon
Na sodium	Mg magnesium											Al aluminium	Si silicon	P phosphorus	S sulfur	Cl chlorine	Ar argon
K potassium	Ca calcium	Sc scandium	Ti titanium	V vanadium	Cr chromium	Mn manganese	Fe iron	Co cobalt	Ni nickel	Cu copper	Zn zinc	Ga gallium	Ge germanium	As arsenic	Se selenium	Br bromine	Kr krypton
Rb rubidium	Sr strontium	Y yttrium	Zr zirconium	Nb niobium	Mo molybdenum	Tc technetium	Ru ruthenium	Rh rhodium	Pd palladium	Ag silver	Cd cadmium	In indium	Sn tin	Sb antimony	Te tellurium	I iodine	Xe xenon
Cs caesium	Ba barium	La lanthanum	Hf hafnium	Ta tantalum	W tungsten	Re rhenium	Os osmium	Ir iridium	Pt platinum	Au gold	Hg mercury	Tl thallium	Pb lead	Bi bismuth	Po polonium	At astatine	Rn radon
Fr francium	Ra radium																

metals   non-metals

Note: This periodic table does not include all the elements.

Properties of metals and non-metals

The table shows the properties of typical metal and non-metal elements. Their properties are described in more detail on pages 26–31.

Property	Metals	Typical non-metals
Melting point and boiling point	High – all metals, except mercury, are in the solid state at 20 °C.	Low – many are in the gas state at 20 °C. Bromine is liquid. A few are low-melting point solids. Carbon is an exception – it has a high boiling point.
Appearance	Shiny.	The solids are dull.
Conduction of electricity	Good conductors.	All are poor conductors, except graphite (a form of carbon).
Conduction of heat	Good conductors.	Most are poor conductors, except diamond (a form of carbon).
Other properties	Strong and bendy.	Solids are brittle.

Atom arrangements in metals and non-metals

You can explain the properties in the table by considering:

- how the atoms are arranged
- how the atoms are held together.

104

Metals

In metals, the atoms are arranged in a huge pattern. Strong forces hold the atoms together. The rows of atoms can slide over each other.

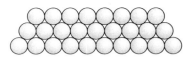
⬆ Part of the structure of a typical metal.

Non-metals

Some non-metal elements exist as single atoms. There are weak forces between an atom and its neighbours.

Some non-metal elements exist as **molecules**. A molecule is a group of atoms that are held together by strong forces. There are weak forces between a molecule and its neighbours.

Carbon is different to other non-metals. Its atoms are joined together in a huge structure. The forces between the atoms are very strong.

Using atom arrangements to explain properties

Melting and boiling points

Metals have high melting and boiling points. This is because, in their solids, strong forces hold the atoms together. Much energy is needed to overcome these forces to form liquids or gases.

Most non-metals have low melting and boiling points. This is because:

- for elements that exist as molecules, there are weak forces between the molecules
- for elements that exist as single atoms, there are weak forces between the atoms.

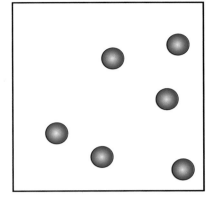
⬆ Helium, neon, argon, krypton, and xenon exist as single atoms.

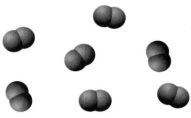
⬆ An oxygen molecule is made up of two atoms. A very strong force holds the atoms together. There are very weak forces between different molecules.

Strength

Metals are strong. This is because strong forces hold their atoms together.

In the solid state, non-metals are weak. This is because there are weak forces between the molecules.

Bendiness

A thin sheet of a metal is bendy. This is because its rows of atoms can slide over each other.

In the solid state, non-metals are not bendy. They are brittle. For example, if you tap an iodine crystal with a hammer it breaks. This is because there are weak forces between its molecules.

Q

1 Describe three differences between metals and non-metals.

2 Explain why a thin sheet of a metal is bendy, and a thin sheet of a non-metal is not.

3 The melting point of chromium is 1890 °C. The melting point of argon is −189 °C. Suggest a reason for this difference.

- Most metals have higher melting and boiling points than non-metals.
- Metals are good conductors of heat and electricity. Non-metals are not.
- Atom arrangements, and forces between atoms, explain metal and non-metal properties.

6.7

What are compounds?

Objectives

- Understand what a compound is
- Give examples of compounds and state how their properties are different from the properties of their elements

What's in a tooth?

The white part of your teeth is called enamel. It contains atoms of three elements:

- calcium – a shiny metal that fizzes in water.
- phosphorus – a poisonous solid that catches fire easily.
- oxygen – a gas that helps things burn.

So why don't your teeth catch fire? Or poison you? Or fizz when you drink water?

⬆ Tooth enamel protects your teeth.

⬆ Calcium in water.

⬆ Burning phosphorus.

Compounds

The elements in tooth enamel are not just mixed up. Their atoms have joined together to make one substance – calcium phosphate. This substance is different from all the elements that are in it.

Most substances are not elements on their own. They are made up of atoms of elements joined to atoms of other elements. These substances are **compounds**.

Compound properties

The properties of a compound are different from the properties of the elements in it.

Sodium chloride

Sodium is a shiny metal. It fizzes in water. Chlorine exists as a green, smelly, poisonous gas at 20 °C. These two elements join together to make a compound, sodium chloride. This is the salt you may add to food.

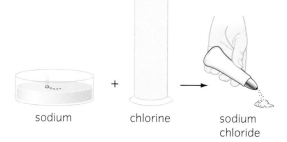
sodium   +   chlorine   sodium chloride

⬆ Sodium and chlorine join together to make sodium chloride.

Carbon monoxide

At 20 °C, carbon exists as a solid. Oxygen is a colourless gas – you can't live without it. Joining together 12 g of carbon and 16 g of oxygen makes carbon monoxide. This compound is a deadly poison.

Carbon monoxide exists as molecules. Each molecule consists of one atom of carbon joined to one atom of oxygen.

⬆ A molecule of carbon monoxide.

Carbon dioxide

You can make another compound from carbon and oxygen. Joining 12 g of carbon with 32 g of oxygen makes carbon dioxide. Carbon monoxide and carbon dioxide have different properties. Carbon dioxide is not poisonous. However, large amounts of carbon dioxide in the air make the Earth hotter.

Carbon dioxide exists as molecules. Each molecule consists of one atom of carbon joined to two atoms of oxygen.

⬆ A molecule of carbon dioxide.

Water

Water is a compound. It is made up of the elements hydrogen and oxygen. Each water molecule has one oxygen atom joined to two hydrogen atoms.

Imagining compounds

Toy bricks can help us imagine compounds.

⬆ A water molecule.

⬆ You can use these bricks to represent carbon atoms…

⬆ … and these bricks to represent oxygen atoms.

⬆ You can join the bricks like this to show the atoms in carbon monoxide (a compound). Each carbon monoxide molecule is made up of one carbon atom and one oxygen atom.

1 What is a compound?

2 Give one difference between an element and a compound.

3 Use the pictures of the toy bricks to help you answer these questions.

   a How many carbon atoms are in one carbon monoxide molecule?

   b How many oxygen atoms are in one carbon monoxide molecule?

   c What is the total number of atoms in one carbon monoxide molecule?

4 Compare the properties of carbon monoxide to the properties of carbon and oxygen.

- A compound is a substance that is made up of atoms of elements joined to atoms of other elements.

- The properties of a compound are different from the properties of its elements.

Making a compound

Developing a question

Zac is doing an investigation. He wants to make a compound of iron. He needs some scientific knowledge, so he makes notes from a text book.

> If I heat iron wool in air, the iron will join with oxygen.
> This will make a compound, iron oxide.

Zac decides to heat iron wool in air. He asks a question:

> How will I know if a compound is made?

Planning an investigation

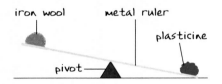

Zac asks his teacher for help. The teacher draws some apparatus that Zac could use.

Zac plans to heat the iron wool with a hot flame. The iron will then react with oxygen from the air. Zac must use a metal ruler because the hot iron wool might set fire to a wooden ruler.

Zac knows that iron atoms have mass. Oxygen atoms have mass too. He makes a prediction.

Hazards:
* iron wool – low hazard to health, but can cut skin
* iron wool catches fire easily when in contact with a flame
* when iron wool burns, pieces of burning iron wool fall off
* the metal ruler may get very hot when heated by the hot iron wool

> If I heat iron in air, iron atoms and oxygen atoms will join together. The mass of iron oxide I make will be greater than the mass of iron I start with. So the ruler will tilt like this:

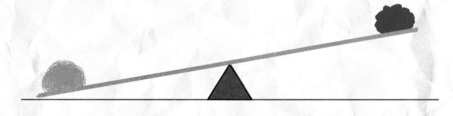

Controlling risks

Zac thinks about the **hazards** of his investigation. A hazard is a possible source of danger. He makes notes from the Internet.

Zac must control the **risks** from these hazards. Risk is the chance of damage or injury from a hazard.

You can plan how to control a risk by thinking about three things:

- time
- distance
- shielding.

Zac makes the decisions below to control risk.

> Time – turn off the Bunsen burner as soon as possible, and wait long enough for the equipment to cool before touching it after the experiment.
>
> Distance – stand back from the burning iron wool.
>
> Shielding – keep spare iron wool in a sealed container. Wear eye protection. Wear gloves when handling iron wool.

Considering evidence

Zac heats the iron wool for one minute. The ruler tilts over like this. Zac's prediction was correct.

Zac writes a conclusion for his investigation.

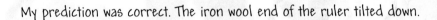

> My prediction was correct. The iron wool end of the ruler tilted down.

Zac's teacher asked Zac to improve his conclusion. She told him to use scientific knowledge and understanding to explain his results.

Zac added the sentences below.

> When I heated the iron, iron atoms joined with oxygen atoms from the air. This made a compound called iron oxide. The mass of iron oxide was greater than the mass of the iron I started with. So the iron oxide end tilted down.

Doing a calculation

Ava did a similar investigation to Zac. But she also made some measurements.

> mass of iron before heating = 4.1 g
>
> mass of iron oxide after heating = 5.6 g

Ava did a calculation to find the mass of oxygen that had joined to the iron.

> mass of oxygen = mass of iron oxide – mass of iron
>
> = 5.6 g – 4.1 g
>
> = 1.5 g

Q

1 Explain the difference between a hazard and a risk.

2 List three things to consider when planning how to control risk.

3 Suggest why it is important to use scientific knowledge when writing a conclusion to an investigation.

When planning an investigation, use scientific knowledge to:

- develop a question, make a plan, and control risks

- consider evidence.

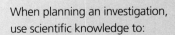

6.9

Naming compounds and writing formulae

Objectives

■ Name compounds

■ Write and interpret formulae

Naming compounds

Compounds of a metal and a non-metal

Many compounds are made up of a metal and a non-metal. Follow the rules below to name these compounds.

1 Write the name of the metal.

2 Write the name of the non-metal, but change the end of its name to -*ide*.

Metal	Non-metal	Name of compound
zinc	oxygen	zinc oxide
sodium	chlorine	sodium chloride
calcium	sulfur	calcium sulfide

Compounds of a metal, a non-metal, and oxygen

To name a compound made up of a metal, a non-metal, and oxygen, follow the rules below.

1 Write the name of the metal.

2 Write the name of the non-metal, but change the end of its name to -*ate*. The -*ate* shows that the compound contains oxygen.

Elements in compound	Name of compound
copper, sulfur, oxygen	copper sulfate
potassium, nitrogen, oxygen	potassium nitrate
magnesium, carbon, oxygen	magnesium carbonate

Compounds containing non-metals only

Some compounds are made up of atoms of non-metals only. To name these compounds, you need to know the numbers of atoms of each element in a molecule of the compound.

This molecule is made up of one carbon atom and one oxygen atom. It is carbon **mon**oxide.

This molecule consists of one carbon atom and two oxygen atoms. Its name is carbon **di**oxide.

Molecule of compound made up of...	Name of compound
1 atom of sulfur and 2 atoms of oxygen	sulfur dioxide
1 atom of sulfur and 3 atoms of oxygen	sulfur trioxide
1 atom of phosphorus and 3 atoms of chlorine	phosphorus trichloride
2 atoms of nitrogen and 4 atoms of oxygen	dinitrogen tetroxide

↑ Carbon monoxide.

↑ Carbon dioxide.

Writing formulae

Each element has its own chemical symbol. You can combine chemical symbols to give the **formula** of a compound. A formula shows the number of atoms of each element in a compound. You can also use formulae to represent elements that exist as molecules.

↑ A nitrogen molecule.

Nitrogen exists as molecules. Each molecule is made up of two atoms. The formula of nitrogen is N_2.

A molecule of carbon dioxide consists of one atom of carbon joined to two atoms of oxygen. Its formula is CO_2.

Follow these rules for numbers in formulae:

- Write each number after (to the right of) its element symbol.
- Write numbers small, and below the line.

Name of element or compound	Number of atoms of each element in one molecule ...	Formula
bromine	2 bromine atoms	Br_2
nitrogen monoxide	1 nitrogen atom and 1 oxygen atom	NO
nitrogen dioxide	1 nitrogen atom and 2 oxygen atoms	NO_2
dinitrogen tetroxide	2 nitrogen atoms and 4 oxygen atoms	N_2O_4

Many compounds do not exist as molecules. Their formulae show the ratio of the number of atoms of each element in the compound.

Name of compound	Ratio of number of atoms of each element in the compound	Formula
iron sulfide	1 iron : 1 sulfur	FeS
sodium chloride	1 sodium : 1 chlorine	NaCl
copper sulfate	1 copper : 1 sulfur : 4 oxygen	$CuSO_4$
sodium carbonate	2 sodium : 1 carbon : 3 oxygen	Na_2CO_3

Interpreting formulae

Formulae show whether a substance is an element or a compound.

- If a formula includes the chemical symbol of one element only, the substance is an element.
- If a formula includes the chemical symbols of more than one element, the substance is a compound.

Q

1 Name the elements in: copper sulfide, silver bromide, aluminium iodide, iron sulfate, sodium carbonate, silicon dioxide.

2 Name these compounds: KCl, ZnO, SO_2, SO_3, $CuSO_4$

3 Which of these formulae represent compounds: P_4, P_2O_5, N_2, S_8, $CaSO_4$?

!

- The name of a compound shows the elements in it.
- A formula shows the ratio of the number of atoms of each element in the substance.

6.10 Oxides, hydroxides, sulfates, and carbonates

Objectives

- Name some common oxides and hydroxides
- Describe one difference in the properties of metal oxides and non-metal oxides

Oxides

A compound of oxygen with another element is called an **oxide**. Many oxides exist naturally in the Earth's crust. They are often mixed with other oxides in rocks.

⬆ Sand is silicon dioxide.

⬆ Haematite is iron oxide.

⬆ Rubies consist of aluminium oxide with tiny amounts of chromium.

Making oxides

An oxide forms when an element joins with oxygen. For example, if you heat magnesium in air, magnesium oxide quickly forms. The oxygen has come from the air. Heating sulfur in air makes sulfur dioxide.

Some elements join to oxygen without heating. As soon as you cut a piece of aluminium, its surface atoms join with oxygen from the air. Aluminium oxide forms. This oxide is useful – it protects the aluminium underneath it.

Metal or non-metal?

Metal oxides and non-metal oxides have different properties.

Most non-metal oxides are acidic. If you bubble carbon dioxide gas into pure water, a solution forms. Its pH is less than 7. The same happens if you bubble oxides of nitrogen, or oxides of sulfur, into pure water.

Metal oxides are **bases**. This means that they neutralise acids. Some metal oxides, for example sodium oxide, dissolve in water to form alkaline solutions.

Using oxides

The uses of oxides depend on their properties. For example:

- Magnesium oxide has a very high melting point. It is used in furnaces.
- Titanium dioxide is bright white. It is used in paints and toothpastes.

Hydroxides

Compounds made up of a metal, hydrogen, and oxygen, are called **hydroxides**.

- Sodium hydroxide contains atoms of sodium, hydrogen, and oxygen.
- Potassium hydroxide contains atoms of potassium, hydrogen, and oxygen.

Some metal hydroxides dissolve in water to form alkaline solutions.

Formulae of oxides and hydroxides

The tables give the formulae of some oxides and hydroxides.

Name of compound	Ratio of number of atoms of each element in the compound...	Formula
Metal oxides		
magnesium oxide	1 magnesium atom and 1 oxygen atom	MgO
sodium oxide	2 sodium atoms and 1 oxygen atom	Na_2O
aluminium oxide	2 aluminium atoms and 3 oxygen atoms	Al_2O_3

Name of compound	Ratio of number of atoms of each element in the compound...	Formula
Non-metal oxides		
carbon monoxide	1 carbon atom and 1 oxygen atom	CO
carbon dioxide	1 carbon atom and 2 oxygen atoms	CO_2

Name of compound	Ratio of number of atoms of each element in the compound...	Formula
Hydroxides		
sodium hydroxide	1 sodium atom, 1 hydrogen atom and 1 oxygen atom	NaOH
potassium hydroxide	1 potassium atom, 1 hydrogen atom and 1 oxygen atom	KOH
calcium hydroxide	1 calcium atom, 2 hydrogen atoms and 2 oxygen atoms	$Ca(OH)_2$

Sulfates

A sulfate is made up of three elements – a metal, sulfur, and oxygen. Its formula is $CuSO_4$. You might have used copper sulfate at school. It exists as blue crystals. Farmers use it to control fungus on fruit crops.

Carbonates

A carbonate is made up of three elements – a metal, carbon, and oxygen. Calcium carbonate exists naturally as limestone and marble. It is a useful building material. Its formula is $CaCO_3$.

⬆ Copper sulfate crystals.

Q

1 Name the elements that make up calcium oxide. Would you expect this compound to be acidic or basic?

2 Name the elements that make up lithium hydroxide.

3 Name the elements that make up sodium sulfate.

4 Name the compounds with these formulae: CaO, SiO_2, KOH, $CaCO_3$, Na_2SO_4

5 **Extension:** Give one use of magnesium oxide, and explain how this use depends on its properties.

- An oxide is a compound of oxygen and another element.

- A hydroxide is a compound of oxygen, hydrogen, and another element.

- A carbonate is a compound of carbon, oxygen, and another element.

- A sulfate is a compound of sulfur, oxygen, and another element.

- A typical non-metal oxide is acidic; a typical metal oxide is a base.

Chlorides

A **chloride** is a compound made up of chlorine and one other element. Examples include sodium chloride and calcium chloride.

Making sodium chloride

Mrs Mtera makes sodium chloride in the laboratory. First, she fills a gas jar with chlorine gas. Then she heats a small piece of sodium until it melts. She places the sodium in the chlorine gas. The sodium burns with a bright yellow flame. Clouds of white sodium chloride form.

How much salt is in the sea?

There is no need to make sodium chloride. Huge amounts of the salt exist naturally, dissolved in seawater.

⬆ Burning sodium in chlorine.

Planning an investigation

Emebet wonders how much salt is in the Red Sea. She decides to do an investigation. Her friend, Berekti, says the investigation is impossible – no one could test so much seawater.

Emebet turns her idea it into a question she can test.

> What mass of salt is dissolved in 20 cm³ of water from the Red Sea?

Emebet writes down a plan.

> * Measure out 20 cm³ seawater
> * Heat until all the water evaporates
> * Find the mass of salt that remains

Obtaining and presenting evidence

Emebet pours seawater into a measuring cylinder. She says its volume is 20 cm³.

Berekti tells Emebet to add more seawater. The bottom, not the top, of the curved surface of the liquid (the **meniscus**) should be level with the 20 cm³ mark.

Next, Berekti finds the mass of the empty evaporating basin. It is 25 g. Emebet points out a mistake. The evaporating dish is wet, so its measured mass is too high. Emebet dries the evaporating basin. She places it on the balance again.

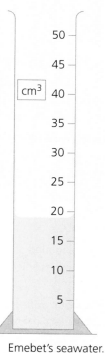

⬆ Emebet's seawater.

Its mass is 25 g.

Emebet is surprised that the mass values are the same for the dry and wet basins. She realises that she needs a balance that measures smaller differences in mass. She fetches a new balance, and finds the mass of the dry evaporating basin.

mass of evaporating basin is 25.10 g

Berekti points out that they will be making several measurements. It would be better to organise them in a table. Then it will be easier to use the data to do calculations. Berekti's table is below. She has given a unit in the column heading.

	mass (g)
mass of empty evaporating basin	25.10
mass of evaporating basin + salt	25.60
mass of salt	

Emebet and Berekti heat the seawater. The water evaporates. Salt remains. The students measure the mass of the evaporating dish and salt.

Considering evidence

They students calculate the mass of salt:

mass of salt = (mass of evaporating basin + salt) − (mass of evaporating basin)
= 25.60 g − 25.10 g
= 0.50 g

The students have set out their calculation clearly. This makes it easy to check, or do a similar calculation later.

The teacher suggests that Emebet and Berekti repeat their investigation three more times. They can then calculate an average value for the mass of salt in 20 cm³ of seawater. This result is more accurate than just one result.

To finish the investigation, Emebet uses a secondary source to help estimate the volume of water in the Red Sea. She then uses this value, and her investigation data, to estimate the mass of salt in the Red Sea.

1 Name the chloride that is made up of potassium and chlorine.

2 Explain why Emebet and Berekti write their results in a table.

3 Explain why repeating an investigation several times can improve the accuracy of data.

4 Suggest why Emebet and Berekti are unlikely to get identical results when they repeat their investigation.

Doing and investigation involves:

- devising a question
- planning
- obtaining, presenting, and considering evidence

Mixtures

Introducing mixtures

Prita spills water in the salt. Prema finds a stone in her rice. Priyam crunches sand in her salad.

Salt and water, stones and rice, and sand and salad are all **mixtures**. The substances in mixtures are not joined to each other. They are just mixed up.

Often, it is easy to separate the substances in a mixture. Prema could pick stones out of her rice. Priyam could wash sand off her salad. Prita could evaporate water from her salt.

⬆ A mixture of elements.

Different mixtures

Mixtures can contain elements, compounds, or both.

Salim has two sorts of nails – iron and copper. He keeps them in a jar. Iron and copper are both elements. So the jar contains a mixture of elements.

The label shows the ingredients in toothpaste. The ingredients are all compounds. So toothpaste is a mixture of compounds.

⬆ A mixture of compounds.

Air – an important mixture

Air is a mixture of substances, including:

- elements – for example nitrogen (N_2), oxygen (O_2), and argon (Ar)
- compounds – for example carbon dioxide (CO_2).

How are elements, mixtures, and compounds different?

Ricardo collects 7 g of iron powder and 4 g of sulfur powder. Iron is an element. It is made up of one type of atom. It cannot be split into anything simpler. Ricardo holds a magnet near the iron powder. It jumps onto the magnet.

Sulfur is also an element. It is made up of one type of atom. Its atoms are different from iron atoms.

⬆ Orange juice is a mixture of compounds.

⬆ Iron filings.

⬆ Sulfur powder.

Ricardo mixes his iron and sulfur. He can see the individual elements. He can separate them with his magnet. Ricardo has a mixture. Its properties are similar to those of the elements in it. The elements have not joined together, so is easy to separate them.

The amounts of iron and sulfur in the mixture are not important. Whatever the amounts of iron and sulfur, it is still a mixture.

↑ A mixture of iron and sulfur.

Ricardo heats his mixture. The two elements join together. A compound, iron sulfide, has formed. Ricardo cannot get iron out of the compound with his magnet. The compound looks different from the elements it is made from. Its properties are different from its elements.

↑ Iron sulfide.

The amounts of elements in a compound are important. Iron sulfide always contains iron and sulfur in the ratio of 7:4 by mass.

The table summarises the differences between mixtures and compounds.

	Compound	Mixture
Number of types of atoms	More than one, joined together.	More than one.
Can it be separated into simpler substances?	Not easily – chemical reaction needed.	Yes
Properties	Different properties from its elements.	Same properties as substances in it.
Amounts	Amounts of its elements are always in the same ratio.	Amounts of substances can change.

1 What is a mixture?

2 Describe three differences between a mixture and a compound.

3 List five mixtures and five compounds.

4 A mixture includes substances with these formulae: CO_2, N_2, SO_3, O_2. Is it a mixture of elements, a mixture of compounds, or a mixture of elements and compounds?

- The substances in a mixture are not joined up, and can be separated.

- A mixture has similar properties to the substances in it.

117

Separating mixtures – filtering and decanting

Objectives

■ Describe how to separate mixtures by decanting and filtering

■ Understand how to plan an investigation

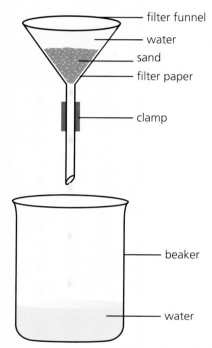

- filter funnel
- water
- sand
- filter paper
- clamp

- beaker

- water

⬆ Filtration separates an insoluble solid from a liquid.

Decanting

Tabia collects water from a pond. The water is muddy. She takes it home and leaves it in the bucket. The mud settles to the bottom. Later, Tabia carefully pours the water into a storage container. This is **decanting**. The mud remains in the bucket.

Tabia used decanting to separate a mixture of a liquid and a solid. You can also use decanting to separate liquids, if one liquid floats on the other.

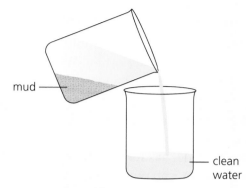

mud —

— clean water

⬆ Decanting involves carefully pouring off a liquid from a mixture.

Filtering

At school, Wira has a mixture of sand and water. Sand does not dissolve in water. It is insoluble. Wira wants to separate the sand from the water. He pours the mixture onto a piece of filter paper. Sand remains in the filter paper. Water passes through tiny holes in the paper.

Wira has **filtered** the sandy water. He has used **filtration** to separate an insoluble solid from a liquid.

Anvita's teacher gives her a mixture of salt and sand. He tells her to separate the sand and salt. Anvita adds hot water to the mixture, and stirs. The salt dissolves in the water.

Next, Anvita filters the mixture. Sand remains in the filter paper. The salt solution passes through the paper. Anvita removes the sand from the paper, and keeps it to show her teacher. Turn over to find out how to separate solid salt from salt solution.

Planning an investigation

Turning ideas into a form that can be tested

Jamal's mum takes iron tablets. Iron tablets contain compounds that contain iron. Jamal plans a project about iron tablets. He wants to investigate their solubility in water of different temperatures.

First, Jamal thinks of a question to test.

What mass of iron tablet dissolves in water at different temperatures?

Considering variables

Jamal lists all the possible variables. He decides which to change, control, and measure.

> Temperature – change this variable
>
> Mass of iron tablet that dissolves – measure this variable
>
> How fast I stir – control this variable
>
> Volume of water – control this variable

Jamal needs to decide what volume of water to use. He tries dissolving a tablet in 10 cm³ of water, then in 100 cm³ of water, and lastly in 1000 cm³ of water at room temperature. He chooses to use 100 cm³ of water for his investigation. With this volume, some – but not all – of the tablet dissolves. This means that, in this volume of water, it is possible that different masses of tablet will dissolve at different temperatures.

Planning what to do

Jamal writes a plan. He decides to use filtering to separate the solution from the solid that does not dissolve.

> 1 Measure out 50 cm³ water. Find its temperature.
>
> 2 Find the mass of a tablet.
>
> 3 Add the tablet to the water. Stir.
>
> 4 Filter the mixture.
>
> 5 Keep the solid in the filter paper. When it dries, find its mass.
>
> 6 Calculate the mass of iron tablet that dissolved.
>
> 7 Repeat at 4 different temperatures.

Making predictions and obtaining evidence

Jamal makes a prediction. He knows that, for many substances, the higher the temperature, the more dissolves. He uses this scientific knowledge to predict that the same will be true in his investigation.

Jamal carries out his investigation. He finds that his prediction is correct.

Q

1 Draw and label two diagrams to show how to separate mud from water by decanting and by filtering.

2 Franco has a mixture of olive oil and water. Suggest how to separate the two liquids.

3 Zumila wants to use filtration to separate salt from salty water. Explain why this will not work.

- Decanting separates a liquid from a solid, or liquids of different densities.

- Filtering separates an insoluble solid from a liquid or solution.

6.14 Separating mixtures – evaporation and distillation

Objective

- Understand how evaporation and distillation separate liquids and solids from solutions

> Use pages 120–3 to review what you learned about Separating mixtures at Primary level. Think about how the rest of this chapter helps you understand how mixtures are separated.

Evaporation

Copper sulfate crystals

Savit is making copper sulfate crystals. He has made copper sulfate solution, which is a mixture of copper sulfate and water. Now he needs to remove water from the mixture.

Savit decides to remove the water by **evaporation**. First, he heats the solution over a Bunsen burner. The water in the solution boils. Some of the water escapes from the solution as bubbles of steam. All the copper sulfate remains in the evaporating dish.

When about half the liquid water has changed state to become steam, Savit stops heating. He leaves the evaporating dish and its contents in a warm, dry room. Water evaporates from the solution. After a few days, all the water has evaporated. Copper sulfate crystals remain.

⬆ Heating copper sulfate solution.

⬆ All the water has evaporated from the solution. Copper sulfate crystals remain.

⬆ Copper sulfate solution.

Sodium chloride

People extract huge amounts of salt from seawater. Seawater is a mixture of water and sodium chloride (salt).

Seawater flows into large shallow ponds, called salt pans. Pure water evaporates from the seawater – the Sun provides energy for this process. Solid salt remains in the ponds.

⬆ Salt pans near Puducherry, India.

Lithium compounds

Every year, companies make more and more electric cars. The cars are powered by lithium-containing batteries. Huge amounts of lithium will be needed.

Up to half of the world's lithium is found in Bolivia. Lithium compounds are dissolved in water under an enormous salt desert.

The Bolivian government plans to bring lithium compound solution to the surface. Then energy from the Sun will make water evaporate. Solid lithium compounds will remain. The process works because the water and the lithium compounds are not joined to each other. They are just mixed up.

⬆ Salar de Uyuni, Bolivia's salt desert.

Distillation

It rains very little in Saudi Arabia. There are no permanent rivers or lakes, so about half the country's drinking water comes from the sea. But you can't drink seawater.

Huge plants like this one supply water to Saudi Arabian homes. The plants take in seawater. They separate pure water from the compounds that are dissolved in it. They use a process called multistage flash distillation.

⬆ This plant separates pure water from seawater.

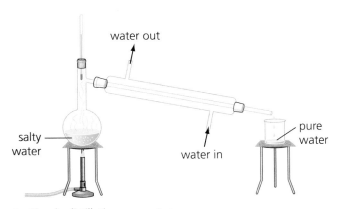

⬆ Simple distillation apparatus.

In the laboratory, you can use the apparatus above to separate pure water from seawater by **distillation**. The salty water boils. Some of the liquid water evaporates, forming steam. Steam travels through the condenser and cools down. It condenses to liquid water. The liquid water goes into the beaker. The compounds that were dissolved in the seawater remain in the flask.

Q

1 Name two important substances that can be obtained by evaporation.

2 Kish has some salt solution. He wants to separate salt from the solution. Should he use distillation or evaporation? Explain your decision.

3 Describe how to separate pure water from a solution of ink in the laboratory. Include a labelled drawing of the apparatus.

- Evaporation removes the solvent from a solution. The solute remains.
- Distillation involves evaporating and condensing the solvent from a solution.

Separating mixtures – fractional distillation

Distillation

Simple distillation can be used to separate pure water from salty water (see page 121). The process also works for other solutions. You can use it to separate pure water from copper sulfate solution, for example.

Fractional distillation

Ethanol and water

Fractional distillation separates mixtures of liquids. It only works if the liquids have different boiling points.

Mr Hassan is a science teacher. He has a mixture of ethanol and water. He sets up the apparatus opposite. He heats the flask gently.

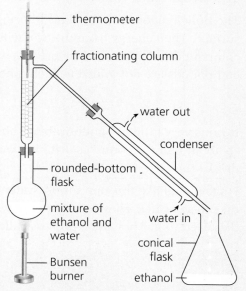

↑ Laboratory apparatus for fractional distillation.

Substance	Boiling point (°C)
ethanol	78
water	100

As the mixture gets hotter, both liquids evaporate. Vapours form. At first, both vapours condense when they reach the cooler fractionating column.

When the fractionating column reaches 78 °C, ethanol vapour does not condense. It enters the condenser. Here, ethanol vapour cools and condenses. Liquid ethanol drips into the beaker. Mr Hassan continues to heat gently, so that the temperature stays at 78 °C.

When all the ethanol has evaporated, Mr Hassan removes the beaker of liquid ethanol. He heats more strongly. The temperature of the fractionating column gets higher.

When the fractionating column reaches 100 °C, water vapour no longer condenses in it. Instead, water vapour enters the condenser. There, it condenses, and drips into the beaker. Mr Hassan has separated his mixture of liquids.

Crude oil

Diesel is a mixture of compounds. Most compounds in diesel are made up of atoms of hydrogen and carbon only. They are called hydrocarbons. Most molecules in diesel contain between 14 and 19 carbon atoms.

Petrol (also called gasoline, or gas) is also a mixture of hydrocarbons, but its molecules are smaller. Most molecules in petrol contain between five and ten carbon atoms.

↑ Diesel is used as a fuel in lorries, buses, and some cars.

Diesel and petrol are separated from crude oil. Crude oil is a mixture of hundreds of hydrocarbons.

Crude oil is heated to more than 450 °C. Its compounds become gases. The gases enter a fractionating column. They move upwards, getting cooler all the time.

As the gases cool, they condense. Because they have different boiling points, they condense at different temperatures. The compounds that make up diesel have high boiling points. They do not need to cool much to turn back into liquids. They condense near the bottom of the column, where the temperature is about 260 °C. The liquid is drained off.

Higher up the column, the temperature is lower. Here, petrol compounds condense.

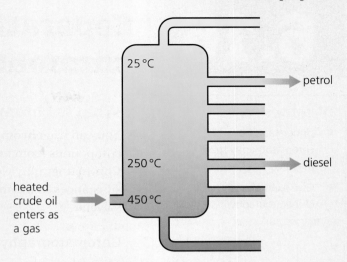

↑ Diagram of an industrial fractionating column.

Considering evidence – interpreting data from secondary sources

Crude oil is hugely important. Most crude oil is used for fuels. But we also use it to make plastics, paints, and medicines.

The bar chart shows the amounts of crude oil produced by the 15 top oil producing countries.

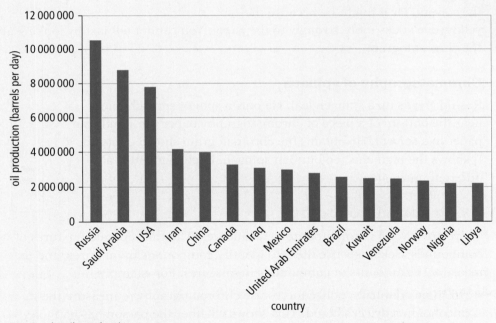

↑ Crude oil production.

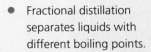

↑ This oil refinery in Nigeria uses fractional distillation to separate useful products from crude oil.

Q
1 What type of mixture can be separated by fractional distillation?
2 Explain why, in fractional distillation, the liquid with the lower boiling point is collected first.
3 Miss Chuma has a mixture of hexane and heptane. The boiling point of hexane is 69 °C. The boiling point of heptane is 98 °C. Which liquid will she collect first during fractional distillation of the mixture?
4 Name the top three crude-oil producing countries shown in the bar chart.

- Fractional distillation separates liquids with different boiling points.

6.16 Separating mixtures – chromatography

Objectives

- Understand how chromatography separates mixtures
- Give examples of uses of chromatography

⬆ Chromatogram from a green felt-tip pen.

What is chromatography?

You can use **chromatography** to separate compounds from mixtures of compounds. Chromatography works if all the substances in the mixture dissolve in one solvent.

Chromatography of ink

Mita sets up the apparatus opposite. The water moves up the paper. It takes the dyes in the ink with it. Different dyes move at different speeds, so they separate. A **chromatogram** is produced.

In the chromatogram, the blue dye goes further up the paper. This might be because the blue dye dissolves better in the solvent. Or it might be because the yellow dye sticks more strongly to the paper. You cannot tell just by looking at the chromatogram.

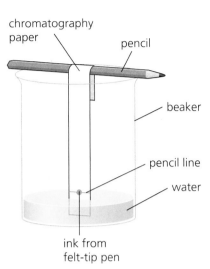

⬆ Chromatography apparatus.

Chromatography of spinach

Rashid grinds up a spinach leaf. He puts a spot of spinach juice near the bottom of a piece of chromatography paper. He stands the paper in a solvent. He obtains the chromatogram shown opposite. It shows the pigments (colours) in spinach. Each pigment is a different nutrient.

Using chromatography

There are several chromatography techniques. They all separate mixtures of compounds. Scientists use them to identify compounds in mixtures, and to measure the amounts of compounds in mixtures. For example:

- In some countries, police forces use chromatography to measure the alcohol in a driver's blood. This shows whether the person has had too much alcohol to drive safely.
- Detectives have used chromatography to look for explosives on the body hair of bomber suspects.
- Scientists use chromatography to identify nutrients in foods.

Ideas and evidence – using chromatography

Developing empirical questions

In Africa and southern Asia, up to 100 000 children go blind each year. A major cause of blindness is lack of vitamin A.

Many people in Africa and southern Asia eat a diet rich in cassava. Nigerian scientist Steve Adewusi and Australian Howard Bradbury wondered if different types of cassava contain different amounts of vitamin A. Would switching to vitamin-A rich cassava prevent childhood blindness?

The scientists developed an empirical question:

How much vitamin A is in the roots and leaves of different types of cassava?

Collecting evidence

The scientists did experiments to collect evidence to help answer their question. They used chromatography to measure the amounts of vitamin A in yellow cassava roots and in white cassava roots. They also measured the amounts of vitamin A in dark green and light green cassava leaves.

The scientists also collected data from a secondary source, the World Health Organisation. The data included the recommended daily vitamin A intake for children.

⬆ Cassava roots are important foods. The leaves of the cassava plant are also a common food in Africa and Asia.

⬆ Yellow cassava roots.

⬆ White cassava roots.

Developing explanations

The scientists studied their results. They concluded that yellow cassava roots are richer in vitamin A than white roots. Dark green leaves are richer in vitamin A than light green leaves.

The scientists thought about their evidence. They calculated the mass of cassava that provides the recommended intake of vitamin A. They worked out that eating yellow cassava root, and cassava leaves, can provide enough vitamin A. White roots alone cannot.

The scientists made a recommendation. To prevent childhood blindness, children should eat yellow cassava, not white.

1 Which of these mixtures can be separated by chromatography: sand and salt; coloured compounds in leaves; dyes in ink; water and salt. Give reasons for your decisions.

2 Explain why, in chromatography, some substances travel further up the paper than others.

3 Describe one use of chromatography.

- Chromatography can separate mixtures of substances that are soluble in the same solvent.

Separating metals from their ores

Objectives

- Describe how to separate metals from ores
- Calculate the mass of metal obtained from an ore sample

Substance	Density (g/cm³)
gold	19.3
quartz (the main substance in sand)	2.7

↑ Tin ore.

Separating gold from sand

Gold exists naturally as an element on its own. It is sometimes found mixed with sand on riverbeds. Gold is separated from its mixture by panning.

Panning works because the substances in the mixture have different densities.

Gold falls to the bottom of the pan. Sand mixes with the water and, on shaking, escapes over the edge of the pan.

↑ Panning for gold.

Extracting tin from its ore

Most metals do not exist naturally as elements on their own. They are found joined to other elements, in compounds. These compounds are mixed with other compounds in rocks. Rocks from which metals are extracted are called **ores**.

It is not easy to extract a metal from its ore. There are often many stages. Much energy is needed for some of these stages.

Tin exists naturally as tin oxide, SnO_2. The tin oxide is mixed with other compounds in tin ore. In China, South America, and Australia, most tin ore is deep underground. In Indonesia most tin ore is in riverbeds, mixed with sand and mud.

Tin is extracted from riverbed ores that contain 0.015% or more tin by mass. First, tin oxide is separated from the substances it is mixed with:

- filtration separates tin oxide from big pieces of unwanted material
- gravity separates tin oxide from sand and mud. This works because tin oxide has a higher density than sand and mud.

The filtration and gravity produce almost pure tin oxide. It contains more than 70% tin by mass.

The tin oxide is placed in a furnace with carbon. The mixture is heated to 1400 °C. Carbon removes oxygen from the tin oxide. Tin metal remains.

The tin metal is not pure. There are small amounts of other elements mixed with it. The table lists some of these elements, and their melting points.

Element	Melting point (°C)
tin	232
iron	1535
copper	1083

The mixture is separated by heating. Tin melts at the lowest temperature. It is poured off. The other elements are left behind.

Considering evidence and approach

Ore calculations

A miner has some tin ore. Its tin content is 0.015%. The miner works out the mass of tin in different masses of ore.

Mass of tin in 100 g of ore = 0.015 g

The mass of tin in 1000 g (1 kg) of ore = 0.015 g × 10
$$= 0.15 \text{ g}$$

The mass of tin in 1000 kg (1 tonne) of ore = 0.15 g × 1000
$$= 150 \text{ g}$$

Interpreting data from secondary sources

The bar chart shows the amounts of tin produced by the top ten tin producing countries.

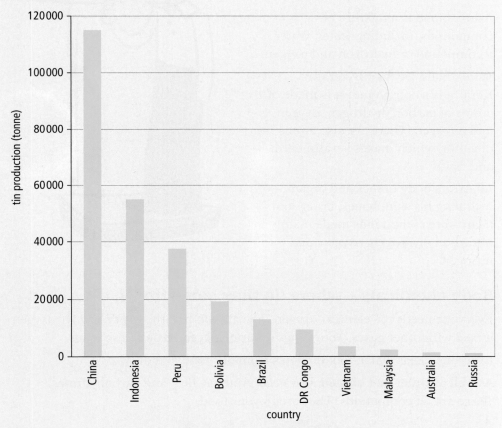

Q

1 Explain how panning separates a dense metal, or metal-containing compound, from the less dense substances it is mixed with.

2 Name two processes used to separate tin ore from the other substances it is mixed with.

3 Describe how tin metal is extracted from its compound.

4 Calculate the mass of tin that can be extracted from 100 kg of tin ore that contains 1% tin by mass. Calculate the mass of waste produced.

5 Name one country that produce more tin than Indonesia.

!

- Panning separates a dense metal, or metal-containing compound, from the less dense substances it is mixed with.

- Tin is separated from tin oxide by heating with carbon.

- Tin is separated from metal impurities by melting.

What are you made of?

Inside Asim

Asim has a mass of 50 kg. His body contains:

- enough hydrogen to fill his classroom
- enough oxygen to fill a room in his house
- enough nitrogen to fill his school bag 85 times
- and enough carbon to make a huge number of pencils.

Asim's body also contains 0.5 kg of phosphorus and small amounts of many other elements. The elements in Asim's body are not just mixed up. They are joined together in hundreds of different compounds.

Asim's blood is a mixture of compounds, including water. Water is a compound of hydrogen and oxygen.

Asim's nails are mainly keratin. Keratin is a compound. It is made of atoms of carbon, hydrogen, oxygen, and nitrogen. There are also atoms of sulfur, which makes keratin hard and rigid.

All Asim's body tissues and organs – including his skin, bones, brain, and heart – are compounds made mainly of carbon, hydrogen, oxygen, and nitrogen.

Body chemicals – where do they come from?

Everyone needs the element oxygen. The air you breathe contains 21% oxygen mixed with other gases. Your lungs separate oxygen from these gases.

Everyone needs water, too. It comes from our food and drink.

As well as water and oxygen, you need proteins, fats, and carbohydrates. These are all compounds. They are in your food.

Other important chemicals

To keep healthy, your body needs small amounts of **vitamins**. Vitamins are compounds made up mainly of the elements carbon, hydrogen, and oxygen.

You also need small amounts of other elements, such as iron and calcium. But it's no use swallowing iron nails or lumps of calcium metal. You need compounds that contain these elements, called **minerals**.

Mineral deficiency

If you do not take in enough of any mineral, you may suffer symptoms of mineral deficiency.

Mineral	Symptoms of deficiency
iron	tiredness, lack of energy, shortness of breath
calcium	weak bones and frequent fractures
zinc	reduced growth in children, problems with senses and memory
iodine	swelling of thyroid gland in neck, tiredness, brain damage

Iodine deficiency

In the 1980s, about 25% of people in Tanzania had iodine deficiency disorders. The government told salt makers to add iodine to all salt sold in Tanzania.

The government wanted to know if its policy had worked. In 2004, scientists investigated two questions:

- What percentage of households use salt with added iodine?
- Did fewer people suffer from iodine deficiency in 2004 than in the 1980s?

The scientists gathered evidence. They tested salt samples from 156 000 households. Iodine had been added to more than 80% of the salt samples.

The scientists tested 166 000 children for iodine deficiency symptoms. The percentage of children with iodine deficiency had decreased from 25% in the 1980s to 7% in 2004.

The scientists studied their evidence and made conclusions. In most areas, the greater the number of people eating iodized salt, the smaller the number of people with iodine-deficiency. This is an **inverse correlation**.

The scientists want the government to make sure that iodine is added to all salt in future. They now want to investigate iodine deficiency in pregnant women.

⬆ This woman has not had enough iodine in her diet.

1 Name the four elements that make up most of the mass of your body.

2 What is a mineral?

3 Describe what may happen if you do not take in enough iron.

4 Give the symptoms of calcium deficiency, iodine deficiency, and zinc deficiency.

- Our bodies are made up of compounds containing mainly the elements carbon, hydrogen, and oxygen.

- Our diet should include proteins, carbohydrates, fats, vitamins, and minerals.

1 Copy and complete the table.

Element name	Chemical symbol
	B
	Be
silicon	
sodium	
sulfur	
chlorine	
fluorine	
potassium	

[8]

2 Copy and complete the table to show whether each substance is an element or a compound.

Name of substance	Formula	Element or compound?
nitrogen	N_2	
carbon dioxide	CO_2	
sulfur	S_8	
argon	Ar	
magnesium oxide	MgO	
copper sulfate	$CuSO_4$	

[6]

3 The table gives data for four elements. Each element is represented by a number.

Element	Melting point (°C)	Does it conduct electricity?	Is its oxide acidic or basic?
1	113	no	acidic
2	850	yes	basic
3	−210	no	acidic
4	1063	yes	does not form an oxide

a Give the numbers of the elements in the table which are metals. [1]

b Give the numbers of the elements in the table which are likely to be shiny. [1]

c Give the numbers of the elements in the table which are likely to be malleable. [1]

4 The diagram shows the atoms in a thin sheet of metal. Use the diagram to help you explain why a thin sheet of metal is easy to bend. [2]

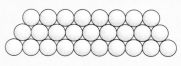

5 The diagrams show some particles of gases.

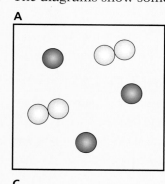
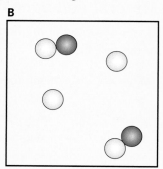
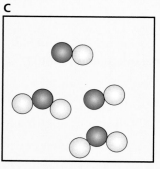
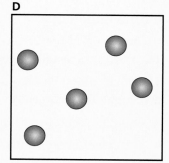
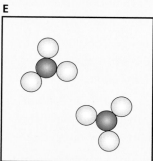

a Write the letters of the diagrams that show gases that exist as single atoms. [3]

b Write the letters of the diagrams that show gases that exist as molecules. [4]

c Write the letter of the diagram that shows a mixture of elements. [1]

d Write the letter of the diagram that shows a mixture of compounds. [1]

e Write the letter of the diagram that shows a mixture of an element and a compound. [1]

f Write the letter of the diagram that shows a single element. [1]

g Write the letter of the diagram that shows a single compound. [1]

6 Copy and complete the sentences below. Use these phrases. You can use each phrase once, more than once, or not at all.

one   more than one   different from the same as   can vary   are always the same

A compound is made up of _____ type of atom. Its properties are _____ the elements that are in it. The amounts of each element in a certain compound _____ .

A mixture contains _____ substance. Its properties are _____ the substances that are in it. The amounts of the substances in a mixture _____ . [6]

7 Copy and complete the table to show the names of the elements that are in each compound. [5]

Compound	Elements in compound
calcium oxide	
sodium chloride	
potassium hydroxide	
iron sulfate	
magnesium carbonate	

8 Write the names of the elements represented by the formulae below.

a $MgSO_4$ [1]

b NaCl [1]

c $CaCO_3$ [1]

d BeO [1]

e KOH [1]

9 The pie chart shows the percentage by mass of the different elements that make up the substances in the Earth's crust.

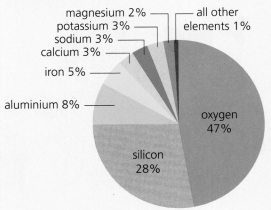

a Write down the names and symbols of 6 metal elements in the Earth's crust. [6]

b Name the metal element in the Earth's crust which is present in the greatest amount. [1]

c Name the two elements which together make up 75% of the mass of the Earth's crust. [1]

d Oxygen exists in the Earth's crust not as an element, but in compounds. Give one difference between an element and a compound. [1]

10 Sahira wants to investigate mass changes when she burns metals in air.

a Sahira writes down two possible questions to investigate.

– how do the masses of all metals change when they burn?

– what is the mass change of magnesium when it burns?

Sahira's teacher tells her to investigate the second question above. Suggest why. [1]

b Sahira draws the apparatus for investigating the mass change of magnesium when it burns to make magnesium oxide.

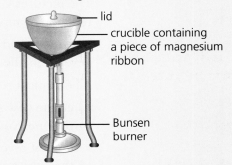

Sahira must open the lid a few times as she heats. Suggest why. [1]

c Sahira writes down some hazards of the investigation. Complete the table to show how she can control the risks from these hazards.

Hazard	How to control risks from hazard
magnesium is highly flammable	
burning magnesium has a very bright flame	

d Sahira writes down her results.

Mass of crucible + lid = 32.00 g

Mass of magnesium = 0.24 g

Mass of crucible + lid + magnesium oxide = 32.40 g

i Calculate the mass of magnesium oxide made. [2]

ii Calculate the mass of oxygen that joined with the magnesium in Sahira's experiment. [2]

e Sahira writes the conclusion below.

In my investigation, the mass increased.

Add a scientific explanation to improve Sahira's conclusion. [2]

Chemical reactions

What is a chemical reaction?

What links the pictures below?

The pictures show places where chemical reactions happen. In fact, chemical reactions happen everywhere, all the time, even inside you!

Scientists study chemical reactions in laboratories, too. They use them to develop medicines, fuels, and materials.

All chemical reactions:

- create new substances – the substances you end up with are different from the ones you started with.
- are not reversible – at the end of the reaction, you cannot easily get back the substances you started with.

The signs of a chemical reaction

You do an experiment in the lab. How do you know if it was a chemical reaction? There are many clues to look out for. You might:

- see huge flames … or tiny sparks
- notice a sweet smell … or a foul stink
- feel the chemicals getting hotter … or colder
- hear a loud bang … or gentle fizzing.

By the end of the reaction, what you see probably looks very different to what you started with.

Combustion reactions

Magnesium

Farah heats a piece of magnesium metal in a Bunsen burner flame. She looks away quickly and shields her eyes. Suddenly, there is a bright white flame.

The flame soon goes out. White ash remains.

Farah explains her observations. She saw a chemical reaction. In the reaction, magnesium reacted with oxygen from the air. The white ash is magnesium oxide. It was made in the chemical reaction.

The substances that react in a chemical reaction are **reactants**. The substances that are made are **products**.

The reaction of magnesium with oxygen is an example of a **burning**, or **combustion**, reaction. Any reaction in which a substance reacts quickly with oxygen, and gives out heat and light, is a combustion reaction.

Halim does a similar experiment. He finds the mass of a piece of magnesium, and heats it in a crucible. He lifts the lid three times during the reaction so that air can get in.

Halim works out the mass of the product. It is greater than the mass of the magnesium he started with. This is evidence that magnesium has joined with another substance – oxygen, from the air.

↑ The combustion reaction of magnesium.

↑ Heating magnesium in a crucible.

Mass of crucible + lid = 30.00 g

Mass of magnesium ribbon = 0.24 g

Mass of crucible + lid + product = 30.40 g

Mass of product   = (mass of crucible + lid + product) – (mass of crucible + lid)

= 0.40 g

Carbon

Chan heats a piece of carbon in the air. It glows red. Its mass decreases.

Chan explains her results. A combustion reaction has happened. Carbon has reacted with oxygen from the air to make carbon dioxide.

The reactants are carbon and oxygen. The product is carbon dioxide. Carbon dioxide is a colourless gas that escapes into the atmosphere as it is produced.

Q

1 Give two characteristics of chemical reactions.

2 List three signs of chemical reactions.

3 Phizz heats some iron in air. It reacts with oxygen to make iron oxide. Name the reactants and products in this reaction.

4 Explain why, if you heat carbon in air, its mass decreases.

5 Kezi heats 0.12 g of magnesium in air. It burns to make 0.20 g of magnesium oxide. What mass of oxygen has joined to the magnesium in this reaction?

- Chemical reactions create new substances.
- Chemical reactions are not reversible.

Writing word equations

Word equations

You can use **word equations** to show reactions simply. This word equation shows the combustion reaction of magnesium:

magnesium + oxygen → magnesium oxide

A word equation shows:

● reactants (starting materials) on the left

● products (what is made in the reaction) on the right.

The arrow means *react to make*. In a chemical equation, the reactants and products are different from each other. So the arrow in a chemical equation has a different meaning to the equals sign (=) in a maths equation.

The word equation below shows the combustion reaction of carbon in plenty of air to make carbon dioxide:

carbon + oxygen → carbon dioxide

Acid reactions

Combustion reactions are not the only type of reaction. There are many others. This section is about acid reactions.

Acids and alkali

Sam adds sodium hydroxide to hydrochloric acid. The alkali reacts with the acid. A **neutralisation** reaction has happened.

The products of the reaction are sodium chloride and water. This word equation shows the reaction:

hydrochloric acid + sodium hydroxide → sodium chloride + water

Sodium chloride is the salt you can add to food.

Acids with metal oxides

You can also neutralise acids with metal oxides. The equation shows an example.

sulfuric acid + copper oxide → copper sulfate + water

Copper sulfate is a **salt**. But it is not the salt in food. Scientists say that a salt is a compound made when a metal replaces hydrogen in an acid.

Making a salt

Maria uses the reaction in the equation above to make copper sulfate crystals. She writes down her plan.

1. Measure 25 cm³ sulfuric acid into a beaker.

2. Add copper oxide powder, one spatula at a time, until no more reacts. This makes a solution of blue copper sulfate solution. It is mixed with black copper oxide powder that has not reacted.

3. Filter to separate copper oxide powder.

4. Heat the copper sulfate solution over a water bath. Stop heating when half its water has evaporated.

5. Leave the solution to stand for a few days. Copper sulfate crystals will form.

Maria draws and labels the apparatus she needs for each stage.

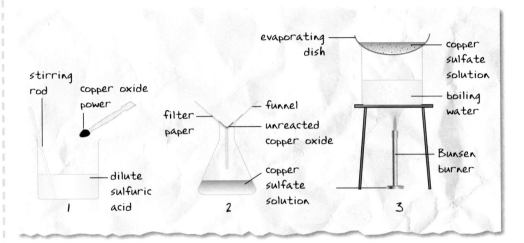

Maria finds out about the hazards in her experiment. She asks her teacher how to reduce the risks from each hazard.

Hazard	How to reduce risk from hazard
Copper oxide is harmful if swallowed. Dust irritates lungs and eyes.	Wear eye protection. Be careful when handling with spatula to prevent dust escaping.
Copper sulfate is harmful if swallowed. Solid irritates eyes and skin.	Wear eye protection. Do not touch with hands.
Glass makes sharp pieces if broken.	Place glass apparatus where it cannot roll off table.
Apparatus is hot.	Do not touch until cool.

Maria carries out her plan. A week later, she looks at her beautiful crystals!

1 Write a word equation to show that iron and sulfur react to make iron sulfide.

2 Write a word equation to represent the combustion reaction of calcium.

3 Identify the reactants and products in the word equation below:
copper oxide + hydrochloric acid → copper chloride + water

4 In a chemical reaction, the reactants are magnesium and hydrochloric acid. The products are magnesium chloride and hydrogen. Write a word equation to represent the reaction.

In a word equation:

- the reactants are on the left of the arrow

- the products are on the right of the arrow

- the arrow means *reacts to make*.

7.3 Corrosion reactions

Objectives

- Understand what corrosion is
- Know how to prevent iron corroding

Reactions – useful or not?

Many chemical reactions are useful. Chemical reactions make medicines, fertilisers and cement. Combustion reactions release energy to cook food and make cars go. Chemical reactions keep living things alive.

But some chemical reactions are not useful. Read on to find out more.

Corrosion

⬆ This car is made from steel, which is mainly iron. It is covered in rust.

⬆ This roof is made from copper. Its surface is covered in green compounds called verdigris.

⬆ These forks are made from silver. Their surfaces are covered in black silver sulfide except for one, which has been cleaned.

Rust, verdigris, and silver sulfide are formed in **corrosion** reactions. A corrosion reaction is a chemical reaction that happens on the surface of a metal. Most corrosion reactions happen slowly – over days and weeks rather than seconds or minutes.

Iron corrosion

Iron corrosion, or **rusting**, is a big problem. It happens when iron reacts with oxygen and water. The oxygen comes from the air. The water may come from the air as vapour, or be in its liquid state.

The product of the rusting reaction is hydrated iron oxide. This is iron oxide with water joined loosely to it.

The word equation below summarises the rusting reaction:

iron + oxygen + water → hydrated iron oxide

Rust forms on the surface of iron. It is soft and crumbly. It easily comes off the surface of the metal. This leaves more iron exposed and ready to rust.

Copper corrosion

Over time, copper reacts with substances from the air, such as carbon dioxide. The reactions make green compounds, for example copper carbonate. The green compounds cover the surface of the copper. They do not easily come off, so the copper underneath is not damaged.

Silver corrosion

Silver does not react with oxygen or water at 20 °C. In clean air, it does not corrode.

Polluted air may contain hydrogen sulfide. Hydrogen sulfide reacts with silver. The product is a black compound – silver sulfide – which forms on the surface of silver.

Preventing corrosion

Steel is mainly iron. Most of the metal things we use are made from steel. So iron corrosion – rusting – is an expensive problem.

Oxygen and water make iron rust. We can prevent rusting by keeping oxygen and water away from iron. Chemists do this by coating iron with:

- paint (on cars)
- oil or grease (in engines)
- another metal.

Ben's bucket is made of steel. It is covered in zinc. Even if Ben scratches the zinc, the iron does not rust. The zinc reacts with oxygen instead of iron.

⬆ This steel bucket has a coating of zinc.

Not all metals corrode

Some metals do not corrode in the air. Gold and platinum do not react with substances from the air, or water. The elements stay shiny for thousands of years.

The surface atoms of a piece of tin react quickly with oxygen from the air. A thin layer of tin oxide forms on the surface of the tin. The tin oxide does not react with substances from the air, or water. The tin beneath is protected.

The word equation shows how the tin oxide layer is formed:

tin + oxygen → tin oxide

Aluminium metal is also covered by a layer of its oxide. The aluminium oxide protects the aluminium underneath. This aluminium cannot take part in reactions.

⬆ Aluminium is covered by a layer of aluminium oxide. It is not easily corroded.

Q

1 Name the two substances that react with iron to form rust.

2 Write a word equation to represent rusting.

3 Explain why rusting is a problem.

4 Describe three ways of preventing rusting, and explain how they each work.

- Iron rusts when it reacts with oxygen and water.
- Rust is hydrated iron oxide.

Doing an investigation

Turning ideas into questions to test

A class plans to investigate rusting. Different students have different ideas.

I want to know why iron goes rusty.

⬆ Ruby

I used to live by the sea. Cars rust quickly there. I think salt might speed up rusting.

⬆ Seb

Rusting costs millions. I want to know how to prevent it.

⬆ Tahlia

The students discuss how to turn their ideas into questions they can test.

Ruby thinks her idea is too big to investigate. She doesn't know where to start. She reads in a text book that iron needs air and water to rust. She writes down a question she can test.

> **Ruby** The textbook says that iron needs air and water to rust. Is this correct?

Seb reads that he is correct – salt does speed up rusting. He realises that his idea is too narrow. He wants to do an investigation that will give him plenty of data. He writes down a question to investigate.

> **Seb** How does the speed of rusting depend on the amount of salt?

Tahlia knows she needs to narrow down her question. She collects evidence from a secondary source. She uses the evidence to help her write a question.

> **Tahlia** Which best prevents rusting – paint, grease, or covering iron in zinc?

Planning an investigation

Ruby plans her investigation. She draws her apparatus. She plans to leave the apparatus set up for a week. Then she will see which nails are rusty.

Before she starts, Ruby thinks about the variables in her investigation. She decides which to change, which to measure or observe, and which variables to control.

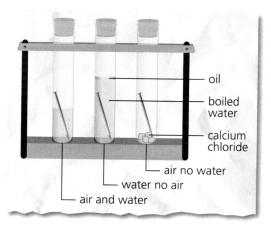

- oil
- boiled water
- calcium chloride
- air no water
- water no air
- air and water

Variable	Change, measure/observe, or control?
Substance in contact with iron	change
Size of nail	control
Type of nail	control
Whether or not the nail goes rusty	observe

Ruby uses her scientific knowledge to make a prediction.

The nail in contact with both air and water will go rusty. The others will not. I predict this because iron reacts with oxygen and water to make rust (hydrated iron oxide).

Obtaining and presenting evidence

Ruby considers the hazards in her investigation. She decides how to reduce the risks from the hazards. Then she sets up her apparatus.

A week later, Ruby looks carefully at the nails in the test tubes. She writes her results in a table. The variable Ruby decided to change is in the left column. The variable she is observing is in the right column.

Substance in contact with iron	Has the nail gone rusty?
air only	no
water only	no
air and water	yes

Considering evidence

Ruby compares her results with her prediction. Her prediction is correct. She writes a conclusion, which includes a scientific explanation for her results.

The nail in contact with both air and water went rusty. The iron on the surface reacted with oxygen from the air, and water, to make hydrated iron oxide. This is rust. The equation for the reaction is:

iron + oxygen + water → hydrated iron oxide.

Q

1 Write a plan that Seb could use to collect evidence to help answer his question. Include a diagram, and identify the variables to change, observe, and control.

2 Write a plan to investigate Tahlia's question. Include a list of apparatus, and explain how to make the investigation fair.

Doing an investigation involves:

- developing a question
- planning, including identifying variables
- obtaining and presenting evidence
- considering evidence.

Using reactions to identify chemicals

Objective

- Know how to use chemical reactions to identify metal elements in compounds

Flame tests

It's festival time! Fireworks light up the sky. How do scientists give fireworks their colours?

Firework colours come from burning reactions of metal compounds. Different metals give different coloured flames.

You can use **flame tests** to help identify metal atoms in compounds:

1. Take a clean nichrome wire.
2. Dip the end of the wire in the compound you are testing.
3. Hold the end of the wire in a hot flame.
4. Observe the flame colour.

The pictures show the flame colours made by compounds of different metals.

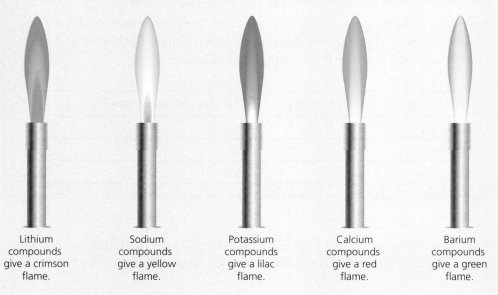

| Lithium compounds give a crimson flame. | Sodium compounds give a yellow flame. | Potassium compounds give a lilac flame. | Calcium compounds give a red flame. | Barium compounds give a green flame. |

Metal hydroxide colours

Flame tests identify some metals in compounds, but not all. You can test with sodium hydroxide to identify some different metals in compounds.

Here is what to do:

1. Dissolve a small amount of the compound in pure water.
2. Add a few drops of sodium hydroxide solution.
3. Write down your observations.

You might see that a **precipitate** forms. A precipitate is a suspension of tiny solid particles in a liquid or solution. In this test, the precipitates are metal hydroxides. Different metal ions make precipitates of different colours.

The pictures show the colours of some precipitates.

⬆ Some metals form coloured precipitates when they react with sodium hydroxide. Here are (from left to right): iron(II) hydroxide, iron(III) hydroxide, copper hydroxide, and nickel hydroxide.

Iron forms two hydroxides:

- iron(II) hydroxide is green
- iron(III) hydroxide is brown.

You can use word equations to summarise reactions that make precipitates. The equation below shows how to make a precipitate of copper hydroxide.

copper chloride + sodium hydroxide → copper hydroxide + sodium chloride

In the equation above:

- the reactants (copper chloride and sodium hydroxide) are solutions
- one product (sodium chloride) is a solution
- one product (copper hydroxide) is solid – it forms as a blue precipitate.

A student writes equations for three more reactions that make precipitates. Use the equations to answer question 3 below.

⬆ Precipitates of aluminium hydroxide, calcium hydroxide, and magnesium hydroxide are white.

1. iron(II) nitrate + sodium hydroxide → iron(II) hydroxide + sodium nitrate

2. iron(III) chloride + sodium hydroxide → iron(III) hydroxide + sodium chloride

3. aluminium chloride + sodium hydroxide → aluminium hydroxide + sodium chloride

Q

1 Describe how to do a flame test.

2 A compound burns with a yellow flame. Which metal atoms are in the compound?

3 a Give the colour of the precipitate formed in reaction 1 above.

  b Name the precipitate formed in reaction 3 above.

4 Write a word equation for the reaction of iron(II) chloride with potassium hydroxide. Name the precipitate formed in the reaction, and give its colour.

- Flame tests help identify metal atoms in compounds
- Sodium hydroxide reacts with some salts to form coloured precipitates

1 Copy and complete the word equations below.

a sodium + chlorine → _____ [1]

b zinc + _____ → zinc oxide [1]

c _____ + sulfur → iron sulfide [1]

d iron + oxygen → _____ [1]

e carbon + _____ → carbon dioxide [1]

f _____ + oxygen → sulfur dioxide [1]

2 What does the arrow (→) mean in a word equation? Choose the best answer from the four below:

are the same as   **are equal to**

react to make   **join up to make** [1]

3 Akono used to live in Abuja, a city far from the sea. He recently moved to Lagos, a city near the sea. He notices more rusty cars in Lagos. He wonders if salt speeds up rusting.

a Akono writes down three possible questions to investigate.

i Does salt speed up rusting?

ii What factors speed up rusting?

iii How does the mass of salt affect the speed of rusting?

Akono decides to investigate question iii. Identify one advantage of this question compared to question ii. [1]

b Akono lists some of the variables in his investigation to answer the question: *How does the mass of salt affect the speed of rusting?*
Variables:

– amount of salt

– how much of the nail has gone rusty?

– type of nail

– time nail is left in test tube

i From the list of variables above, identify the variable Akono should change. [1]

ii From the list of variables above, identify the variable Akono should measure. [1]

iii The list above includes two variables that Akono should control. Suggest one other variable that Akono should control. [1]

iv Explain why Akono should control the variables he is not changing or measuring. [1]

c Akono plans how to set up his apparatus.

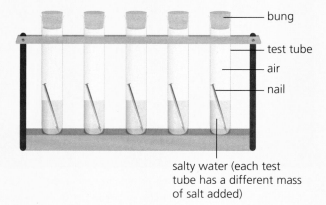

bung

test tube

air

nail

salty water (each test tube has a different mass of salt added)

Explain why the nail is in contact with both air and water. [1]

d Akono draws a table for his results. Copy and complete the missing column heading.

_____ (g)	How much of the nail has gone rusty?
0	
1	
2	
3	
4	

[1]

4 Name the reactants and products in the reactions shown by the word equations below.

a sodium + iodine → sodium iodide [2]

b carbon + oxygen → carbon dioxide [2]

c sulfuric acid + copper oxide → copper sulfate + water [2]

d magnesium + hydrochloric acid → magnesium chloride + hydrogen [2]

e copper carbonate → copper oxide + carbon dioxide [2]

5 Write word equations to summarise the reactions below.

   a Heating sodium in bromine to make sodium bromide. [3]

   b Heating sulfur in air to make sulfur dioxide. [3]

   c Heating calcium carbonate so that it makes two products – calcium oxide and carbon dioxide. [3]

   d Adding zinc to hydrochloric acid to make zinc chloride and hydrogen. [3]

   e Adding copper oxide to hydrochloric acid to make copper chloride and water. [3]

6 A scientist investigates the question: *How does temperature affect the speed of rusting?* She places six identical iron nails in boiling tubes. The nails are exposed to both air and water. She places each boiling tube in an oven or fridge at a different temperature. She observes the nails regularly.

Her results are in the table.

Temperature (°C)	Time for rust to appear on iron nail (hours)
10	240
20	120
30	100
40	30
50	15
60	7

   a Finish labelling the axes on a copy of the graph axes below. [2]

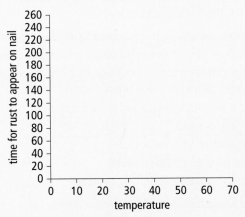

b Plot the data in the table onto your graph. [2]

c Draw a line of best fit on your graph. [1]

d Identify the anomalous result. [1]

e Suggest a reason for this result being anomalous. [1]

7 Purnomo sets up the apparatus below.

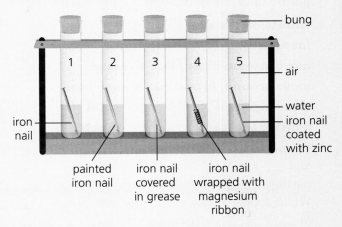

Copy and complete the table below. Predict the results you would expect for the investigation. Give a reason for each prediction. The second one has been done for you.

Test tube number	Prediction	Reason for prediction
1		
2	Nail will not rust.	Paint prevents air and water being in contact with the nail.
3		
4		
5		

[8]

1 Use the words and phrases to copy and complete the sentences below. You may use each word or phrase once, more than once, or not at all.

vibrate on the spot	**gas**
far apart	**liquid**
move around from place to place	
move around, in and out of each other	
close together	**solid**
a little	**much**

Copper exists in three states, solid, liquid, and _____. In the solid state, its particles _____. The particles are _____. When copper melts, it changes state from _____ to _____. Its particles start to _____. They get _____ further apart.

If copper is heated to 1083 °C it changes from the liquid to the _____ state. Its particles get _____ further apart, and they start to _____. [10]

2 Match the names of the substances to their formulae.

Name	Formula
carbon dioxide	He
copper sulfate	CO_2
carbon monoxide	N_2
nitrogen	$CuSO_4$
helium	CO

[5]

3 Copy and complete the word equations below.

a _____ + bromine → iron bromide [1]

b copper + _____ → copper oxide [1]

c magnesium + chlorine → _____ [1]

d nitrogen + _____ → nitrogen dioxide [1]

4 Tamara investigates diffusion. She sets up the apparatus below.

Petri dish —

pure water

lead nitrate crystal

potassium iodide crystal

The lead nitrate crystals and potassium iodide crystals are colourless. They dissolve in the water, and then diffuse.

a Explain what diffusion is. [1]

b As a result of diffusion, lead particles and iodide particles meet. They react to form a yellow solid. The yellow solid is called lead iodide.

i Name the reactants in the reaction. [1]

ii Name the product in the reaction. [1]

iii Write a word equation for the reaction. [3]

c The yellow solid forms along the line shown in the diagram below.

— lead nitrate

potassium — iodide

— lead iodide

Choose the best two reasons from the list below to explain why solid lead iodide forms nearer the lead nitrate crystal than the potassium iodide crystal.

Reason 1: Lead particles have a greater mass than iodide particles.
Reason 2: The lead particles are at a higher temperature than the iodide particles.
Reason 3: Iodide particles diffuse more slowly than lead particles.
Reason 4: Lead particles diffuse more slowly than iodide particles. [2]

d Tamara wants to investigate how the rate of diffusion changes at different temperatures. She lists the important variables in her investigation.
– temperature
– time from adding crystals to formation of yellow solid
– amount of water
– size of lead nitrate crystal
– size of potassium iodide crystal

i Name the variable Tamara needs to change. [1]

ii Name the variable Tamara needs to measure. [1]

iii Explain why Tamara needs to control the other variables. [1]

e Tamara writes a list of her results.

At 20 °C the precipitate formed after 60 seconds. When I used water at 30 °C it took 30 seconds. And then at 40 °C it was only 15. At 50 °C the time was about 14 seconds. And when the water was at 60 °C it only took 3 seconds to make the yellow solid.

   i Write a table for Tamara's results. Include units in the column headings. [2]

   ii Write Tamara's results in the table. [2]

f Copy and complete the axes below. Plot a graph of Tamara's results.

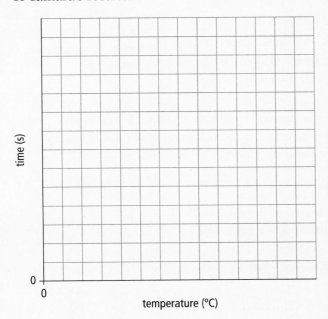

g Describe the correlation shown by the graph. [1]

h Identify the anomalous result on the graph. [1]

i What do you think Tamara should do about the anomalous result? Give a reason for your suggestion. [1]

j Write a conclusion for Tamara's investigation. Suggest a scientific reason that explains the correlation shown on the graph. [2]

5 The bar chart shows the melting points of some elements. Each element is represented by a letter. The letter is not the chemical symbol of the element.

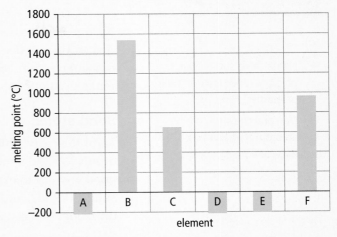

a Give the letters of the three elements on the bar chart with the lowest melting points. [1]

b Give the letters of three elements on the bar chart which are most likely to be metals. [1]

c Give the letters of three elements on the bar chart which are least likely to conduct electricity. [1]

6 A student has a block of chromium. Its volume is 4 cm³. It has a mass of 28 g. Use the equation below to calculate its density.

$$density = \frac{mass}{volume}$$ [3]

7 The table gives the melting and boiling points of some elements.

Element	Melting point (°C)	Boiling point (°C)
argon	-189	-186
bromine	-7.2	59
calcium	850	1487
gallium	30	2400
zirconium	1850	3580
technetium	2200	3500

a Which elements are in the solid state at 20 °C? [1]

b Which elements are in the liquid state at 40 °C? [1]

Atomic structure

Models of atoms

No one can see inside an atom. Scientists have developed **models** of atoms. A scientific model describes an object or a system. It is simpler than the real object or system. Scientists use models to explain things that happen, or to make predictions.

Solid atoms

Until the early 1900s, scientists imagined atoms as solid spheres. This model is good enough to explain the behaviour of solids, liquids, and gases. It also explains diffusion, density, and gas pressure.

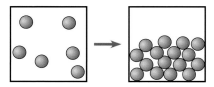

⬆ The solid atom model explains changes of state such as condensing.

You can also use the solid atom model to make predictions. For example, how will a substance behave when it changes state from solid to liquid?

But the solid atom model cannot explain everything in chemistry. It cannot explain how atoms join together. It cannot explain chemical reactions. Scientists need a more detailed model.

1932: a new model

In the early 1900s, scientists wanted to find out what is inside an atom. They collected evidence and thought about it creatively. You can find out more about what they did on pages 148–9.

By 1932, scientists had developed a new model. The model explains how atoms join together. It also explains chemical reactions.

The model states that atoms are made up of tiny **sub-atomic particles**. There are three types of sub-atomic particle – **protons**, **neutrons**, and **electrons**.

Protons and neutrons make up the nucleus. The **nucleus** is in the centre of an atom. Electrons whizz around the outside.

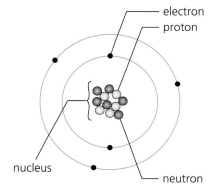

⬆ Atoms are made up of three types of sub-atomic particle: protons, neutrons, and electrons. *Not to scale.*

More on sub-atomic particles

The table gives the masses and charges of protons, neutrons, and electrons.

Type of sub-atomic particle	Relative mass	Charge
proton	1	+1
neutron	1	0
electron	$\frac{1}{1840}$	-1

The table compares the masses of protons, neutrons, and electrons. Their actual masses are tiny. The mass of a proton is about:

0.000 000 000 000 000 000 000 000 001 7 kg

The mass of an electron is even smaller.

Almost all the mass of an atom is in its nucleus. But a nucleus is tiny compared to its atom. This means that a nucleus has a very high density. For example, the density of a fluorine atom nucleus is about 60 000 000 000 000 g/cm³.

⬆ A nucleus is tiny compared to its atom. If you imagine an atom to be the size of a football stadium, the nucleus is the size of a pea.

Why do atoms have no electric charge?

Atoms contain charged particles. But atoms have no overall electrical charge. They are neutral. This is because, in any atom, the number of protons is the same as the number of electrons.

For example, a helium atom is made up of:

- 2 positive protons
- 2 negative electrons
- 2 neutral neutrons.

A lithium atom is made up of:

- 3 positive protons
- 3 negative electrons
- 4 neutral neutrons.

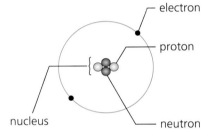

⬆ A helium atom. *Not to scale.*

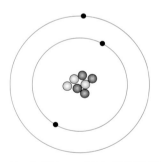

⬆ A lithium atom. *Not to scale.*

1 Give the relative charge and mass of each of the following: a proton, a neutron, and an electron.

2 Name the two types of sub-atomic particle in the nucleus of an atom.

3 Draw a beryllium atom. It is made up of four protons, four electrons, and five neutrons.

4 Explain why a beryllium atom is electrically neutral.

- Atoms are made up of sub-atomic particles called protons, neutrons, and electrons.

- Protons and neutrons make up the nucleus of an atom. Electrons whizz around the outside.

Finding electrons

Scientists cannot look inside atoms. So how did they discover sub-atomic particles? How did they create the models of atomic structure that we use today?

Finding electrons

In the late 1800s scientists investigated gases. They took sealed tubes containing tiny amounts of gas. They set up an electric circuit and supplied huge voltages.

Amazingly, the gases conducted electricity. In 1869 Johann Hittorf noticed a green glow on the screen. The glow, he said, was caused by rays from the negative electrode. The rays travelled through the gas and hit the screen. These were cathode rays.

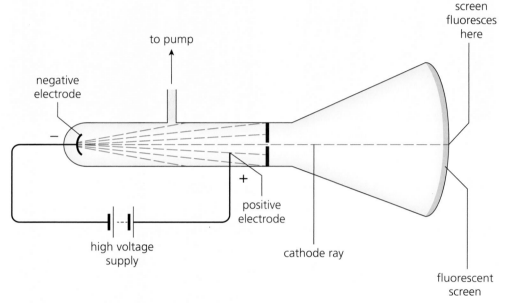

When the voltage is high, cathode rays travel through the gas.

Scientist Joseph John Thomson thought about cathode rays. He asked a question.

Thomson thought creatively about his question. He suggested an explanation. Maybe cathode rays are electrically charged.

Thomson collected evidence to test his idea. He passed cathode rays between electrically charged pieces of metal. The rays bent towards the positively charged metal.

Thomson was pleased. The evidence supported his explanation. Cathode rays are charged. Their charge is negative.

What *are* cathode rays?

Thomson asked more questions. He did some more thinking. He collected more evidence. He concluded that cathode rays are made up of particles. All the particles have the same – tiny – mass. They all have the same electrical charge. By 1897 Thomson had discovered the first sub-atomic particle, the electron.

New models of the atom

Scientists thought about electrons. They knew that electrons come from materials. Materials are made up of atoms. Electrons must be part of atoms.

Scientists suggested models for the atom.

Thomson's plum pudding model

Thomson knew that electrons are negatively charged. He also knew that atoms have no overall electrical charge.

In 1904, Thomson used this evidence to suggest a new atomic model. Negative electrons, he said, are placed throughout a positively-charged sphere. The electrons move around in rings.

Other people called Thomson's model the plum pudding model. The electrons reminded people of plums in a pudding.

Nagaoka's Saturn model

Hantaro Nagaoka was a Japanese scientist. He thought about the evidence for Thomson's model. He read about evidence collected by other scientists.

Thomson's model, said Nagaoka, could not be correct. It is not possible for negative charges to be spread out in a positively-charged sphere.

In 1904, Nagaoka suggested a new model. An atom consists of a positively-charged centre. Electrons orbit around the centre in rings, like those of the planet Saturn. Nagaoka used his model to predict that an atom has a nucleus with a large mass.

The story of the discovery of atomic structure does not end here. Turn the page to find out more.

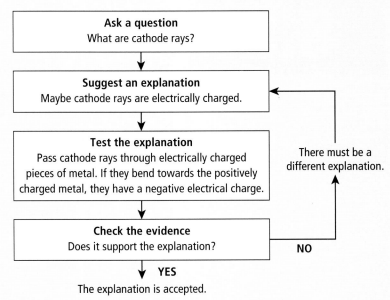

Thomson found out that cathode rays are negatively charged by asking a question, thinking creatively, and collecting evidence.

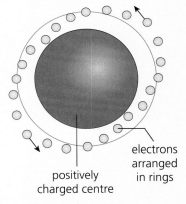

Nagaoka imagined an atom as having a positively-charged centre surround by electrons in rings, like those of Saturn.

1 Thomson suggested that cathode rays are electrically charged. Describe the evidence that supports this explanation.

2 Compare Thomson's plum pudding model with Nagaoka's Saturn model.

3 Explain why Nagaoka thought that Thomson's model for the structure of an atom is incorrect.

To develop explanations, scientists:
- ask questions
- use creative thought
- do experiments and make observations to collect evidence.

Discovering the nucleus

Testing the plum pudding model

Scientists thought about Thomson's plum pudding model. There was good evidence for the existence of negatively-charged electrons. But what about their arrangement in a positively-charged sphere? Was there evidence for this?

Ernest Rutherford lived and studied in New Zealand until he was 23. In 1895, he moved to Cambridge, England, to study under Thomson. He later worked in universities in Montreal, Canada, and Manchester, England.

Rutherford wanted to test Thomson's plum pudding model. He made a prediction, based on the model.

> We are going to fire positively-charged particles at a piece of gold foil. If the plum pudding model is correct, most of the positive particles will go straight through the foil. A few will pass close to negative electrons. These positive particles will change direction slightly.

Rutherford worked with two other scientists to test his prediction. The scientists, Hans Geiger and Ernest Marsden, set up the apparatus below.

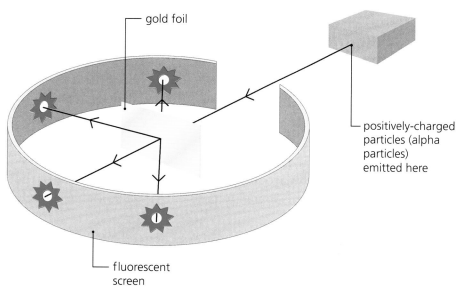

gold foil

positively-charged particles (alpha particles) emitted here

fluorescent screen

⬆ Geiger and Marsden used this apparatus to test the plum pudding model in 1909.

The scientists started firing positive particles at the foil. The results were amazing. About one positive particle in every 10 000 bounced backwards off the foil. Rutherford wrote:

We have been able to get some of the alpha-particles coming backwards!

> It was quite the most incredible event that has ever happened to me in my life. It was almost as incredible as if you fired a 15 inch [38 cm] artillery shell at a piece of tissue paper and it came back and hit you.

Rutherford evaluated the evidence. His prediction was wrong. He had based his prediction on the plum pudding model. This, said Rutherford, means the plum pudding model must be wrong.

Rutherford thought creatively about the problem. Could he come up with a better model to explain the evidence?

A new model for the atom

By 1911, Rutherford had created a new model:

- Atoms have a central nucleus. Most of the mass of an atom is in its nucleus. The nucleus is positively charged.
- The nucleus is surrounded by a big empty space in which electrons move.

Rutherford's model explained Geiger and Marsden's observations:

- The positive particles that bounced backwards had hit a nucleus.
- The positive particles that travelled straight through the foil had passed through empty space between nuclei.

Rutherford told other scientists about his work. Niels Bohr wondered how electrons move in the empty space around a nucleus. He suggested an explanation. Electrons move in orbits, or shells.

Inside the nucleus

Scientists thought about the nucleus. Was it made up of smaller particles?

Rutherford collected evidence. He fired positive particles into the air. Tiny positive particles were formed. Where did they come from? Rutherford realised that the tiny positive particles came from the nuclei of nitrogen atoms. The tiny particles were protons.

A year later, in 1920, Rutherford suggested that protons were not the only particles in the nucleus. Did nuclei also contain particles with mass, but no charge?

By 1932, James Chadwick had an answer. His experiments showed that nuclei contain neutrons as well as protons.

In chemistry, you will use the atomic model of 1932. This explains chemical reactions. It also explains patterns in the properties of elements.

Scientists did not stop studying the atom in 1932. They wanted to find out what makes up protons and electrons. Turn to pages 166–7 to find out more.

1 Describe Rutherford's model of the atom.

2 Describe how Rutherford, Geiger, and Marsden collected evidence for the nucleus.

3 Describe Rutherford's evidence for protons.

Rutherford discovered that:

- atoms have a central nucleus
- most of the mass of an atom is in its nucleus
- the nucleus contains protons.

Protons, electrons, and the periodic table

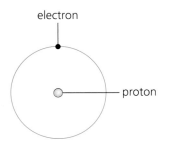

↑ The electron in a hydrogen atom.

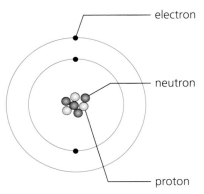

↑ The electrons in a lithium atom.

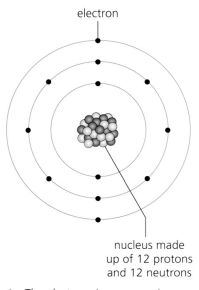

↑ The electrons in a magnesium atom.

Protons

The nucleus of an atom is made up of protons and neutrons. All atoms of an element have the same number of protons. For example, all oxygen atoms have eight protons, and all nitrogen atoms have seven protons.

In the modern periodic table, the elements are arranged in order of their number of protons.

Electrons in atoms

Electrons whizz around an atom outside its nucleus. The electrons occupy **shells**. Shells are also called **energy levels**, or **orbits**.

Each shell can hold a maximum number of electrons:

● the first shell can hold up to two electrons

● the second shell can hold up to eight electrons.

Electrons fill the shells that are closest to the nucleus first.

Hydrogen has one electron. It occupies the first shell.

Lithium has three electrons. Two electrons occupy the first shell. This shell is full. The other electron occupies the second shell.

A magnesium atom has 12 electrons. Two electrons occupy the first shell. Eight electrons occupy the second shell. The first two shells are now full. The other two electrons are in the third shell.

You can also use numbers to represent electron arrangements. The numbers show the **electronic structure** of an atom. The first number of an electronic structure shows the number of electrons in the first shell. The second number gives the number of electrons in the second shell, and so on.

The table shows the electronic structures of the atoms drawn opposite.

Element	Number of electrons	Electronic structure
hydrogen	1	1
lithium	3	2,1
magnesium	12	2,8,2

The first twenty elements

The diagrams on the next page show the electrons in the atoms of the first 20 elements of the periodic table. They do not show the number of protons and neutrons.

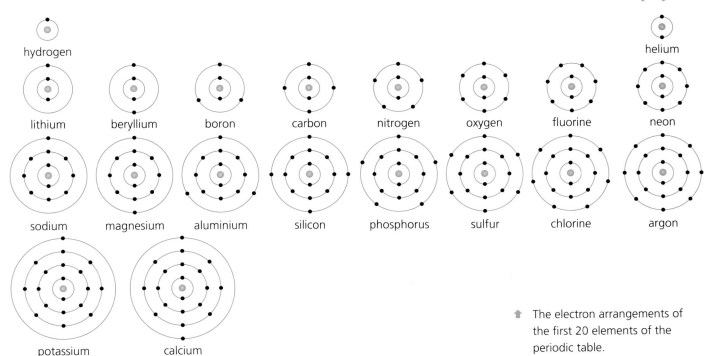

The electron arrangements of the first 20 elements of the periodic table.

The diagram below gives the symbols and electronic structures of the first 20 elements of the periodic table. The elements are arranged as they are in the periodic table.

H 1							
							He 2
Li 2,1	Be 2,2		B 2,3	C 2,4	N 2,5	O 2,6	F 2,7	Ne 2,8
Na 2,8,1	Mg 2,8,2		Al 2,8,3	Si 2,8,4	P 2,8,5	S 2,8,6	Cl 2,8,7	Ar 2,8,8
K 2,8,8,1	Ca 2,8,8,2						

Can you see a pattern in the electronic structures? The elements in the column on the left (Group 1 of the periodic table) have one electron in their outermost shell (the shell that is furthest from the nucleus). The elements in the next column (Group 2) have two electrons in their outermost shell. In all groups, atoms of each element have the same number of electrons in their outermost shell.

Q

1 Draw the electron arrangements in atoms of lithium, sodium, and potassium. Describe what the arrangements have in common.

2 Write down the electronic structures of helium, neon, and argon. Describe how the arrangements are similar.

3 Write down the electronic structures of the elements from lithium to neon in the periodic table. Describe the pattern you see.

- Electrons in atoms are arranged in shells.

- Each shell holds a maximum number of electrons.

Proton number, nucleon number, and isotopes

Proton number

Every atom of hydrogen has one proton in its nucleus. Every atom of oxygen has eight protons in its nucleus. Every atom of magnesium has 12 protons in its nucleus.

The number of protons in the nucleus of an atom is its **proton number**. The table gives the proton numbers of some elements. Every atom of a certain element has the same proton number.

Element	Proton number
hydrogen	1
oxygen	8
magnesium	12

In modern periodic tables, elements are arranged in order of proton number.

1.0 H hydrogen 1																	4 He helium 2
7 Li lithium 3	9 Be beryllium 4										11 B boron 5	12 C carbon 6	14 N nitrogen 7	16 O oxygen 8	19 F fluorine 9	20 Ne neon 10
23 Na sodium 11	24 Mg magnesium 12										27 Al aluminium 13	28 Si silicon 14	31 P phosphorus 15	32 S sulfur 16	35.5 Cl chlorine 17	40 Ar argon 18
39 K potassium 19	40 Ca calcium 20	45 Sc scandium 21	48 Ti titanium 22	51 V vanadium 23	52 Cr chromium 24	55 Mn manganese 25	56 Fe iron 26	59 Co cobalt 27	59 Ni nickel 28	63.5 Cu copper 29	65 Zn zinc 30	70 Ga gallium 31	73 Ge germanium 32	75 As arsenic 33	79 Se selenium 34	80 Br bromine 35	84 Kr krypton 36
85.5 Rb rubidium 37	88 Sr strontium 38	89 Y yttrium 39	91 Zr zirconium 40	93 Nb niobium 41	96 Mo molybdenum 42	(98) Tc technetium 43	101 Ru ruthenium 44	103 Rh rhodium 45	106 Pd palladium 46	108 Ag silver 47	112 Cd cadmium 48	115 In indium 49	119 Sn tin 50	122 Sb antimony 51	128 Te tellurium 52	127 I iodine 53	131 Xe xenon 54
133 Cs caesium 55	137 Ba barium 56	139 La lanthanum 57	178.5 Hf hafnium 72	181 Ta tantalum 73	184 W tungsten 74	186 Re rhenium 75	190 Os osmium 76	192 Ir iridium 77	195 Pt platinum 78	197 Au gold 79	201 Hg mercury 80	204 Tl thallium 81	207 Pb lead 82	209 Bi bismuth 83	210 Po polonium 84	(210) At astatine 85	222 Rn radon 86
(223) Fr francium 87	(226) Ra radium 88	(227) Ac actinium 89	(261) Rf rutherfordium 104	(262) Db dubnium 105	(266) Sg seaborgium 106	(264) Bh bohrium 107	(277) Hs hassium 108	(268) Mt meitnerium 109	(271) Ds Darmstadtium 110	(272) Rg roentgenium 111							

Note: This periodic table does not include all the elements.

⬆ For each element, the lower number is the proton number. The upper number gives the relative atomic mass of the element.

Atoms are neutral. This is because an atom has an equal number of protons and electrons. So the proton number of an element tells you the number of protons, which is also the number of electrons in one atom of the element.

Nucleon number

Protons and neutrons make up the nucleus of an atom. Particles in the nucleus – protons and neutrons – are called **nucleons**. The total number of protons and neutrons in an atom is its **nucleon number**. For example, an atom of oxygen has eight protons and eight neutrons. Its nucleon number is sixteen.

The nucleon number of an atom is also called its **mass number**. It gives the relative mass of an atom compared to other atoms.

The table gives the numbers of protons and neutrons in some atoms. It also shows their nucleon numbers.

Atom of the element	Number of protons	Number of neutrons	Nucleon number
fluorine	9	10	(9 + 10) = 19
magnesium	12	12	(12 + 12) = 24
argon	18	22	(18 + 22) = 40

If you know the proton number and the nucleon number of an atom, you can work out how many protons and neutrons are in its nucleus.

Worked example

An atom of boron has a proton number of 5 and a nucleon number of 11. How many protons and neutrons does it contain?

The proton number shows that the number of protons in a boron atom is 5.

The number of neutrons = nucleon number – proton number

$$= \quad 11 \quad - \quad 5$$
$$= \quad 6$$

Isotopes

Every carbon atom has 6 protons. Every carbon atom also has 6 electrons. Most carbon atoms have 6 neutrons. However, some carbon atoms have 8 neutrons, and some have 7 neutrons.

Atoms of the same element that have different numbers of neutrons are called **isotopes**. The different isotopes of an element have different nucleon numbers. The table shows the nucleon numbers of the three isotopes of carbon.

Atom of the element...	Number of protons	Number of neutrons	Nucleon number
carbon	6	6	12
carbon	6	7	13
carbon	6	8	14

Every chlorine atom has 17 protons and 17 electrons. About 75% of chlorine atoms have 18 electrons. The other 25% of chlorine atoms have 20 electrons. There are two isotopes of chlorine. The nucleon number of one isotope is (17 + 18) = 35. The nucleon number of the other isotope is (17 + 20) = 37.

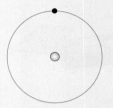

hydrogen-1
(1 proton)

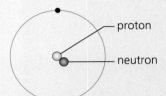

hydrogen-2
(1 proton and
1 neutron)

proton

neutron

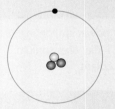

hydrogen-3
(1 proton and
2 neutrons)

⬆ Hydrogen has three isotopes.

1 Explain what an isotope is.

2 An atom of an element has 15 protons and 16 neutrons. What is its proton number? What is its nucleon number?

3 An atom has a proton number of 19 and a nucleon number of 39. Calculate the number of protons and neutrons in the atom.

- Proton number is the number of protons in an atom of an element.

- Nucleon number is the total number of protons and neutrons in an atom of an element.

- Isotopes are atoms of the same element with different numbers of neutrons.

The Group 1 elements

The Group 1 elements

The columns of the periodic table are called **groups**. The elements of a group have similar properties to each other.

The periodic table below shows Group 1. The group includes the elements lithium, sodium, and potassium.

Group 1

Li	Be											B	C	N	O	F	He Ne
Na	Mg											Al	Si	P	S	Cl	Ar
K	Ca	Sc	Ti	V	Cr	Mn	Fe	Co	Ni	Cu	Zn	Ga	Ge	As	Se	Br	Kr
Rb	Sr	Y	Zr	Nb	Mo	Tc	Ru	Rh	Pd	Ag	Cd	In	Sn	Sb	Te	I	Xe
Cs	Ba	La	Hf	Ta	W	Re	Os	Ir	Pt	Au	Hg	Tl	Pb	Bi	Po	At	Rn
Fr	Ra	Ac	Rf	Db	Sg	Bh	Hs	Mt	Ds	Rg							

H

⬆ Group 1 is on the left of the periodic table.

⬆ Lithium and its compounds are used in cell phone batteries.

Properties and patterns

The Group 1 elements are metals. In some ways, they are like other metals:

- they conduct electricity
- they are shiny when freshly cut.

The Group 1 elements are softer than most other metals. They can be easily cut with a knife.

⬆ This nuclear power station in Kalpakkam, India, uses sodium metal as a coolant.

Melting point and boiling point

The Group 1 elements have low melting points compared to most other metals. The table gives some examples.

Metal	Is the metal in Group 1?	Melting point (°C)
lithium	yes	180
sodium	yes	98
potassium	yes	64
rubidium	yes	39
iron	no	1535
copper	no	1083
gold	no	1063

⬆ Group 1 metals are soft.

There is a pattern in the melting points of the Group 1 elements. Going down the group, from lithium to rubidium, melting point decreases. A gradual change in a property is called a **trend**.

The boiling points of the Group 1 elements also decrease from top to bottom of the group.

Density

The Group 1 elements have low densities compared to most other metals. A 1 cm³ cube of sodium has a mass of 0.97 g. Iron has a much higher density than sodium. A 1 cm³ cube of iron has a mass of 7.86 g.

This bar chart compares the densities of Group 1 elements with three other metals.

The bar chart shows a trend in density values for the Group 1 elements. Overall, going down the group, from lithium to caesium, density increases. The density of potassium does not fit the pattern.

Reactions with water

The Group 1 elements have exciting reactions with water. As they react, they zoom around on the surface of the water. The reactions make hydrogen gas and an alkaline solution. Universal Indicator solution becomes blue or purple in the solution.

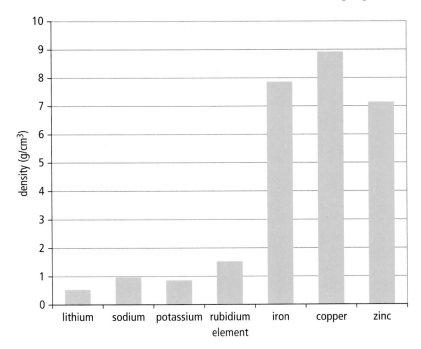

These word equations summarise the reactions of sodium and potassium with water:

sodium + water → sodium hydroxide + hydrogen

potassium + water → potassium hydroxide + hydrogen

There is a trend in these reactions. They get more vigorous going down the group.

Why do Group 1 elements have similar properties?

The atoms of the Group 1 elements have similar electron arrangements. They all have one electron in the outermost shell. This explains their similar properties.

Q

1 Describe the trend in melting point for the Group 1 elements.

2 Describe the trend in density for the Group 1 elements.

3 Write word equations to summarise how three Group 1 elements react with water. Describe the trend in these reactions.

From top to bottom of Group 1:

- melting point and boiling point decrease
- density increases, overall
- the reactions with water get more vigorous.

The Group 2 elements

A rare element

What links the items in the pictures?

⬆ An emerald from India.　　⬆ Part of the James Webb Space Telescope.　　⬆ Special tools for using on an oil rig.

They all include beryllium. Beryllium is joined to other elements in the main compound of emerald.

The space telescope has 18 beryllium mirrors. Beryllium has perfect properties for this job. It is shiny, has a low density, and does not change shape at low temperatures.

An alloy of two metals – beryllium and copper – is used to make tools for workers on oil rigs. The alloy is strong and will not be damaged by seawater. It will also not cause sparks that could start a fire on an oil rig.

The Group 2 elements

Beryllium is in Group 2 of the periodic table. The other members of the group are magnesium, calcium, strontium, barium, and radium.

Group 2

Li	Be												B	C	N	O	F	Ne
Na	Mg												Al	Si	P	S	Cl	Ar
K	Ca	Sc	Ti	V	Cr	Mn	Fe	Co	Ni	Cu	Zn	Ga	Ge	As	Se	Br	Kr
Rb	Sr	Y	Zr	Nb	Mo	Tc	Ru	Rh	Pd	Ag	Cd	In	Sn	Sb	Te	I	Xe
Cs	Ba	La	Hf	Ta	W	Re	Os	Ir	Pt	Au	Hg	Tl	Pb	Bi	Po	At	Rn
Fr	Ra	Ac	Rf	Db	Sg	Bh	Hs	Mt	Ds	Rg							

(H is shown in a separate box at the top; He at the top right.)

⬆ Group 2.

The electronic structures of some Group 2 elements are shown below:

beryllium	2,2
magnesium	2,8,2
calcium	2,8,8,2

The atoms of all Group 2 elements have 2 electrons in their outermost shell. Their similar electron arrangements give the elements similar properties.

Reactions with water

Calcium reacts vigorously with water. The products are hydrogen gas and calcium hydroxide solution:

calcium + water → calcium hydroxide + hydrogen

Strontium and barium react even more vigorously with water. The products are similar:

strontium + water → strontium hydroxide + hydrogen

barium + water → barium hydroxide + hydrogen

Magnesium does not react vigorously with water. If you put a piece of magnesium ribbon in a test tube of cold water, tiny hydrogen bubbles form slowly on its surface.

The reactions of Group 2 metals with water show a trend. They get more vigorous going down the group. The Group 1 metals show a similar trend (see page 157).

⬆ Calcium reacts vigorously with water.

Reactions with acid

The Group 2 elements react with dilute hydrochloric acid. Smita wants to answer this question:

> Which reacts more vigorously with acid – magnesium or calcium?

She makes a prediction, based on her scientific knowledge.

> I predict that calcium will react more vigorously than magnesium. I think this because the reactions of the Group 2 metals with water get more vigorous going down the group.

Smita sets up the apparatus opposite.

Both reactions produce bubbles of hydrogen gas. The reaction of calcium is more vigorous. Smita's prediction is correct.

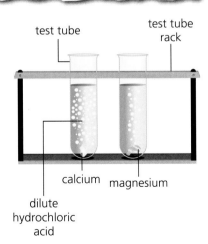

test tube

test tube rack

calcium   magnesium

dilute hydrochloric acid

⬅ Calcium and magnesium reacting with dilute hydrochloric acid.

Q

1 Write word equations for the reactions of calcium, strontium, and barium with water.

2 Predict how beryllium reacts with water, compared to the other elements of the group.

3 Suggest how you could investigate which reacts more vigorously with dilute hydrochloric acid – beryllium or magnesium.

From top to bottom of Group 2:

- the reactions of the elements with water get more vigorous

- the reactions of the elements with acids get more vigorous.

159

The Group 7 elements

Deadly elements

Chlorine gas killed 5000 people in the First World War. Fluorine poisons all living things. Fluorine, chlorine, bromine, and iodine destroy bacteria.

These deadly elements can also save lives. Chlorine and its compounds destroy viruses and bacteria in water, making it safe to drink. Iodine solution destroys bacteria around cuts.

Fluorine, chlorine, bromine, and iodine are in Group 7 of the periodic table. They are the **halogens**.

⬆ Iodine solution destroys bacteria around cuts.

Group 7 the halogens

													H						He
Li	Be													B	C	N	O	F	Ne
Na	Mg													Al	Si	P	S	Cl	Ar
K	Ca	Sc	Ti	V	Cr	Mn	Fe	Co	Ni	Cu	Zn			Ga	Ge	As	Se	Br	Kr
Rb	Sr	Y	Zr	Nb	Mo	Tc	Ru	Rh	Pd	Ag	Cd			In	Sn	Sb	Te	I	Xe
Cs	Ba	La	Hf	Ta	W	Re	Os	Ir	Pt	Au	Hg			Tl	Pb	Bi	Po	At	Rn
Fr	Ra	Ac	Rf	Db	Sg	Bh	Hs	Mt	Ds	Rg									

⬆ Group 7 is towards the right of the periodic table.

Group trends

⬆ A chlorine molecule, Cl_2.

The Group 7 elements are non-metals. They do not conduct electricity. They are poor conductors of heat.

The table shows some properties of the Group 7 elements.

Element	Melting point (°C)	Boiling point (°C)	State at 20 °C	Colour
fluorine	-220	-188	gas	yellow
chlorine	-101	-35	gas	green
bromine	-7	59	liquid	dark red
iodine	114	184	solid	solid – shiny grey-black vapour – purple

The Group 7 elements have low melting and boiling points compared to most metals. This is because they exist as molecules.

A strong force holds the two atoms of the molecule together. The forces between a molecule and its neighbours are weak. It is easy to separate the molecules of chlorine in the liquid state to form a gas.

The table above shows a trend in melting and boiling points. They increase from top to bottom of the group. This is because the atoms (and molecules) of the elements get bigger.

Reactions of the Group 7 elements

Mr Ali is planning to teach about trends in the reactions of Group 7 elements. He decides to show his students how the elements react with iron.

Mr Ali sketches some apparatus.

Mr Ali writes down some hazards of some of the substances in the reactions. He notes how to control the risks from these hazards.

substance	hazards	how to control risks from hazard
chlorine gas	• toxic	• use a fume cupboard • wear eye protection
bromine liquid	• very toxic • corrosive	• use a fume cupboard • wear eye protection • wear gloves

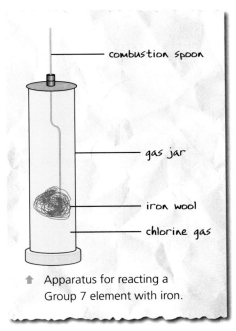

↑ Apparatus for reacting a Group 7 element with iron.

Mr Ali thinks about the risks. He does not have a fume cupboard to remove toxic gases from the laboratory. He decides not to demonstrate the reactions himself. His students will not learn about the reactions from first-hand experience. Instead, he will show videos of the reactions. His students will learn about the reactions from secondary sources.

A student watches the videos. She writes down her observations.

Reactants	Observations	Word equation
iron and chlorine	Very fierce reaction. Bright flame. Makes brown solid.	iron + chlorine → iron chloride
iron and bromine	Less fierce reaction.	iron + bromine → iron bromide
iron and iodine	Even less fierce reaction.	iron + iodine → iron iodide

The reactions are similar. This is because all the Group 7 elements have seven electrons in the outermost shell.

For the Group 7 elements, reactions get less vigorous going down the group. This is different from Groups 1 and 2, in which the reactions get more vigorous going down the group.

1 Describe and explain the trends in melting and boiling point for the Group 7 elements.

2 Write word equations for the reactions of three Group 7 elements with iron. Describe how the vigour of these reactions changes from top to bottom of the group.

From top to bottom of Group 7:

- melting point and boiling point increase
- the reactions with iron get less vigorous.

161

Looking at secondary data – chlorinating water

Why add chlorine?

Dirty water kills. The World Health Organization estimates that 3.4 million people die every year from diseases that are spread by untreated water. The diseases include cholera, typhoid fever, and dysentery.

Adding chlorine to drinking water destroys the bacteria, viruses, and parasites that cause these diseases. However, people have not always known this.

In 1894 a German scientist, Moritz Traube, investigated the effects of adding calcium chloride to bacteria-rich water. After two hours, the bacteria had been destroyed. The water was safe to drink.

Since 1900, chlorine and its compounds have been added to drinking water in many places. Fewer people have died from waterborne diseases.

⬆ Adding chlorine and its compounds to water destroys disease-causing microbes.

A dangerous by-product?

When chlorine is added to water, it may react with substances dissolved in water. The products are trihalomethanes (THMs). Drinking THM-containing water may slightly increase the risk of cancer.

Studying the effects of chlorinated water

Asking a question

Scientists from West Bengal, India, decided to investigate the long-term effects of drinking chlorinated water. They asked a question:

What are the health effects of drinking chlorinated drinking water?

Obtaining evidence

The scientists, Ritesh Sharma and Sudha Goel, collected evidence from three groups of people:

- Group 1 had been drinking chlorinated water for at least 30 years.
- Group 2 had had little access to chlorinated water at home.
- Group 3 had had no access to chlorinated water at home.

The scientists asked many people to join their study – there were 1085 people in Group 1. The big sample size would help to make the evidence reliable.

The scientists did not collect evidence from people younger than 30. They only wanted to investigate people who had been drinking chlorinated water – or any water at all – for 30 years.

The scientists collected evidence by talking to people in their homes. They asked questions about many things:

- how long they had lived in their home
- their age
- their education
- their income (how much money they earned)
- their health.

The scientists asked the first two questions to check whether a person should be included in the study. They asked about education and income because these two variables affect health, as well as drinking water quality.

The scientists asked many questions about health. They wanted to know if people had had cancer. They asked about waterborne diseases such as cholera, typhoid, and dysentery. They also asked about skin infections and kidney diseases.

Considering evidence

The scientists thought about their evidence. They used their data to do calculations. They made two conclusions:

- Drinking chlorinated water did not significantly increase the chance of cancer.
- Drinking chlorinated water reduced the chance of cholera, typhoid, and dysentery. It also reduced the chance of skin infections and kidney diseases.

Thinking about secondary evidence

The scientists wrote about their work in a scientific journal. They reported exactly what they did, and included their results and calculations.

The large number of people in the study, and the care with which the study was done, mean that other scientists are likely to trust its conclusions.

Q

1 Suggest why the scientists investigating chlorinated water and health in India questioned many people.

2 Suggest why the scientists did not question an even bigger number of people.

3 Suggest why chlorine is added to water supplies where possible, even though chlorine may form trihalomethanes, which may increase the risk of cancer.

- Scientists report studies in scientific journals.
- In studies on health, large group sizes help make data reliable.

Periodic trends

Groups and periods

Groups

In the periodic table, the vertical columns are called **groups**. The elements in a group have similar properties. There are trends in these properties. For example, in Groups 1, 2, and 7 the melting points of the elements increase going down the group.

Periods

The horizontal rows of the periodic table are called **periods**.

						H											He	← Period 1
Li	Be											B	C	N	O	F	Ne	← Period 2
Na	Mg											Al	Si	P	S	Cl	Ar	← Period 3
K	Ca	Sc	Ti	V	Cr	Mn	Fe	Co	Ni	Cu	Zn	Ga	Ge	As	Se	Br	Kr	← Period 4
Rb	Sr	Y	Zr	Nb	Mo	Tc	Ru	Rh	Pd	Ag	Cd	In	Sn	Sb	Te	I	Xe	← Period 5
Cs	Ba	La	Hf	Ta	W	Re	Os	Ir	Pt	Au	Hg	Tl	Pb	Bi	Po	At	Rn	← Period 6
Fr	Ra	Ac	Rf	Db	Sg	Bh	Hs	Mt	Ds	Rg							

⬆ The periodic table shows Periods 1, 2, 3, 4, 5, and 6.

Metal elements are on the left of a period. Non-metal elements are on the right.

Periodic trends

Vipasa asks a scientific question.

Vipasa decides not to measure the melting points herself. She does not have all the elements she needs, or the equipment to measure their melting points.

Instead, Vipasa collects data from a data book. The data book is the secondary source. Vipasa writes her data in two tables.

> Is there a trend in melting points across the periods of the periodic table?

Period 2 element	Melting point (°C)
lithium	180
beryllium	1280
boron	2300
carbon	3730 (sublimes)
nitrogen	−210
oxygen	−218
fluorine	−220
neon	−249

Period 3 element	Melting point (°C)
sodium	98
magnesium	650
aluminium	660
silicon	1410
phosphorus (white)	44
sulfur	113
chlorine	−101
argon	−189

Vipasa cannot see a pattern in her data. She decides to present it on two bar charts. This will make it easier to see if there is a trend in melting points.

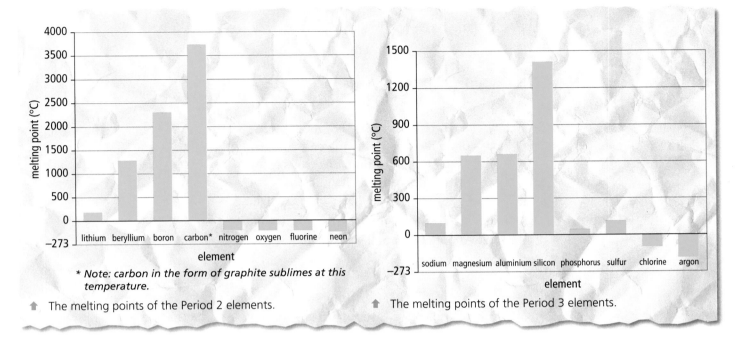

* Note: carbon in the form of graphite sublimes at this temperature.

↟ The melting points of the Period 2 elements.

↟ The melting points of the Period 3 elements.

Vipasa describes the trends shown on the bar charts. She writes a conclusion.

Trends

- For Period 2, the melting point increases from left to right for the first four elements of the period. The melting points of the other elements are very low.

- For Period 3, the trend is similar.

Conclusion

In every period of the periodic table, the melting point increases from left to right for the first four elements. The melting points of the other elements are very low.

Another student looks at Vipasa's data and conclusion. She says that Vipasa's data supports her conclusion for Periods 2 and 3. But how does she know if the conclusion is true for other periods?

Vipasa decides to collect melting point data for Periods 4 and 5. If the two periods show the same trend, she will be more confident in her conclusion. If they do not show the same trend, she will need to change her conclusion.

1 Name the elements in Period 2 of the periodic table.

2 Explain why Vipasa did not use evidence from first-hand experience to find out about trends in periods.

3 Describe the trend in melting points for Period 3 of the periodic table.

From left to right of periods 1 and 2:

- melting points increase for the first four elements

- melting points of the other elements in the periods are lower.

How scientists work: inside sub-atomic particles

What's in a proton?

By 1920, scientists knew that most of the mass of an atom is in its nucleus. The nucleus contains protons. Electrons move around an atom, outside its nucleus.

Scientists continued to ask questions. What makes up protons and electrons? Are they made up of even smaller particles?

Suggesting explanations

Scientists used creative thought to suggest explanations. They used maths to support their ideas. Satyendra Nath Bose thought about sub-atomic particles and energy. He wrote to Albert Einstein about his ideas. Together, Bose and Einstein predicted a new state of matter. They called it the Bose-Einstein condensate. The new state would exist only at very low temperatures.

Other scientists built on the ideas of Bose and Einstein. In 1964, six scientists, including Peter Higgs, suggested an explanation. There is a particle, they said, that gives sub-atomic particle their mass. They called this particle the Higgs boson, in honour of Satyendra Nath Bose.

In Pakistan, Mohammed Abdus Salam used ideas about the Higgs boson to develop explanations about forces between sub-atomic particles.

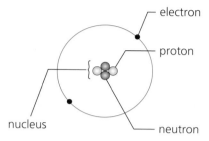

⬆ A helium atom has two protons and two neutrons in its nucleus. Two electrons move around the atom, outside its nucleus.

⬆ Satyendra Nath Bose was born in Kolkata, India, in 1894.

Testing the explanation

Scientists look for evidence to test explanations. They started looking for the Higgs boson.

In Europe, 10 000 scientists from more than 100 countries worked together. They had one purpose. To design and build apparatus to detect the Higgs boson. The result of their work – the Large Hadron Collider (LHC) – was ready to use by 2010.

The LHC is a 27 km long circular tunnel, deep underground. It produces beams of high energy protons. Inside the tunnel, huge magnets guide the protons around the circle, in both directions.

⬆ Archana Sharma of India worked on the Higgs boson team.

The protons travel faster and faster. They collide with each other, and break up. Four huge detectors follow the collisions. They detect the particles made in the collisions. Teams of scientists from India made important parts of these detectors.

The detectors send data to computers all over the world. The computers process the data. Scientists in many countries study the evidence. Does the evidence support the explanation? Do Higgs bosons exist, and do they give sub-atomic particles their mass?

Evidence for the Higgs boson

On 4 July 2012 LHC scientists made an exciting announcement. They had detected a new boson. The boson, they said, behaved as they had predicted a Higgs boson would.

Their evidence supported the explanation put forward nearly 50 years earlier. There is a particle that gives sub-atomic particles their mass. This particle is the Higgs boson.

Of course, scientists cannot be sure that the evidence supports the explanation. They need to spend many more years studying the data that they already have. They also need to do more experiments, to collect more evidence. Will the new evidence support the explanation, or not?

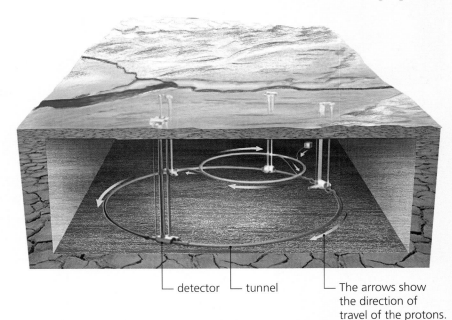

detector — tunnel — The arrows show the direction of travel of the protons.

⬆ The Large Hadron Collider.

⬆ The picture represents two protons colliding.

Q

1 Suggest two advantages of scientists working in international teams.

2 Suggest one disadvantage of working in an international team.

3 Suggest why it easier for scientists to collaborate in international teams today than it was 100 years ago.

!

To develop explanations scientists:

- ask questions
- use creative thought to suggest ideas
- collect and consider evidence
- collaborate with each other, often in international teams.

1 Copy the diagram below and fill in the missing labels. Choose from the words below. Use each word once, more than once, or not at all.

nucleus   proton   electron   neutron

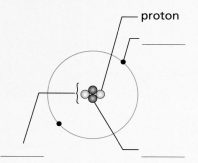

— proton

[3]

2 Complete the table to show the relative mass and charge of each sub-atomic particle.

Sub-atomic particle	Charge	Relative mass
proton	+1	
neutron		
electron		$\frac{1}{1840}$

[4]

3 A phosphorus atom is made up of 15 protons, 15 electrons, and 16 neutrons. Explain why it is electrically neutral. [1]

4 Ernest Rutherford fired tiny positively-charged particles at thin gold foil.

  a Explain why most of the tiny particles travelled straight through the gold foil. [1]

  b Explain why a few tiny particles bounced backwards off the foil. [1]

5 Draw the electronic structures of the following atoms.

  a A helium atom, with 2 electrons. [1]

  b A sodium atom, with 11 electrons. [1]

  c A phosphorus atom, with 15 electrons. [1]

6 The electronic structure of lithium is 2,1.

  a Write the electronic structures for sodium and potassium. [1]

  b Describe one way in which the electronic structures are similar. [1]

  c Describe the link between the atomic structure of an element, and the periodic table group the element is in. [1]

7 The table gives the melting points of four elements in Group 1 of the periodic table.

Element	Melting point (°C)
lithium	180
sodium	98
potassium	64
rubidium	39

  a Draw a bar chart to show the melting points of the Group 1 elements. [3]

  b Describe the trend in the melting points of Group 1 elements. [1]

8 Katya watches as her teacher adds a small piece of sodium to water. She makes these observations.

The sodium moves around on the surface of the water. Bubbles are formed.
After the reaction finished, the teacher added Universal Indicator to the solution. The indicator went purple.

  a Explain what the bubbles show. [1]

  b Explain why the indicator went purple. [1]

  c Write a word equation for the reaction of sodium with water. [2]

  d Potassium also reacts with water.

    i Describe one way in which this reaction is similar to the reaction of sodium with water. [1]

    ii Describe one way in which the reaction of potassium with water is different from the reaction of sodium with water. [1]

  e Describe the trend in the reactions of the first three Group 1 elements (lithium, sodium, and potassium) with water. [1]

9 The table gives the relative sizes of the atoms of the Group 1 elements.

Element	Relative size of atom
lithium	16
sodium	19
potassium	24

  a Describe the trend shown in the table. [1]

  b Use ideas about the electronic structures of the elements to suggest a reason for the trend you described in part (a). [1]

10 The bar chart shows the boiling points of four Group 2 elements. Beryllium is at the top of the group, followed by magnesium, calcium, and strontium.

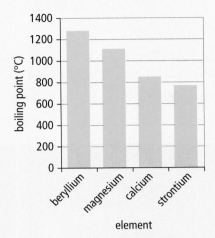

a Describe the trend shown by the bar chart. [1]

b Barium is under strontium in the periodic table. Use the bar chart to predict its boiling point. [1]

c Predict one other trend shown by the Group 2 elements. Give a reason for your prediction. [2]

11 Paulo investigates how vigorously the Group 2 elements react with water. He wants to find out if there is trend in these reactions.

a Name the variable he changes and the variable he observes. [1]

b Identify one variable Paulo should keep constant. [1]

c Suggest what preliminary work Paulo could do before starting his investigation. [1]

d Paulo decides to collect evidence from first-hand experience for the reactions of magnesium and calcium with water. He collects evidence from secondary sources for the reaction of strontium with water. Suggest why he decides not to add strontium to water himself. [1]

12 The Group 7 elements are non-metals.

a Name two elements in Group 7. [2]

b From the list below, choose two properties of the Group 7 elements.

- **do not conduct electricity**
- **good conductors of heat**
- **all have high melting points**
- **all are solid at room temperature**
- **poor conductors of heat**
- **good conductors of electricity.** [2]

c The table gives most of the melting and boiling points of four Group 7 elements.

Element	Melting point (°C)	Boiling point (°C)
fluorine	-220	-118
chlorine		-35
bromine	-7	59
iodine	114	184

i Name the element in Group 7 that is liquid at 20 °C. [1]

ii Describe the trend in boiling points in Group 7. [1]

iii Use the trend in melting points to predict the melting point of chlorine. [1]

d Chlorine has 17 electrons. Its electronic structure is 2,8,7. Draw the electronic structure of chlorine. [3]

13 This question is about the elements in Period 3 of the periodic table.

a The electronic structure of sodium is 2,8,1. Write the electronic structures of the other seven elements in Period 3. [7]

b Name two metals in Period 3. [1]

c Name two elements in Period 3 that do not conduct electricity. [1]

d The table gives the relative size of the atoms of the Period 2 elements. Describe the trend shown in the table. [1]

Element	Relative size
sodium	16
magnesium	14
aluminium	13
silicon	12
phosphorus	11
sulfur	10
chlorine	10

Energy changes in chemical reactions

Fuels for cooking

Kemala cooks over kerosene. Wani uses wood. Grace burns gas to heat her food. Kerosene, wood, and gas are **fuels**. Fuels release useful heat when they burn.

Burning reactions release heat. Reactions that release, or give out, heat are called **exothermic reactions**.

⬆ Burning wood is an exothermic reaction.   ⬆ Burning gas is an exothermic reaction.

Melting and evaporation

Some changes take in heat from the surroundings. These are **endothermic** processes.

Imagine a block of ice on your hand. The ice starts to melt. Your hand feels cold. This is because the ice takes heat from your hand. Its particles use this energy to leave their places in the pattern of solid ice, and start moving around, in and out of each other. Melting is endothermic.

⬆ Melting is an endothermic process.

Evaporation is endothermic, too. The particles of a liquid take in heat from the surroundings. They use this energy to leave the liquid.

Exothermic or endothermic?

All chemical reactions and changes of state involve energy changes. You can use temperature changes to work out whether a change is exothermic or endothermic.

A neutralisation reaction

Tim pours 50 cm³ of hydrochloric acid into a plastic cup. He measures its temperature. He adds 50 cm³ of sodium hydroxide solution. A neutralisation reaction takes place. Tim measures the temperature again.

hydrochloric acid + sodium hydroxide → sodium chloride + water

	Temperature (°C)
hydrochloric acid, before reaction	21
sodium hydroxide, before reaction	21
reaction mixture, immediately after reaction	52
reaction mixture, 1 hour after reaction	21

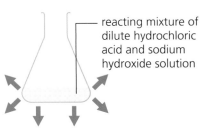

⬆ In an exothermic reaction, heat is released to the surroundings. At first, the temperature of the reaction mixture increases.

The reaction releases energy. It is exothermic. At first, the energy that is released heats up the reaction mixture. Then the energy is transferred to the surroundings. The mixture cools to room temperature. Most neutralisation reactions are exothermic.

The reaction of sodium hydrogencarbonate with citric acid

Meg pours sodium hydrogencarbonate solution into a plastic cup. She measures its temperature. She adds citric acid powder. The mixture fizzes, and a reaction takes place. Meg measures the temperature again. The temperature is lower.

During the reaction, the reacting mixture uses heat from the solution. That's why its temperature decreases. Afterwards, the mixture of products takes in heat from the surroundings. The mixture warms to room temperature. The reaction is endothermic.

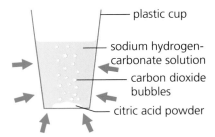

⬆ In an endothermic reaction, heat is taken in from the surroundings. The temperature decreases.

Dissolving – exothermic or endothermic?

Caz dissolves four substances in water. She records the temperature changes in a table.

Substance dissolved	Temperature change (°C)	Exothermic or endothermic?
ammonium chloride	−3	endothermic
potassium nitrate	−9	endothermic
copper sulfate	+7	exothermic
ammonium nitrate	−6	endothermic

The results show that dissolving can be exothermic or endothermic. If the temperature decreases, the reaction is endothermic. The reaction takes in heat.

1 Name two types of reaction that are usually exothermic.

2 Give an example of a change which is endothermic.

3 Name one type of change that can be exothermic or endothermic.

4 Explain why the temperature increases during an exothermic reaction.

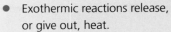

- Exothermic reactions release, or give out, heat.
- Endothermic reactions take in heat.

Investigating fuels

Planning an investigation

Ideas for testing

Fatima thinks about fuels. She asks herself some questions.

Which fuel makes water hottest?

Which fuel is cheapest?

Which fuel is best?

Fatima decides to investigate three fuels. She plans to find out which fuel makes water hottest.

Preliminary work

Fatima sketches her apparatus. She considers the variables in her investigation. She makes some notes.

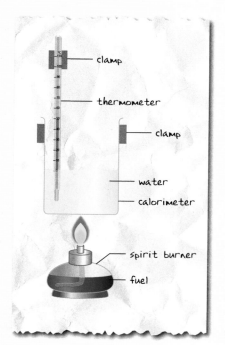

clamp

thermometer

clamp

water

calorimeter

spirit burner

fuel

Variable to change – type of fuel

Variable to measure – temperature change of water

Variables to control – mass of fuel burned, volume of water

Fatima does not know what volume of water to use. She decides to do some preliminary work. She tries heating different volumes of water with 1 g of one of her fuels.

Volume of water (cm³)	Temperature change (°C)
10	water boiled
100	about 50
1000	about 5

Fatima decides to heat 100 cm³ of water in her investigation. The temperature change for this volume is likely to be measurably different for each fuel.

Obtaining evidence

Reducing error and increasing reliability

Fatima sets up her apparatus. She thinks about her investigation.

Fatima decides to repeat her investigation three times.

- If the values for temperature increase are similar each time, she will know that her investigation is **reliable**.

How can I make sure my results are reliable?

- If one temperature increase is very different from the other two, she will check it again. This will reduce error.

Presenting results

Fatima draws a table for her results.

How can I reduce error?

Fuel	Temperature change (°C)			
	first time	second time	third time	average
ethanol	60	40	40	
propanol	50	53	56	53
butanol	55	51	53	55

Fatima looks at the results in her table. She notices that the first result for ethanol is very different from the other two. She thinks she must have made a mistake.

Fatima repeats the test for ethanol again. This time, the temperature change is 43 °C. It is much closer to the other two results for ethanol. By repeating the investigation, Fatima has reduced error and increased the reliability of her results.

Drawing conclusions

Fatima calculates average values for the temperature changes. She writes a conclusion for her investigation.

The temperature change for ethanol was smallest, with an average value of 41 °C. This means that ethanol releases less heat on burning than the other two fuels.

The average value for the temperature change of propanol is 53 °C and for butanol is 55 °C, so propanol and butanol release more heat on burning than ethanol.

Q

1 Explain why Fatima repeated her investigation.

2 Explain how Fatima's results show that ethanol releases less heat on burning than the other two fuels in her investigation.

3 Suggest why Fatima does not investigate the question. *Which fuel is best?*

- Repeating measurements in an investigation reduces error and makes results more reliable.

- Temperature change gives an indication of how much heat is released in an exothermic reaction – the greater the temperature change, the more heat is released.

Choosing fuels

What is a fuel?

Tinho lives in Brazil. His car runs on ethanol. Lorne is Canadian. His car is fuelled by hydrogen. Mila lives in Angola. Her car runs on diesel.

Ethanol, hydrogen, and diesel are **fuels**. A fuel is a substance that releases useful heat when it burns. Burning fuel reactions are exothermic.

Best fuel

Which fuel is best? There is no easy answer. There are many factors to consider when comparing fuels, including:

- How much heat do they release on burning?
- What products are produced when they burn?
- Where – and how – are the fuels produced?
- How convenient are the fuels to use?
- What are the hazards of using the fuels?

How much heat?

The table shows the heat released on burning three fuels.

Fuel	Heat released on burning (kJ/g)
ethanol	29.8
hydrogen	143.0
diesel	45.0

The table shows that 1 g of hydrogen releases more heat on burning than the other fuels in the table. Ethanol releases the least heat.

What are the products of combustion?

The products of combustion are the substances made when a fuel burns. Hydrogen has only one combustion product – water.

hydrogen + oxygen → water

Ethanol is a compound of hydrogen, carbon, and oxygen. It produces carbon dioxide and water on burning. Carbon dioxide is a **greenhouse gas**. In the atmosphere, it causes climate change.

ethanol + oxygen → carbon dioxide and water

Diesel is a mixture of compounds. Most of its compounds are made up of carbon and hydrogen only. When diesel burns, the main products are carbon dioxide and water. Burning diesel also makes small amounts of compounds that are solid at 20 °C. Some of these products may increase the risk of getting cancer, or heart disease.

How are the fuels produced?

Diesel is separated from crude oil. Crude oil was formed over millions of years from dead sea animals. Crude oil is a non-renewable resource. We are using crude oil much faster than it can be replaced.

↑ Tinho lives in Brazil. His car is fuelled by ethanol.

Most hydrogen fuel is made from methane. Methane is formed from animal waste, and on rubbish dumps. Methane from these sources is renewable.

Most ethanol fuel is made from plants, such as sugar cane. This means that ethanol is renewable. However, the plants are grown on land that could be used to grow food. The top eight ethanol fuel-producing countries and regions in 2009 were USA, Brazil, the European Union, China, Thailand, Canada, India, and Colombia.

⬆ Much ethanol fuel is produced from sugar cane.

Convenience and safety

Diesel and ethanol are liquid at 20 °C. They are convenient to transport and store. Hydrogen is a gas at 20 °C. It is more difficult to store and transport. Mixtures of hydrogen and air are explosive. Hydrogen must be stored away from flames and sparks.

Which fuel is best?

There is no single right answer to this question. Different people – and organisations – will make different decisions depending on the factors that are most important to them.

⬆ A hydrogen filling station.

Q

1 What is a fuel?

2 Name the products of combustion of hydrogen, and of ethanol.

3 Draw a table to compare the advantages and disadvantages of three fuels – ethanol, hydrogen, and diesel.

● There are many factors to consider when choosing fuels.

Calculating food energy

Nut energy

Nku buys some cashew nuts. How much energy will they provide? He uses the Internet to find out, and makes some notes. You can find out more about the energy in food in your *Complete Biology for Cambridge Secondary 1* Student Book.

> Eating 100 g of cashew nuts provides 2200 kJ of energy.

Nku wants to check this piece of data. He decides to do an experiment.

Measuring the energy in food

Planning investigative work

Nku sets up the apparatus below. He will burn a 1 g piece of cashew. The burning cashew will heat the water. Nku will measure the temperature increase of the water.

↑ Cashew nuts

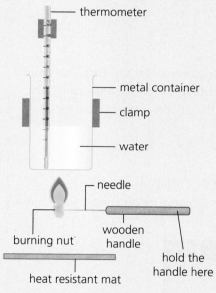

- thermometer
- metal container
- clamp
- water
- needle
- burning nut
- wooden handle
- hold the handle here
- heat resistant mat

↑ Apparatus to measure the energy released as heat when food burns.

Obtaining and presenting evidence

Nku decides to repeat his test three times. This will help to reduce error, and make his results more reliable. He writes a table for his results.

Test number	Water temperature before heating (°C)	Water temperature after heating (°C)	Water temperature change (°C)
1	21	61	40
2	22	65	43
3	22	59	37

Nku looks at his data. The water temperature change was similar for each test. This shows that the results are reliable.

Nku calculates the mean (average) value for the water temperature change:

$$\text{mean temperature change} = \frac{40 + 43 + 37}{3}\,°C$$
$$= 40\,°C$$

Considering evidence

The greater the temperature increase of the water, the more energy a food or fuel has released as heat. But temperature is not the same as heat. Nku needs to do a calculation to find out the amount of heat the cashew released.

The equation for the energy transferred to the water as heat is:

$$H = m \times c \times \Delta T$$

In the equation:

- H is the energy transferred to the water as heat
- m is the mass of the water
- c is the specific heat capacity of the water, 4.2 J/g °C
- ΔT is the temperature change of the water

Nku does his calculation. The answer gives the energy transferred as heat by 1 g of burning cashew.

$$H = m \times c \times \Delta T$$
$$H = 100\,g \times 4.2\,J/g\,°C \times 40\,°C$$
$$H = 16800\,J$$
$$H = 16.8\,kJ$$

This gives a value of 1680 kJ for burning 100 g of cashew nuts. Nku compares his result to the value he found on the Internet. His value is lower.

Nku thinks about the two values, and discusses them with his teacher. He writes an evaluation.

My value is less than the value given on the Internet. I trust the data from the Internet site. I think my value was lower because not all the heat from the burning cashew was transferred to the water. Some was transferred to the surroundings and to the apparatus.

Nku decides to continue his investigation. He burns other foods, and uses the heat released to heat water.

Q

1 A mass of 1 g of a burning food heats 100 g of water from 20 °C to 80 °C. Calculate the heat transferred to the water.

2 Explain why the value you calculated in question 1 might be less than the heat released on burning the food.

3 Explain the difference between temperature and heat.

- Use the equation $H = m \times c \times \Delta T$ to calculate the heat transferred to water.

Investigating endothermic changes

Dissolving ammonium nitrate

When ammonium nitrate dissolves in water, it takes in heat from the surroundings. The process is endothermic.

A teacher places a drop of water on a block of wood. She places a conical flask on the drop of water. She pours water into the conical flask, and dissolves ammonium nitrate in this water. The dissolving mixture takes heat energy from the drop of water on the wood. The drop of water becomes ice. The ice sticks the block of wood to the flask.

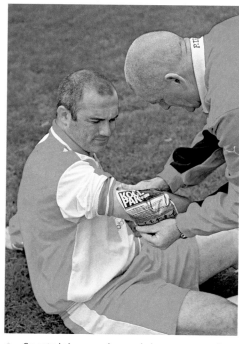

⬆ Dissolving ammonium nitrate in water is an endothermic process.

⬆ Sports injury packs cool damage muscles. They take in energy from muscles when the solid inside the packs dissolves in water.

Scientific enquiry

Asking questions

Jaka, Kali, and Legi investigate endothermic dissolving processes. They ask some questions.

Does the mass of substance that dissolves affect the amount of heat taken in?

Does the volume of solvent affect the amount of heat taken in when a substance dissolves?

Which substances take in the most heat when they dissolve in water?

⬆ Jaka

⬆ Kali

⬆ Legi

Planning investigative work – variables

The students list the variables in their investigation:

- substance used as solute (a solute is the substance that dissolves)
- mass of solute
- volume of water
- temperature change (the greater the temperature change, the greater the amount of heat taken in).

The students decide to investigate Jaka's question. The variable they change is the mass of substance. The variable they measure is the temperature change. The students will keep the other variables constant:

- the solute is ammonium chloride
- the volume of water – they will need to choose a suitable volume.

They do some preliminary work and decide to use 100 cm³ of water. This volume gives a suitable temperature change between 1 g and 15 g of ammonium chloride.

Planning investigative work – choosing equipment

The students use a balance to measure masses of ammonium chloride. They choose a balance that measures small differences in mass.

They use a thermometer to measure temperature change. They choose a thermometer than measures 0.5 °C changes in temperature.

Planning investigative work – assessing hazards and controlling risk

The students use a secondary source to find out about the hazards of using ammonium chloride. The solid is harmful. They wear eye protection during their experiment.

Obtaining and considering evidence

The students collect their evidence. They repeat their measurements three times to reduce error and make their results more reliable.

They look for a pattern in their results. Then they make a conclusion. The conclusion describes the pattern linking the variable they changed (the mass of ammonium chloride) and the variable they measured (the temperature change).

⬆ The students choose a balance that measures small differences in mass. This balance gives the mass to the nearest 0.1 g.

1 Some students investigate Kali's question. Identify the variables they should change, measure, and control.

2 Some students investigate Legi's question.
  a Suggest what preliminary work they need to do.
  b Draw a table for their results. Include column headings.

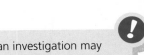
Planning an investigation may involve:

- identifying variables
- doing preliminary work
- choosing equipment
- assessing hazards and controlling risk.

1 Choose words and phrases from the list to copy and complete the sentences below. You may use each word or phrase once, more than once, or not at all.

given out   **taken in**   **increases**
decreases   **stays the same**

In an exothermic reaction, heat is _____. The temperature _____. In an endothermic reaction, heat is _____. The temperature _____.   [4]

2 Tick a copy of the table to show which changes are exothermic and which changes are endothermic.

Type of change	Is the change exothermic?	Is the change endothermic?
combustion (burning)		
neutralisation		
evaporation		
melting		
freezing		
[5]

3 The table gives the temperature changes when different substances dissolve in water. The same mass of solid was used in each test, and the same volume of water.

Substance	Temperature change (°C)
ammonium chloride	−5
ammonium nitrate	−6
copper sulfate	+5
potassium nitrate	−9

a Identify the substances that release (give out) heat when they dissolve in water.   [1]

b Identify the substance that takes in the most heat when it dissolves in water.   [1]

4 Mr Mushi sets up the apparatus below.

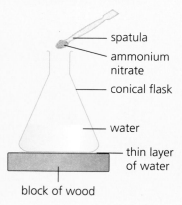

spatula
ammonium nitrate
conical flask
water
thin layer of water
block of wood

He adds ammonium nitrate to the water, and stirs until it dissolves.

a The water between the flask and the wooden block freezes. Explain why.   [1]

b Does ammonium nitrate dissolve exothermically or endothermically? Explain how you know.   [2]

5 Zoza investigates a neutralisation reaction. She adds 50 cm³ potassium hydroxide solution to 50 cm³ of nitric acid. Her results are in the table below.

	Temperature (°C)
potassium hydroxide, before reaction	23
nitric acid, before reaction	23
reaction mixture, immediately after reaction	56
reaction mixture, two hours after reaction	23

a Use data from the table to calculate the temperature change during the reaction.   [1]

b Explain how the data show that the neutralisation reaction is exothermic.   [2]

6 Josie investigates four fuels. She sets up the apparatus below. She uses the fuels to heat water.

She measures the temperature change of the water when she burns different fuels in the spirit burner.

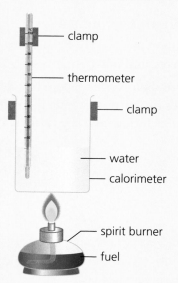

clamp
thermometer
clamp
water
calorimeter
spirit burner
fuel

a Identify the variable Josie changes.   [1]

b Identify the variable Josie measures.   [1]

c Josie heats the same volume of water with each fuel. Name two other variables that Josie should control.   [2]

d Josie does some preliminary work to help her decide what volume of water to heat with the fuels. Suggest why. [1]

e Josie's results are in the table.

fuel	temperature at start (°C)	temperature at end (°C)	temperature change (°C)
ethanol	19	56	37
propanol		63	43
butanol	20	65	
pentanol	21	68	47

i Copy and complete the table. [2]

ii Which fuel released least energy on burning? [1]

f Josie decided to repeat her investigation. Suggest why. [1]

g Josie thinks that some of the heat released by the burning fuels was not transferred to the water. Where else might the heat have been transferred to? [1]

7 Ashok compares the heat released in different neutralisation reactions. He uses the apparatus below.

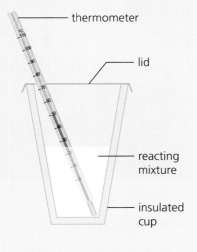

thermometer

lid

reacting mixture

insulated cup

Ashok repeats his investigation three times. The table below summarises his results.

Reactants	Temperature change (°C)			
	First time	Second time	Third time	Average
nitric acid and sodium hydroxide	50	32	32	32
hydrochloric acid and potassium hydroxide	34	33	35	34
sulfuric acid and sodium hydroxide	30	34	32	32
sulfuric acid and potassium hydroxide	33	33	33	33

a Suggest why Ashok repeated his investigation three times. [1]

b Ashok ignored his first result for the first pair of reagents. Suggest why. [1]

c Use the data to write a conclusion for the investigation. [1]

181

10.1 The reactions of metals with oxygen

Objective

- Investigate the burning reactions of metals

Burning metals

Ships and sailing boats often carry flares on board. They use these to attract the attention of the emergency services if they are in distress. When lit, flares emit a bright white or red light that can be seen for miles.

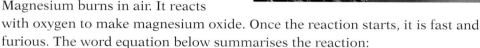

Some flares contain magnesium. Magnesium burns in air. It reacts with oxygen to make magnesium oxide. Once the reaction starts, it is fast and furious. The word equation below summarises the reaction:

magnesium + oxygen → magnesium oxide

Burning metals in the laboratory

⬆ Burning magnesium ribbon.

Martha burns a small piece of magnesium ribbon. She sees a bright, white flame. She shields her eyes and does not look at the flame directly, since it will damage her eyes.

Next, Martha sprinkles tiny pieces of iron (iron filings) in a flame. She sees bright sparks. Then she tries burning an iron nail. Nothing happens.

Martha's teacher burns a piece of sodium metal. The flame is very bright, and the reaction very fast.

Comparing burning reactions

Planning an investigation

⬆ Burning iron filings.

Martha wants to investigate burning metals in more detail. She wants to compare how vigorously they react.

Martha has already observed some metals burning. This is her **preliminary work**. She will use this to help plan her investigation. She writes down some ideas.

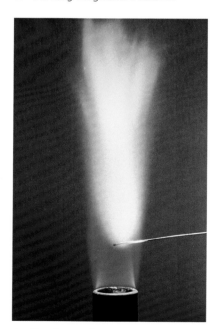

⬆ Burning sodium.

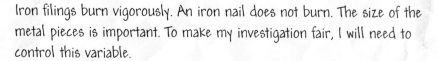

Iron filings burn vigorously. An iron nail does not burn. The size of the metal pieces is important. To make my investigation fair, I will need to control this variable.

My preliminary work shows that big pieces of some metals do not burn. I will compare the burning reactions of tiny pieces of metal.

Making observations and presenting results

Martha decides to sprinkle tiny metal pieces into a hot flame. She plans to observe how vigorously they react.

Martha uses secondary sources to collect data about hazards. She decides not to use sodium – the risks are too great. She asks her teacher to do the magnesium reaction in a fume cupboard.

Martha draws a table. She sprinkles the metals in the flame. She writes down her observations.

Metal	Observations
magnesium	Bright white sparks. Crackling sounds. Very vigorous.
zinc	Bright white sparks. More vigorous than iron?
copper	No signs of a reaction.
iron	Burned – bright yellow sparks.

Interpreting results

Martha describes the pattern in her results, and writes a conclusion.

> From my results, I conclude that magnesium reacts most vigorously with oxygen. Next is zinc, then iron. Copper does not react at all.

Martha thinks about her investigation. It was difficult to judge whether zinc or iron reacted more vigorously. She cannot be sure that her order is correct. She writes the comment below.

> **Evaluation:**
>
> From my investigation, I cannot be sure that the order is correct. I need to do another investigation to collect more evidence.

Martha also realises that she has not used scientific knowledge to explain her results. She plans to use secondary sources to find out why magnesium reacts more vigorously than the other metals she tested.

1 Describe two signs that show that a chemical reaction happens when magnesium burns in air.

2 Name the product formed when iron burns in air.

3 Write a word equation for the burning reaction of zinc in air.

4 List these three metals in order of how vigorous their reactions with oxygen are, most vigorous reaction first: iron, magnesium, copper.

- Some metals burn in air.
- On burning, metals react with oxygen to make metal oxides.
- The burning reactions of sodium and magnesium are very vigorous.

The reactions of metals with water

Calcium and water

Do metals react with water? Not the ones we use most often. There would be a problem if metal taps reacted with water, or if metal cars reacted with rain.

But some metals do react with water. Winton drops a small piece of calcium into a beaker of water. It bubbles quickly. After a while, the bubbling stops. The piece of calcium seems to have disappeared.

The calcium has reacted with the water. The bubbles contained hydrogen gas. The equation below shows the reactants and products:

calcium + water → calcium hydroxide + hydrogen

Even more exciting reactions

Calcium is not the only metal that reacts with water. Other metals have even more vigorous reactions.

Lithium whizzes around on the surface of a big bowl of water. It makes bubbles of hydrogen gas, like calcium. The other product is lithium hydroxide.

lithium + water → lithium hydroxide + hydrogen

On page 157 we learned that sodium and potassium react with water more vigorously than lithium. Potassium gets so hot that it sets fire to the hydrogen made in the reaction.

Not all metals react with water...

Magnesium ribbon reacts with cold water. The reaction is so slow that you hardly notice it. Zinc does not react with cold water, but it does react with steam.

▲ Calcium reacts vigorously with water.

▲ Lithium reacts with water very vigorously.

23 December 2007

Yesterday, Chinese archaeologists raised the wreck of an 800-year-old ship from the depths of the South China Sea. The ship, which sank in heavy storms, was carrying exquisite treasures to sell overseas. The treasure includes gold, silver, and tin pots, and 6000 copper coins. There's even a sailor's gold belt buckle and silver rings.

Why did the treasure survive under the sea for so long? It's because gold, silver, copper, and tin do not react with cold water.

Metals that do not react with water are very useful. Copper makes excellent water pipes. Gold and silver rings are very attractive, and you can't damage them by washing your hands.

An order of reactivity

The table below summarises how vigorously some metals react with water.

Metals	Comment	
potassium	most vigorous reactions	reactions get less vigorous
sodium		
lithium		
calcium		
magnesium		
zinc		
copper	do not react with water under normal conditions	
silver		
gold		
platinum		

⬆ This gold fan was found in Egypt. It is 3300 years old. It has not reacted with water, so it is still shiny.

All the metals that react with water form two products:

- an oxide or hydroxide
- hydrogen.

The metals that react vigorously with oxygen also react vigorously with water. Is there a similar pattern for the reactions of metals with acids? Turn over to find out.

Q

1 Name three metals which react vigorously with water.

2 Name the products of the reaction when potassium reacts with water. Write a word equation for the reaction.

3 Explain why gold coins stay shiny for hundreds of years.

!

- Some metals react with water to make hydrogen and a metal oxide or hydroxide.
- Potassium, sodium, lithium, and calcium react most vigorously with water.
- Gold, silver, and copper do not react with cold water.

Objective

■ Describe how metals react with acids

Ring reaction?

Sundara has a ring. It is an alloy of three metals – gold, silver, and copper. Sundara drops her ring in dilute hydrochloric acid. Nothing happens. She rinses the ring and puts it back on her finger. The ring survives because its metals do not react with dilute acids.

Investigating acid reactions

Many metals do react with acids. Dan wants to investigate which metals react most vigorously. His teacher gives him small pieces of five metals.

Assessing hazards and controlling risks

Dan assesses the hazards of the substances he will use. He writes down how to control the risks from the hazards.

Substance	Hazard	How to control risks from hazard
dilute hydrochloric acid	Low hazard, but may cause harm in eyes or cuts.	Wear eye protection, and take care not to spill on skin.
hydrogen (made in reactions)	Makes explosive mixtures with air.	Make small quantities. Do not use bung in test tube.
iron	Low hazard.	
zinc	Low hazard.	
magnesium	Catches fire easily.	Keep away from flames.
lead	Low hazard, harmful if swallowed.	Wash hands after use.
copper	Low hazard.	

Obtaining evidence

Dan sets up the apparatus below. To make the test fair, he controls these variables:

● concentration of hydrochloric acid

● size of metal pieces.

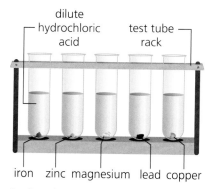

dilute hydrochloric acid

test tube rack

iron zinc magnesium lead copper

⬆ Reacting metals with dilute hydrochloric acid.

Testing for hydrogen

Magnesium bubbles vigorously with hydrochloric acid. Dan collects the gas by placing another test tube over the top of the first one.

Dan lights a splint. Keeping the test tube containing the hydrogen upside down, he quickly places the lighted splint in to the test tube. The splint makes a squeaky pop, and goes out. This shows that the reaction makes hydrogen gas.

↑ In hydrogen gas, a lighted splint goes out with a squeaky pop.

Considering evidence

Dan lists the metals in order of how vigorously they react.

Metal	Comment	
magnesium	vigorous reaction	reactions get less vigorous ↓
zinc		
iron		
copper	did not react	

In Dan's experiment, the piece of magnesium gets smaller. It disappears. Only a colourless solution remains in the test tube.

The magnesium and hydrochloric acid have reacted to make hydrogen gas and magnesium chloride. The hydrogen gas leaves the test tubes in bubbles. The magnesium chloride dissolves in water, so you cannot see it. This word equation summarises the reaction:

magnesium + hydrochloric acid → magnesium chloride + hydrogen

Magnesium chloride is a salt. A salt is a compound made when a metal replaces the hydrogen in an acid.

Every metal that reacts with hydrochloric acid makes a salt and hydrogen gas. The equations for the reactions in Dan's experiment are given below.

zinc + hydrochloric acid → zinc chloride + hydrogen

iron + hydrochloric acid → iron chloride + hydrogen

Look back at pages 182–5. Can you see any similarities in how vigorously the metals react with oxygen, water, and hydrochloric acid?

Q

1 Name two metals that react vigorously with dilute acid.

2 Name the products of the reaction when magnesium reacts with dilute acid and write a word equation for the reaction.

3 Describe the test for hydrogen gas. Write down what you would see and hear if hydrogen gas is present.

4 Explain why, in his investigation, Dan used pieces of metal of the same size.

!

- Many metals react with dilute acids to make salts and hydrogen gas.
- Magnesium and zinc react vigorously with dilute acids.
- Copper and gold do not react with dilute acids.

10.4 The reactivity series

A pattern of reactions

The pattern of metal reactions with acids is similar to their pattern of reactions with water, and with oxygen.

Potassium, sodium, and lithium react vigorously with water and oxygen, and violently with dilute acids. Calcium and magnesium have the next most vigorous reactions.

Objective

■ To understand the reactivity series

potassium
sodium
lithium
calcium
magnesium
aluminium
zinc
iron
lead
copper
silver

⬆ The reactivity series of metals.

← Sodium reacts vigorously with water. The indicator phenolphthalein has been added to this water. The indicator turns pink when it detects sodium hydroxide, the alkaline product of the reaction.

Zinc, iron, and lead react slowly (or not at all) with dilute acids and cold water. They burn in air, but their reactions are less vigorous than those of magnesium.

Silver, gold, and platinum do not react with water, dilute acids, or oxygen at normal conditions.

The **reactivity series** describes this pattern of metal reactions. It lists the metals in order of how vigorously they react. The metals at the top have very vigorous reactions. They are the most reactive. Going down the reactivity series, the metals get gradually less reactive. The metals are the bottom are unreactive.

The reactivity series and the periodic table

The metals at the top of the reactivity series are in Groups 1 and 2 of the periodic table. Most of the unreactive metals are transition metals, in the middle of the periodic table.

1	2											3	4	5	6	7	0
						H											He
Li	Be											B	C	N	O	F	Ne
Na	Mg				transition elements							Al	Si	P	S	Cl	Ar
K	Ca	Sc	Ti	V	Cr	Mn	Fe	Co	Ni	Cu	Zn	Ga	Ge	As	Se	Br	Kr
Rb	Sr	Y	Zr	Nb	Mo	Tc	Ru	Rh	Pd	Ag	Cd	In	Sn	Sb	Te	I	Xe
Cs	Ba	La	Hf	Ta	W	Re	Os	Ir	Pt	Au	Hg	Tl	Pb	Bi	Po	At	Rn
Fr	Ra	Ac															

Groups 1 and 2

⬆ The metals at the top of the reactivity series are in Groups 1 and 2 of the periodic table.

Using the reactivity series

Predicting corrosion

Metals near the top of the reactivity series burn vigorously in air when they are heated. They react with oxygen to form oxides. For example:

lithium + oxygen → lithium oxide

Metals at the top of the reactivity series react with oxygen at normal temperatures, too. Lithium is shiny when freshly cut. In air, a dull white substance forms quickly on its surface. The white substance is lithium oxide. It forms when surface lithium atoms react with oxygen.

The reaction of surface atoms of a metal with oxygen, or other substances, is called **corrosion**. Metals at the top of the reactivity series corrode easily. Metals at the bottom of the reactivity series do not corrode.

⬆ Lithium corrodes quickly in air. The shiny surface has been freshly cut. It will soon go grey, like the rest of the surface of the metal.

Preventing corrosion

Samindee's dad is buying a boat. Should he buy one made from aluminium, or steel? Steel is mainly iron.

⬆ Which corrodes quicker – steel, or aluminium?

Samindee sees that aluminium is above iron in the reactivity series. She predicts that aluminium will corrode more quickly. But this is not the case.

Freshly-cut aluminium immediately reacts with oxygen from the air. A thin, hard aluminium oxide coating forms. This stops water and oxygen molecules hitting the aluminium atoms below. The aluminium cannot react. It is protected from corrosion.

Steel corrodes more easily. Its iron atoms react with water and oxygen molecules to make hydrated iron oxide. This is red-brown rust, which flakes off. Holes may form and let water in.

It is vital to protect steel boats. Paint offers good protection, except when scratched. Many steel boats have a piece of zinc attached to them. Zinc is more reactive than iron. It reacts with water and oxygen instead of iron. The zinc is sacrificed to save the iron, so this is called **sacrificial protection**.

⬆ Zinc is bolted onto the boat's hull. It corrodes instead of the steel.

1 Use the reactivity series to name two metals that are more reactive than magnesium, and three metals that are less reactive.

2 Predict what would happen if a scientist added potassium to a dilute acid.

3 Zinc protects steel boats by sacrificial protection. Explain why magnesium also protects boats in this way.

- The reactivity series is a list of metals in order of how vigorous their reactions are.

Nickel in the reactivity series

Asking questions

Objective

■ Plan an enquiry and interpret evidence to work out the position of nickel in the reactivity series

Priti wears a watch with a metal strap. It makes her wrist go red and itchy. The watchstrap includes nickel. Priti is allergic to this metal.

Priti wonders about the properties of nickel. She decides to investigate. She asks a question.

Where is nickel in the reactivity series?

Planning an investigation

Priti knows that the reactions of a metal with oxygen, water, and dilute acids show the position of a metal in the reactivity series.

First, Priti does some research on the Internet and finds out that the salts formed by reaction of nickel with acids can be toxic. She decides to use evidence from secondary sources.

Priti collects evidence from secondary sources to compare the reaction of nickel with acid to the reactions of other metals. She writes her findings in a table.

metal	observations on adding to dilute acid
nickel	bubbles form slowly
magnesium	bubbles vigorously
zinc	bubbles vigorously
copper	no reaction

potassium
sodium
lithium
calcium
magnesium
aluminium
zinc
iron
lead
copper
silver
gold

⬆ The reactivity series.

Priti thinks about her findings so far. She concludes that nickel must be between zinc and copper in the reactivity series. She decides to compare the reactions of nickel to two other metals in this part of the reactivity series – iron and lead.

Obtaining evidence

Priti assesses the hazards of the metals she plans to use – nickel, iron, and lead. Then she starts collecting evidence.

Priti judges that the hazards of burning powdered nickel, iron, and lead are too great. She also uses secondary sources to find out about these reactions.

Metal	Reaction of powdered metal with air
nickel	reacts quickly to make nickel oxide
iron	reacts quickly to make iron oxide
lead	reacts quickly to make lead oxide

Next, Priti adds samples of the metals to water. A week later, she notes her observations.

Metal	Observations after leaving the metal in water and air for one week
nickel	no reaction
iron	red-brown flaky substance formed
lead	no reaction

Finally, Priti adds pieces of iron and lead to dilute sulfuric acid. She writes down her observations.

Metal	Observations on adding to dilute sulfuric acid	Notes
nickel	slowly, bubbles form	evidence from a secondary source (text book)
iron	bubbles form, more vigorous than reaction of nickel	evidence from first-hand experience
lead	no reaction	evidence from first hand experience

Considering the evidence

Priti studies the evidence. She uses her knowledge and understanding to interpret the results. She writes a conclusion.

> The reactions of the metals with water show that nickel may be less reactive than iron. The reactions of the metals with dilute sulfuric acid support this conclusion.
>
> The reactions of the metals with dilute sulfuric acid show that nickel may be higher in the reactivity series than lead. However, I need more evidence to be confident in this conclusion.
>
> On the basis of the evidence I have, nickel is between iron and lead in the reactivity series.

1 Explain why Priti collected most of her evidence from secondary sources.

2 Explain why the reactions of oxygen with iron, nickel, and lead did not help Priti to find the position of nickel in the reactivity series.

3 Suggest why Priti wants more evidence to be confident that nickel is higher in the reactivity series than lead.

- You can compare the reactions of metals to find their positions in the reactivity series.

Metal displacement reactions

Copper – a vital metal

Copper is an important metal. Its properties make it perfect for electrical equipment, water pipes, and heat exchangers. Worldwide, we produce about 15 million tonnes of the metal each year. In 2009 Indonesia alone produced nearly 1 million tonnes of copper.

⬆ About 60% of copper is used to make electrical equipment.

World reserves of copper will not last forever. This is why we recycle copper. Companies also extract copper from copper ore waste. This is how they do it:

- Spray dilute sulfuric acid onto copper ore waste. This makes copper sulfate solution.

- Add waste iron to the copper sulfate solution. The products of the reaction are copper and iron sulfate.

The equation below shows the reaction of iron with copper sulfate solution:

iron + copper sulfate → copper + iron sulfate

This is an example of a **displacement reaction**. Iron is more reactive than copper. It has **displaced** – or pushed out – copper from its compound.

More displacement reactions in solution

A more reactive metal will displace a less reactive metal from its compounds in solution.

Mandeep adds magnesium to blue copper sulfate solution. In a few minutes, she notices copper metal in the test tube. The blue solution becomes paler.

There has been a displacement reaction. Magnesium is higher in the reactivity series than copper. It displaces copper from copper sulfate solution.

magnesium + copper sulfate → copper + magnesium sulfate

Mandeesha adds copper to magnesium chloride solution. Nothing happens. There is no reaction, because copper is less reactive than magnesium. Copper cannot displace magnesium from its compounds.

Displacing metals from metal oxides

Alex wonders if metals displace other metals from their oxides. He uses science knowledge to make a prediction.

⬆ Iron is more reactive than copper. The iron is displacing copper from copper sulfate solution. Copper is being formed.

> I predict that a more reactive metal will displace a less reactive metal from its oxide.

Alex plans to heat pairs of substances. He will look for signs of reaction, and observe any products made. He draws a table for his results.

lid

crucible containing a mixture of metal and metal oxide powders

Bunsen burner

⬆ Alex heats a mixture of a metal and a metal oxide.

Metal element	Metal oxide	Observations
iron	copper oxide	glows red, pink-brown metal formed
copper	iron oxide	no reaction
zinc	copper oxide	glows red, pink-brown metal formed
copper	zinc oxide	no reaction
zinc	iron oxide	glows red, silver-coloured metal formed

Alex looks for patterns in his results. If the metal element is more reactive than the metal in the oxide, there is a reaction. He writes a conclusion.

A more reactive metal displaces a less reactive metal from its oxide.

iron + copper oxide → copper + iron oxide

zinc + copper oxide → copper + zinc oxide

zinc + iron oxide → iron + zinc oxide

⬆ The thermite reaction.

The thermite reaction

Aluminium is more reactive than iron. Aluminium reacts with iron oxide. The products are iron and aluminium oxide. Aluminium displaces iron from its oxide. This is the **thermite reaction**:

aluminium + iron oxide → aluminium oxide + iron

The thermite reaction gives out lots of heat. The heat melts the iron. Railway workers use liquid iron from the thermite reaction to join rails together.

⬆ Liquid iron from the thermite reaction joins rails together.

Q

1 What is a displacement reaction?

2 Decide which of these pairs of reactants react, and write word equations for the reactions: magnesium and copper oxide; zinc and magnesium oxide; zinc and copper sulfate solution.

3 Describe one displacement reaction that is useful, and explain why it is useful.

!

● More reactive metals displace less reactive metals from solutions of their salts, and, from their oxides.

Using the reactivity series: extracting metals from their ores

Metal compounds and the reactivity series

The higher a metal in the reactivity series, the more strongly its atoms are joined to atoms of other elements in compounds.

The more strongly the atoms of a compound are joined, the more difficult it is to extract an element from the compound.

Extracting gold

Gold is unreactive. It is found as an element in the Earth's crust. The metal is easily separated from the substances it is mixed with.

Some gold is found in stream beds, mixed with sand and gravel. You can separate gold by placing the mixture in a pan, and adding water. Gold is more dense than sand and gravel. It sinks to the bottom of the pan.

↑ Panning for gold.

Extracting metals in the middle of the reactivity series

Iron

Most metals are not found as elements in the Earth's crust. They are joined to other elements in compounds. The compounds must be broken down to get metals out of them.

Iron is a vital metal. It is in nearly all the metal objects we use. Most iron exists as oxides in the Earth's crust. The oxides are heated with carbon. Carbon is more reactive than iron. It removes oxygen from iron oxide.

↑ This ship is made from steel. Steel is mainly iron.

Lead

People have used lead for up to 8000 years. Lead beads were made in Turkey in about 6400 BCE. Skilled craftspeople made lead objects in the Indus valley about 4000 years ago.

Lead exists as lead sulfide in the Earth's crust. Lead is extracted like this:

- Heat lead sulfide in air:
  lead sulfide + oxygen → lead oxide + sulfur dioxide
- Heat the lead oxide with carbon. Carbon is more reactive than lead. It removes oxygen from lead oxide:
  lead oxide + carbon → lead + carbon dioxide

A pattern of reactions

Zinc, and metals below zinc in the reactivity series, can be extracted from their oxides by heating with carbon. The reactions work because carbon is more reactive than these metals.

Carbon is chosen because it is cheap, and there is plenty of it. It is possible to extract iron from iron oxide by heating with a more reactive metal, like magnesium. But magnesium is rarer than iron. It is much more expensive.

⬆ This lead statuette was made in Greece over 3000 years ago.

Extracting metals at the top of the reactivity series

Aluminium is near the top of the reactivity series. In the Earth's crust, it exists as aluminium oxide. The aluminium and oxygen atoms are strongly joined together. Carbon is not reactive enough to remove oxygen from aluminium oxide.

Aluminium is extracted from its oxide by **electrolysis**:

- Dissolve pure aluminium oxide in a special solvent.
- Pass a 100 000 amp electric current through the solution. The electricity splits up aluminium oxide. Liquid aluminium is produced.

Other reactive metals are also extracted from their compounds by electrolysis. Sodium is extracted by passing an electric current through seawater.

⬆ Aluminium is near the top of the reactivity series. An electric current separates the metal from its oxide.

Q
1 Name two elements that are extracted from their compounds by electrolysis.
2 Explain why iron is extracted from its ore by heating with carbon.
3 Describe the link between the position of a metal in the reactivity series, and how the metal is extracted from its ore.

- Metals near the top of the reactivity series are extracted from their compounds by electrolysis.
- Metals below aluminium are extracted from their oxides by heating with carbon.

Writing symbol equations

Why write symbol equations?

Word equations summarise chemical reactions. They show the reactants and products.

A balanced symbol equation tells us more about a reaction. It shows:

- the formulae of the reactants and products
- how the atoms are rearranged in the reaction
- the relative amounts of reactants and products.

How to write a symbol equation

Zinc and copper oxide

Zinc reacts with copper oxide in a displacement reaction. The products are copper and zinc oxide.

Follow the steps below to write a balanced symbol equation for the reaction.

1 Write a word equation. Put the correct chemical symbol or formula under each reactant and product. You cannot guess these – look them up, or ask your teacher.

zinc + copper oxide $\rightarrow$ zinc oxide + copper
Zn + CuO $\rightarrow$ ZnO + Cu

2 Balance the equation. There must be the same number of atoms of each element on each side of the equation. The equation above shows one atom of zinc on each side of the arrow, one atom of copper on each side of the equation, and one atom of copper on each side of the equation. The equation is balanced.

Burning magnesium

Magnesium burns in oxygen. The product is magnesium oxide. Follow the steps below to write a balanced symbol equation.

- Write a word equation. Write a formula under each substance.
  magnesium + oxygen $\rightarrow$ magnesium oxide
  Mg + O_2 $\rightarrow$ MgO

- Balance the amounts of oxygen. There are two atoms of oxygen on the left, and one on the right. Write a big number 2 to the left of the formula of magnesium oxide. Do not change or add any little numbers.

  $Mg + O_2 \rightarrow 2MgO$

- The big 2 applies to every atom in the formula that follows it. Here it means that there are two atoms of magnesium and two atoms of oxygen. There are now two oxygen atoms on each side of the equation. The amounts of oxygen are balanced.

- Balance the amounts of magnesium. Add a big 2 to the left of the chemical symbol for magnesium. There are now two atoms of magnesium on each side. The equation is balanced.

  $2Mg + O_2 \rightarrow 2MgO$

↑ Burning magnesium

Burning lithium

Lithium reacts with oxygen to make lithium oxide. The formula of the product is Li_2O.

Write a balanced symbol like this:

- Write a word equation, and a formula under each substance.
  lithium + oxygen → lithium oxide
  $$Li + O_2 \rightarrow Li_2O$$

- Balance the amounts of oxygen.
  $$Li + O_2 \rightarrow 2Li_2O$$
  There are two oxygen atoms on each side of the arrow.

- Balance the amounts of lithium.
  $$4Li + O_2 \rightarrow 2Li_2O$$
  There are four lithium atoms on each side of the arrow.

State symbols

You can add **state symbols** to an equation. State symbols show the states of the substances in a reaction. They are given below. Do not use capital letters.

- (s) for solid
- (l) for liquid
- (g) for gas
- (aq) to show that a substance is dissolved in water.

Zinc reacts with dilute hydrochloric acid to make zinc chloride solution and hydrogen gas. The balanced equation below shows the state of each reactant and product.

$$Zn\ (s) + 2HCl\ (aq) \rightarrow ZnCl_2\ (aq) + H_2\ (g)$$

Q

1 Write a balanced symbol equation for the reaction of sodium and oxygen to form sodium oxide, Na_2O.

2 Write a balanced symbol equation for the displacement reaction of zinc with copper sulfate solution. Include state symbols. The formula for copper sulfate is $CuSO_4$.

3 Write a balanced symbol equation for the reaction of potassium with water to make potassium hydroxide (KOH) and hydrogen (H_2).

- Balanced symbol equations show formulae, how atoms are rearranged, and the relative amounts of reactants and products.

1 Some metals react with oxygen. Write word equations for the reactions of the metals below with oxygen.

  a magnesium   [1]

  b zinc   [1]

  c potassium   [1]

2 The list below shows part of the reactivity series of metals.

  sodium

  magnesium

  zinc

  iron

  lead

  silver

  platinum

  a Name the most reactive metal in the list above. [1]

  b Name one metal that is more reactive than lead. [1]

  c Predict what you would observe if you added platinum to dilute hydrochloric acid. [1]

  d Predict what you would observe if you left a piece of platinum in a beaker of water for a week. Give a reason for your prediction. [2]

  e From the list, suggest a metal that could be attached to a steel ship so that the metal would corrode instead of the steel (mainly iron). [1]

3 A teacher demonstrates the reactions of water with three metals. A student writes her observations in the table below.

Metal	Observations
lithium	Moves around on surface of water. Bubbles produced quickly. Alkaline solution formed.
magnesium	Tiny bubbles form slowly on surface of metal.
potassium	Moves around on surface of water. Bubbles produced quickly, and burn. Alkaline solution formed.

  a Name the gas formed in each reaction. [1]

  b Describe how the teacher could show that the solution formed in a reaction is alkaline. Describe the changes the student would expect to see. [2]

  c Name the alkaline solution formed when lithium reacts with water. [1]

  d Write a word equation for the reaction of potassium with water. [2]

  e List the metals in the table in order of reactivity, most reactive first. [1]

  f Name another metal that reacts with water in a similar way to potassium. [1]

  g Suggest why the teacher did not add the metals in the table to dilute acid. [1]

4 Nadish wants to investigate the reactions of metals with dilute hydrochloric acid. He has the apparatus shown in the pictures below.

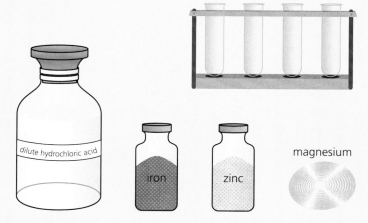

  a Nadish thinks about the variables in his investigation.

    i Identify the variable Nadish will change. [1]

    ii Identify two variables Nadish must control. [2]

    iii Explain why Nadish must control these variables. [1]

  b Write an outline plan for the investigation. [2]

  c Draw a results table for the investigation. [2]

  d Nadish decides to repeat the investigation with a different dilute acid. Suggest why. [1]

  e Nadish wants to show that hydrogen gas is produced when metals react with acids. Describe how to do a test to show that hydrogen gas is made. Write down the results you expect. [2]

5 This question is about displacement reactions. The list below shows part of the reactivity series. Use it to help you answer the question.

zinc
iron
lead
copper

a Predict which of the pairs of substances below will react. [2]

   i Copper and zinc oxide.

   ii Lead and copper oxide.

   iii Zinc and lead oxide.

   iv Lead and iron oxide.

b Write word equations for the pairs of substances in part (a) that react. [2]

6 Caz puts a piece of zinc in some copper sulfate solution.
A reaction takes place.
The word equation for the reaction is:
zinc + copper sulfate
   → copper + zinc sulfate

a Name the products of the reaction. [1]

b Explain why the reaction is a displacement reaction. [1]

c Caz places a piece of zinc in some nickel nitrate solution.
A displacement reaction takes place.

   i Which metal is more reactive, nickel or zinc? Explain how you know. [2]

   ii Write a word equation for the reaction. [2]

   iii Predict what would happen if Caz placed a piece of nickel in zinc chloride solution. Give a reason for your prediction. [2]

7 Mary wants to find the position of tin in the reactivity series. She has the materials listed below.

Solutions	Metals
iron chloride solution	iron
lead nitrate solution	lead
tin chloride solution	tin
zinc chloride solution	zinc

a Mary adds a small piece of zinc to each solution in turn. She writes her observations in the table below.

Solution	Observations on adding zinc metal
iron chloride	silvery metal formed
lead nitrate	grey metal formed
tin chloride	grey metal formed

   i What conclusion can Mary make from the observations in the table? [1]

   ii Suggest why Mary did not add a piece of zinc to zinc chloride solution. [1]

b Mary adds a small piece of tin to each solution in turn. She writes her observations in the table below.

Solution	Observations on adding tin metal
iron chloride	no reaction
lead nitrate	grey metal formed
zinc chloride	no reaction

Write a conclusion that Mary can make from the observations in this table. [1]

c Suggest one more investigation that Mary could do to confirm the position of tin in the reactivity series. [2]

11.1 Making salts – acids and metals

What are salts?

These pictures show some crystals. What do they have in common?

↑ Copper sulfate crystals.

↑ Manganese chloride crystals.

↑ Nickel nitrate crystals.

The crystals are all samples of **salts**. A salt is a compound made when a metal replaces the hydrogen in an acid.

Different acids make different salts:

- hydrochloric acid makes chlorides
- sulfuric acid makes sulfates
- nitric acid makes nitrates.

Making magnesium chloride

Choosing reactants

Seeta wants to make magnesium chloride. She needs two reactants. One is hydrochloric acid. The other reactant must include magnesium. Seeta could use magnesium metal, magnesium oxide, or magnesium carbonate. She decides to use magnesium metal.

There is a pattern in the reactions of metals with acids. When a metal reacts with an acid, there are two products – a salt and hydrogen.

So when magnesium reacts with hydrochloric acid, the products are magnesium chloride and hydrogen. The word equation for the reaction is:

magnesium + hydrochloric acid → magnesium chloride + hydrogen

The chemical reaction

Seeta measures out 25 cm³ of dilute hydrochloric acid. She uses a measuring cylinder. A measuring cylinder measures smaller differences in volume than a beaker. Seeta pours the acid into a beaker.

↑ There is 25 cm³ of hydrochloric acid in the measuring cylinder.

Seeta adds a small piece of magnesium ribbon to the acid in the beaker. The magnesium reacts with the acid. Bubbles of hydrogen gas form. After a few seconds, the bubbles stop. All the magnesium has reacted with the acid.

Seeta adds another piece of magnesium to the acid. She continues to add magnesium until there are no more bubbles. A piece of magnesium remains. It has not reacted, because all the acid has been used up.

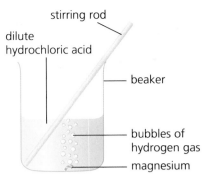

↑ Magnesium reacts with hydrochloric acid. Bubbles of hydrogen gas form.

Separating magnesium chloride from the mixture

Seeta's beaker contains a mixture. The mixture includes:

- magnesium chloride solution
- solid magnesium.

Seeta wants to make pure magnesium chloride. First, she filters the mixture. This removes the solid magnesium.

Next, Seeta pours the magnesium chloride solution into an evaporating dish. She heats the solution. Water evaporates. When about half the water has evaporated, Seeta stops heating. She places the evaporating dish in a warm place.

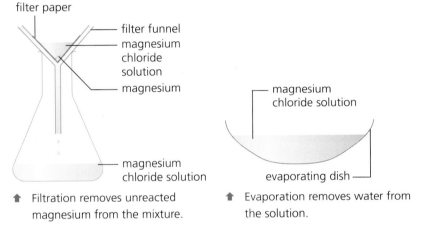

↑ Filtration removes unreacted magnesium from the mixture.

↑ Evaporation removes water from the solution.

A few days later, Seeta looks into the evaporating dish. She sees beautiful white crystals. She has made her salt, magnesium chloride.

Q

1 Jay makes a salt from a metal and an acid. Name the process used to separate the salt solution from unreacted metal.

2 Write a word equation for the reaction of zinc with hydrochloric acid. Name the salt made in this reaction.

3 Name the metal and acid that you could react to make magnesium nitrate crystals.

Make salts from acids and metals by:

- reacting an acid with excess metal
- filtering to remove unreacted metal
- heating to remove water.

Making salts – acids and carbonates

Objective

- Describe how to make salts by reacting acids with carbonates

Killing fungi

Fungi can seriously damage crops. They reduce crop yield and crop quality.

Fungicides destroy fungi. Some farmers use fungicides from natural sources, such as the neem tree. Some farmers use fungicides that are made in factories, such as copper sulfate.

↑ Different fungi attack different plants causing damage to their leaves, seeds or fruit, and roots.

↑ The fungus on these grapes can be controlled using copper sulfate.

Making copper sulfate

Choosing reactants

Copper sulfate is a salt. It is made in the reactions below.

- **Reaction 1**
  sulfuric acid + copper → copper sulfate + hydrogen
  The acid must be concentrated and the temperature high.

- **Reaction 2**
  sulfuric acid + copper oxide → copper sulfate + water
  Dilute acid may be used.

- **Reaction 3**
  sulfuric acid + copper carbonate → copper sulfate + water + carbon dioxide
  Dilute acid may be used.

On a large scale, copper sulfate is made in reactions 1 and 2. At school, you can use reactions 2 or 3 to make copper sulfate solution. Reaction 1 is too hazardous.

The chemical reaction

Sisira plans to make copper sulfate solution from sulfuric acid and copper carbonate.

— stirring rod
— copper carbonate powder
— dilute sulfuric acid

↑ Copper carbonate and sulfuric acid react together to make copper sulfate solution, water, and bubbles of carbon dioxide gas.

He measures out 25 cm³ of acid. He pours it into a beaker. He adds one spatula measure of copper carbonate powder. Carbon dioxide gas forms, and the reacting mixture bubbles. Sisira continues to add copper carbonate. Eventually, no more bubbles form. The reaction has finished.

Separating copper sulfate from the mixture

The beaker now contains a mixture of:

- copper sulfate solution
- solid copper carbonate that has not reacted.

Sisira filters the mixture to remove solid copper carbonate from the mixture. He collects the copper sulfate solution in an evaporating dish.

Sisira heats the copper sulfate solution over a flame. Some of its water evaporates. Some of the mixture spits out.

Sisira removes the evaporating dish from the heat, and places it in a warm room for a few days. The remaining water evaporates. Blue copper sulfate crystals are formed.

Evaluating and improving methods

Sisira makes a smaller mass of copper sulfate crystals than expected. He lost some of the product when heating the copper sulfate solution.

Sisira decides to improve his method. He repeats the whole experiment. This time, he does not heat the copper sulfate solution over a flame. Instead, he uses a water bath. This heats the solution more evenly. The solution does not spit. Sisira ends up with a greater mass of crystals.

A pattern of reactions

When a metal reacts with a carbonate, three products are formed:

- a salt
- carbon dioxide
- water.

The equations show some examples:

hydrochloric acid + copper carbonate → copper chloride + carbon dioxide + water

nitric acid + magnesium carbonate → magnesium nitrate + carbon dioxide + water

sulfuric acid + zinc carbonate → zinc sulfate + carbon dioxide + water

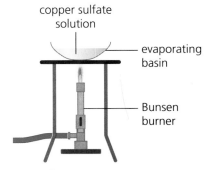
↑ On heating, water evaporates from the copper sulfate solution.

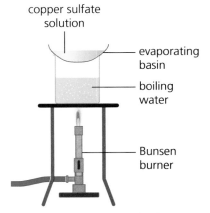
↑ Heating over a water bath.

Q
1 Maddie makes a salt from a metal carbonate and an acid. Name the process used to separate the salt solution from water.

2 Write a word equation for the reaction of zinc carbonate with hydrochloric acid, and name the salt made in this reaction.

3 Name the metal carbonate and acid that you could react to make zinc nitrate crystals.

Make salts from acids and carbonates by:

- reacting an acid with excess metal carbonate
- filtering to remove unreacted metal carbonate
- heating to remove water.

Making salts – acids and alkalis

Objective

- Describe how to make salts by reacting acids with alkalis

↑ In 2010, India produced more than 15 million tonnes of sodium chloride. Egypt produced 2.4 million tonnes.

Sodium chloride

Sodium chloride preserves and flavours food. It helps to dye clothes. It is used to make other important chemicals, such as chlorine and sodium hydroxide.

On a large scale, sodium chloride is extracted from the sea, or mined as rock salt. But you can make sodium chloride in the laboratory – read on to find out how.

Making salt

Choosing reactants

How to make sodium chloride from its elements is described on page 114. But burning sodium in chlorine is hazardous and the sodium chloride produced is not pure.

sodium + chlorine → sodium chloride

You can also make sodium chloride by neutralising an acid with an alkali.

hydrochloric acid + sodium carbonate → sodium chloride + water

How much sodium carbonate?

When dilute hydrochloric acid reacts to neutralise sodium carbonate, there is nothing to see. Both reactants are soluble in water. How do you know how much acid to add?

Azalee follows the stages shown in the pictures below to make sodium chloride crystals.

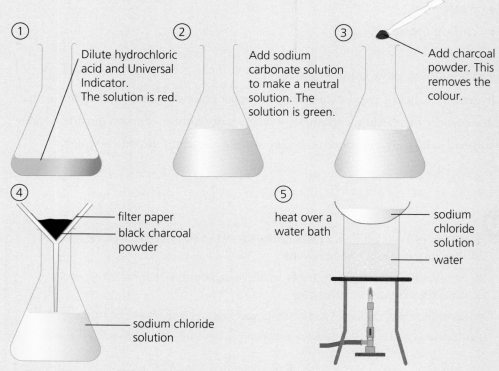

① Dilute hydrochloric acid and Universal Indicator. The solution is red.

② Add sodium carbonate solution to make a neutral solution. The solution is green.

③ Add charcoal powder. This removes the colour.

④ filter paper
black charcoal powder
sodium chloride solution

⑤ heat over a water bath
sodium chloride solution
water

↑ Azalee's method for making sodium chloride crystals.

Bem uses a different method to make sodium chloride solution. He uses a burette and pipette, and indicator solution, to measure the volume of acid needed to exactly neutralise 25.00 cm³ of sodium carbonate solution. He pours away this mixture, and repeats the method without indicator. Then he heats the sodium chloride solution over a water bath.

Evaluating the two methods

Both Azalee and Bem started with the same amounts of reactants. Bem made more sodium chloride than Azalee. The students evaluated their methods to work out why.

Azalee filtered her mixture to remove the charcoal powder. Some of the sodium chloride solution soaked into the filter paper. Azalee lost some of her product.

Bem did not need to filter his mixture. He did not lose any product in the first stages of his method.

Bem and Azalee heated their sodium chloride solutions over a water bath. Some of the water evaporated. They both lost very little sodium chloride at this stage. This stage does not explain why they made different amounts of sodium chloride. The difference is explained only by Azalee's filtering.

Azalee and Bem discussed their results further.

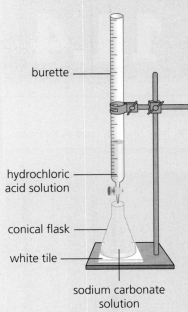

burette
hydrochloric acid solution
conical flask
white tile
sodium carbonate solution

⬆ Some of Bem's apparatus for making sodium chloride crystals.

I only had to do my reaction once. I lost some sodium chloride when filtering. That's all.

I did my reaction twice. I had to throw away my first mixture of sodium chloride solution and indicator. So I wasted lots of chemicals. Azalee removed the indicator from her solution, so she wasted less. Maybe Azalee's method was better, after all!

Q
1 Julia makes a salt by reacting an acid and an alkali. She uses an indicator to find out the volumes of solutions that react together. Describe how to separate the indicator from the salt solution.
2 Write a word equation for the reaction of potassium hydroxide with nitric acid, and name the salt made.
3 Name the acid and alkali that you could react to make potassium chloride crystals.

Make salts from acids and alkalis by:
- reacting an acid with an alkali – use an indicator
- heating to remove water.

Making salts – fertilisers

Objective
- Identify salts used as fertilisers

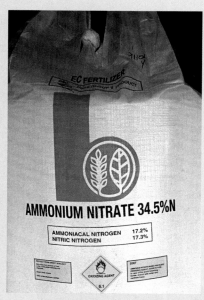

↑ The bag shows the elements in a fertiliser.

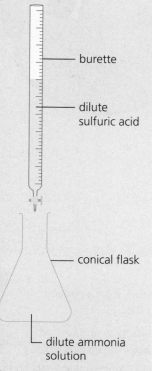

↑ Madu's apparatus.

Why add fertiliser?

Plants use water, and carbon dioxide from the air, to make glucose. Glucose is a compound made up of the elements carbon, hydrogen, and oxygen. Its formula is $C_6H_{12}O_6$.

Plants need other elements, too. They need nitrogen to make proteins. They need phosphorus to form flowers and seeds. They need potassium to protect them against disease.

Plants get nitrogen, phosphorus, and potassium minerals from the soil. Farmers increase crop yields by adding fertiliser to the soil. Some fertilisers, such as manure and compost, occur naturally. Other fertilisers are made in factories.

Making fertilisers

Most nitrogen fertilisers are made from ammonia. Ammonia is a compound of nitrogen and hydrogen. Its formula is NH_3.

Ammonia dissolves in water to make an alkaline solution. In the laboratory, you can react ammonia solution with acids. These neutralisation reactions make salts. The salts are used as fertilisers.

Which salts?

The equations show the reactions of ammonia solution with acids.

ammonia + sulfuric acid → ammonium sulfate + water

ammonia + hydrochloric acid → ammonium chloride + water

ammonia + nitric acid → ammonium nitrate + water

Ammonium nitrate contains more nitrogen than the other ammonium salts. Farmers add ammonium sulfate to alkaline soil. The salt provides nitrogen for plant growth, and makes the soil less acidic.

Making ammonium sulfate

Madu plans to make ammonium sulfate. He pours 25 cm³ of ammonia solution into a conical flask. He pours sulfuric acid into a burette.

Madu adds 1 cm³ of acid to the ammonia solution in the flask. The acid reacts with some of the ammonia solution. Madu removes a drop of the mixture. He drops it onto blue litmus paper. The paper remains blue. The flask contains some ammonia solution that has not reacted.

Madu repeats the step above several times. He adds more and more acid. Eventually, the litmus goes red. Madu has now added enough acid to neutralise all the ammonia. The flask now contains a mixture of ammonium sulfate and water. There is a tiny bit of extra acid, too.

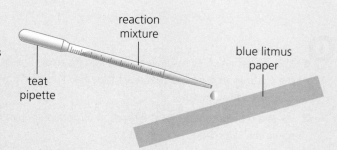

↑ Madu removes a drop of mixture from the flask. He drops it onto blue litmus paper.

Separating ammonium sulfate from the mixture

Madu uses evaporation to remove water from the ammonium sulfate solution.

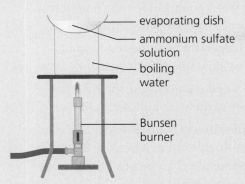

↑ Evaporation removes water from ammonium sulfate solution.

When about half the water has evaporated, Madu stops heating. He leaves the ammonium sulfate solution in a warm place. The rest of the water evaporates. Ammonium sulfate crystals remain.

Fertiliser production

We use huge amounts of fertiliser. One common fertiliser that is made from ammonia is urea. In 2009, factories made about 190 000 million tonnes of urea. The pie chart shows the five countries that produced the most urea.

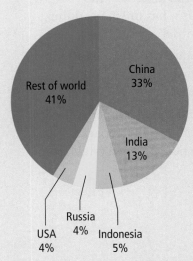

↑ The top five urea-producing countries in 2009.

1 Name the fertiliser made by reacting ammonia solution with dilute nitric acid.

2 Name the process that removes water from a solution of a fertiliser.

● Ammonium nitrate and ammonium sulfate are useful fertilisers.

1 From the list below, choose the one best definition of a salt.

   A compound made when an element replaces the hydrogen in an acid.

   A compound made when a metal replaces the hydrogen in an acid.

   A substance that preserves and flavours food.

   Chloride and sulfate compounds. [1]

2 Name the salts made when the following pairs of substances react.

   a Magnesium and sulfuric acid. [1]

   b Zinc and hydrochloric acid. [1]

   c Magnesium and nitric acid. [1]

   d Copper carbonate and hydrochloric acid. [1]

   e Zinc oxide and sulfuric acid. [1]

   f Copper oxide and nitric acid. [1]

3 Hydrogen gas is produced when a metal reacts with an acid.

   a Describe how to test for hydrogen gas. [1]

   b Describe what you would observe in your test if hydrogen is present. [1]

4 Copy and complete the word equations below.

   a magnesium + nitric acid → [1]

   b zinc + sulfuric acid → [1]

   c magnesium + hydrochloric acid → [1]

   d copper carbonate + hydrochloric acid → [1]

   e zinc oxide + nitric acid → [1]

5 Zafira wants to make some copper sulfate crystals.

   a Name the acid she needs. [1]

   b Zafira has a choice. She could add either copper carbonate or copper oxide to the acid to make her crystals.

   i Name the products of the reaction of copper carbonate with sulfuric acid. [1]

   ii Write a word equation for the reaction of copper carbonate with sulfuric acid. [1]

   iii Name the products of the reaction of copper oxide with sulfuric acid. [1]

   iv Write a word equation for the reaction of copper oxide with sulfuric acid. [1]

   c Zafira decides to use copper oxide. She places 25 cm³ of sulfuric acid in a beaker. She adds black copper oxide powder until the copper oxide stops reacting.

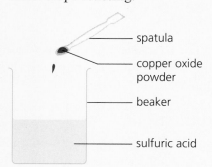

spatula

copper oxide powder

beaker

sulfuric acid

   i Name the three substances in the beaker when Zafira has finished adding copper oxide powder. [3]

   ii Describe how Zafira can separate the copper oxide powder from the other substances in the mixture. [1]

   d Zafira now has a solution of copper sulfate. Describe how she can use the apparatus below to obtain copper sulfate crystals from the solution.

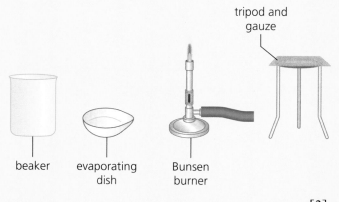

tripod and gauze

beaker   evaporating dish   Bunsen burner

[3]

6 Rizki uses the apparatus below to make copper chloride crystals.

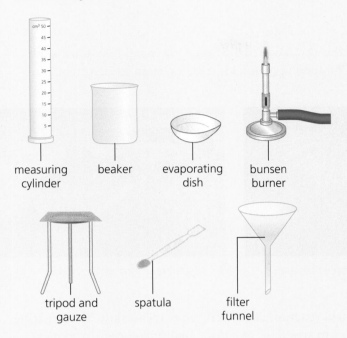

measuring cylinder   beaker   evaporating dish   bunsen burner

tripod and gauze   spatula   filter funnel

a Rizki makes copper chloride from copper carbonate and hydrochloric acid.

  i Name the gas made in the reaction. [1]

  ii Write a word equation for the reaction. [2]

b Rizki follows the steps below for making his crystals, but they are not in the correct order.

A	Measure out 25 cm³ of hydrochloric acid.
B	Pour the solution into an evaporating dish.
C	Heat the solution until about half its water has evaporated.
D	Add copper carbonate, spatula by spatula, until there is no more bubbling.
E	Place the evaporating dish on a water bath.
F	Filter the mixture. Keep the solution.
G	Place the evaporating dish and its contents in a warm room.
H	Wait for a few days to allow the rest of the water to evaporate.

Write the correct order for the steps above. The first one is A. [5]

7 Lia plans to make zinc chloride crystals. She decides to react zinc metal with hydrochloric acid.

a The products of the reaction are zinc chloride solution and hydrogen gas. Write a word equation for the reaction. [2]

b Lia uses a secondary source to list the hazards of the reactants and products.

Substance	Hazard
zinc metal	Low hazard
dilute hydrochloric acid	Low hazard. May cause harm in eyes or in a cut.
hydrogen gas	Extremely flammable. Forms explosive mixture with air.
zinc chloride solution (dilute)	Low hazard.
zinc chloride crystals and concentrated solutions of zinc chloride	Corrosive. Burns skin. Harmful if swallowed.

Lia takes the precautions below to reduce risks from the hazards. Give one reason for each precaution.

  i Be careful not to spill the acid. [1]

  ii When adding zinc metal to the acid, make sure there are no flames nearby. [1]

  iii Wear eye protection at all stages of the experiment. [1]

  iv Do not touch the zinc chloride crystals. [1]

c Lia makes zinc chloride solution. She pours the solution into an evaporating dish. She does not heat the solution directly. Instead, she heats the solution over a water bath. Suggest why.

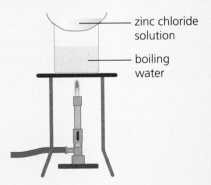

zinc chloride solution

boiling water

[1]

Rates of reaction

Fast or slow?

Fireworks explode in the sky. A car rusts. Some chemical reactions, such as those in fireworks, happen very quickly. Others, such as rusting, are much slower.

⬆ Chemical reactions in fireworks are very fast.

⬆ Rusting reactions are very slow.

Chemists need to control reaction rates. They may try to slow down rusting reactions. They may try to speed up reactions that make useful chemicals, such as soap, fertilisers, or medicines.

Following a reaction

Before chemists can control reaction rates, they need to find out how fast a reaction is. You cannot tell how quickly a reaction happens just by looking at its equation. You need to do an experiment to find out – how quickly is a reactant used up? How quickly does a product form?

Vijay wants to find out about the rate of the reaction of magnesium with hydrochloric acid. The equation for the reaction is below.

magnesium + hydrochloric acid → magnesium chloride + hydrogen

Obtaining and presenting evidence

Vijay sets up the apparatus on the right. He drops a piece of magnesium into the acid. He observes bubbles. The bubbles contain hydrogen gas. As the hydrogen gas forms, it goes into the gas syringe. The plunger moves out.

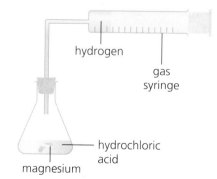

Vijay measures the total volume of gas that has been produced by the reaction at the end of each minute.
He draws a table for his results:

● The variable he changes (time) is in the left column.

● The variable he measures (volume of gas) is in the big right column.

Vijay wants to reduce error and make sure his results are reliable, so he decides to repeat his investigation. His table has space for three results for each test, and for an average value.

Time (minutes)	Total volume of gas formed by the end of this minute (cm³)			
	1	2	3	average
0	0	0	0	0
1	31	30	32	31
2	45	47	49	47
3	64	68	66	66
4	69	69	66	68
5	76	76	79	77
6	83	85	81	83
7	83	83	83	83
8	84	82	83	83

Vijay chooses how to present his results. The variable he changes, and the variable he measures, are continuous. This means he can plot a line graph:

- The scale for the variable he changes is on the *x*-axis.
- The scale for the variable he measures is on the *y*-axis.

Vijay makes sure the numbers on each axis are evenly spaced.

Vijay draws a cross for each point. He then draws a line of best fit. This is a smooth curve. The number of points above and below the line are similar.

Describing patterns and interpreting results

At first, the graph rises steeply. This shows that hydrogen is formed quickly at the start of the reaction. The rate of the reaction is fast. Then the slope of the graph gets less steep. This shows that the reaction is slowing down. The rate of the reaction is slower.

From the sixth minute onwards, the graph does not go up any more. No more hydrogen gas is being made. This shows that the reaction has finished. All the magnesium has been used up, so there is nothing left for the acid to react with.

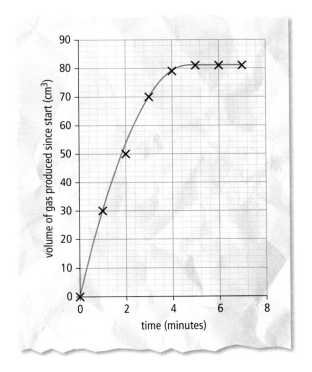

Q

1 Give an example of a very fast reaction, and a very slow reaction.

2 Use the graph above to estimate the volume of gas made during the first 2.5 minutes of the reaction.

3 Explain how the graph shows when the reaction has finished.

!

- In a reaction that makes a gas, the total amount of gas made by the end of each minute shows how the rate of reaction changes over time.

12.2 Concentration and reaction rate

Objective

- Describe and explain how concentration affects reaction rate

↑ Companies employ chemists to tell them how to speed up reactions.

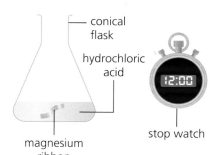

↑ Apparatus for investigating the effect of acid concentration on rate of reaction.

Why speed up reactions?

Tara is a chemist. She works for a company that makes medicines. The company wants to make its medicines as quickly as possible, and as cheaply as possible. Tara investigates the conditions that speed up reactions that make medicines.

Questioning reaction rates

Some students ask questions about reaction rates.

How can I make reactions faster?

↑ Junaid

↑ Alaur

In acid reactions, what difference does the concentration of the acid make?

The students decide to investigate Alaur's question. It is focused. They can get an answer to the question in just one hour.

Planning an investigation

The students decide to investigate the reaction of magnesium with hydrochloric acid. Their teacher gives them the apparatus below.

The students list the variables in the investigation:

- time for magnesium ribbon to finish reacting
- amount of magnesium ribbon
- concentration of acid
- temperature
- volume of acid

The students decide to change the concentration of acid. They will measure the time for the magnesium ribbon to finish reacting. They will keep the other two variables constant, so that their test is fair.

The students wonder how much magnesium ribbon to use. They do some preliminary work to find out. This involves adding different lengths of magnesium ribbon to acids of different concentration. They find the length of ribbon that reacts with the most and least concentrated acids in a sensible time.

212

Presenting evidence

The students write their results in a table. Next, they plot the points on a graph, and draw a line of best fit.

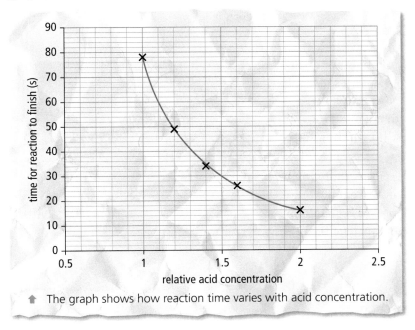

⬆ The graph shows how reaction time varies with acid concentration.

Considering evidence

The students write a conclusion for their investigation.

> The graph shows a correlation between acid concentration and reaction time. As acid concentration increases, reaction time decreases. This means that when the acid concentration is higher, the rate of reaction is faster.

The students need to improve their conclusion. They must give a scientific explanation for the correlation.

Explaining the correlation between concentration and rate

The concentration of a solution tells you how much solute is dissolved in the solvent. The more concentrated an acid solution, the greater the number of acid particles dissolved in a certain volume of solution.

Substances only react when their particles hit each other, or collide. The more concentrated an acid, the more frequently its particles collide with magnesium particles … and the faster the reaction.

⬆ If the beaker on the left represents a less concentrated acid … then the beaker on the right represents a more concentrated acid. Water particles are not shown on the diagrams. *Not to scale.*

Q

1 Explain why the students displayed their results on a line graph, not a bar chart.

2 Describe the correlation between acid concentration and reaction rate.

3 Use ideas about particles to explain the correlation you described in question 2.

4 A student wonders whether the results would be similar if they used a different acid. Suggest how they could investigate.

● For reactions involving solutions, the more concentrated the solution, the faster the reaction.

Temperature and reaction rate

Cooking temperatures

Farai and Ibrahim chop potatoes. Ibrahim adds his potatoes to boiling water, at 100°C. They cook in 12 minutes. Farai adds potatoes to boiling oil, at 200°C. They cook more quickly.

The chemical reactions that happen when potatoes cook are quicker at higher temperatures. The reaction rates are faster. Is this true for other reactions?

⬆ The higher the temperature, the faster food cooks.

Investigation rates and temperature

Ideas and evidence

Reactions happen when moving particles collide. At higher temperatures, particles move more quickly, and collide more frequently.

Farai uses this scientific explanation to make a prediction.

Prediction:
The higher the temperature, the more frequently particles collide.
I predict that the higher the temperature, the faster the reaction.

Planning an investigation

Sodium thiosulfate solution reacts with hydrochloric acid to make four products. The word equation summarises the reaction:

sodium thiosulfate + hydrochloric acid → sodium chloride + water + sulfur dioxide + sulfur

The sulfur is formed as a solid. It is insoluble in water, so it makes the reaction mixture cloudy.

Farai draws a cross on a piece of paper. He stands a conical flask on the cross. He pour sodium thiosulfate solution into the flask. Then he adds hydrochloric acid. He starts the timer.

Gradually, solid sulfur forms. Soon, the mixture is so cloudy that Farai can no longer see the cross. He does the same experiment using acid at four different temperatures. He repeats the whole investigation twice more, to reduce error and make his results more reliable. Will his prediction be correct?

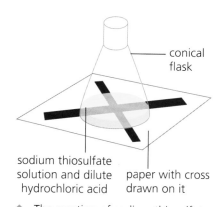

conical flask

sodium thiosulfate solution and dilute hydrochloric acid

paper with cross drawn on it

⬆ The reaction of sodium thiosulfate solution with hydrochloric acid makes solid sulfur. Soon, Farai will not be able to see the cross under the flask.

Presenting results

Farai writes his results in a table.

Temperature of acid (°C)	Time to cover cross (seconds)			
	1	2	3	average
20	244	240	242	242
30	119	117	118	118
40	59	61	63	61
50	67	32	30	31
60	13	16	16	15

Farai notices that the first result for 50 °C is very different from the other results at this temperature. The result is anomalous. He decides not to include this result when calculating the average time for 50 °C.

Farai knows that both the variable he changes (temperature) and the variable he measures (time) are continuous. He decides to draw a line graph. Drawing a graph makes it easier to spot patterns in results.

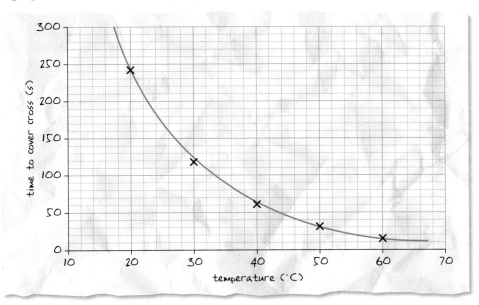

Considering evidence

The graph shows a correlation – the higher the temperature, the faster the reaction. As temperature increases, so does the rate of reaction.

This finding agrees with Farai's prediction. He is now more confident that the explanation on which he based his prediction is correct.

Q

1 Describe the correlation between temperature and rate of reaction.

2 Use ideas about particles to explain the correlation between temperature and rate of reaction.

3 Farai wants to investigate whether increasing temperature increases the rate of the reaction of magnesium with hydrochloric acid. Describe an investigation he could do to find out.

- Increasing temperature increases reaction rate.

Surface area and reaction rate

Flour tragedy

In 1965 in London, England, an explosion at a flour mill killed four people and injured 31. Why does flour explode?

Flour is made up of tiny grains. In the air, the grains spread out, as dust. Particles from the air – including oxygen molecules – surround the flour grains. Then someone lights a match. Instantly, a flour grain catches fire. It lights the other grains near it. A flame flashes through the flour cloud. This is the explosion. Other powders form explosive mixtures with air, too, including fine sugar, coal dust, and sawdust.

⬆ Flour and other powders can explode in the laboratory.

Surface area and reaction rate

Making a prediction

Catherine wants to investigate reactions involving powders. She asks a question.

Catherine decides to investigate the reaction of dilute hydrochloric acid with calcium carbonate. The equation below summarises the reaction.

calcium carbonate + hydrochloric acid →

calcium chloride + carbon dioxide + water

Catherine knows that substances react when their particles collide. In the reaction above, particles from hydrochloric acid react only with particles on the surface of a piece of calcium carbonate. Ten grams of calcium carbonate powder has a bigger surface area than ten grams of calcium carbonate lumps. This means that the powder has more particles that are available to react.

Catherine uses this knowledge to make a prediction.

Do powders react faster than bigger lumps of solid?

Calcium carbonate powder will react with dilute acid more quickly than big lumps of calcium carbonate.

Obtaining evidence

Catherine sets up the apparatus in the diagram. As carbon dioxide is made, it escapes from the apparatus. The mass of the flask and its contents decreases.

Catherine adds a big lump of calcium carbonate to dilute hydrochloric acid. She measures the time for the mass to decrease by 1.0 g.

Next, Catherine adds calcium carbonate powder to dilute hydrochloric acid. She uses the same mass of calcium carbonate as before. She measures the time for the mass to decrease by 1.0 g.

Finally, Catherine adds small lumps of calcium carbonate powder to dilute hydrochloric acid. Again, she keeps the other variables constant. She measures the time for the mass to decrease by 1.0 g.

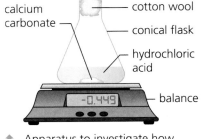

↑ Apparatus to investigate how surface area affects reaction rate.

Presenting evidence

The table shows Catherine's results.

Size of calcium carbonate pieces	Time for total mass to decrease by 1.0 g (mins)
big lump	10
powder	1
small lumps	5

Catherine wants to draw a graph. This will make it easier to spot patterns in her results. The variable she changes (the size of the pieces of calcium carbonate) is discrete. This means she must draw a bar chart.

Considering evidence

The bar chart shows that, as surface area increases, the time for the reaction decreases. Therefore, increasing surface area increases reaction rate.

Catherine's prediction is correct. Increasing the surface area increases the number of particles available for reaction. Acid particles collide with solid particles more frequently, so the reaction rate increases.

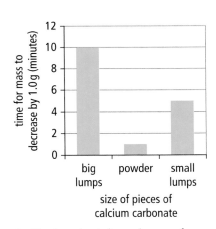

↑ The bar chart shows how surface area affects reaction time.

Q

1 Identify the variables Catherine needs to control in her investigation.

2 Describe the correlation between surface area and rate of reaction.

3 Use ideas about particles to explain the correlation between surface area and rate of reaction.

● Increasing the surface area of solid reactants increases reaction rate.

Catalysts and reaction rate

A natural catalyst

Sarah chews a piece of bread. She chews it for a long time. After a while, there is a sweet taste in her mouth.

There has been a chemical reaction in Sarah's mouth. Starch molecules from the bread have broken down to form glucose. Glucose is a sugar. The reaction happens very, very slowly on its own.

In our mouths there is a substance that makes the reaction happen more quickly. This substance is an **enzyme** called salivary amylase. All enzymes are examples of **catalysts**. A catalyst is a substance that speeds up a reaction without being used up in the reaction.

Another natural catalyst

Hydrogen peroxide is a bleach. It makes paper white. Hydrogen peroxide is normally diluted with water. It breaks down very slowly to make water and oxygen gas. The reaction is called a decomposition reaction.

hydrogen peroxide → water + oxygen

Amber has a test tube of hydrogen peroxide solution. She adds a small piece of chicken liver to the solution. It bubbles vigorously. A substance in the liver catalyses the decomposition reaction. The catalyst is an enzyme called catalase. It speeds up the reaction without being used up.

Testing for oxygen gas

Amber puts a glowing splint into the foam above the reaction mixture. The glowing splint relights. This shows that the gas produced in the reaction is oxygen.

Testing catalysts

Amber wants to test some other substances. Which will be the best catalyst for the decomposition of hydrogen peroxide? She sets up the apparatus below.

Objective

■ Describe and explain how catalysts affect reaction rate

↑ Chewing white bread for a long time makes a substance with a sweet taste.

↑ Catalase in liver catalyses the decomposition reaction of hydrogen peroxide.

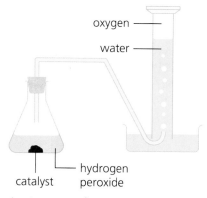

↑ Apparatus for measuring the volume of oxygen produced when hydrogen peroxide decomposes.

Amber draws a table for her results.

Name of substance	Volume of oxygen gas produced in 1 minute (cm³)
manganese(IV) oxide	25.0
lead(IV) oxide	28.0
iron(III) oxide	0
copper(II) oxide	1.0
zinc oxide	0
hydrogen peroxide only	0

She studies her data, and writes a conclusion.

Manganese(IV) oxide and lead(IV) oxide are the best catalysts for the decomposition reaction. I know this because they produced the biggest volumes of oxygen gas in 1 minute.

Iron(III) oxide and zinc oxide do not catalyse the decomposition reaction of hydrogen peroxide.

How do catalysts work?

Catalysts make it easier for a reaction to start. The decomposition reaction of hydrogen peroxide happens on the surface of the catalyst powders.

Using catalysts

Catalysts are vital in the chemical industry. They speed reactions up, meaning that more product is made in a shorter time. For example, iron catalyses the reaction of hydrogen with nitrogen to make ammonia. Ammonia makes fertilisers and explosives.

Catalytic converters in car exhaust systems contain metal catalysts such as platinum, rhodium, and palladium. The metals catalyse reactions such as the one below, in which poisonous carbon monoxide is converted to carbon dioxide, which is not poisonous.

carbon monoxide + oxygen → carbon dioxide

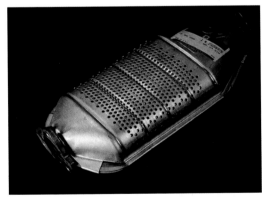

⬆ Catalytic converters in cars convert harmful gases to less harmful ones.

Q
1 Explain what catalysts do.

2 Give examples of three catalysts.

3 Explain how catalysts speed up reactions.

!
● Catalysts speed up reactions without themselves being used up in the reaction.

1 Abbas investigates the reaction of zinc with
hydrochloric acid. He pours 25 cm³ of the acid
into a conical flask. He adds small pieces of zinc.
He collects the gas in a syringe.

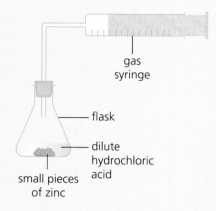

gas
syringe

flask

dilute
hydrochloric
acid

small pieces
of zinc

a The products of the reaction are zinc chloride
and hydrogen. Write a word equation for
the reaction. [1]

b Abbas measures the volume of gas collected
every minute. He plots a graph of his results.

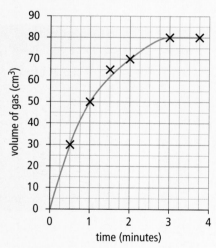

i Between which times is the reaction fastest?
Choose from the list below. [1]

Between 0 and 1 minute.
Between 2 and 3 minutes.
Between 3 and 4 minutes.

ii After how many minutes does the reaction
finish? [1]

iii What is the total volume of gas made in the
investigation? [1]

c Abbas wants to find out how the rate of reaction
changes if he increases the concentration of acid.

i Name two variables he should keep
the same in his investigation. [2]

ii Explain why he should keep these
variables the same. [1]

iii Draw a table in which Abbas could
write his results. [1]

2 Arifa investigates the reaction of sodium thiosulfate
solution with hydrochloric acid.

One of the products of the reaction is sulfur. This
forms as a solid.

As sulfur is made, it hides the cross under the
conical flask. Arifa measures the time taken for
the cross to disappear.

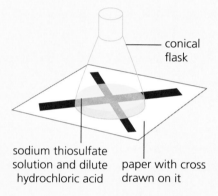

conical
flask

sodium thiosulfate
solution and dilute
hydrochloric acid

paper with cross
drawn on it

a Arifa wants to find out how changing the
temperature affects the rate of the reaction.

i Name the variable Arifa changes. [1]

ii Name the variable Arifa measures. [1]

iii Name three variables Arifa should control. [3]

b Arifa's results are in the table.

Temperature (°C)	Time for cross to disappear (s)			
	1	2	3	average
20	400	403	397	400
30	200	202	198	
40	104	100	102	102
50	47	50	47	48
60	24	27	27	26
70	148	13	13	58

i Suggest why Arifa measures the time
for the cross to disappear three times
at each temperature. [1]

ii Calculate the missing average. [1]

iii Plot Arifa's results on a graph, and draw
a line of best fit. [1]

iv Identify the anomalous result in the investigation. [1]

v Describe the correlation shown by the graph. [1]

c Use ideas about particles and collisions to help you explain the correlation shown by the graph. [2]

3 Rashid investigates the reaction of hydrochloric acid with calcium carbonate.

The equation for the reaction is

hydrochloric acid + calcium carbonate → calcium chloride + carbon dioxide + water

a Predict which product of the reaction is formed as a gas. [1]

b Rashid sets up the apparatus below.

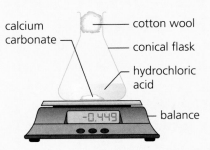

i Rashid predicts that, as the reaction progresses, the mass of the reaction mixture in the flask will decrease.

Which of the reasons below best explains why the mass decreases?

The product that is formed as a gas dissolves in the reaction mixture.
The product that is formed as a gas escapes into the air.
The product that is formed as a gas is made up of atoms of two elements. [1]

ii Rashid records the mass of the reactant mixture every minute. He plots a graph of his results.

Predict which of the graphs below best represents Rashid's results.

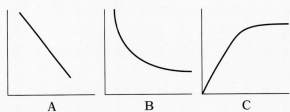

[1]

c Rashid wants to investigate how the size of the pieces of calcium carbonate affect the reaction rate.

He has three sizes of calcium carbonate pieces – big lumps, small lumps, and powder.

He decides to measure the time taken for 1.0 g of gas to be made with each size of calcium carbonate pieces.

i Name the variable he changes. [1]

ii Name the variable he measures. [1]

iii Name two variables Rashid must keep constant. [1]

iv Draw a table for Rashid's results. [2]

v Rashid finds that the powder reacts most quickly.

Which of the reasons below best explains why?

For a certain mass of calcium carbonate, the powder has the smallest surface area.
For a certain mass of calcium carbonate, the powder has the biggest surface area.
For a certain mass of calcium carbonate, the powder has the highest concentration.

4 The equation below shows the products when hydrogen peroxide decomposes:

hydrogen peroxide → water + oxygen

Manganese(IV) oxide catalyses the reaction.

a What is a catalyst? [2]

b Salama wants to investigate the effects of different catalysts on the reaction. She measures the volume of oxygen gas produced in one minute by four different catalysts. Draw a table for Salama's investigation. [2]

1 The diagram shows the sub-atomic particles in an atom of an element.

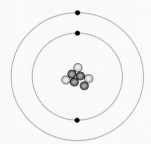

a Give the number of sub-atomic particles in the nucleus of the atom. [1]

b Name the two types of particles found in the nucleus. [2]

c Predict which group of the periodic table the element is in. [1]

2 Three scientists, Geiger, Marsden, and Rutherford, fired small positively-charged particles at thin sheet of gold foil.
The diagram shows the paths of some of the particles.

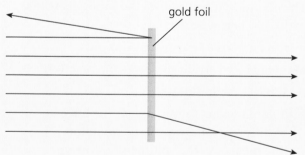

gold foil

a Explain why some of the particles travelled straight through the foil. [1]

b Give the name of the part of the atom which causes some particles to change direction. [1]

c Explain why more particles travel straight through the foil than change direction. [1]

3 The diagrams below show the electron arrangements of atoms of four elements.

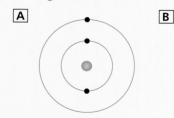

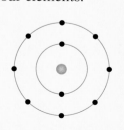

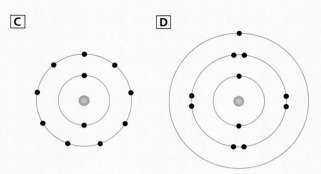

a Which electron arrangement is incorrect? [1]

b Which two elements are in the same group of the periodic table? [1]

c Which element is in period three of the periodic table? [1]

4 The table below shows the densities of some group 2 elements.

Element	Density (g/cm³)
calcium	1.54
strontium	
barium	3.51
radium	5.00

a Plot the data in the table on a bar chart. [3]

b Use your bar chart to predict the density of strontium. [1]

5 The tables give data for elements in two groups of the periodic table.

Table A.

Element	Boiling point (°C)
lithium	1330
sodium	890
potassium	774

Table B.

Element	Boiling point (°C)
chlorine	−35
bromine	59
iodine	184

a Use the periodic table to give the group numbers of the elements in Table A and Table B. [2]

b Describe the trend in boiling points for the elements in Table A. [1]

c Compare the trend you described in part (b) with the trend in boiling points for the elements in Table B. [2]

6 Iveta neutralises an acid with an alkali. She records the temperatures of the solutions before and after the reaction.

She writes her results in a table.

Temperature of acid before reaction (°C)	21
Temperature of alkali before reaction (°C)	23
Maximum temperature reached after reaction (°C)	69

a Explain how the results show that the neutralisation reaction is exothermic. · [1]

b Name one other type of reaction that is usually exothermic. [1]

7 Artem investigates the energy given out by four fuels. He sets up the apparatus below.

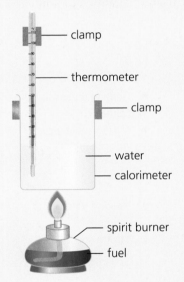

- clamp
- thermometer
- clamp
- water
- calorimeter
- spirit burner
- fuel

He measures the temperature change of the water when he burns 1 g of each fuel.

a Name the variable Artem changes, and the variable he measures. [1]

b Name two variables Artem must control in the investigation. [1]

c Artem obtains the results in the table.

Fuel	Temperature before heating (°C)	Temperature after heating (°C)	Temperature change (°C)
butanol	20	35	15
pentanol	21	33	
hexanol	22	44	22
heptanol	21		21

i Calculate the two missing values in the table. [2]

ii Which fuel heated up the water the most? [1]

d Artem writes a conclusion for his investigation.

The temperature change was similar for all the fuels. I think 1 g of each fuel releases similar amounts of heat when they burn.

Do you agree with Artem's conclusion? Explain why, or why not. [2]

8 Part of the reactivity series is given below.

sodium	iron
calcium	lead
magnesium	copper
zinc	gold

a Use the reactivity series to predict which of the following pairs of substances will react when they are heated together. [1]

calcium and zinc oxide
iron and zinc oxide
copper and lead sulfate solution
lead and copper sulfate solution

b Write word equations for the reactions in part (a) that you predict will react. [2]

c Use the reactivity series to help you explain the following:

i Why gold is used to make jewellery. [1]

ii Why water taps are not made from calcium. [1]

iii Sodium is stored under oil. [1]

9 Name the salts made by the following pairs of substances.

a Copper oxide and hydrochloric acid. [1]

b Magnesium and sulfuric acid. [1]

c Zinc and nitric acid. [1]

10 Copy and complete the word equations below.

a calcium + water → [1]

b magnesium + oxygen → [1]

c zinc + hydrochloric acid → [1]

11 Zara wants to make zinc chloride. She adds zinc to hydrochloric acid, until a little zinc remains unreacted. Then she filters the mixture.

a Explain why she filters the mixture. [1]

b Describe how Zara can make zinc chloride crystals from her zinc chloride solution. [2]

Choosing apparatus

There are many different types of scientific apparatus. The table below shows what they look like, how to draw them, and what you can use them for.

Apparatus name	What it looks like	Diagram	What you can use it for
test tube			• Heating solids and liquids. • Mixing substances. • Small-scale chemical reactions.
boiling tube			• A boiling tube is a big test tube. You can use it for doing the same things as a test tube.
beaker			• Heating liquids and solutions. • Mixing substances.
conical flask			• Heating liquids and solutions. • Mixing substances.
filter funnel			• To separate solids from liquids, using filter paper.
evaporating dish			• To evaporate a liquid from a solution.
condenser			• To cool a substance in the gas state, so that it condenses to the liquid state.

stand, clamp, and boss			• To hold apparatus safely in place.
Bunsen burner			• To heat the contents of beakers or test tubes. • To heat solids.
tripod			• To support apparatus above a Bunsen burner.
gauze			• To spread out heat from a Bunsen burner. • To support apparatus such as beakers over a Bunsen burner.
pipette			• To transfer liquids or solutions from one container to another.
syringe			• To transfer liquids and solutions. • To measure volumes of liquids or solutions.
spatula			• To transfer solids from one container to another.
tongs and test tube holders			• To hold hot apparatus, or to hold a test tube in a hot flame.

Working accurately and safely

Using measuring apparatus accurately

You need to make accurate measurements in science practicals. You will need to choose the correct measuring instrument, and use it properly.

Measuring cylinder

Measuring cylinders measure volumes of liquids or solutions. A measuring cylinder is better for this job than a beaker because it measures smaller differences in volume.

To measure volume:

1. Place the measuring cylinder on a flat surface.

2. Bend down so that your eyes are level with the surface of liquid.

3. Use the scale to read the volume. You need to look at the bottom of the curved surface of the liquid. The curved surface is called the **meniscus**.

Measuring cylinders measure volume in cubic centimetres, cm³, or millilitres, ml. One cm³ is the same as one ml.

Thermometer

The diagram to the left shows an alcohol thermometer. The liquid expands when the bulb is in a hot liquid and moves up the column. The liquid contracts when the bulb is in a cold liquid.

To measure temperature:

1. Look at the scale on the thermometer. Work out the temperature difference represented by each small division.

2. Place the bulb of the thermometer in the liquid.

3. Bend down so that your eyes are level with the liquid in the thermometer.

4. Use the scale to read the temperature.

Most thermometers measure temperature in degrees Celsius, °C.

Balance

A **balance** is used to measure mass. Sometimes you need to find the mass of something that you can only measure in a container, like liquid in a beaker. To use a balance to find the mass of liquid in a beaker:

1. Place the empty beaker on the pan. Read its mass.

2. Pour the liquid into the beaker. Read the new mass.

3. Calculate the mass of the liquid like this:

    (mass of liquid) = (mass of beaker + liquid) – (mass of beaker)

Balances normally measure mass in grams, g, or kilograms, kg.

— column of liquid

— bulb

⬆ The different parts of a thermometer.

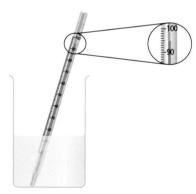

⬆ The temperature of the liquid is 95 °C.

⬆ The balance measures mass.

Working safely

Hazard symbols

Hazards are the possible dangers linked to using substances or doing experiments. Hazardous substances display **hazard symbols**. The table shows some hazard symbols. It also shows how to reduce risks from each hazard.

Hazard symbol	What it means	Reduce risks from this hazard by...
	Corrosive – The substance attacks and destroys living tissue, such as skin and eyes.	• Wearing eye protection • Avoiding contact with the skin
	Irritant – The substance is not corrosive, but will make the skin go red or form blisters.	• Wearing eye protection • Avoiding contact with the skin
	Toxic – Can cause death, for example, if it is swallowed or breathed in.	• Wearing eye protection • Wearing gloves • Wearing a mask, or using the substance in a fume cupboard
	Flammable – Catches fire easily.	• Wearing eye protection • Keeping away from flames and sparks
	Explosive – The substance may explode if it comes into contact with a flame or heat.	• Wearing eye protection • Keeping away from flames and sparks
	Dangerous to the environment – The substance may pollute the environment.	• Taking care with disposal

Other hazards

The table does not list all the hazards of doing practical work in science. You need to follow the guidance below to work safely. Always follow your teacher's safety advice, too.

- Take care not to touch hot apparatus, even if it does not look hot.
- Take care not to break glass apparatus – leave it in a safe place on the table, where it cannot roll off.
- Support apparatus safely. For example, you might need to weigh down a clamp stand if you are hanging heavy loads from the clamp.
- If you are using an electrical circuit, switch it off before making any change to the circuit.
- Remember that wires may get hot, even with a low voltage.
- Never connect wires across the terminals of a battery.
- Do not look directly at the Sun, or at a laser beam.
- **Wear eye protection – *whatever* you are doing in the laboratory!**

Recording results

A simple table

Results are easier to understand if they are in a clear table.

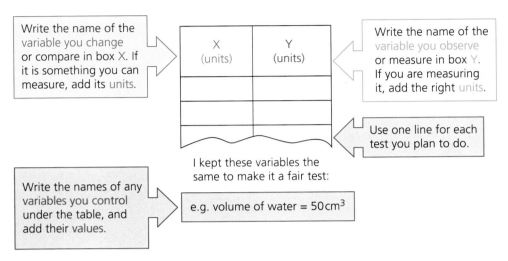

Write the name of the variable you change or compare in box X. If it is something you can measure, add its units.

X (units)	Y (units)

Write the name of the variable you observe or measure in box Y. If you are measuring it, add the right units.

Use one line for each test you plan to do.

Write the names of any variables you control under the table, and add their values.

I kept these variables the same to make it a fair test:

e.g. volume of water = 50cm³

Units

It is very important to use the correct units.

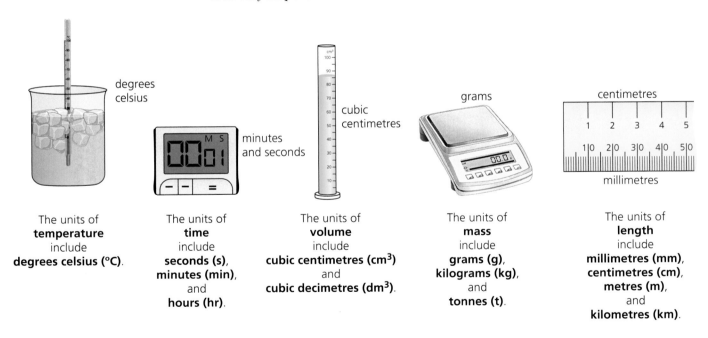

degrees celsius

minutes and seconds

cubic centimetres

grams

centimetres

millimetres

The units of **temperature** include **degrees celsius (°C)**.

The units of **time** include **seconds (s)**, **minutes (min)**, and **hours (hr)**.

The units of **volume** include **cubic centimetres (cm³)** and **cubic decimetres (dm³)**.

The units of **mass** include **grams (g)**, **kilograms (kg)**, and **tonnes (t)**.

The units of **length** include **millimetres (mm)**, **centimetres (cm)**, **metres (m)**, and **kilometres (km)**.

Making results reliable, and reducing error

You should always try to repeat observations or measurements. Never rely on a single result. If repeat results are similar, they are more **reliable**. Repeating results also helps to reduce error. If the results keep changing, try to find out why. It could be a mistake, or there might be another variable you need to control.

When you collect similar measurements, you should calculate their average value.

Three students find the time it takes to draw a table. Jamil takes 75 seconds, Abiola takes 35 seconds, and Karis takes 73 seconds.

Abiola's result is **anomalous** because it is very different from the others. Jamil and Karis find out why. Abiola's table is very messy. She did not use a ruler. They decide to leave it out of the average.

$$\textbf{average time} = \frac{\textbf{sum of the measurements}}{\textbf{number of measurements}} = \frac{\textbf{75 + 73}}{\textbf{2}} = \frac{\textbf{148}}{\textbf{2}} = \textbf{74 seconds}$$

A table for repeat results

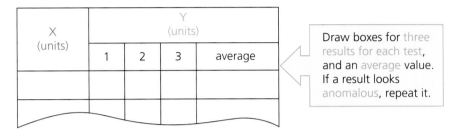

X (units)	Y (units)			
	1	2	3	average

Draw boxes for three results for each test, and an average value. If a result looks anomalous, repeat it.

A table for results that need to be calculated

Some variables can't be measured. They need to be calculated from two different results. Do all the calculations before you calculate an average value.

X (units)	Result 1 (units)	Result 2 (units)	Y (units)	Average (units)

Draw boxes for three sets of measurements, three calculated values, and an average. If a result looks anomalous, repeat it.

Displaying results

Drawing a bar chart

Three students timed how long they spent doing homework. The results are in the table.

A bar chart makes results like these easier to compare.

Students	Time spent on homework (hours)
Deepak	2
Jamila	4.5
Kasim	1

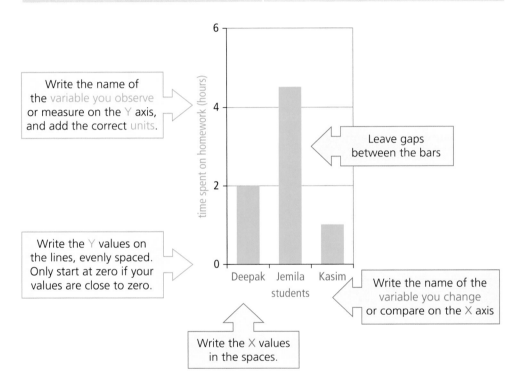

Write the name of the variable you observe or measure on the Y axis, and add the correct units.

Leave gaps between the bars

Write the Y values on the lines, evenly spaced. Only start at zero if your values are close to zero.

Write the X values in the spaces.

Write the name of the variable you change or compare on the X axis

Categoric or continuous

If the values of the variable you change (X) are words, then X is a **categoric** or **discrete** variable. You can only draw a bar chart for this type of variable.

Variables like shoe size are also categoric variables. They are numbers, but there are no inbetween sizes.

Other variables are **continuous** variables. Their values can be any number. Height is a continuous variable and so is temperature.

If the variables you change and measure are both continuous variables, display the results on a line graph or scatter plot.

Drawing a line graph

A line graph makes it easier to see the **relationship** between two continuous variables – the variable you change or compare and the variable you observe or measure.

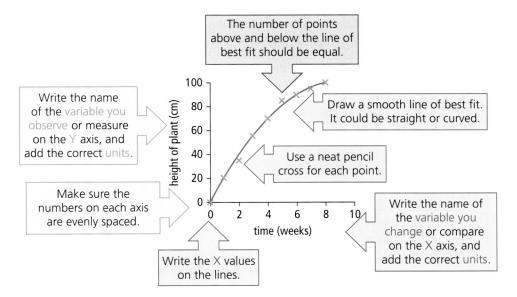

The number of points above and below the line of best fit should be equal.

Write the name of the variable you observe or measure on the Y axis, and add the correct units.

Make sure the numbers on each axis are evenly spaced.

Draw a smooth line of best fit. It could be straight or curved.

Use a neat pencil cross for each point.

Write the X values on the lines.

Write the name of the variable you change or compare on the X axis, and add the correct units.

Drawing a scatter graph

A scatter graph shows whether there is a **correlation** between two continuous variables. In the graph below, all the points lie close to a straight line. That means there is a correlation between them.

A correlation does not mean that one variable affects the other one. Something else could make them both increase or decrease at the same time.

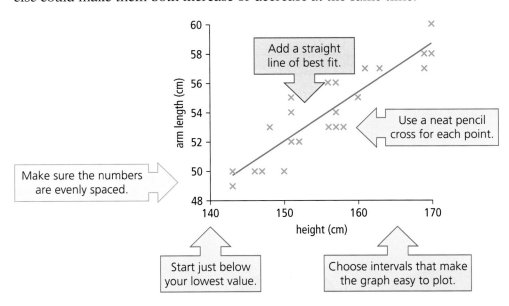

Add a straight line of best fit.

Use a neat pencil cross for each point.

Make sure the numbers are evenly spaced.

Start just below your lowest value.

Choose intervals that make the graph easy to plot.

Analysing results: charts and diagrams

Describe the pattern.
(e.g. A is bigger than B)

Use the numbers to
compare results.
(e.g. A is three times bigger than B)

Suggest a reason using
scientific knowledge.
(e.g. This is because...)

Charts and diagrams help you to analyse results. They show differences between results clearly. The flow chart shows you how to analyse results.

Here is a bar chart to show how long it takes three students to get to school.

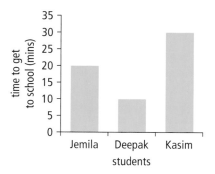

The first stage of analysing your results is to **describe the pattern**.

"Deepak takes the shortest time to get to school. Kasim takes the longest time to get to school."

The next stage it to **use the numbers** on the *y*-axis of the bar chart to **make comparisons**.

"Deepak takes 10 minutes to get to school, but Kasim takes 30 minutes. Kasim takes three times longer.

Finally, **suggest reasons** for any differences that you have found.

"This could be because Kasim lives further away or because Deepak walks more quickly."

When you do an experiment, use **scientific knowledge** to explain differences between results. Here are some examples of scientific reasons.

I think that the powdered sugar dissolved faster than the normal sugar because the pieces were much smaller.

I think that the plant near the window grew more quickly than the plant away from the window because there was more sunlight there.

I think that the shoe on the carpet needed a bigger force to move it than the shoe on the wooden floor because there was more friction between the shoe and the carpet.

Analysing results – line graphs

Line graphs show correlations between continuous variables. When you have plotted the points on a line graph, draw a line of best fit. Then analyse the graph. The flow chart on the right shows how to do this.

In the graphs below the line of best fit is shown, but not the points.

Describe the pattern by saying what happens to B as A increases. (e.g. As A increases B increases)

Choose pairs of values to illustrate the pattern and compare them. (e.g. When A is 3, B is 2, and when A is 6 B is 4 so doubling A will double B)

Suggest a reason using scientific knowledge. (e.g. This is because...)

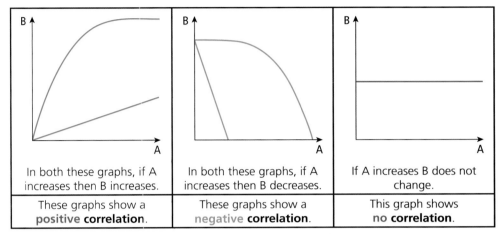

In both these graphs, if A increases then B increases.	In both these graphs, if A increases then B decreases.	If A increases B does not change.
These graphs show a **positive correlation**.	These graphs show a **negative correlation**.	This graph shows **no correlation**.

On some graphs the line of best fit is a straight line. You can say 'B changes by the same amount for each increase in A'. The blue line in Graph 1 shows that B increases by the same amount for each change in A. The red line shows that B decreases by the same amount for each change in A. You can choose values to illustrate this. Graph 2 on the right shows how.

A graph with a positive correlation where the line of best fit is a straight line that *starts at zero* is a special case. In this case B is **directly proportional** to A. You can say 'if A doubles then B will also double'. (See Graph 3.) You can choose values to illustrate this.

A graph that has a curved shape with a negative correlation may show that B is **inversely proportional** to A. Choose pairs of values. If you get the *same number* every time you multiply A by B then B is inversely proportional to A. This is the same as saying 'if you double A then B will halve'. (See Graph 4.) You can choose values to illustrate this.

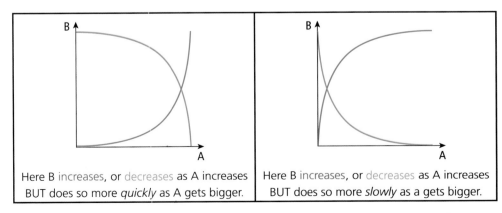

Here B increases, or decreases as A increases BUT does so more *quickly* as A gets bigger.	Here B increases, or decreases as A increases BUT does so more *slowly* as a gets bigger.

When you have described the pattern in your results, try to use scientific knowledge to explain the pattern.

Detecting gases

Hydrogen gas

To find out whether a reaction in a test tube has produced hydrogen gas:

1. Collect a small quantity of gas by holding an empty test tube upside down over the top of the test tube containing the reaction mixture.
2. Place a lighted splint in the gas.
3. If the splint goes out with a squeaky pop, hydrogen gas is present.

Oxygen gas

To find out whether a reaction in a test tube has produced oxygen gas:

1. Collect a small quantity of gas by holding an empty test tube upside down over the top of the test tube containing the reaction mixture.
2. Place a glowing splint in the gas.
3. If the splint relights, oxygen gas is present.

Carbon dioxide gas

To find out whether a reaction in a test tube has produced carbon dioxide gas:

• Bubble the gas through limewater solution.
• If the limewater solution turns milky or cloudy, carbon dioxide is present.

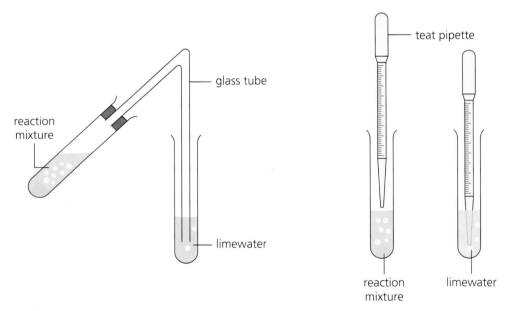

↑ The diagrams show two ways of bubbling gases through limewater.

Periodic Table

The periodic table shows all of the elements in order of the number of protons they have in their nucleus – the proton number.

1.0 H hydrogen 1																	4 He helium 2
7 Li lithium 3	9 Be beryllium 4											11 B boron 5	12 C carbon 6	14 N nitrogen 7	16 O oxygen 8	19 F fluorine 9	20 Ne neon 10
23 Na sodium 11	24 Mg magnesium 12											27 Al aluminium 13	28 Si silicon 14	31 P phosphorus 15	32 S sulfur 16	35.5 Cl chlorine 17	40 Ar argon 18
39 K potassium 19	40 Ca calcium 20	45 Sc scandium 21	48 Ti titanium 22	51 V vanadium 23	52 Cr chromium 24	55 Mn manganese 25	56 Fe iron 26	59 Co cobalt 27	59 Ni nickel 28	63.5 Cu copper 29	65 Zn zinc 30	70 Ga gallium 31	73 Ge germanium 32	75 As arsenic 33	79 Se selenium 34	80 Br bromine 35	84 Kr krypton 36
85.5 Rb rubidium 37	88 Sr strontium 38	89 Y yttrium 39	91 Zr zirconium 40	93 Nb niobium 41	96 Mo molybdenum 42	(98) Tc technetium 43	101 Ru ruthenium 44	103 Rh rhodium 45	106 Pd palladium 46	108 Ag silver 47	112 Cd cadmium 48	115 In indium 49	119 Sn tin 50	122 Sb antimony 51	128 Te tellurium 52	127 I iodine 53	131 Xe xenon 54
133 Cs caesium 55	137 Ba barium 56	139 La lanthanum 57	178.5 Hf hafnium 72	181 Ta tantalum 73	184 W tungsten 74	186 Re rhenium 75	190 Os osmium 76	192 Ir iridium 77	195 Pt platinum 78	197 Au gold 79	201 Hg mercury 80	204 Tl thallium 81	207 Pb lead 82	209 Bi bismuth 83	210 Po polonium 84	(210) At astatine 85	222 Rn radon 86
(223) Fr francium 87	(226) Ra radium 88	(227) Ac actinium 89	(261) Rf rutherfordium 104	(262) Db dubnium 105	(266) Sg seaborgium 106	(264) Bh bohrium 107	(277) Hs hassium 108	(268) Mt meitnerium 109	(271) Ds Darmstadtium 110	(272) Rg roentgenium 111							

Note: This periodic table does not include all the elements.

Glossary

Acid a solution with a pH of less than 7

Acidic a substance is acidic if its pH is less than 7

Acid rain rain that is more acidic than usual because substances such as sulfur dioxide are dissolved in it

Air pressure the force exerted by air particles when they collide with 1 m² of a surface

Alkali a solution with a pH of more than 7

Alkaline a solution is alkaline if its pH is more than 7

Alloy a mixture of two or more elements, at least one of which is a metal

Anomalous an odd result, or piece of data, that does not fit the pattern of results

Atom the smallest particle of an element which can exist

Balance an instrument for measuring mass

Basalt an igneous rock formed from liquid rock that cooled quickly. Its crystals are relatively small.

Base metal oxides are bases. They neutralise acids.

Beaker a container that you can use for mixing, reacting, and heating chemicals

Best-fit line a smooth line on a graph that travels through or very close to as many plotted points as possible

Biological weathering the breaking up or wearing down of a rock by the action of living things

Boil when a substance changes from the liquid state to the gas state at its boiling point

Boiling point the temperature at which a substance in the liquid state boils and changes to the gas state. Every substance has its own boiling point.

Brittle a substance is brittle if it breaks easily when you hit it with a hammer

Bunsen burner a piece of apparatus that burns gas to heat things in the laboratory

Burning a reaction in which a substance reacts quickly with oxygen and gives out light and heat. Also called combustion.

Carbonates a group of compounds which make carbon dioxide when they react with acid. Carbonates are made up of atoms of carbon, oxygen, and a metal element. There are 3 oxygen atoms for every 1 carbon atom.

Catalyst a substance which speeds up a reaction without itself being used up in the reaction

Cementation the 'gluing together' of particles of sediment by different minerals

Change of state the change that happens when a substance changes from one state to another, for example from solid to liquid or from gas to liquid

Chemical reaction an event which creates new substances and which is not easy to reverse

Chemical symbols letters which represent elements (usually one or two letters) which are understood in all languages. Each element has its own chemical symbol.

Chemical weathering the breaking up or wearing down of rocks by the action of chemicals such as those in rainwater

Chloride a compound that is made up of chlorine and one other element, for example sodium chloride, NaCl

Chromatogram a record obtained from chromatography

Chromatography a method of separating mixtures of liquids

Clay soil in clay soil, at least 40% of the rock fragments are clay

Claystone an example of a sedimentary rock

Collision when a particle bumps into another particle, or the inside of its container

Combustion a burning reaction, in which a substance reacts quickly with oxygen and gives out light and heat

Compaction when sediments are squashed together to make new rocks by the weight of layers above

Compound a substance made up of atoms of two or more elements chemically joined together

Concentrated a solution that contains a lot of solute dissolved in very little solvent

Concentration the amount of a substance that is dissolved in a certain volume of a solution

Condense when a substance changes from the gas state to the liquid state at the boiling point of the substance or below

Continuous variable a variable which can have any value within a range, for example time, temperature, length, mass

Contracts gets smaller

Correlation a link between two variables

Corrosion a reaction that happens on the surface of a metal when the metal reacts with substances from the air or water around it. Corrosion reactions happen slowly.

Corrosive a corrosive substance destroys living tissue

Creative thinking thinking in a new way

Crude oil a thick black liquid formed underground, or under the sea, from the remains of plants and animals that died millions of years ago. Crude oil is used to make fuels, such as petrol and diesel, and many plastics.

Crust the outer layer of the Earth. It is made up of different types of rock, and is thinner than the other layers of the Earth.

Crystal a substance in the solid state with its atoms arranged in a regular pattern, for example salt and diamond

Data measurements taken from an investigation

Decanting carefully pouring off a liquid from a mixture of the liquid with a solid, in which the solid has settled to the bottom; or pouring off the top liquid from two liquids that have settled one on top of the other.

Density the mass of a substance in a certain volume. A substance with a high density feels heavy for its size.

Deposition the settling of sediments that have moved away from their original rock

Diffusion the spreading out and mixing of particles from areas with many particles to areas with fewer particles

Discrete variable a variable whose values are words, or whose values can only have certain numerical values

Diesel a fuel separated from crude oil

Dilute a solution that contains very little solvent dissolved in a lot of solvent

Dissolve when a substance (the solute) mixes with a liquid (the solvent) to make a solution

Displacement reaction a reaction in which a more reactive metal displaces a less reactive metal from a compound of the less reactive metal

Distillation a method of separating a solvent from a solution, for example water from salty water

Ductile a material is ductile if it can be pulled into wires

Electric balance an instrument for measuring mass that is powered by electricity

Electron a sub-atomic particle that moves around the outer parts of an atom. It has a single negative charge. Its relative mass is 1/1840.

Element a substance consisting of atoms of only one type. It cannot be split into new substances.

Empirical question a question that can be answered scientifically, by collecting evidence and using creative thought

Endothermic change a change in which energy is taken in from the surroundings.

Energy levels electrons in atoms occupy energy levels. Energy levels are also called shells, or orbits.

Erosion the processes of weathering and transportation together make up erosion

Evaporation when a substance changes from the liquid state to the gas state. Evaporation can happen at any temperature.

Evidence observations or measurements that support a scientific explanation

Exothermic change a change in which energy is released to the surroundings.

Expand get bigger

Explanation a scientific idea that explains evidence and which scientists have developed using creative thought

Fair test an investigation in which all the variables are kept constant except the variable which the investigator changes

Filter a way of removing pieces of solid that are mixed with a liquid or solution by pouring through filter paper

Filtration separating pieces of solid from a mixture with a liquid or solution

Fluid a substance that has no fixed shape and that flows to fill a container or space

Fossil the remains or traces of a plant or animal that lived many years ago

Fossil fuels fuels made from the remains of animals and plants that died millions of years ago, for example coal, oil, and natural gas

Formula (plural formulae) a formula uses symbols and numbers to show the relative number of atoms of each element in a compound. For example, the formula of water is H_2O. This shows that water is made up of atoms of hydrogen and oxygen, strongly joined together. In a sample of water, there are two hydrogen atoms for every one oxygen atom.

Fractional distillation heating a liquid mixture to separate it into fractions with different boiling points

Freeze when a substance changes from the liquid state to the solid state

Freezing point the temperature at which a substance changes from the liquid state to the solid state. Each substance has its own freezing point.

Fuel a store of energy which burns to release useful heat, for example coal and diesel

Gas a fluid with no fixed volume that takes the shape of its container

Gas pressure the force exerted by gas particles when they collide with 1 m² of a surface

Geologist a scientist who studies the origin, structure, and composition of the Earth

Global warming the gradual increase in the Earth's average surface temperature

Gneiss an example of a metamorphic rock

Granite an igneous rock formed from liquid rock that cooled slowly. Its crystals are relatively large.

Greenhouse gases gases that contribute to climate change, for example carbon dioxide

Group the elements in one vertical column of the periodic table

Group 1 elements the elements in the left vertical column of the periodic table

Group 2 elements the elements in the vertical column that is second from the left of the periodic table

Group 7 elements the elements in the vertical column that is second from the right of the periodic table. They are also called the halogens.

Halogens the elements in the vertical column that is second from the right of the periodic table. They are also called the group 7 elements.

Hard a material is hard if it is difficult to scratch

Hazard a possible source of danger

Hazard symbols warning symbols on chemicals that show what harm they might cause if not handled properly

Hummus decayed plant and animal matter in the soil

Hydroxide a compound made up of a metal, hydrogen, and oxygen.

Index fossil a fossil type that identifies the geological time period in which a rock was formed. Every time period has its own index fossil.

Inner core the solid iron and nickel at the centre of Earth

Insoluble a substance that does not dissolve in a solvent

Inverse correlation a link between two variables in which when one variable increases, the other variable decreases

Igneous rock rock made when liquid rock (called magma below the surface of the Earth, and lava above the surface of the Earth) cooled and solidified

Isotope atoms of the same element which have different numbers of neutrons are called isotopes

Joule (J) the unit of energy

Kilogram unit of mass

Kilojoule (kJ) 1000 joules

Lava hot liquid rock that is on – or above – the surface of the Earth

Limestone an example of a type of sedimentary rock. It is mainly calcium carbonate

Liquid a fluid with a fixed volume that takes the shape of its container

Litmus indicator an indicator which tells you if a substance is acidic or alkaline. If a substance is alkaline, it makes red litmus become blue. If a substance is acidic, it makes blue litmus paper red.

Loam in a loam soil the rock fragments are 40% sand, 40% silt, and 20% clay

Magma hot liquid rock that is beneath the Earth's surface

Malleable a material is malleable if it can be hammered into shape without cracking

Mantle the layer of the Earth that is beneath the crust. It is solid but can flow very slowly. It goes down almost halfway to the centre of the Earth.

Marble a metamorphic rock formed from limestone

Mass the amount of matter in something

Materials the different types of matter that things are made of

Matter stuff that takes up space and has mass

Measuring cylinder a piece of apparatus that measures volumes of liquids or solutions

Melt when a substances changes from the solid state to the liquid state

Melting point the temperature at which a substance changes from the solid to liquid state. Every substance has its own melting point.

Meniscus the surface of a liquid

Metalloid an element with properties that are between those of metals and non-metals

Metals elements which are good conductors of heat and electricity. Most elements are metals. They are to the left of the stepped line on the periodic table.

Metamorphic rock a type of rock formed by the action of heat and/or pressure on sedimentary or igneous rock

Minerals substances that occur naturally. They are usually made up of crystals.

Mixture a mixture contains two or more elements or compounds mixed together. The substances in a mixture are not chemically joined together.

Molecule a particle of a substance made from two or more atoms that are strongly joined together

Mudstone a type of sedimentary rock

Natural polymer a polymer that exists naturally, often made by plants or animals

Neutral a substance or solution with a pH of 7 which is neither acidic nor alkaline

Neutralise to add acid or alkali to a solution to make a solution of pH 7

Neutralisation the process of making a solution neutral

Non-metals elements that are not metals. They do not conduct electricity. They are to the right of the stepped line of the periodic table.

Non-porous a non-porous material does not have small gaps containing gases or liquids. Water cannot soak into a porous material.

Nucleon number the number of protons and neutrons in the nucleus of an atom. It is also called mass number.

Nucleus (plural **nuclei**) the central part of an atom. Most of the mass of an atom is in its nucleus. The nuclei of all elements are made up of protons and neutrons, except for the nuclei of most hydrogen atoms which are made up of one proton only.

Neutron a sub-atomic particle found in the nucleus of an atom. It has no electric charge. Its relative mass is 1, the same as the mass of a proton.

Observations the results of looking carefully at something and noticing properties or changes

Oil a fossil fuel formed from sea creatures over millions of years

Orbits electrons in atoms occupy orbits. They are also called energy levels, or shells.

Ore a rock that contains natural minerals from which useful substances, for example metals, can be extracted

Outer core the liquid iron and nickel between the Earth's mantle and inner core

Oxide a compound of oxygen with another element

Palaeontologists scientists that study fossils and use evidence from them – and creative thinking – to understand the history of life on Earth

Particle theory a theory that uses ideas about particles to explain how matter behaves

Particles tiny pieces of matter from which everything is made

Period a horizontal row of the periodic table

Periodic table an arrangement of all the elements in order of increasing number of protons (proton number). In the periodic table, the elements are grouped with those that have similar properties.

pH a way of measuring how acidic or alkaline a solution is

pH scale the range of levels of acidity and alkalinity

Physical weathering the breaking up or wearing down of rocks, for example, by the effects of changing temperature

Polymer a substance with large molecules made up of atoms joined together in long chains

Porous a porous material has small gaps which may contain gases or liquids. Water can soak into a porous material.

Predict suggest what you think will happen

Prediction a suggestion of what will happen

Preliminary work observations or measurements done at the start of an investigation to work out appropriate values for control variables

Primary data data collected directly for a particular investigation

Products the new substances that are made in a chemical reaction

Property a characteristic of a substance; how it behaves

Proton a tiny sub-atomic particle with a positive charge. Protons are found in the nuclei of atoms. The relative mass of a proton is 1, the same as that of a neutron.

Proton number the number of protons in the nucleus of an atom

Radiometric dating this uses the natural decay of particles in a rock to measure the age of a rock

Range the difference between the biggest value and the smallest value in a series of data

Rate of reaction how fast a reaction is. The faster a reaction, the greater its rate.

Reactants the starting materials, or substances that react together, in a chemical reaction

Reactivity series a list of metals placed in order of their reactivity

Risk the chance of damage or injury from a hazard

Rock cycle the rock cycle explains how rocks change and are recycled into new rocks over millions of years

Rusting the corrosion reaction of iron. Oxygen and water are needed for iron to rust. The product of the reaction – rust – is hydrated iron oxide.

Sacrificial protection putting a more reactive metal in contact with a less reactive one so that the more reactive metal corrodes. The more reactive metal is sacrificed to protect the less reactive one.

Salt a compound in which the hydrogen atom of an acid has been replaced by a metal atom. Salts may be formed in neutralisation reactions or in reactions of acids with metals or metal oxides.

Sandstone an example of a type of sedimentary rock

Sandy soil in sandy soil, most of the rock fragments are sand

Saturated solution a solution in which no more solute can dissolve

Scientific journal a collection of papers, written by scientists, which describe their work and which have been carefully checked by other scientists

Scientific model an idea that explains observations, and that you can use to make predictions. A scientific model of an object or phenomenon is simpler than the real thing.

Secondary source a source such as a book or the Internet which provides evidence or data that you have not collected yourself

Sedimentary (rock) rock made from sediments joined together by pressure or chemicals

Sedimentation the settling of solid particles that were mixed with a liquid

Sediments pieces of matter which have settled to the bottom of a liquid

Semiconductor a material is a semi-conductor if it conducts electricity less well than conductors, but better than insulators

Semi-metal an element with properties that are between those of metals and non-metals

Shells electrons in atoms occupy shells. Shells are also called energy levels, or orbits

Slate a metamorphic rock made from mudstone

Solid a state of matter in which the substance has a fixed shape and volume

Solubility the maximum mass of solute that can dissolve in 100 g of solvent

Soluble a substance is soluble in a solvent if it can dissolve in that solvent

Solute a substance which dissolves in a solvent to make a solution

Solution a mixture of solvent and solute, in which the solute has dissolved.

Solvent in a solution, the liquid in which the solute is dissolved

Sonorous a material is sonorous if it makes a ringing sound when hit

States of matter most substances can exist as a solid, a liquid, and a gas. These are the states of matter.

Stirring rod a rod, usually made from glass, that is used to stir chemicals

Strata the layers of sedimentary rocks and soils that have built up over time

Strong a material is strong if a large force is needed to break it

Sub-atomic particles the particles that make up an atom, including protons, neutrons, and electrons

Sublimation when a substance changes from the solid state directly to the gas state

Sublime when a substance changes from the solid state directly to the gas state

Sulfate a compound that includes atoms of the elements sulfur and oxygen. There are four oxygen atoms for every one sulfur atom.

Symbol equation an equation in which the reactants and products are represented by their formulae. It gives the relative amounts of the substances in the reaction, and their states.

Synthetic polymer a polymer made by people and machines in factories or science laboratories

Temperature a measure of how hot something is

Thermite reaction the displacement reaction of iron oxide with aluminium. The products are iron and aluminium oxide. The reaction releases a great amount of energy as heat and light.

Thermometer an instrument you can use to measure temperature

Transportation the processes by which sediments of rock that have been removed from their original rock by weathering are moved away from the original rock

Universal Indicator (UI) a solution that changes colour to show the pH of the solution it is mixed with

Uplift uplift happens when huge forces from inside the Earth push rocks upwards. The process makes mountains.

Variable a quantity which can change in an investigation, for example time, temperature, length, mass

Vulcanologist a scientist who studies volcanoes

Weathering weathering breaks up all types of rock into smaller pieces, called sediments

Word equation a word equation summarises a chemical reaction in words. It shows the reactants and products. The arrow means 'react to make'.

Index

OXFORD
UNIVERSITY PRESS

Great Clarendon Street, Oxford OX2 6DP

Oxford University Press is a department of the University of Oxford. It furthers the University's objective of excellence in research, scholarship, and education by publishing worldwide in

Oxford New York

Auckland Cape Town Dar es Salaam Hong Kong Karachi Kuala Lumpur Madrid Melbourne Mexico City Nairobi New Delhi Shanghai Taipei Toronto

With offices in

Argentina Austria Brazil Chile Czech Republic France Greece Guatemala Hungary Italy Japan Poland Portugal Singapore South Korea Switzerland Thailand Turkey Ukraine Vietnam

First published in 2013

British Library Cataloguing in Publication Data

Data available

ISBN 978-0-19-839018-3

20 19 18 17 16 15

Printed by Repro India Ltd.

Acknowledgments

®IGCSE is the registered trademark of Cambridge International Examinations.

Cover photo: Olivier Le Queinec / Shutterstock; **p8(l):** Toniflap / Shutterstock; **p8(m):** Galyna Andrushko / Shutterstock; **p8(r):** Andrew Lambert Photography / Science Photo Library; **p9(tr):** John Cleare Mountain; **p9(m):** Cris Kelly / Shutterstock; **p9(ml):** digitalr / istock; **p10(tr):** Tina Rencelj / Shutterstock; **p10(ml):** sgm / shutterstock; **p10(bl):** anilakduygu / istock; **p12(l):** AISPIX by Image Source / Shutterstock; **p12(r):** Wikimedia Commons; **p14(ml):** Russ Lappa / Science Photo Library; **p14(bl):** SunChan / istock; **p14(r):** Andrew Lambert Photography / Science Photo Library; **p15(tl):** sailfasterman / istock; **p15(tr):** Keith Kent / Science Photo Library; **p15(bl):** Charles D. Winters / Science Photo Library; **p15(br):** Claude Nuridsany & Marie Perennou / Science Photo Library; **p16(t):** SilviaJansen / istock; **p16(m):** David Taylor / Science Photo Library; **p16(b):** Chris R. Sharp / Science Photo Library; **p17:** mtoker / Shutterstock; **p18:** Lynsey Addario/VII / Corbis; **p20:** Hemis / Alamy; **p27(tr):** Elenamiv / Shutterstock; **p27(bm):** Ulkastudio / Shutterstock; **p27(bm):** imagebroker / Alamy; **p27(br):** Andraž Cerar / Shutterstock; **p27(tl):** Primož Cigler / Shutterstock; **p27(bl):** anaken2012 / Shutterstock; **p28(t):** sansara / istock ; **p28(b):** nycshooter / istock ; **p29(tl):** Corbis; **p29(tr):** Look and Learn / Bridgeman; **p29(m):** John Warburton-Lee Photography / Alamy; **p29(br):** fotko/ istock; **p29(bl):** dan_prat / istock; **p29(bm):** light_fire / istock; **p30(tl):** pukach / shutterstock; **p30(tm):** photocritical / shutterstock; **p30(tl):** Ingvald Kaldhussater / shutterstock; **p30(bl):** Leslie Garland Picture Library / Alamy; **p30(br):** Corbis; **p31(l):** mikeuk / istock; **p31(r):** hxdbzxy / shutterstock; **p34(t):** MC_PP / shutterstock; **p34(bl):** Middle East / Alamy; **p34(br):** Thomas Cockrem / Alamy; **p35(m):** Dmitry Kalinovsky / shutterstock; **p35(bl):** Corbis; **p35(br):** British Library; **p36(tm):** Images of Africa Photobank / Alamy; **p36(tr):** wavebreakmedia ltd; **p36(ml):** Ctatiana / shutterstock; **p36(mr):** Chirtsova Natalia / shutterstock; **p36(b):** Lokibaho / istock; **p37(t):** AnglianArt/ istock; **p37(m):** Elnur / shutterstock; **p37(bl):** svera / istock; **p37(br):** azotov / istock; **p38(tr):** Kheng Guan Toh/ shutterstock; **p38(tl):** Sergieiev / shutterstock; **p38(m):** Chris Howes/Wild Places Photography / Alamy; **p38(b):** RichPhotographics / istock; **p39(tl):** Pedro Salaverría / shutterstock; **p39(tr):** Karin Smeds / Getty; **p39(ml):** jayjayoo7_com / istock; **p39(mr):** Shvaygert Ekaterina / shutterstock; **p39(bl):** roset / istock; **p39(br):** Bryan Busovicki / Shutterstock; **p40:** ziprashanti / istock; **p42:** Testbild / shutterstock; **p43(t):** Andrew Lambert Photography/Science Photo Library; **p43(m):** Africa Studio / Shutterstock; **p43(b):** Getty Images; **p44(l):** Jerry Mason / Science Photo Library; **p44(r):** Andrew Lambert Photography / Science Photo Library; **p45:** Robert Brook / Alamy; **p46:** louise murray / Alamy; **p47(t):** Birkholz / istock; **p47(b):** Mati Nitibhon / shutterstock; **p48(l):** danhughes / istock; **p48(m):** eyenigelen / istock; **p48(r):** Brian Weed / Shutterstock; **p52(l):** Neil Fraser / Alamy; **p52(r):** NASA; **p53(t):** Science Photo Library; **p53(b):** Charles O'Rear/Corbis; **p54(tl):** Herve Conge, ISM / Science Photo Library; **p54(tm):** alanphillips / istock; **p54(tr):** Scientifica, Visuals Unlimited / Science Photo Library; **p54(bm):** Oxford Scientific / Getty; **p54(br):** Miguel Cabezón / shutterstock; **p54(bl):** Pyma / shutterstock; **p55(t):** tropicalpixsingapore / istock; **p55(ml):** menonsstocks / istock; **p55(m):** Bridgeman Art Library; **p55(mr):** ivstiv / istock; **p56(t):** PASIEKA/Science Photo Library; **p56(br):** Leslie Garland Picture Library / Alamy; **p56(ml):** PEDRE / istock; **p56(bl):** Wayne Hutchinson / Alamy; **p57(l):** alanphillips / istock; **p57(r):** Adrea / Dreamstime; **p58:** Yory Frenklakh / Shutterstock; **p59(t):** Jorge Moro / Shutterstock; **p59(ml):** Mike Truchon / Shutterstock; **p59(m):** Pgiam/ istock; **p59(mr):** Mac99 / istock; **p59(b):** Vitamin / Shutterstock; **p60(l):** Lance Rider / Shutterstock; **p60(r):** JeremyRichards / shutterstock; **p61(tl):** Dirk Wiersma / Science Photo Library; **p61(tr):** Glugwine / shutterstock; **p61(b):** Dirk Wiersma / Science Photo Library; **p62(t):** Roger Ressmeyer / Corbis; **p62(b):** The Art Archive / Alamy; **p64:** AFP / Getty Images; **p65(l):** Wikimedia Commons; **p65(r):** James King-Holmes / Science Photo Library; **p68:** Nigel Cattlin / Alamy; **p69:** Michael Dwyer / Alamy; **p70(l):** JohnArcher / istock; **p70(m):** John Reader / Science Photo Library; **p70(r):** Marcio Jose Bastos Silva / Shutterstock; **p71(t):** DR Morley Read / Science Photo Library; **p71(m):** University of St Andrews; **p71(bl):** Annoyz View / Wordpress; **p71(br):** Natural History Museum, London / Science Photo Library; **p72(t):** David A. Hardy / Science Photo Library; **p74(t):** Anthropology.net; **p74(b):** AFP / Getty Images; **p75(tl):** D. Roberts / Science Photo Library; **p75(tm):** Kennis and Kennis/MSF / Science Photo Library; **p75(tr):** John Reader / Science Photo Library; **p75(b):** Christelle Orluc/Look At Sciences / Science Photo Library; **p76:** Massimiliano Gallo / Shutterstock; **p79:** Ammit Jack / Shutterstock; **p80:** Pallava Bagla / Corbis; **p81:** Charles D. Winters / Science Photo Library; **p83(t):** Andrew Lambert Photography / Science Photo Library; **p83(b):** Joerg Boethling / Alamy; **p85:** Ewa Studio/ Shutterstock; **p89:** Wikimedia Commons; **P97:** The Art Archive; **p98(tl):** Khoroshunova Olga / Shutterstock ; **p98(tm):** SOMMAI / Shutterstock; **p98(tr):** www.BibleLandPictures.com / Alamy; **p98(ml):** Wikimedia Commons; **p98(mr):** Robert Harding/Robert Harding World Imagery / Corbis; **p98(b):** Iron Age/ Getty; **p100(tl):** Andrew Lambert Photography / Science Photo Library; **p100(tr):** Tom Grundy / Shutterstock; **p100(ml):** immelstorm/ Shutterstock; **p100(mr):** papa1266 / Shutterstock; **p100(b):** Ria Novosti / Science Photo Library; **p106(l):** Jason Stitt / Shutterstock; **p106(m):** Andrew Lambert Photography / Science Photo Library; **p106(r):** Science Photo Library; **p112(l):** David Steele / Shutterstock; **P112(m):** Natural History Museum, London / Science Photo Library; **P112(r):** Manamana / Shutterstock; **p113:** immelstorm / Shutterstock; **p114:** Charles D. Winters / Science Photo Library; **p115:** elen_studio / Shutterstock; **p116:(tl)** Photographers Direct / Mark Lane; **p116(bl):** studiomode / Alamy; **p116(br):** Martyn F. Chillmaid / Science Photo Library; **p117(t):** Getty; **p117(b):** Arnold Fisher / Science Photo Library; **p120(tr):** Martyn F. Chillmaid / Science Photo Library; **p120(tl):** Martyn F. Chillmaid / Science Photo Library; **p120(bl):** Andrew Lambert Photography / Science Photo Library; **p120(br):** Hornbil Images / Alamy; **p121(t):** LaiQuocAnh / Shutterstock ; **p121(b):** shao weiwei / Shutterstock; **p122:** travelib sulawesi / Alamy; **p123:** Getty; **p125(t):** Christine Osborne Pictures / Alamy; **p125(bl):** Bon Appetit / Alamy; **p125(br):** Helen Sessions / Alamy; **p126(t):** Danita Delimont / Alamy; **p126(b):** RF Company / Alamy; **p128:** Tom Grill/Corbis; **p129:** Jake Lyell / Alamy; **p132(l):** Dinodia Photos / Alamy; **p132(m):** Sergey Dubrov / Shutterstock; **p132(r):** Corbis Cusp / Alamy; **p133(t):** sciencephotos / Alamy; **p133(b):** Andrew Lambert Photography / Science Photo Library; **p135:** Andrew Lambert Photography / Science Photo Library; **p136(l):** Mikael Goransson / Shutterstock; **p136(m):** Massimiliano Pieraccini / Shutterstock; **p136(r):** Kai Schwabe/ Westend61 / Corbis; **p137(t):** keith morris / Alamy; **p137(b):** Keith Wilson / Shutterstock; **p140:** Andrew Lambert Photography / Science Photo Library; **p141(t):** Andrew Lambert Photography / Science Photo Library; **p141(b):** Andrew Lambert Photography / Science Photo Library; **p147:** Picture Contact BV / Alamy; **p149:** Lucie-Anne / Shutterstock; **p156(t):** Mykira / dreamstime; **p156(m):** Pallava Bagla / Corbis; **p156(b):** Charles D. Winters / Science Photo Library; **p157(l):** Andrew Lambert Photography / Science Photo Library; **p157(m):** Andrew Lambert Photography / Science Photo Library; **p157(r):** Andrew Lambert Photography / Science Photo Library; **p158(l):** Boykung / Shutterstock; **p158(m):** NASA / Science Photo Library; **p158(r):** Guy Immega/ Wikimedia Commons; **p159:** Andrew Lambert Photography / Science Photo Library; **p160:** cstar55 / istock; **p162:** Borderlands / Alamy; **p163:** Shutterstock; **p166:** Wikimedia Commons; **p158(l):** only low-res - no contact from author; **p167:** Getty Images; **p170(tl):** Zvonimir Luketina / Shutterstock; **p170(tr)** vovan / Shutterstock; **p170(b):** gvictoria / istock; **p174:** David R. Frazier / Science Photo Library; **p175(t):** santosha / istock; **p175(b):** Martin Bond / Science Photo Library; **p176:** ALEAIMAGE / istock; **p178(l):** Charles D. Winters / Science Photo Library; **p178(r):** Koolpak; **p182(t):** Getty Images; **p182(ml):** Lawrence Migdale / Science Photo Library; **p182(mr):** Charles D. Winters / Science Photo Library; **p182(b):** E. R. Degginger / Science Photo Library; **p184(t):** Andrew Lambert Photography / Science Photo Library; **p184(m):** Andrew Lambert Photography / Science Photo Library; **p184(b):** Associated Press; **p185:** Ancient Art & Architecture Collection Ltd / Alamy; **p186:** Peter Amsden / Photographers Direct; **p187:** Martyn F. Chillmaid / Science Photo Library; **p188:** Andrew Lambert Photography / Science Photo Library; **p189(t):** Martyn F. Chillmaid / Science Photo Library; **p189(ml):** Rigucci / Shutterstock; **p189(mr):** BergmannD / istock; **p189(b):** holbox / Shutterstock; **p192(t):** luismmolina / istock; **p192(b):** Andrew Lambert Photography / Science Photo Library; **p193(t):** Charles D. Winters / Science Photo Library; **p193(b):** Horizon International Images Limited / Alamy; **p194(t):** oscarcalero / istock; **p194(b):** Rigucci / Shutterstock; **p195(t):** Bildarchiv Steffens Henri Stierlin / Bridgeman Art Library; **p195(b):** Anthony Collins Cycling / Alamy; **p196:** Lawrence Migdale / Science Photo Library; **p197(t):** Charles D. Winters / Science Photo Library; **p197(b):** Charles D. Winters / Science Photo Library; **p200(l):** raiwa / istock; **p200(m):** Ralf Neumann / Shutterstock; **p200(r):** Martyn F. Chillmaid / Science Photo Library; **p201:** MARKA / Alamy; **p202(l):** Nigel Cattlin / Science Photo Library; **p200(r):** Jack Clark / Agstockusa / Science Photo Library; **p204:** dbimages / Alamy; **p206:** geogphotos / Alamy; **p207:** Health Protection Agency / Science Photo Library; **p210(l):** PapaBear / istock; **p210(r):** EricHood / istock; **p212:** Science Photo Library; **p214:** Photobunnyuk/ Dreamstime; **p216:** Martyn F. Chillmaid / Science Photo Library; **p218(t):** enciktat / Shutterstock; **p218(b):** Martyn F. Chillmaid / Science Photo Library; **p219:** Astrid & Hanns-Frieder Michler / Science Photo Library; **p230:** LSOphoto / istock